Contents

This is dedicated to my father
Dr Charles Sims
who, more than anyone else,
taught me to be observant

10-95

SYMPTOMS IN THE MIND

An Introduction
to Descriptive Psychopathology

ANDREW SIMS MA MD FRCPsych

Professor of Psychiatry
University of Leeds

Baillière Tindall   London   Philadelphia
Toronto   Sydney   Tokyo

Baillière Tindall   24–28 Oval Road
W. B. Saunders   London NW1 7DX, England

West Washington Square
Philadelphia, PA 19105, USA

1 Goldthorne Avenue
Toronto, Ontario M8Z 5T9, Canada

ABP Australia Ltd, 44 Waterloo Road
North Ryde, NSW 2064, Australia

Harcourt Brace Jovanovich Japan Inc.
Ichibancho Central Building, 22–1 Ichibancho
Chiyoda-ku, Tokyo 102, Japan

© 1988 Bailière Tindall

First published 1988

Typeset by Scribe Design, 123 Watling Street, Gillingham, Kent
Printed and bound in Great Britain by Alden Press, Osney Mead, Oxford

British Library Cataloguing in Publication Data

Sims, Andrew
  Symptoms in the mind: an introduction
  to descriptive psychopathology.
  1. Psychology, Pathological
  I. Title
  616.89′07   RC454
  ISBN 0-7020-1237-8

Foreword

The time has certainly come for the publication of a new textbook of psychopathology written initially in English and directed primarily at English-speaking readers. This is such a book. It is more than ordinarily comprehensive, up-to-date, fluently written and easy to read. While there may still be some who would regard Karl Jaspers's *Allgemeine Psychopathologie* (General Psychopathology) as the phenomenologist's 'bible', it is, while a classic work, off-puttingly heavy going for the newcomer to psychiatry. Also having first been published in 1913 (although not translated into English until 1962, when in its 7th edition) it must now be seen as becoming somewhat outdated, for psychopathology is still to be considered as an evolving subject. Professor Andrew Sims's new book will, therefore, go a long way to remedy a deficiency not entirely overcome by the publication of a number of smaller texts during the intervening years.

Just as internal medicine and surgery and their subspecialties cannot properly be studied without a thorough grounding in morbid anatomy and other types of physiopathology, so does an understanding of psychiatry depend on a detailed knowledge of psychopathology. However, this analogy should not be pushed too far. Physiopathology is concerned largely with the anatomical, physiological and biochemical anomalies produced by disease. While such things have some and possibly slightly growing relevance to psychiatry, particularly in the realm of organically determined mental illnesses, this is not yet extensive and is unlikely ever to loom very large in our understanding of the overall nature of psychiatric disorders except in a quantitative as opposed to a qualitative sense. Professor Sims defines psychopathology as 'the systematic study of abnormal experience and behaviour' and goes on to suggest that 'using phenomenology diagnostically may be compared with scanning the field of a microscope'. What he is pointing out, of course, is that phenomenology primarily concerns itself with the examination in detail of the minutiae of mental symptoms with a view to determining their exact nature and defining them and their place within the general range of abnormal mental phenomena with which the psychiatrist has to deal. This is not merely an academic exercise, or as he himself says 'archaic, hair-splitting or hare-chasing', as some may still mistakenly maintain, but is indeed an ever-fascinating task which, properly undertaken, leads to the acquisition of skills essential to diagnosis.

It could, of course, be argued that if the essential cause of a disorder such as schizophrenia was discovered tomorrow and turned out to be such that a specific remedy could be applied which would *cure* the condition, then there would no longer be a need for a detailed analysis of the phenomenology of this disorder. Not only does this seem very unlikely to happen, but even if it did, diagnosis would probably still have to be made extremely early for the supposed specific remedy to be really effective. Here again, a detailed knowledge of the phenomenology of schizophrenia would be required, there being no substitute for this.

There also remains the matter of differential diagnosis. For example: how often does the experienced psychiatrist run across a case of mixed affective psychosis wrongly diagnosed as schizophrenia by someone not sufficiently familiar with the phenomenology of both these complaints who is led into error more often than not by the bizarre appearance of the mixed state? Many other examples could be cited – two such being the tendency of those who are phenomenologically naive to over-diagnose schizo-affective disorders, or to fail to differentiate depression from dementia in ageing patients.

A number of years have passed since Professor Sims first began plans for this book, some of which he discussed with me at the time, particularly, if I remember rightly, his views on how he should deal with the psychopathology of delusions, of which he has an extensive knowledge. Now that his project has come to fruition it is both a pleasure and a privilege to have been asked to contribute the foreword to a new and important book such as this.

Sir William Trethowan

Preface

'If the word *mind* means anything, it means that which feels' (John Stuart Mill, 1811). That is the sense in which this book investigates the mind and its disturbances – emphasizing subjective experience and its description by the sufferer and the behaviour that results. The title *Symptoms or Signes in the Mind* is 'Partition 1, Section 3, Member 1, Subsection 2' of Robert Burton's *Anatomy of Melancholy* (1621). Burton claimed that one can dissect and display the *essential elements* of 'melancholy'. This is what I have attempted in this account of psychopathology in order to learn about them for subsequent research and treatment.

This book is aimed specifically at the recruit to psychiatry in his or her first year of training in the specialty. Such a person will have received some teaching in psychiatry as a medical undergraduate and some experience in dealing with those with emotional disturbance or personality difficulties in their medical practice since qualification, but is unlikely to have experience of the vast range of symptoms that patients present; nor is it likely he will have acquired a system for structuring abnormal subjective phenomena. I hope others, both in psychiatry and in related disciplines, will also find this book helpful; there has been a healthy revival of interest in descriptive psychopathology in the last few years, especially in British psychiatry. This has resulted in no small part from the enormous encouragement to high standards in the training of psychiatrists consequent upon the inception of the Royal College of Psychiatrists. Changes in the examination for membership of the College to be implemented in 1987 will further emphasize the importance of clinical training in psychiatry and hence the need for a thorough grasp of descriptive psychopathology.

Psychopathology is a very complicated subject and the texts have not always been remarkable for their lucidity and conciseness. Writing about mental illness is a forlorn task, a matter of trying to describe the ultimately indescribable. Having had the temerity to attempt it, I have gone further and tried occasionally to represent the abstract visually and in tabular form. My apologies to those who are offended by this, but I hope that by over-simplifying, I may help some to start looking at mental illnesses in a more observant and comprehending way. This is not ordered as a textbook of psychiatry; the classical syndromes are not usually dealt with in a simple section but scattered, according to the different elements of their psychopathology, in many chapters. This book has taken some fifteen years to write; the first few years were spent collecting information to fill it up and the latter few discarding it to slim it down.

For the sake of clarity some arbitrary lines have had to be drawn. The material of many chapters is not discrete but overlaps. There are still enormous areas of uncertainty in psychopathology; I hope these have not been spuriously simplified and that my own continuing quest for understanding is apparent. To this end I invite the reader to comment on any specific topics so that we (he/she/I) can work together towards a more authoritative second edition.

In the words of the Oxford English Dictionary the word *he* is used 'of things not sexually distinguished ... any man, any one, a person'. This convention has been used throughout; it reads more easily than interminable 'he or shes' or genderless 'theys'.

There are very many people who have helped me in preparation and without whom this would never have appeared; they are not responsible for my errors. Dr Ruth Sims has helped throughout. I am very grateful for discussion with and useful suggestions from Professor Robert Bluglass, Mrs Marian Greenwood, Dr Peter McKenna, Professors Clive Mellor, Richard Mindham and Kenneth Rawnsley, Drs Keith Rix, Paula Salmons, Charles Sims and Philip Snaith, Professor Sir William Trethowan and Dr Alfred White.

I acknowledge the help of successive groups of Leeds and Birmingham postgraduate and undergraduate students who have asked difficult questions and also perused my drafts with admirable astringency. Mrs Monika O'Connor, and at an earlier stage Mrs Barbara Rudge, have been endlessly patient in preparing repeated drafts. I am grateful to the Medical Illustration Department at St James's University Hospital, Leeds, for all their work over the years, some of which is included. The libraries of the Universities of Leeds and Birmingham, and especially the staff at St James's Hospital library have been extremely helpful at all stages of preparation.

I suppose I should thank British Rail, who have been my hosts while much of this has been written, and who, by their relaxed attitude to punctuality, have given me much more time for work than I could have anticipated.

Many patients over the years have taken the trouble to explain to me exactly how they feel; they have taught me what I know, and also that I know little. I acknowledge my indebtedness to them and I hope that this work will partly repay my debt by improving understanding of their successors. Perhaps the chief difference between this book and others on this topic that have gone before is that it aims to put descriptive psychopathology in its social, psychological and biological contexts.

Andrew Sims

1

Fundamental Concepts of Descriptive Psychopathology

As one takes up mental alienation as a separate object of investigation, it would be making a bad choice indeed to start a vague discussion on the seat of reason and on the nature of its diverse aberrations; nothing is more obscure and impenetrable. But if one wisely confines one's self to the study of the distinctive characteristics which manifest themselves by outward signs and if one adopts as a principle only a consideration of the results of enlightened experience, only then does one enter a path which is generally followed by natural history.

Philippe Pinel (1801)

The intricacies of different mental illnesses are of absorbing interest, but it is necessary to remind oneself that such illness is damaging to the individual sufferer, and very disruptive to his social situation and a powerful and frequent cause of human misery. This account describes the patterns of illnesses based on their symptoms.

Phenomenology and psychopathology

The range of experiences described by the mentally ill is categorized by defining terms. Classification is the starting point for studying differences in natural history and, hence, efficacy of different treatment methods. Understanding the subjective experiences of a sufferer will help the patient himself: to know that the therapist has demonstrated his interest by trying to understand him will increase his confidence in treatment.

Symptoms aggregate in particular patterns and so we can talk about different *mental illnesses*. We do not know how treatment will develop over the next few years, but it is certain that precise methods of *diagnosis*, or defining the problem, will remain important. The way ahead demands a return to accurate observation of the phenomena with which we are confronted.

What is a person, demonstrably disturbed with a mental illness, actually experiencing? In what ways are his own experience like and unlike the experience of others—both those who are well and those who are ill? It is important for the professional worker to have a scheme for organizing the phenomena that occur.

Psychopathology is the systematic study of abnormal experience, cognition and behaviour. *Descriptive psychopathology* avoids theoretical explanations for these psychic events: it describes and categorizes the abnormal experiences as recounted by the patient and observed in his behaviour. In its historical context, Berrios (1984) defines it as a cognitive system constituted by terms, assumptions and rules for its application—'the identification of classes of abnormal mental acts'. *Phenomenology* is the study of events, either psychic or physical, without

1

embellishing those events with explanation of cause or function. As used in psychiatry, phenomenology involves the observation and categorization of abnormal psychic events, the internal experiences of the patient and his consequent behaviour. An attempt is made to observe and understand the psychic event or phenomenon, so that the observer can, as far as possible, know for himself what the patient's experience must feel like.

How can one use the word *observer* about someone else's internal experience? This is where the process of *empathy*, described later, becomes relevant. Descriptive psychopathology therefore includes subjective aspects (phenomenology) and objective aspects (description of behaviour). It is concerned with the variety of human experience but it is deliberately limited in its scope; for example, it can say nothing about the religious validity of what James (1902) has called 'saintliness'.

How does this work in practice? Mrs Jenkins complains that she is unhappy. It is the business of *descriptive psychopathology* both to describe her thoughts and actions without trying to explain them and to observe her behaviour—the listless sagging of her shoulders, the tense gripping and wringing of her hands. *Phenomenology* demands a very precise description of exactly how she feels inside herself–'that horrible feeling of not really existing', and 'not being able to feel any emotion'.

Some psychiatrists have held phenomenology in derision as archaic, hair-splitting or hare-chasing pedantry, but the diagnostic evaluation of symptoms is a task that the psychiatrist omits at his own and his patient's peril. Studying phenomenology whets diagnostic tools, sharpens clinical acumen and improves communication with the patient. The patient and his complaints deserve our scrupulous attention. If 'the proper study of mankind is man' the proper study of his mental illness starts with the description of how he thinks and feels inside–'chaos of thought and passion, all confused' (Pope, 1688–1744).

A cavalier neglect of phenomenology can have serious repercussions for care of the patient. In 1973 eight people were sent separately to twelve admission units in American mental hospitals complaining of hearing these words said aloud: 'empty, hollow, thud' (Rosenhan, 1973). In all cases save one, they were diagnosed as schizophrenic. They produced no further psychiatric symptoms after admission to hospital but acted as normally as they could, answering questions truthfully except to conceal their name and occupation. The ethics and good sense of the experiment can certainly be questioned, but what comes out most clearly is not that psychiatrists should refrain from making a diagnosis, but that their diagnosis should be made on a sound psychopathological basis. Neither Rosenhan, nor his colleagues, nor the admitting psychiatrists gave any information as to what symptoms could reasonably be required for making a diagnosis of schizophrenia (Wing, 1978). It could be predicted that with adequate use of phenomenological psychopathology this failure of diagnosis would not have occured.

Jaspers (1963) wrote, 'Phenomenology, though one of the foundation stones of psychopathology, is still very crude.' One of the great problems in using this method is the muddled nature of terminology. Almost identical ideas may be assigned different names by people from different theoretical backgrounds–for example, the plethora of descriptions of how a person may conceptualize himself: self-image, cathexis, body awareness and so on.

Phenomenology, the *empathic* method for the eliciting of symptoms, can never be learned from a book. Patients are the best teachers, but it does help to know what one is looking for, the practical, clinical aspects in which the patient describes himself, his feelings and his world. The doctor tries to unravel the nature of the sufferer's experience–to understand it well enough and to feel it so poignantly that the account of his findings evokes recognition from the patient. The method of phenomenology in psychiatry is entirely subjugated to its single purpose of rendering the patient's experience *understandable* (this is a technical word in phenomenology and is described in more detail on p.9; however, it implies the capacity for putting oneself in the patient's place), so that classification and rational therapy may proceed.

'The barrier to conspicuous advance in psychiatry has not been stinginess and prejudice on the part of those who decide whether a research project submitted to them should live or die; nor has it been lack of ability among those who are engaged in psychiatric research: it lies in the inherent toughness of the problems' (Lewis, 1963). It is not the assimilation of abstruse facts or the accumulation of foreign eponyms which is most difficult in phenomenology, although either of these may be hard: it is the comprehension of a method of investigation and the ability to use new concepts. In an attempt to avoid the obscure and obvious, I have described some of these concepts in contrasted pairs for the rest of this chapter.

Normal health

Some words are used very commonly, but inconsistently; so, although we know what we mean by them, we are unable to assume that other people are using them in the same way. Two such words are *normal* and *healthy*. In a discussion of mental illness they occur so frequently that they should be examined briefly before further excursion into psychopathology.

HEALTH : ILLNESS

Psychopathology concerns itself with *illness of the mind*, but what is illness? This is a vast subject that has received discussion from philosophers, theologians, administrators and lawyers as well as from physicians. Doctors who spend most of their working time straddled between health and illness rarely ask this question, and even less frequently attempt to answer it.

1   The World Health Organization definition states: 'Health is a state of complete physical, mental and social well-being and not merely the absence of disease or infirmity' (1946). If total well-being is required perhaps virtually all of us are excluded.
2   Illness may be thought of in physical terms, as in Griesinger's (1845) dictum that mental diseases are diseases of the brain. Although this statement reasonably fits the organic psychiatric states and can be broadened to encompass mental subnormality, one is less comfortable trying to include the functional psychoses and the neuroses; and personality disorders just do not fit at all.
3   Similarly diseases may be described in terms of *what doctors treat*. In defining this, Kräupl Taylor (1980) states 'the diagnosis of patienthood has as its

sufficient and necessary condition the experience of therapeutic concern by a person for himself and/or the arousal of therapeutic concern for him in his social environment.' Mental illness becomes, then, a term to describe the symptoms and condition of those people who are referred to a psychiatrist. This tautologous description of illness has some practical advantage, as it does not prevent therapeutic skills from being used over a wide spectrum of human problems. It does, however, have the disadvantage of allowing society to choose whom it will call mentally ill; and with a malignant social system, the state may direct that those who are politically deviant should be deemed ill (Bloch & Reddaway, 1977).

4   Illness may be considered as a statistical variation from the norm, carrying biological disadvantage. This was formulated by Scadding (1967) for physical illness and developed for psychiatric disease by Kendell (1975). Biological disadvantage implies reduced fecundity and/or shortened life. This state of disadvantage becomes difficult to apply to modern man, as he has learned to control his environment and procreativity to such an extent that the very term *biological disadvantage* becomes arguable. What is biological advantage for the individual may be a disadvantage for the species, and vice versa.

5   Illness has legal implications. For instance, the circumstances that result in illness may merit compensation at law; the behaviour that arises from illness may mitigate punishment. Similarly, mental illness is a concept that can justify compulsory detention in hospital (Mental Health Act, 1983), and mentally ill offenders are dealt with by the law in a different way from other criminals (Bluglass, 1983).

This distinction between normality and disease, health and illness, is by no means trivial. 'A large part of medical ethics and much of the whole underpinning of current medical policy, private and public, are squarely based on the notion of disease and normality. Left to himself the physician (whether he realizes it or not) can do very well without a formal definition of disease.... Unfortunately, the physician is not left alone to work his common sense. He is attacked from two angles: the predatory consumers and the pretentious advisors' (Murphy, 1979).

NORMALITY : ABNORMALITY

The word *normal* is used correctly in at least four senses in the English language (Mowbray, Rodger & Mellor, 1979). These are the *value* norm, the *statistical* norm, the *individual* norm and the *typological* norm. *Normal* is abused when it replaces unjustifiably the words *usual* or *usually*.

The *value* norm takes the ideal as its concept of normality. Thus, the statement, 'It is normal to have perfect teeth', is using normal in a value sense–in practice most people have at least something wrong with their teeth.

The *statistical* norm is, of course, the preferred use the word retains in the scientific vocabulary; the abnormal is considered to be that which falls outside the average range. If a normal Englishman is 5 feet 8 inches tall, to be either 6 feet 2 inches or 5 feet 2 inches tall is equally abnormal statistically. 'Normal' implies being within a limited range around the mean or average value.

The *individual* norm is the consistent level of functioning that an individual maintains over time. Following brain damage, a person may experience a decline in intelligence which is certainly a deterioration from their previous individual norm but may not represent any statistical abnormality (for example, a decline in IQ from 110 to 90).

Typological abnormality is a necessary term to describe the situation when a condition is regarded as normal in all the three meanings above and yet represents *abnormality*, perhaps even disease. The example given by Mowbray *et al.* is the infective condition of *pinta*. The mottling of the skin is highly prized in the South American Indians who suffer from it, to the extent that non-sufferers are excluded from the tribe. Thus, having the condition is normal in a value, statistical and individual sense, and yet is clearly pathological.

PSYCHIATRIC SAMPLE: GENERAL POPULATION

Whilst discussing health and normality, it is important to point out those dangerous generalizations which arise when the psychiatrist, usually against his will, is thrust into the position of being the expert on the whole conduct of life. We cannot extrapolate from the abnormal to the normal. They are unlikely to be on a continuum, but rather are qualitatively different. Because of his detailed knowledge of abnormal psychic processes and symptoms and their management, the psychiatrist is not necessarily an expert on bringing up children or providing a recipe for a tranquil mind.

The sample of people seeing a psychiatrist is different in many respects from those consulting their family doctors with psychological symptoms; and this general-practice population varies from the population at large (Goldberg & Huxley, 1980). While it is very necessary to concentrate on the individual and his symptoms, it is also useful to bear in mind the characteristics of the remainder of the population from which he comes. His behaviour and his understanding of the world has roots within his own individual psychopathology, and also in the social milieu which is his usual context.

Very often one wants to argue from the particular to the general. On the basis of our experience with young schizophrenic patients in a teaching hospital, we make assertions about *schizophrenia*. To be able to do this we must know that the patients we have seen (our sample population) are representative of the target population (schizophrenia). We can only make this claim if our sample was randomly selected from all schizophrenics, so that all schizophrenics had a known, equal and greater than zero probability of getting into our sample. In practice, of course, this can never be so and we must restrict our target population to a more limited group (the sample), and our claims for knowledge about them must be similarly restricted. The axiom bears repeating: different populations have different characteristics.

THE COMMON: THE ESOTERIC

Descriptive psychopathology is in danger of indulging in the esoteric, i.e. excessive interest in rare syndromes. To be of practical use, it needs to concentrate on the universal:

1 Observation of phenomena without preconceived theory is useful in reconciling different schools of psychopathology.
2 The requirement of precise definition forms a groundwork for sound research. Rare syndromes have their value in learning psychopathological skills,

but interest in them should not detract from the more important, if more mundane, uses of this method of enquiry (Sims, 1982).

Understanding the patient's symptoms

Understanding, in both an everyday and a phenomenological sense, cannot be complete unless the doctor has a detailed knowledge of the patient's background culture and specific information about his family and immediate environment. Neither can phenomenology concentrate solely on the individual isolated in a moment of time. It must be concerned with the person in a social setting: after all, a person's experience is largely determined by his interactions with others.

The method of phenomenology facilitates communication; its use makes it easier for the doctor to understand his patient. His patient is also helped to have confidence in the doctor, because he realizes his symptoms are understood and therefore accepted. The precise description and evaluation of symptoms also helps communication between doctors.

SYMPTOM : SIGN

Clinical medicine makes a clear distinction between signs and symptoms. The patient complains of *symptoms:* feeling agitated, uncomfortable in hot weather, with thyrotoxicosis. Physical *signs* are elicited on examination: soft goitre with audible bruit, loss of weight, rapid pulse and exophthalmos.

This distinction is not usually made with the phenomena of the mental state. The patient's description of an abnormal mental phenomenon is usually called a *symptom* whether he is complaining about something that distresses him, or simply describing his mental experience which appears pathological to an observer. In his account of his experiences, they are therefore considered as symptoms. When these symptoms are aggregated, they may be regarded as the *signs* of whatever diagnosis is indicated.

Symptom then, which is taken to include sign, may be either an item of complaint (for example, a feeling of misery) or an item of phenomenological description that may represent no complaint from the patient (for example, hearing quiet voices who discuss the patient with admiring awe). The feeling of misery may be a sign of depressive illness; the auditory hallucinations may be a sign of schizophrenia. There are also behavioural symptoms or signs, such as the patient who shouts at the ceiling–this may be regarded as a *sign* suggesting auditory hallucinosis. Schneider (1959) considers that a *symptom* in schizophrenia is a 'frequent and therefore a prominent characteristic of that state'. For a symptom to be used diagnostically, its occurrence must be typical of that condition and it must occur relatively frequently.

THE METHOD OF EMPATHY : THE METHOD OF OBSERVATION AND EXPERIMENT

The classical method in medicine of gaining information about the patient is from the history and by physical examination. The use of phenomenology in psychiatry is an extension of the history in that it amplifies the description of the present complaint to give more detailed information. It is also an examination in that it reveals the mental state. It is not possible for me, the doctor, to observe my patient's hallucination nor in any direct way to measure it. However, what I can do to comprehend him is to use those human characteristics I hold in common with him: my ability to perceive and to use language I share with him. I can endeavour to create in my own mind what his experience must be like. I then test to see if I am correct in my reconstruction of his experience, by asking him to affirm or deny my description. I also use my observation of his behaviour—the sad expression of his face or his thumping the desk with his fist—to reconstruct his experiences.

Listening and observing are crucial for understanding. Great care must be taken with asking questions. Doctors not infrequently identify symptoms incorrectly and come to the wrong diagnosis because they have asked leading questions with which the patient, through his submissiveness to the doctor's status and anxiety to co-operate, is only too willing to concur.

This is *the method of empathy*. Empathy is the ability to feel oneself into the situation of the other person. It consists of asking appropriate, persistent, insightful questions; rephrasing and reiterating where necessary until being sure that one understands what he is describing. The process runs something like this:

Question–'You describe your thoughts changing; what happens to them?'
Answer–a description of how he has a recurring thought to kill people and this results from a pain in his stomach.
Question–(trying to isolate the elements of his experience) 'What is your thought of killing people like?' (obsession, delusion, fantasy, is it likely to be acted on, etc.). 'Do you believe that your stomach affects your thinking?'; 'Is this different from a person who knows that they become irritable when hungry?'; 'In what way is it different from that?'; 'What causes your pain in the stomach?'; etc.
Answer–he describes the details, which will include amongst irrelevant material the sort of information I require for determining what symptoms are present.
Question–(the invitation for empathy) 'Am I right in thinking that you are describing an experience in which rays are causing pain in your stomach, and that your stomach in some way quite independent of yourself causes this thought, which frightens you, that you must kill somebody with a knife?' This is an account of the relevant symptoms that he has described in language he should be able to recognise as his own.
Answer–'Yes' (we have then achieved our goal); 'No' (therefore I must try again to elicit the symptoms, experience them for myself and describe them back to him again.

Perhaps an analogy from general medicine would be helpful here. The experienced physician palpates an enlarged kidney in his patient's abdomen (Figure 1.1). He invites the medical students to palpate the abdomen bimanually so that they too can learn to experience that barely perceptible, yet important, sensation. The phenomenological method of empathy employed in psychiatry is even more difficult to teach than this. It is like the doctor having to carry out his examination without hands. First, he has to train the patient to palpate his own abdomen bimanually in the required fashion and then, accurately describe what he feels. The doctor then interprets the patient's

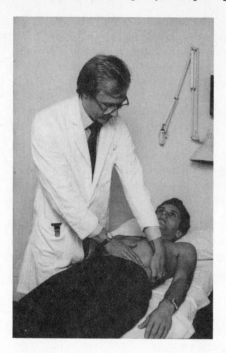
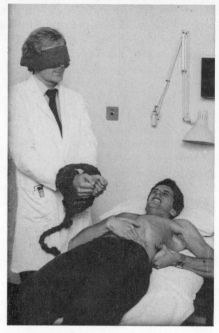

Figure 1.1 Bimanual palpation and phenomenology

description to decide whether the kidney is enlarged without being able to put a hand on the abdomen himself.

It is the purpose of the phenomenological method therefore: (i) to describe inner experiences; (ii) to order and classify them; and (iii) to create a reliable terminology. Empathy is invaluable therapeutically in establishing a relationship with the patient. Knowing that the doctor understands, and is even to some extent able to share his feelings, gives him confidence and a sense of relief. This empathy is also useful as a way of extending knowledge more generally in the field of psychiatry as it allows a diagnostic terminology to be developed.

THE UNDIFFERENTIATED WHOLE: THE SIGNIFICANT PART

Generally, classification of any sort requires detailed scanning of a large amount of material to find the small, but significant, clue. This is true for phenomenology where the significant part of psychic material for phenomenological evaluation may occur within a lengthy history and examination, in which most of the patient's conversation does not reveal any evidence of illness. One patient talked for several minutes and various things he said seemed rather strange but I could not be sure that he was psychotic. However, when he said, 'I shaved my eyebrows because they were ginger and when people saw ginger eyebrows they knew I was queer' (homosexual–in practice, he was not homosexual), it became obvious that he was deluded, and this symptom was explored in more detail.

Using phenomenology diagnostically in the mental state may be compared with scanning the field of the microscope. One cannot expect to find the blood film meaningful by simply focusing and looking. One has to move the slide about and pick out a good example to demonstrate the point of interest from the undifferentiated mass. So the patient's conversation may have demonstrated many odd ideas and bizarre allusions, but perhaps only once can the interviewer obtain a description that satisfies him completely as being an example of a particular psychopathological symptom of diagnostic significance.

RANDOM BEHAVIOUR : MEANING

A man cycling along a canal towpath met a large man walking in the opposite direction carrying a length of rubber pipe. The large man lifted his rubber pipe and thumped the cyclist on the shoulder, nearly knocking him into the canal. When he reached the next village, the cyclist reported the assault to the local policeman who duly arrested the assailant. The police considered this behaviour senseless and therefore asked for a psychiatric opinion. When asked why he had assaulted the cyclist, the man said that he had had a pain in his stomach. He had heard a voice saying, 'Hit the man on the bicycle and the pain will go', and so he had done just that!

The casual layman, commenting on 'mad' behaviour, may say that it is meaningless because this is not always apparent to an observer or even a victim, it does not negate its real, although psychotic, meaning to the patient. 'An action is on principle intentional' (Sartre, 1943).

It is important to try and reach the patient's subjective meaning and not just be satisfied that the response is abnormal. Phenomenological meaning is sometimes revealed in the type of response; for instance, when a schizophrenic patient was asked to explain the difference between a *wall* and a *fence*, he answered: 'You can see through a fence, but walls have ears' (Rawnsley, 1985, pers. comm.).

UNDERSTANDING : EXPLANATION

We start with the premise that behaviour means something, that is, it arises with internal consistency from psychic events. Although a patient's behaviour is meaningful to him, it may not be possible for us, the outside observers, to understand it. There are different levels at which we may understand. For example, we may get some insight into the sexual difficulties of a recidivist exhibitionist from knowing about his very disturbed childhood; but it still does not explain why he regularly indulges in behaviour that brings him into conflict with the law, and damages him socially. Wittgenstein (1953) has stated: 'We explain human behaviour by giving reasons not causes'.

Jaspers has contrasted understanding (*verstehen*) with explaining (*erklären*) and has shown how these terms may be used in both a static and genetic sense. *Static* implies understanding or explaining the present situation from information which is available now; *genetic* how it reached this state by examining antecedents. This is represented in Table 1.1. Understanding is the perception of personal meaning.

1 If we want to find meaning at a particular moment in time, the method of phenomenology is appropriate. The patient's subjective experience is dissected out and a static picture is formed of what that thought or event meant to him at

Table 1.1 Diagram of Understanding and Explanation

	Understanding	*Explanation*
Static	(1) Phenomenological description	(3) Observe through external sense perception
Genetic	(2) Empathy established from what emerges	(4) Cause and effect of scientific method

that particular time. No comment is made on how the event arose and no prediction is made as to what will happen next. The meaning is simply extracted as a description of what the patient is experiencing and what this signifies to him now. A man feels angry: static understanding uses empathy to describe in detail exactly what it is like for him to feel angry. Have I, the examiner, experienced phenomena like these? Are they known to me through the experiences I have had in my lifetime?

2   Genetic understanding, as opposed to static understanding, is concerned with a *process*. It is understood that when this man is insulted, he reacts with violence; when that woman hears voices commenting on her actions, she draws the curtains. For understanding of the way psychic events emerge one from another in the patient's experience, the therapist uses *empathy* as a method or a tool. He *feels himself into* the patient's situation. If that first event were to have occured to him personally in the patient's total circumstances, the second event, which was the patient's reaction to it, might reasonably be expected to have followed. He understands the feelings he ascribed to the patient in terms of the action that results from these feelings. So, if I were the patient with the same history, do I feel I would have the same experiences and behave in the same way? An example would help to demonstrate the humanity of this approach and the universality of human experience: I must put myself into the shoes of a young woman, aged 19, raised in an isolated fishing community, the eldest of eight siblings, who becomes stuporose during her second pregnancy. She is married to an alcoholic man aged 35, and her father is also alcoholic. I must understand how she dealt with her father's alcoholic behaviour as a child; what her pregnancy meant to her; how she regarded her mother's behaviour during her pregnancies; and so on.

Explanation is concerned with accounting for events from a point of observation outside them; understanding from inside them. One understands another person's anger and its consequences; one explains the occurrence of snow in winter. Explanations also can be described as static or genetic.

3   *Static* explanation is concerned with external sense perception, observing an event.

4   *Genetic* explanation consists of unravelling causal connections: it describes a chain of events and why they follow that sequence. Understanding and explanation are both necessary parts of the psychiatric investigation.

Jaspers makes an important distinction between that which is *meaningful* and allows empathy, and that which is ultimately *un-understandable*–the essence of the psychotic experience. Although one can possibly empathize with the *content* of a patient's delusion in any particular situation, one cannot understand or see a meaningful connection in the occurrence of the delusion itself. The delusion as an event is not understandable: it seems to the doctor incomprehensible and unreal. We can understand from a knowledge of the patient's background why, if her thinking is going to be disordered in form, the topic or content of that thinking should be concerned with persecution by the Nazis–perhaps because her parents escaped from Germany in 1937. But we can have no understanding of why she should believe something that is demonstrably false: that her persecutors are putting a tasteless fluid into her drinking water that makes her feel ill. The delusion itself, as psychopathological form, is *un-understandable.*

PRIMARY : SECONDARY

Jaspers discusses the different meaning which can be given to the terms *primary* and *secondary* when applied to symptoms. The distinction may be in terms of understanding in that what is primary can be reduced no further by understanding, for example, hallucinations; while what is secondary is what *emerges* from the primary in a way which can be understood, for example, delusional elaboration arising from the healthy part of the psyche in response to hallucinations arising from the unhealthy part of the psyche. Again, the distinction between primary and secondary may be one of *causality*, in that what is primary is the cause, while what is secondary is the effect: sensory aphasia is primary, the resulting disruption of relationships with other people is secondary.

These two distinct meanings of the term *primary* overlay the crucial distinction between meaningful connections and causal connections. For the avoidance of doubt in physics and chemistry we make observations by experiment and then formulate causal connections and causal laws; whereas, in psychopathology, we experience another sort of connection wherein psychic events emerge out of one another in a way which can be understood–so-called meaningful connections (Robinson, 1984, pers. comm.).

The analysis of experience

Certain features of the patient's experience are of considerable importance in his clinical evaluation by the doctor, but he himself would not volunteer them. Thus the distinction between form and content is vital to understanding the nature of the patient's condition. It is also important to discriminate between subjective and objective aspects of symptom evaluation.

PREDICTION : QUANTIFICATION

There are two misapprehensions in the accusation levelled at psychopathology that it is unscientific because it is not quantifiable. First, quantification is not fundamental to science but secondary. The first essential for factual knowledge or science is that it be of good enough quality to be predictive. For example, to know that the apple, unattached, will fall, is the first essential of science: measuring and so quantifying its speed is dependent on the initial observation and prediction. Secondly, it *is* possible to quantify subjective psychology which has used phenomenology at the stage of forming hypotheses. Examples of this will be described in more detail later, including: self-rating assessments for depression; depicting the location of self within semantic space in the Repertory

Grid; and self-measurement of width by patients with anorexia nervosa. It requires indirect and ingenious methods to quantify psychopathology but it is possible, and sometimes worthwhile.

Popper (1959) has introduced the test of *falsifiability* for science: a theory must be falsifiable as a criterion of demarcation. Phenomenology, the description of the individual's subjective state, is falsifiable: it is available for refutation, and part of the empathic method is to invite the patient to refute the interviewer's account of the former's experience. Hence, phenomenological theories may be falsified by asking the patient to comment.

FORM:CONTENT

Like warp and woof, form and content are essentially different but inextricably woven together. The *form* of a psychic experience is the description of its structure in phenomenological terms, for example, a delusion. Viewed in this way, *content* is the colouring of the experience. The patient is concerned because he believes people are stealing his money. His concern is that 'people are taking my money', not that 'I hold on unacceptable grounds a false belief that people are taking my money'. He is concerned about the content. Clearly, form and content are both important, but in different contexts. The patient is only concerned with the content, 'that I am pursued by ten thousand hockey sticks'. The doctor is concerned with both form and content, but as a phenomenologist only with form, in this case, a false belief of being pursued. As far as form is concerned, the hockey sticks are irrelevant. The patient finds the doctor's interest in form unintelligible and a distraction from what he regards as important, and he often demonstrates his irritation.

In Chapter 6, a patient is described who said, 'When I turn the tap on I hear a voice whispering in the water pipe, "She's on her way to the moon. Let's hope she has a soft landing"'. The *form* of this experience is what demands the attention of the phenomenologist and is useful diagnostically. She is describing a *perception*: it is an auditory perception and a false or disordered auditory perception. It has the characteristics of an hallucination, and specifically of a *functional* hallucination. This is the form. Whilst the psychiatrist is busy clarifying the form, the patient is getting very irritated because 'he is not taking any notice of what I am saying'. She is worried that she is being sent to the moon. What will happen when she gets there? How will she get back again? So the *content* is all important to her, and the doctor's absorption with form is incomprehensible and frustrating in the extreme.

The form is dependent upon, and is therefore a diagnostic key to, the particular mental illness from which the patient suffers. For example, *delusional percepts* occur in schizophrenia, and when demonstrated as the form of the experience they indicate this condition. The finding of a visual hallucination suggests the likelihood of an organic psychosyndrome (Chapter 6). The nature of the content of these two examples is irrelevant in coming to a diagnosis. The content can be understood in terms of the patient's life situation with regard to culture, peer group, status, sophistication, age, sex, life events and geographical location. For example, another patient described himself as having been sent to the moon and back during the night within a fortnight of the first landing by man on the moon. Describing one's thoughts as being controlled by television is necessarily confined to those parts of the world with that invention. A colleague has informed me that in the fortnight following Elvis Presley's death, three self-confessed reincarnations of the famous singer attended his Emergency Room.

Hypochondriasis is a disorder of content rather than of form. The form can be various. It could take the form of an auditory hallucination in which the patient hears a voice saying, 'You have cancer'. It could be a delusion, in that he believes falsely and with delusional evidence that he has cancer. It could be an overvalued idea, in that he spends a major part of every day checking on his health believing himself to be ill. It could be an abnormality of affect that manifests itself in extreme hypochondriacal anxiety or in depressive hypochondriacal despondency. Similarly, morbid jealousy is a disorder of content in which the form could be hallucinatory, delusional, an over-valued idea, compulsive behaviour or obsessional thought; but the content is comprehensible in terms of the patient's life situation.

SUBJECTIVE : OBJECTIVE

Objectivity in science has come to be revered as the ideal, so that only what is external to the mind is considered to be real, measurable and valuable. This is a mistake, because objective assessments are necessarily subjectively value-laden in what the observer decides is worth measuring; and this subjective aspect can be made more precise and reliable. There are always value judgements associated both with subjective and objective assessments. The process of making a scientific evaluation consists of various stages: receiving a sensory stimulus, perceiving, observing (making the percepts meaningful), noting, coding and formulating hypotheses. This is a progressive process of throwing away information, and it is the subjective judgement of what is valuable which determines the small amount of each stage which is retained for transmission to the next part of the process. 'There is no such thing as an unprejudiced observation' (Popper, 1974).

Objective assessments in psychiatry have covered many aspects of life. A few examples are the measurement of body movements, facial expression, patients' writings, learning capacity, responses in an operant conditioning programme, memory span, work efficiency and evaluation of logical content of the patients' statements. All these can be quantified and analysed objectively. Subjective analysis can be made, for example, from facial expression, from the patient's description of himself, of his own writing or of his inner events. When a doctor says about a patient, 'she looks sad', he is not measuring objectively the patient's facial expression in 'units of sadness' by some objective yardstick. He is going through these stages: 'I associate her facial expression with the affect that I recognize in myself as feeling sad: seeing her expression makes me feel sad'. *Rapport* is this quality which the patient establishes with the doctor during the clinical interview. In order for it to happen, the doctor has to be receptive to this communication. He has to be able to establish rapport himself; to have a capacity for human understanding. This is necessarily a subjective experience for the doctor, but that is not to say that it is unreal or even that it cannot be measured. The method of phenomenology tries to increase our knowledge of subjective events so that they can be classified and ultimately quantified.

Aggernaes (1972) has defined subjectivity and objectivity for immediate everyday experiences:

'When an experienced something has a quality of 'sensation', it is also said to have a quality of 'objectivity' if the experiencer feels that under favourable circumstances, he would be able to experience the same something with another modality of sensation than the one giving the quality of sensation. When an experienced something has a quality of 'ideation', i.e. is not being directly sensed at the moment, it is also said to have a quality of 'objectivity' if the experiencer feels that under favourable circumstances, he would nevertheless be able to experience the same something with at least two modalities of sensation.

An experienced something has a quality of 'subjectivity' if the experiencer feels that under no circumstances would he be able to experience this something with two or more modalities of sensation'.

Thus I can look at the table in front of me as a visual perception or I can turn my head and still fantasize it as a visual image. As I 'see' it, in either way, the fact that I can imagine both hearing a sound if I were to hit it with a spoon and bruising my knuckles if I were to punch it, confirms its quality of objectivity. If I use my imagination to create in my mind a visual image of a Chippendale chair that I have never actually seen but is a composite of objects and pictures I have seen, I know that I will never be able to feel or hear this actual chair—it is a subjective image without external, objective reality.

PROCESS : DEVELOPMENT

In the same way that understanding or explaining depend upon the perspective of the interviewer—empathically from inside or observing from the outside—so process or development depends upon whether the person experiences an event as within their usual pattern of life or outside. Development implies that an experience is understandable in terms of the person's constitution and history; personality aberrations would be seen as disorders of development. Process is seen as the imposition of an event from outside; epilepsy would be experienced as an occurrence of disease quite separate from normal development—the disease process has interrupted the normal course of life. Similarly, the onset of a schizophrenic illness often produces a definite 'break' in the life history of a late adolescent.

Theoretical stances of psychopathology

There are myriad psychopathologies. Any explanation for abnormal behaviour has the germ of a theory of psychopathology. *Descriptive psychopathology* tries to avoid the countless arguments of aetiology by being satisfied with a description of what occurs, without seeking further explanation. I have discussed already the assumption that the phenomena of mental illness are meaningful. A radically different opinion finds no subjective experience important. Thoughts, including moods and drives, are regarded as *epiphenomena*, that is, thinking has no meaning or goal but is like the froth on top of the beer. Thoughts are regarded as the accidental by-products of the chemical activities occurring in the brain: not causes of behaviour but merely products. The significance the thinker attaches to them subjectively is purely illusory. Such an extreme position negates any possibility of psychological treatment.

DESCRIPTIVE : DYNAMIC PSYCHOPATHOLOGY

Psychopathology is the study of abnormal psychic processes. Descriptive psychopathology is concerned with describing the subjective experiences and also the resultant behaviour during mental illness. It does not venture explanations accounting for these experiences or behaviour, nor does it attempt to discover the aetiology or the process of development.

This approach to abnormal psychic phenomena contrasts quite sharply with other theoretical frameworks of psychopathology, for example, the psychoanalytic. In psychoanalysis at least one of several basic mechanisms are assumed to be taking place and the mental state becomes understandable within this framework. Explanations of what occurs in thought or behaviour are based on these underlying theoretical processes, such as *transference* or *ego defence mechanisms*. For example, with a delusion, descriptive psychopathology tries to describe what it is that the person is believing; how he describes his experience of believing; what evidence he gives for its veracity; and what is the significance of this belief to his life situation. An attempt is made to assess whether this belief has the exact characteristics of a delusion and, if so, of what type of delusion. Having made this phenomenological evaluation the information gained can be used diagnostically, prognostically and, hence, therapeutically. Some of the contrasts between descriptive and dynamic psychopathology are summarized in Table 1.2.

Table 1.2 Psychopathology – Descriptive v. Psychoanalytic

	Descriptive	*Psychoanalytic*
Summary	Empathic evaluation of patient's subjective experience	Study of the roots of current behaviour and conscious experience through unconscious conflicts
Terminology	Description of phenomena	Theoretical processes demonstrated
Methods	Understanding the patient's subjective state through empathic interview	Free association, dreams, transference
Differences in practical application	1. Makes distinction between understanding and explanation: understanding through observation and empathy	Understanding in terms of notional theoretical processes
	2. Form and content clearly separated: form of importance for diagnosis	Concerned with content
	3. Process and development distinguished: process interferes with development	No distinction made; psychiatric symptoms seen as having unconscious psychological basis

Analytic or dynamic psychopathology, however, would be more likely to attempt to explain the delusion in terms of early conflicts repressed into the unconscious and now only able to gain expression in psychotic form, perhaps on a basis of projection. The content of the delusion would be considered an important key to the nature of the underlying conflict which has its roots in early development. Descriptive psychopathology makes no attempt to say why a delusion is present: it solely observes, describes and classifies. Dynamic psychopathology aims to describe how the delusion occurred and why it should be that particular delusion, on the evidence of that person's experience in early life. This is related to genetic understanding as described above, and has been called *prescient understanding* by Mellor (1985, pers. comm.)–indicating presumed foreknowledge of how the events of mental life must unfold because they will necessarily conform with theoretical postulates for development.

CONSCIOUS : UNCONSCIOUS

Phenomenology cannot be concerned with the unconscious because the patient cannot describe it, and so the doctor cannot empathize. Descriptive psychopathology has no theory of the unconscious, nor does it deny its existence. Unconscious mind is simply outside its terms of reference and psychic events are described without recourse to explanations involving the unconscious. Dreams, the contents of hypnotic trance and slips of the tongue are described according to how the patient experiences them, that is, according to how they manifest in consciousness.

ORGANIC : SYMPTOMATIC

Psychopathology is essentially a non-biological approach to abnormal mental processes so that, even when the organic causes of a condition are known, psychopathology is involved in ordering the symptoms and the experience of the patient rather than with its organic pathology. There are now many links known between different psychiatric illnesses and identifiable organic pathology. However, it is not with these links that psychopathology is concerned, and its usefulness is not dependent upon ultimately finding the localization in the brain of a delusion or any other psychic event. Early, organically orientated psychiatrists, such as Griesinger and Wernicke, were not concerned with the psychopathological in psychiatry but much more with charting the diseased brain. This paid a rich dividend, for example, in elucidating the nature and treatment of cerebral syphilis. Similarly, modern behaviourists have generally been uninterested in phenomenology. Phenomenology is not ultimately concerned with organic pathology or with behaviour *per se* but with the patient's subjective experience of his world.

I have not contrasted *organic* with the conventionl *functional*, because functional is a most misleading term. It causes conceptual fog rather than enlightenment: a logical person who is innocent of medical jargon would be baffled to know why disturbance of human function by psychological mishap should be called functional, while similar disturbance of function from organic disease is not. It is the *symptomatic* elements of disease that phenomenology can explore: the nature of the symptoms and with what they are associated.

BRAIN : MIND

René Descartes (1596–1650) examined, formulated and restated views on the separation of body and soul. He described '*l'âme raisonable*'–the reasonable soul lodged in the machine and having its principal seat in the brain. He described the soul as the engineer who altered the movements of the machine, the body (1649). Descartes was a man of his time, reflecting as well as developing the dichotomous views of his time. An example of this Cartesian dualism occurring before Descartes is the following obituary inscription to Lady Doderidge who died in 1614:

'As when a ruinous clocke is out of frame
a workman takes in peeces small the same
and mendinge what amisse is to be found,
the same rejoynes and makes itt treppe and gow
so god this ladie into two partes tooke
too soone her soule her mortall corse forsooke
But by his might att length her bodie sound shall rise
rejoynd unto her soule now crownd
Till then they rest in earth and heaven sundred
att which conjoined all such as live we then wondred'

This clear affirmation of an absolute separateness between body and soul occurs on her tomb which is to be found in Exeter Cathedral.

From this dualism comes our tendency to think in terms of body and mind–mental and physical illness. The whole discipline of psychiatry tacitly accepts a dualistic background for its very existence, although it resents this and tries hard to teach medicine of the whole person. Our language continually brings us back to dualistic words and expressions.

The method of phenomenology has in this regard the advantage of being a bridge across this otherwise irreconcilable chasm. As it is concerned with subjective experience it is involved with mind not body, but the mind can only perceive the stimuli that the body has received and there can be no perception without the state of consciousness of the mind. 'The body is not just a *caused mechanism*, but essentially an *intentional* entity always goal-directed... The *lived-body* is that experience of our body which cannot be objectified' (Gold, 1885; Gold's italics). The term *mind* is not intended to represent some psychological homunculus resident, perhaps upside down, in the cerebral cortex; it is purely an abstraction referring to one aspect of our humanity. Like any other aspect or view, what is held in focus is fairly clear, but the edges of the field are blurred and so we cannot say what precisely lies within the furbelows of *mind*. Neither can we discriminate absolutely between body and mind, nor can we say that mankind is wholly explicable in terms of body and mind.

Popper and Eccles (1977) have developed Cartesian dualism further and elaborated a trichotomous concept–mind, body and self. Body–mind theories and their relationships to psychiatry have been well summarized by Granville-Grossman (1983). *Mind* is used hereafter as an abstraction, a way of looking at part of the phenomena of man. These issues have necessarily been dealt with summarily in this opening chapter, where the purpose has been to look at illness, and not to dissect the mind–'the study of the distinctive characteristics which manifest themselves' (Pinel). This chapter states what phenomenology is and why it is useful in clinical psychiatry. The method concentrates on the subjective experience of the patient–trying to understand his own inner state. Various constellations of ideas have been discussed; and the concepts are listed in pairs as constructs, health and normality, and the ways a psychiatric population differs from a normal population are discussed.

The background ideas to understanding the patient's symptoms are elaborated using the method of empathy and the meaning of behaviour, understanding and explaining psychic events. The patient's behaviour is further analysed in terms of form and content, subjective and objective assessment. The theoretical stances of descriptive psychopathology have been discussed and contrasted with psychoanalytic methods and with the biological approach to illness. The concept of the mind has been briefly considered.

References

Aggernaes A (1972) The experienced reality of hallucinations and other psychological phenomena. *Acta Psychiatrica Scandinavica 48*, 220–238

Berrios GE (1984) Descriptive psychopathology: conceptual and historical aspects. *Psychological Medicine 14*, 303–13

Bloch S and Reddaway P (1977) *Russia's Political Hospitals*. London: Victor Gollancz.

Bluglass RS (1983) *A Guide to the Mental Health Act*. Edinburgh: Churchill Livingstone.

Descartes R (1649) Les Passions de l'Âme. In *Descartes' Philosophical Writings* (transl. Kemp Smith N, 1952). London: Macmillan.

Ebmeier KP (1987) Understanding and explanation in psychopathology. *British Journal of Psychiatry* (in press).

Gold J (1985) Cartesian dualism and the current crisis in medicine–a plea for a philosophical approach: discussion paper. *Journal of the Royal Society of Medicine 78*, 663–6.

Goldberg D and Huxley P (1980) *Mental Illness in the Community: A Pathway to Psychiatric Care*. London: Tavistock.

Granville-Grossman K (1983) Mind and body. In Lader MH (ed.) *Mental Disorders and Somatic Illness: Handbook of Psychiatry 2*, 5–13. Cambridge: Cambridge University Press.

James W (1902) *The Varieties of Religious Experience*.

Jaspers K (1959) *General Psychopathology*, 7th Edn (transl. Hoenig J and Hamilton MW, 1963). Manchester: Manchester University Press.

Kendell RE (1975) The concept of disease and its implications for psychiatry. *British Journal of Psychiatry 127*, 305–315.

Lewis AJ (1963) Medicine and the affections of the mind. *British Medical Journal ii*, 1549–57.

Mental Health Act (1983) London: HMSO.

Mowbray RM, Ferguson Rodger T and Mellor CS (1979) *Psychology in Relation to Medicine*, 5th Edn, Edinburgh: Churchill Livingstone.

Murphy EA (1979) The epistemology of normality. *Psychological Medicine 9*, 409–415.

Pinel P (1801) *Traite Médico-philosophique sur la Manie*, 2nd Edn (transl. Zilboorg G and Henry GW, 1941)

Pope A (1688–1744) *An Essay on Man*. New York: WW Norton.

Popper K (1959) *The Logic of Scientific Discovery*, 9th Impression.

Popper K (1974) *Unended Quest*. Harmondsworth: Penguin.

Popper KR & Eccles JC (1977) *The Self and its Brain*. Berlin: Springer-Verlag.

Rawnsley K (1985) Personal Communication

Robinson ML (1984) Personal Communication

Rosenhan DL (1973) On being sane in insane places. *Science 179*, 250–258.

Sartre JP (1943) Being and Nothingness. (transl. by Barnes HE, 1958) London: Methuen.

Scadding JG (1967) Diagnosis: the clinician and the computer. *Lancet ii*, 877–82.

Schneider K (1959) *Clinical Psychopathology*, 5th edn (transl. Hamilton MW). New York: Grune & Stratton.

Sims ACP (1982) The renaissance of descriptive psychopathology. *University of Leeds Review*, 191–213.

Taylor FK (1980) The concepts of disease. *Psychological Medicine 10*, 419–424.

Wing JK (1978) Clinical concepts of schizophrenia. In Wing JK (ed.) *Schizophrenia: Towards a New Synthesis*. London: Academic Press.

Wittgenstein L (1953) *Philosophical Investigations*. (transl. Anscombe GEM). Oxford: Blackwell.

World Health Organization (1946) Constitution of the World Health Organization. *Official Record of the World Health Organization 2*, 100.

2

Consciousness and Disturbed Consciousness

Psychiatry and neuropathology are not merely two closely related fields, they are but one field in which only one language is spoken and the same laws rule. Wilhelm Griesinger (1868)

Cardinal principle: When all is finished, take care of the conscious, and leave the unconscious to take care of itself.   Parry (1975)

The logical starting place for the study of symptoms from a subjective standpoint is that which allows subjectivity to exist–consciousness. To be able to experience, one must be conscious. Terminology in this area is appallingly confused. This and subsequent chapters have attempted to clarify the terminology; sometimes at the expense of terms with a long history, and sometimes lumping as a single concept terms between which are only minute differences of meaning. The disturbances of consciousness described in this chapter are specific to organic psychosyndromes.

Conscious and unconscious experiences

The words 'consciousness', 'conscious mind' and 'awareness' are used very freely in psychiatry but often without a precise meaning. *Consciousness* 'is a state of awareness of the self and the environment' (Fish, 1967). Consciousness 'is to be conscious, to know about oneself and the world' (Scharfetter, 1980). The word is, in fact, better used as an adjective than a noun: 'The conscious man does not possess consciousness, but is a conscious being, he is himself conscious in an unmistakable way. Consciousness cannot be separated from that which one is conscious of; it implies knowing, understanding something–the object of consciousness is its essential social dimension.'

The term as used by clinicians refers first to the inner *awareness* of experience as opposed to the categorizing of events as they occur. Secondly, it refers to the subject reacting to the objects *intentionally*. Thirdly, it denotes a knowledge of a conscious *self*.

UNCONSCIOUSNESS

Unconscious, according to Jaspers (1962), 'means something that is not an inner existence and does not occur as an experience; secondly, something that is not thought of as an object and has gone unregarded; thirdly, it is something which has not reached any knowledge of itself.'

   In clinical practice, the term *unconscious* is used in three quite different ways that only have in common the phenomenological element in that there is *no* subjective experience (Figure 2.1). A person suffering from serious brain disease may be unconscious–consciousness in this instance being seen on a continuum, with a normal state of consciousness at one end–and death at the other. Someone who is asleep is unconscious–again there is a continuum from full wakefulness to deep sleep. An alert and healthy person is only aware of certain parts of his environment both externally and internally; of the rest he is unconscious. There is also a continuum here from full vigilance towards the immediate object of awareness to total unawareness. The organic state of the brain as, for instance, demonstrated by the electroencephalogram is utterly different in these three situations.

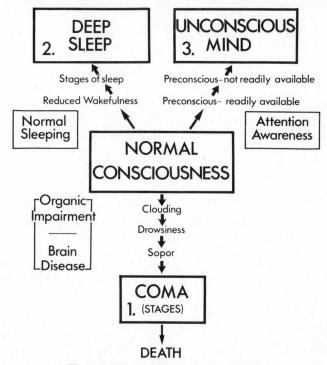

Figure 2.1 Three meanings of unconsciousness

   This third meaning of unconsciousness implies that certain mental processes cannot be observed by introspection. Amongst such processes, for which there is good evidence of their existence, frequency and complexity, there are some which have been, or may yet become, conscious. This is what Freud called the *preconscious* (Frith, 1979). Whereas there is a strict limit to the number of items available in the conscious state and therefore capable of being memorized (approximately seven; for example, a number with seven digits), there is very much more information stored at the preconscious level. If a stimulus is ambiguous, only one interpretation is possible in consciousness at any one time, however, multiple meanings are available preconsciously. It is very difficult to carry out more than one task at a time consciously, but undertaking parallel tasks is normal at a preconscious level. Preconscious processes are automatic, whereas conscious ones are flexible and strategic. Consciousness is executive in its nature and is dominant to, and has the capacity to override, the perceptions and functions of preconscious processes.

This function of the preconscious was well-known long before Freud, for example, Brodie (1854):

'But it seems to me that on some occasions a still more remarkable process takes place in the mind, which is even more independent of volition than that of which we are speaking; as if there were in the mind a principle of order which operates without our being at the time conscious of it. It has often happened to me to have been occupied by a particular subject of inquiry; to have accumulated a store of facts connected with it; but to have been able to proceed no further. Then, after an interval of time, without any addition to my stock of knowledge, I have found the obscurity and confusion, in which the subject was originally enveloped, to have cleared away; the facts have all seemed to have settled themselves in their right places, and their mutual relations to have become apparent, although I have not been sensible of having made any distinct effort for that purpose.

DIMENSIONS OF CONSCIOUSNESS

Consciousness, then, is the awareness of experience. There may be awareness of objects or self-reflection. Awareness of objects includes the capacity to be aware of oneself as an object (see Chapter 12); self-reflection refers to the subjective experiencing of self. The three dimensions of consciousness are vigilance, lucidity and self-consciousness.

Vigilance (wakefulness): drowsiness (sleep)

Vigilance is taken to mean the faculty of deliberately staying alert when otherwise one might be drowsy or asleep. This is not uniform or unvarying, but fluctuating. Factors inside the individual that promote vigilance are interest, anxiety, extreme fear or enjoyment; whereas boredom encourages drowsiness. The situation in the environment and the way the individual perceives that situation also affects the vigilance–drowsiness axis. Some abnormal states of health increase vigilance, and many diminish it.

As well as the contrast between vigilance and drowsiness, there are qualitative differences in the nature of wakefulness. The vigilant state of mind of a person scanning a radar screen for a possible enemy interceptor is very different from the rapt attention of a music lover listening to a symphony. These aspects of attention and their abnormalities are discussed in Chapter 3.

Lucidity: clouding

Consciousness is inseparable from the object of conscious attention: lucidity can only be demonstrated in clarity of thought upon a particular topic. The *sensorium*, the total awareness of all internal and external sensations presenting themselves to the organism at this particular moment, may be clear or clouded. Obviously, vigilance is not unrelated; unless the person is fully awake, he cannot be clear in consciousness.

Clouding of consciousness denotes the mildest stage of impairment of consciousness on a continuum from full alertness and awareness to coma

(Lishman, 1978). The patient may be drowsy or agitated, and is likely to show memory disturbance and disorientation. In clouding, most intellectual functions are impaired: attention and concentration; comprehension and recognition; understanding; forming associations; logical judgement; communication by speech; and purposeful action.

Consciousness of self

Alongside full wakefulness and clear awareness is an ability to experience self, and an awareness of self, that is both immediate and complex. This is considered in more detail in Chapter 11.

Pathology of consciousness

Most abnormal states of consciousness show a lowering or diminution of consciousness. However, *heightened* consciousness occurs in which there is a subjective sense of richer perception: colours seem brighter, and so on; there are changes in mood–usually exhilaration perhaps amounting to ecstasy; there is subjective experience of increased alertness, and a capacity for intellectual activity, memory and understanding; there may also be *synaesthesiae* (a sensory stimulus in one modality resulting in sensory experience in another; for example, hearing a finger nail drawn down a blackboard results in a cold feeling down the spine). Such states may occur in normal, healthy people, especially in adolescence or at times of emotional, social or religious crisis: when falling in love, on winning a large sum of money, at sudden religious conversion. Heightened awareness is not uncommon with certain drugs; notably with the hallucinogens (for example, lysergic acid diethylamide (LSD), cannabis) and central nervous system stimulants (for example, amphetamine). A similar state of awareness may occur occasionally in early psychotic illness, especially mania or schizophrenia.

QUANTITATIVE LOWERING OF CONSCIOUSNESS

As mentioned above, consciousness may be considered a continuum from full alertness and awareness to coma. In that sense consciousness may be regarded as quantitative (Figure 2.2). Impairment of consciousness is the primary change in acute organic reactions and holds a fundamentally important place in the detection of acute disturbance of brain function and in assessment of severity (Lishman, 1978).

Some conditions may produce a variable level of diminution of consciousness: that with migraine, for example, may range from blunted awareness through lethargy and drowsiness to loss of consciousness (Lishman, 1978).

Clouding of consciousness

This is the mildest stage of impairment with deterioration in thinking, attention, perception and memory, and, usually, drowsiness and reduced awareness of the environment. There are important differences between the reduced wakefulness before falling asleep and clouding in an organic state (Lipowski, 1967). Although the patient's awareness is *clouded*, he may be agitated and excitable rather than drowsy. Clouding may be seen in a wide variety of acute organic conditions, including drug and alcohol intoxication, head injury, meningeal irritation such as may occur with infection, and so on.

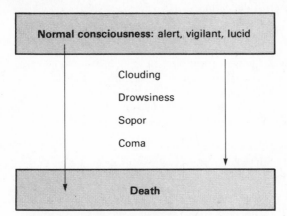

Figure 2.2 Levels or stages of diminished consciousness

The term *clouding* should be used for the psychopathological state: impairment of consciousness, slight drowsiness with or without agitation, and difficulty with attention and concentration. This will usually occur with organic impairment of function; for instance, with cerebral tumour, after head injury or with raised intracranial pressure. If it occurs in schizophrenia, it is as a part of the cognitive deficit that has been shown sometimes to occur in schizophrenia (Frith). It is suggested that in this condition there is an awareness of automatic processes that normally occur below the level of consciousness. These processes are concerned with the selection of appropriate interpretation of stimuli and of response.

Drowsiness

This is the next level of progressive impairment. The patient is 'awake', but will drift into 'sleep' if left without sensory stimulation. He is slow in actions, slurred in speech, sluggish in intention and sleepy in subjective experience. There is an attempt at avoidance of painful stimuli; reflexes, including coughing and swallowing are present but reduced; muscle tone is also diminished.

In psychiatric practice, this is commonly seen following overdosage with drugs that have a central nervous system depressant effect (for example, barbiturates). From the psychiatrist's point of view, it will, of course, mean that interviewing the patient is impossible. These levels of diminished consciousness are quite non-specific and occur whatever the nature of the cause: head injury, tumour, epilepsy, infection, cerebrovascular disorder, metabolic disorder, or toxic state.

Sopor

Whereas the drowsy patient is conscious but lapsing at times into unconsciousness, in sopor the patient is unconscious but may, with strong stimuli, momentarily appear conscious. There are no verbal responses or responding to painful stimuli. Righting response of posture has been lost; reflexes and muscle tone are present but greatly reduced; breathing is slow, deep and rhythmic; face and skin may be flushed.

Coma

The patient is no longer rousable; he is deeply unconscious. These stages of coma have identifiable physical signs ultimately culminating in brain death (Conference of Medical Royal Colleges, 1976).

These stages have all been those that occur progressively and quantitatively with lowering of consciousness. *Qualitative* variations are now discussed further.

QUALITATIVE CHANGES OF CONSCIOUSNESS

Various other organic disturbances in brain function are recognized. These are virtually always associated with a degree of quantitative impairment. The use of terminology in this whole area of discourse is, unfortunately, very muddled; with the same term having different meanings and similar phenomena being described by different words.

Delirium

This term is used appropriately in two quite different ways at present. Lishman restricts the meaning to describe a syndrome of impairment of consciousness along with intrusive abnormalities of perception and affect. *The Diagnostic & Statistical Manual of Mental Disorders* (DSM III), (American Psychiatric Association, 1980) uses the term in a global sense to describe cognitive impairment in a state of clouded consciousness or 'reduction in the clarity of awareness of the environment.' This has replaced the previous term of *acute brain syndrome* and is contrasted in *DSM III* with dementia, which is generally chronic in form. This comprehensive use of the term is well reviewed by Lipowski (1980).

If the term is used in the more limited sense, with disturbance in perceptual and affective functions, the following description applies. The patient is preoccupied with his inner experiences so that only fluctuating attention is paid to the outside world. Perceptual changes include illusions (for instance, cracks in the wall seen as snakes) and hallucinations (especially visual); delusions, especially of a persecutory nature, may occur (these are quite different from the delusions that occur in schizophrenia, which are more complex, and from those in mania and depression); there are marked abnormalities of mood which may vary from stark terror to a fatuous jocularity. There may be a high level of arousal with anxiety, bewilderment and marked motor restlessness and excitability. There is usually considerable clouding of awareness which fluctuates very markedly in intensity over twenty-four hours; being worse in the evening and at night. The patient is highly suggestible to spoken comments and perceptual cues, but there is a loss of grasp: mis-identifications and mis-interpretations occur–one patient thought that nurses were coming to his bed to lay him out, cover him with a sheet and put him in his coffin.

Delirium tremens occurs in the withdrawal stage of alcohol abuse, from twenty-four hours to seven days after ceasing to drink. Tactile and auditory hallucinations may occur. They may be associated with visual, *Lilliputian* hallucinations (seeing little men), so that the patient describes little creatures walking over him. He feels their footsteps and hears them shouting obscene jokes and abusive remarks in his ear. Physical symptoms may include tachycardia, sweating, coarse tremor, dehydration and raised temperature.

A sufferer from delirium tremens described the terrifying, but also humorous, experiences of his nightmarish existence (Anon, 1971):

> 'They were following me in a green car. I went into Woolworth's and bought a saw with six different blades. I laid the blades one by one in various streets to put them off my trail and went home to luncheon... I went up some stairs to see if any of my friends could let me have any money. There were two of them lying across the steps, much diminished in size, their bodies made of the brown stair carpet. They would not speak and made cautionary gestures.
>
> Suddenly I got it. I had not any magic gifts. It had been a rag.... I raced up to the bedroom and, looking out of the window I could see the practical jokers on a flat roof opposite. They were also on our own roof, because one of them lowered a big green, red and gold gargoyle down on a rope to a van in the street. I dictated an insertion in *The Times* personal column, congratulating the revellers on their success.
>
> I awoke in absolute terror. I knew that some time in the night I had given away the code name...'.

Another superb, detailed and lengthy description of the condition is contained in 'The Stroller's Tale' in *Pickwick Papers* (Dickens, 1837). The mood in this account is also a mixture of frivolous buffoonery and abject terror. Illusions and hallucinations abound: 'There were insects too, hideous crawling things with eyes... The walls and ceiling were alive with reptiles–the vault expanded to an enormous size–frightful figures flitted to and fro–and the faces of men he knew, rendered hideous by gibing and mouthing, peered out from among them...'.

Confusion

Confusion is a term, imprecisely defined, referring to subjective symptoms and objective signs indicating loss of capacity for clear and coherent thought. It is purely a descriptive word and does not only apply to clouding of consciousness. When physicians, psychiatrists and nurses were asked what *confusion* meant, marked discordance was found. The term should only be used if clearly defined (Simpson, 1984). It occurs with impairment of consciousness in acute organic states; with disruption of thought processes due to brain damage in chronic organic states; but also is seen in non-organic disturbance. Thus, confusion of thinking may occur as part of the picture in functional psychoses, and also in association with powerful emotion in neurotic disorders. It should therefore be used simply to describe these disturbances of thought, and not as a term pathognomonic of organic psychosyndromes.

The term *acute confusional state* is often used as a synonym for acute organic psychosyndrome (or *delirium* in *DSM III*) in medical literature. The term *confusion* was originally introduced in French psychiatric literature in the latter part of the nineteenth century and is used in a different way in Freudian psychiatric classification. It is referred to a more comprehensive syndrome with chaotic thinking and cognitive failure that included delirium as a subcategory (Berrios, 1981a).

Twilight state

Twilight state refers usually to an organic condition, and most often epilepsy, characterized by: (i) abrupt onset and end; (ii) variable duration from a few hours to several weeks; and, (iii) the occurrence of unexpected violent acts or emotional outbursts during otherwise normal, quiet behaviour (Lishman, 1978). If the term is reserved for these three features in combination as a psychopathological entity, then it should be used whenever they concur, irrespective of cause.

The forensic implications of this condition are therefore important, and it has been used as a legal defence for violent behaviour for which the person had subsequent amnesia.

Consciousness may be markedly impaired or relatively normal between episodes. There may be associated dreamlike states, delusions or hallucinations. It is sometimes associated with temporal lobe seizures of epilepsy; it may occur with other organic states without epilepsy; similar behaviour may occur in apparent hysterical dissociation, and is also described as an acute reaction to massive catastrophe. In the forensic context, it is important to demonstrate: (i) the occurrence of similar episodes with inexplicable behaviour before the key happening; and (ii) other, objective evidence of physical or mental illness. The Ganser state (described with memory disorders in Chapter 4) is, in practice, a sort of twilight state, in which the organic element is often doubtful.

Fluctuation of consciousness

Fluctuation in conscious level is seen in various conditions. It occurs in health, in sleep and in fatigue. In epileptics there is fluctuation in relation to fits. Alterations of conscious level are described with third ventricle tumours (Sim, 1974). In delirious states there may be considerable diurnal fluctuation of consciousness. Characteristically, the patient becomes more disorientated, disturbed in mood and distracted perceptually, with illusions and hallucinations in the late evenings, and shows greatest lucidity mid-morning. Such variation of conscious level is also described and observed with drugs, for instance, mescalin in which there may also be fluctuations of time sense.

Impairment of consciousness associated with organic states may at times be very slight and difficult to demonstrate; especially if the patient's previous level of cognitive functioning is unknown. Fluctuation of consciousness is associated with sensory imput, and impairment is especially likely to occur at night in a darkened room.

Dream-like (oneiroid) state

This is again an unsatisfactory term not clearly differentiated from delirium. The patient is disorientated, confused and experiences elaborate hallucinations, usually visual. There is impairment of consciousness and marked emotional change to terror, or to enjoyment of the hallucinatory experiences; and there may also be auditory or tactile hallucinations. The patient may appear to be living in a dream world and so-called *occupational delirium* could be mentioned in this context: for instance, the ship's petty officer, admitted after a head injury at sea (associated with excess alcohol intake), who kept shouting 'Man the boats'.

It is important to look for other symptoms of organic state to make the important distinction between physical illness and a dissociative non-organic condition.

Stupor

Stupor names a symptom complex whose central feature is a reduction in, or absence of, *relational* functions: that is, action and speech (Berrios, 1981b). This term should therefore be reserved for the syndrome in which mutism and akinesis occur: that is, an inability to initiate speech or action in a patient who appears awake and even alert. It usually occurs with some degree of clouding of consciousness, but does not refer solely to a diminished level. The patient may look ahead or his eyes may wander, but he appears to take nothing in.

This syndrome is characteristic of lesions in the area of the diencephalon and upper brain stem, and also frontal lobe and basal ganglia, and the term *akinetic mutism* has sometimes been reserved by neurologists to describe a much more narrowly defined organic syndrome. It is important to realize, however, that the symptoms of akinesis and mutism in a conscious patient also occurs with schizophrenia, affective psychoses (both depressive and manic) and in hysteria.

The difference between psychogenic (so-called functional) and neurological (organic) causes of stupor can be clinically extremely perplexing. Psychiatric definitions have demanded that the condition is 'a complete absence, in clear consciousness, of any voluntary movements' (Wing *et al.*, 1974). Of course, it is not possible at the time of observation to know whether consciousness is clear or not; and even for functional stupors subsequent amnesia is common. A phenomenological definition of stupor must, therefore, exclude the state of consciousness of a mute patient, and diagnosis of stupor must then be followed by investigation of the differential diagnosis which includes both organic and non-organic condition.

Sleep disorders

These are discussed in Chapter 3.

Automatism

Epileptic automatism may be defined as a state of clouding of consciousness which occurs during, or immediately after, a seizure and during which the individual retains control of posture and muscle tone, and performs simple or complex movements and actions without being aware of what is happening (Fenton, 1975). It occurs as part of the clinical presentation of psychomotor epilepsy, most often arising from discharge in the temporal lobes. It is particularly common in those chronic epileptic patients resident in epileptic colony or mental hospital.

An *aura* may be the first sign of the attack with temporal lobe automatism and may be manifested as abdominal sensations, feelings of confusion with thinking, sensations elsewhere in the body especially the head, hallucinations or illusions (especially olfactory or gustatory), motor abnormalities such as tonic contracture, masticatory movement, salivation or swallowing.

Behaviour during automatism is usually purposeful and often appropriate; for instance, continuing to dry the dishes. Awareness of the environment is impaired: the patient appears to be only partly aware of being spoken to and does not reply appropriately. Initially, activity is diminished with staring eyes, slumped posture; it then becomes stereotyped with repetitive movements, lip smacking, fumbling and other actions. Finally, more complex purposeful behaviour occurs such as walking about, making irrelevant utterances, removing clothing and so on. Sometimes the patient may continue, during automatism, with whatever he was doing before, for example, driving his car; although there is subsequent amnesia and the behaviour or speech at the time never appears entirely normal. Violence is rare during automatism and when it occurs usually amounts to resisting restraint. *Speech automatism* occurs when there is utterance of identifiable words or phrases at some stage during the epileptic attack, for which the patient has no memory later.

Mania à potu (pathological intoxication)

It is important to distinguish this syndrome of acute pathological intoxication with alcohol from delirium tremens, which is a symptom of *withdrawal*. Keller (1977) has defined mania à potu as:

> an extraordinarily severe response to alcohol, especially to small amounts, marked by apparently senseless violent behaviour, usually followed by exhaustion, sleep and amnesia for the episode. Intoxication is apparently not always involved and for this reason *pathological reaction to alcohol* is the preferred term. The reaction is thought to be associated with exhaustion, great strain or hypoglycaemia, and to occur especially in people poorly defended against their own violent impulses.

Coid (1979) describes four components:
(1)   the condition follows the consumption of a variable quantity of alcohol;
(2)   senseless, violent behaviour then ensues;
(3)   there is then prolonged sleep;
(4)   total or partial amnesia for the disturbed behaviour occurs.

Because there is often doubt as to whether intoxication really followed an inappropriately small amount of alcohol, and because several of the other causal factors are diagnostic categories in their own right (hypoglycaemia, epilepsy), Coid would do away with the diagnostic category of *pathological* intoxication leaving only either acute drunkenness or another condition associated with alcohol intake.

References

American Psychiatric Association (1980) *Diagnostic and Statistical Manual of Mental Disorders*, 3rd Edn (DSM III). Washington: American Psychiatric Association.

Anon (1971) 'Or do all doctors know enough about it already?' *World Medicine* Oct. 20, 22–25.

Berrios GE (1981a) Delirium and confusion in the 19th century: a conceptual history. *British Journal of Psychiatry 139*, 439–49.

Berrios GE (1981b) Stupor: a conceptual history. *Psychological Medicine 11*, 677–688

Brodie BC (1854) *Psychological Inquiries: in a series of essays*. London: Longman, Brown, Green & Longman.

Coid J (1979) Mania à potu: a critical review of pathological intoxication. *Psychological Medicine 9*, 709–719.

Conference of Medical Royal Colleges and their Faculties (1976) Diagnosis of brain death. *British Medical Journal 2*, 1187–1188.

Dickens C (1837) *The Posthumous Papers of the Pickwick Club*.

Fenton GW (1975) Epilepsy and automatism. In Silverstone T and Barraclough B (eds; *Contemporary Psychiatry*, 429–439. Ashford: Headley Brothers.

Fish F (1967) *Clinical Psychopathology*. Bristol: John Wright.

Frith CD (1979) Consciousness, information processing and schizophrenia. *British Journal of Psychiatry 134*, 225–35.

Griesinger W (1868) *A History of Medical Psychology* (Zilboorg G & Henry GW (eds), 1941). New York: WW Norton.

Jaspers K (1959) General Psychopathology (transl. Hoenig J & Hamilton MW, 1963). Manchester: Manchester University Press.

Keller M (1977) A lexicon of disablements related to alcohol consumption. In *Alcohol Related Disabilities*. Geneva: World Health Organization.

Lipowski ZS (1967) Delirium, clouding of consciousness and confusion. *Journal of Nervous & Mental Diseases 145*, 227–255.

Lipowski ZJ (1980) *Delirium. Acute Brain Failure in Man*. Springfield, Illinois: Charles C. Thomas.

Lishman WA (1978) *Organic Psychiatry: The Psychological Consequences of Cerebral Disorder*. Oxford: Blackwell Scientific.

Parry R (1975) *A Guide to Counselling and Basic Psychotherapy*. Edinburgh: Churchill Livingstone.

Scharfetter C (1980) *General Psychopathology: An Introduction*. Cambridge: Cambridge University Press.

Sim M (1974) *Guide to Psychiatry*. Edinburgh: Churchill Livingstone.

Simpson CJ (1984) Doctors and nurses use of the word 'confused'. *British Journal of Psychiatry 145*, 441–3.

Wing JK, Cooper JE & Sartorius N (1974) *The Measurement and Classification of Psychiatric Symptoms*. Cambridge: Cambridge University Press.

3

Attention, Concentration and Orientation

Do not adjust your mind, there is a fault in reality

Graffito, University of Birmingham

Attention is the active or passive focusing of consciousness upon an experience. The concept overlaps with the terms 'alertness', 'awareness' and 'responsiveness'. *Voluntary* attention occurs when the subject focuses his attention on an internal or external event; *involuntary* when the event attracts the subject's attention without his conscious effort. *Concentration* is maintaining this focusing of consciousness upon an experience or on the task in hand. *Orientation* is an awareness of one's setting in time and place, and of the realities of one's person and situation. It is not a discrete function, but closely bound up with memory and the clarity or coherence of thought.

This chapter is concerned with cognitive function, but is not limited to the functions which are disturbed by organic lesions, and covers a wider field than just consciousness and its disorders.

Attention, awareness and concentration

Attention is a different function from consciousness, but dependent upon it. Thus, variable degrees of attention are possible with full consciousness, but complete attention and concentration is impossible with diminished consciousness. Attention and awareness are not precisely distinguished but *attention* refers to the objective observation of another person, object or event, whilst *awareness* is the subjective description of the state in which percepts may be received. This is demonstrated by the dialogue: 'Are you paying attention?' 'Yes, I am aware of all that's going on'. Concentration implies attention sustained for some duration of time.

Voluntary (active) attention occurs, for example, as you read this book: you are choosing to direct your attention to it. Your involuntary (passive) attention is drawn to the screech of brakes in the road outside your window. The degree of attention is variable according to the object: the greater the degree of voluntary attention, the less is involuntary attention likely. With voluntary attention there is a clear focus and this guides the *determining tendency* of thought (Chapter 9). With involuntary attention more associations of thought become conscious. These differences, comparing watching a radar screen with thinking while sitting in a deckchair, are represented, with pathological variants, in Figure 3.1.

30

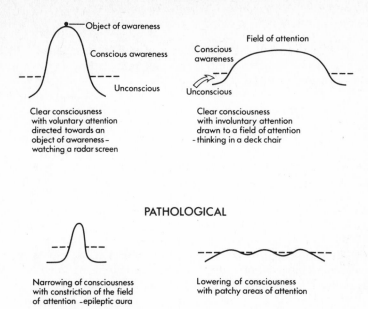

Figure 3.1 Variations in level of awareness

The object at the 'centre of attention' or 'focused' upon is held there by voluntary attention. The further away any object is from this focus within the field of attention, the more involuntary is its command of attention and the less its clarity, until eventually there is no demarcation between what is made consciously aware and what is not conscious at this moment (preconscious).

Kräupl Taylor (1983) has contrasted *vigilance* with *absorption*. The attention of the vigilant person moves freely from one object to another. In absorption, attention is reduced so that the person appears absent-minded; the content of this absorption is, however, usually remembered afterwards. These abnormal states of awareness and attention (there is no organic lowering of consciousness) are of two kinds—*transcendental meditation* and *trance*. In transcendental meditation, the person becomes absorbed by an experience that results in the physiological pattern of sleepiness; in trance, this physiological state need not occur and the person may be physiologically active. Trance may be induced by individual or group hypnotic suggestion, autosuggestion or in mass experiences associated with high emotion (political rallies, religious ceremonies).

ALTERATION OF THE DEGREE OF ATTENTION

Attention is decreased in normal people in sleep, dreams, hypnotic states, fatigue and boredom. It may be pathologically decreased in organic states, usually with lowering of consciousness, for instance: in head injury; acute toxic confusional states such as drug and alcohol-induced conditions; epilepsy; raised intracranial pressure; and brain stem lesions. In psychogenic states, attention may be altered, for example, in hysterical dissociation. Narrowing of attention is also prominent in depressive illness, where the morbid mood state results in attention being limited to a restricted number of themes.

A severe deficit of attention is a prominent feature in the hyperkinetic syndrome of childhood (Attention deficit disorder in DSM III: American Psychiatric Association, 1980). Observation of the child's behaviour by adults such as parents or teachers concentrates on the three aspects: inattention, impulsiveness and hyperactivity. Inattention is shown in that the child, most often a boy and usually aged between 3 and 10, fails to finish activities he starts, appears not to listen, is easily distracted, has difficulty in concentrating on any task requiring sustained attention, and has difficulty sticking to a play activity.

Lack of attention denotes an inability to focus on an object in a purposeful way, and disturbance of concentration an inability to retain this attention, implying weakening of the determining tendency. This is a feature of mania and hypomania, and also occurs in organic states. These are combined to show the symptom of *distractability* which is prominent in mania and some organic states.

Narrowing of attention entails the ability of the subject to focus on a small part of the field of awareness, and occurs in conditions where involuntary attention is directed elsewhere–by hallucinations, by delusions or by strong emotion. After an unprofitable conversation with a schizophrenic patient in which she repeatedly ignored questions, she said, 'I wish you would not interrupt when I am being given my instructions'.

PSYCHOSIS AND ATTENTION

Alteration of external perception depends upon attention. For instance, as the auditory hallucinations gradually disappear with successful treatment in schizophrenia, the patient sometimes describes having to concentrate fully to hear the voices anymore, 'and even then they seem faint and unimportant'. In other situations, psychotic experiences only occur with lowered attention. Thus *functional hallucinations* (Chapter 6, p.78) tend to occur associated with a normal perception which is in the background and not the focus of attention: 'I only hear the voices when the water pipes are noisy'. A *visual pseudo-hallucination* (Chapter 6, p.74) may be removed by directly looking at it. *Pareidolic illusions* become more clear-cut with a greater degree of attention.

Depressed mood is often associated with preoccupation with gloomy thoughts to such an extent that concentration and attention are impaired. In such a situation misinterpretations of perception influenced by the mood state frequently arise. Every hearse is believed to be there to carry the patient to the graveyard and a passing black car is noticed just sufficiently to be considered as strengthening this belief. Similarly, acute anxiety often results in diminished attention.

Sleep disorders

Here, most often, we are dealing with normal phenomena, about which some people make complaint, rather than definite pathology, although there are definite sleep disorders. The loss of consciousness that occurs in sleep is quite different from that occurring in organic states, for example, following head injury. The alerting and arousal mechanisms are suspended but can readily be brought into action, and the psychic self remains in touch with meaningful stimuli. Many doctors have experienced the extraordinarily selective mechanism of waking instantly to the sound of the telephone when they are on duty, but excluding entirely other extraneous noises and the sound of a telephone in a neighbouring room when they are not on call. The sense of time is also preserved in sleep and can be demonstrated by the accuracy with which a person may wake at a predetermined hour.

INSOMNIA

Insomnia implies subjective dissatisfaction with the duration or quality of sleep (Oswald, 1981). It is more common in women and in older people, and is more often associated with a feeling of excessive mental arousal than bodily disorder. Causes of dissatisfaction include unrealistic expectations from the elderly that they will sleep for as long as when they were younger; and, from the sedentary, that they will sleep as deeply as after exhausting physical activity. Complaints of sleeping poorly are extremely common, being among the most frequent symptoms in neuroses and affective disorders. Comparing neurotic patients with a normal population, Jovanovic (1978) found that neurotic patients complained of more wakefulness in the first third of the night; they spent more time lying awake in bed; they awoke during the night more frequently; they spent a relatively shorter period in deep sleep; and their sleep was more likely to be impaired by unfamiliar surroundings. *Early insomnia*, or difficulty in getting off to sleep, occurs in normal people who are aroused through anxiety or excitement. Their thoughts tend to dwell on the affect-laden experiences of the immediate past, and also to rehearse ways of dealing with problems. Fatigue is experienced, but there is also a high level of arousal which prevents the necessary relaxation and withdrawal from perception required for sleeping.

Late insomnia is particularly characteristic of the depressive phase of affective disorders. The patient may wake frequently in the night after getting off to sleep satisfactorily and thenceforward only sleep fitfully and lightly. Alternatively, he may wake early in the morning and be unable to get to sleep again. The important characteristic of depression is that there is a marked change in sleep rhythm from the normal pattern for that person. In depression, the early morning wakening is often associated with marked diurnality of mood with the most severe feelings of despondency and retardation occurring in the early morning. There is also often a marked reduction of sleep requirement in mania.

The mean sleep requirement diminishes with increasing age. It is usually about seven to eight hours through the middle adult years but is markedly reduced from about age 50 onwards. With insomnia, intermediate stages of light, restless sleep occur. These are often associated with abnormal experience in the sleepy state such as *hypnagogic* and *hypnopompic* hallucinations (Chapter 6). Pseudo-hallucinations also occur, and vivid imagery that is difficult to distinguish from hallucination. Normally, passage into sleep is rapid and occurs passively rather than with active intention to sleep. Waking is also normally rapid, and the slowing of this process of becoming awake may be described as a symptom: a complaint of feeling drowsy, being incompetent and incoordinated for an excessive time upon wakening; in other words, *sleep drunkenness*.

HYPERSOMNIA

Hypersomnia may occur either as sleeping for significantly longer periods at night or episodes of somnolence during the day. These cases are more often seen by a neurologist than a psychiatrist and are only reported briefly here.

In the *Kleine–Levin syndrome* attacks of somnolence occur usually in young men. The condition is very rare and usually the attack ends spontaneously. The patient sleeps excessively by day and night, but is rousable as from normal sleep. When awake the patient eats voraciously (megaphagia) and may show marked irritability (Critchley, 1962).

Hypersomnia with sleep drunkenness is more common: the patient has difficulty in achieving complete wakefulness and exhibits confusion, disorientation, a readiness to return to sleep and motor incoordination (Lishman, 1978). Such patients may sleep for seventeen hours or more and always require vigorous stimulation to wake. The condition may persist throughout life.

In the *Pickwickian syndrome*, named after the fat boy of Pickwick Papers (Dickens, 1837), profound daytime somnolence is associated with gross obesity and cyanosis due to hypoventilation. Breathing is periodic during sleep and somnolence, with apnoeic phases that may last for up to a minute, occur.

Sustained drowsiness may occur with organic lesions of the mid brain or hypothalamus of various causes. Hunger, weight gain, excessive thirst and polyuria may also occur.

Hypersomnia may also occur as a psychogenic symptom. There may be a state amounting to hysterical stupor and other conversion symptoms may occur. Other neurotic patients complain persistently of daytime somnolence and an inability to concentrate.

SOMNAMBULISM

Sleepwalking usually occurs in children and in males more often than females. Activity is usually confined to aimless wandering and purposeless repetitive behaviour for a few minutes. The boy may reply monosyllabically to questions and there is little awareness of the environment, but injury is unusual. Frequently there is a family history and enuresis is often associated. As sleepwalking occurs in deep sleep (Stages 3 and 4), usually during the first third of the night, it is unlikely to be the acting out of dreams. It is not the same phenomenon as epileptic automatism, which may also result in a person, who is apparently asleep, getting up and walking around. It is important to establish the diagnosis.

Night terrors also occur in deep sleep early in the night and often in the same individual who sleep walks. Intense anxiety is manifested, the subject may shout, and there is rapid pulse and respiration. Usually there is complete amnesia for the experience on waking. It is not the same experience as a nightmare since this is a type of dream, occurring in lighter stages of sleep, and is remembered vividly if the person awakes immediately after the experience. Most children grow out of night terrors and sleepwalking.

It has been claimed that automatic, violent behaviour has taken place during a night terror. A person who commits a criminal act while asleep is not conscious of his actions and cannot be held legally responsible for them: what the law calls *sane automatisms* (Fenwick, 1986). If the act, for instance homicide, is remembered by its perpetrator as following a chain of psychic events ('being chased by Japanese soldiers'), these images are most likely to have occurred in the context of a nightmare and the act therefore took place on waking and would be regarded as motivated. During the nightmare itself sleep paralysis (see below) will prevent violent emotions being acted upon. For the act to be convincingly ascribed to night terror neither the act nor its antecedent storyline should be remembered and all the evidence should point to the individual being asleep at the time. Previous evidence of night terror and sleep activity is important for corroboration.

NARCOLEPSY

Narcoleptic attacks usually occur first during adolescence and persist through life; they are short episodes of sleep (ten to fifteen minutes) which occur irresistibly during the day. It is often associated with *cateplexy* during which the subject falls down due to sudden loss of muscle tone provoked by strong emotion. *Hypnagogic hallucinations* and *sleep paralysis* may also occur, but less commonly, in the syndrome. There is usually no structural brain disease present. Hypnagogic hallucinations are usually auditory but may be visual or tactile. They occur between wakefulness and sleep; less commonly between sleep and wakening (hypopompic hallucination). Sleep paralysis is an episode of inability to move occurring between wakefulness and sleep–in either direction.

Dreams

Orthodox sleep and *paradoxical* sleep have been distinguished from each other using sleep electroencephalographic tracings in human subjects (Oswald, 1980). Normal reflex activity occurs in the stages of orthodox sleep, but localized activity is seen in paradoxical sleep whilst other muscle actions are paralysed. Rapid eye movements in paradoxical sleep are to some extent associated with dreaming. Nightmares are unpleasant dreams: often the particular horror of a nightmare is that there is nothing the sufferer can do about the terrifying experience. Dreaming occurs in rapid eye movement (paradoxical) sleep and the transfixed sensation of the nightmare is an accurate representation of the sleep paralysis that occurs in that phase.

Dreams have been used to establish elaborate psychiatric theories concerning the origins of conflict; it is outside the scope of this book to enter into any discussion of this area. It is, of course, a topic that was extensively written about by Sigmund Freud (1976). More recently the meaning of dreams has been explored empirically by Kramer *et al.* (1976). Dreams are remembered and described as a psychic event: nightmares (unpleasant dreams) are often complained of and may be a prominent symptom, for instance, in depression. Dreams are highly complex experiences and, so far, have defied adequate analysis and explanation. However, certain characteristics can be described.

There is a loss of some of the structures of waking consciousness; thus there is a loss of self-awareness and awareness of the confines of one's own body. The margin between self and not-self becomes indefinite. The dreamer may dream of himself merging or transforming into someone else without contradiction. Time sense is also lost: there is no sense of progression of events but only immediate awareness of the present. Events occurring in the dream include those in which the dreamer himself is instrumental. There is often a loss of the sense of his having circumstances within his control, and there is also a loss of the physical and mental associations between the different parts of a whole experience. There are, therefore, gaps unaccounted for in space, as well as in time and causation.

As well as the loss of temporal and spatial connections, there is a loss of the psychological associations between events. There is no progressive sequence of serial ideas or pictures. The dream is often like a group of short excerpts from very different films.

In addition to the loss of structure which is typical of the dreaming state, fresh elements also obtrude. These are best called dream-images as they are not accurately delusions, hallucinations, false memories, or other abnormalities of perception or ideation characteristic of the waking state. These images are more vivid than fantasy, and have a characteristic of immediacy and importance; so it is not surprising that from the beginnings of time, people have acted on their dreams as if they were instructions.

To regard dreaming as a symptom, rather than merely a remembered experience, it has to become invested with unpleasant affect. A patient may describe pleasant dreams if requested, but he does not usually complain of these as symptoms, or ask for their removal. However, if the dream is associated with anxiety, terror, gloom, foreboding, and especially if the content or the theme is recurrent, it will be complained of and will indicate a prevailing affect; possibly the areas of conflict which have precipitated the distress will be revealed in the content of the dream. Unpleasant dreams in which the traumatic event is re-experienced are very characteristic of post-traumatic stress disorder (aftermath neurosis) following major disaster or catastrophe.

Hypnosis

There is very great difficulty in understanding and Marcuse (1959) suggests that we 'define hypnosis by what it does rather than by what it is'. At one extreme hypnosis is considered to be a very different state of awareness from normal waking consciousness. At the other extreme Merskey (1979) considers that '...the phenomena of hypnosis are identical with those of hysteria: they involve self-deception and the production of alternative symptoms or behaviour to solve a problem, even if not a conflict.' Merskey further goes on to propose as definition:

> Hypnosis is a manoeuvre in which the subject and hypnotist have an implicit agreement that certain events (e.g. paralysis, hallucinations, amnesias) will occur, either during a special procedure or later, in accordance with the hypnotist's instructions. Both try hard to put this agreement into effect and adopt appropriate behavioural rules and the subject uses mechanisms of denial to report on the events in accordance with the implicit agreement. This situation is used to implement various motives whether therapeutic or otherwise, on the part of both participants. There is no trance state, no detectable cerebral physiological change, and only such peripheral physiological responses as may be produced equally by non-hypnotic suggestions or other emotional changes.

Superficially, hypnosis appears to resemble sleep, but there are no electroencephalographic findings to distinguish hypnosis from other states of relaxed wakefulness. The trance in hypnosis is produced, therefore, in a waking state by one person upon another using suggestion with compliance (Marcuse). It has been claimed to occur in non-human species, but this state cannot be truly regarded as hypnosis. Hypnosis has been used for the control of pain, in the treatment of hyperemesis gravidarum, for various sexual difficulties, and especially in the control of anxiety (Waxman, 1984).

The induction of hypnosis requires the implicit contract Merskey implies. The subject must be willing and co-operative; he or she relaxes and exercises imagination. The field of consciousness is narrowed to include only the instructions of the hypnotist. The subject relinquishes some degree of control to the hypnotist and accepts reality distortion. Following the successful induction of hypnosis autohypnosis can become established. Marcuse considers the following to be the characteristics of an hypnotic state:

(1) the subject ceases to make his own plans;
(2) attention is selectively directed, for example, towards the voice of the hypnotist;
(3) reality testing is diminished and distortions are accepted;
(4) suggestibility is increased;
(5) the hypnotized subject readily enacts unusual roles;
(6) post-hypnotic amnesia is often present.

Suggestion, for the hypnotic subject, is straightforward and obvious; it does not imply gullibility or loss of will-power. It describes the emotion of trust occurring within the implicit relationship in which the subject accepts the hypnotist's statements, acts upon his commands and denies evidence from his senses which would contradict those statements.

A capacity for fantasy is necessary for hypnosis to take place. The relaxation which accompanies hypnosis may progress to normal sleeping, even during a hypnotic session. The alteration in conscious awareness occurring in hypnosis is similar to that in dissociative states, but different from the fluctuations of conscious level occurring in organic psychosyndromes.

Suggestion has been used to produce many physical sequelae, for example blisters, alterations in pulse and blood pressure, levitation of an arm, opisthotonus, absence of pain sensation, and so on. The psychological effects are equally variable and include alterations to perception, cognition, ideation, memory and affect. The subject enters a dramatically altered state in which he temporarily surrenders responsibility for his actions to the hypnotist. In his turn, the hypnotist retains the confidence of the subject only as long as he keeps within the limits of behaviour that the subject finds acceptable; beyond this the subject will relinquish his dependent relationship and come out of the hypnotic state.

Orientation

Orientation is the capacity of a person to know what is real in his current setting in time, space and person. This enables him to make sense of, and be at home in, his environment. This is virtually the same faculty as intellectual grasp in that various perceptual cues are used, and with correct sense of time and place the person is able to come to appropriate conclusions from his context. A man suffering from an advanced dementia was being interviewed by a doctor in the presence of a dozen student nurses, who were taking notes with pen and notebook. When asked where he was, he looked around the rather dingy hospital classroom and said, 'Well, we're waiting to see the doctor'. He had picked up certain clues that reminded him of a general practitioner's waiting room; he had totally missed that all the nurses were in uniform, that they were taking notes, that he was being asked formal questions; and he was disorientated in place and in person.

Orientation in *time* is labile and quite readily disturbed by rapt concentration, strong emotion or organic brain factors (for example, alcoholic intoxication). Milder degrees of disorientation are shown in being inaccurate by more than half an hour for the time of day or duration of interview. More advanced states are demonstrated with incorrect day of the week, year or period of day. Yet further disturbance is shown when the season of the year is not known.

Orientation in *space* is disturbed later in the disease process than time. A patient may be unable to find his way, especially in an area which is relatively new to him. It may take him an inordinate length of time to learn his way to the dining table in the ward after admission. Disorientation in time and place are, when clearly established, evidence of an organic mental state–they may be the earliest signs in a dementing process.

In disorientation for *person*, the patient fails to remember his own name. Loss of knowledge of the patient's own name and identity occurs at a very late stage of organic deterioration. Loss of intellectual grasp (apprehension) occurs in organic states as a form of disorientation, usually combined with other evidence of deterioration. Such a person cannot understand the context of his present situation and connects outside objects and events with himself. Disorientation may occur with a disturbance of consciousness, attention, perception or intelligence. In severe intellectual defect and severe disturbances of memory, orientation is impaired even when consciousness is clear (Scharfetter, 1980).

DISORIENTATION

Orientation may fluctuate in some organic conditions; for example, a patient with an acute toxic state associated with congestive cardiac failure was disorientated in time every evening, but quite clear mentally in the morning.

Disorientation in time and loss of intellectual grasp (situational disorientation) usually occur first in a progressive illness; disorientation in place usually occurs later and, in person, last of all. Disorientation for one's own identity occurs at a later stage than for that of other people. An elderly woman who knew who she was and her previous status as a professor's wife, kept on referring to her daughter as 'that minx who comes in every time the doctor visits'.

Delusions which mimic disorientation

It is, of course, important to understand the phenomenological distinction between disorientation and a delusion which results in misinterpretation of place, of situation or of person. Disorientation is usually associated with other organic features such as lowering of consciousness or disturbance of memory. Delusions of misorientation have the features of a delusion (Chapter 8): a patient on the ward may believe himself to be in prison and a visiting relative may be considered to be an interrogator from the Gestapo.

Dissociation and disorientation

Definite, undisputed disorientation is indicative of either an acute organic brain syndrome, if coupled with lowering of consciousness, or chronic organic deterioration. Hysterical dissociation may mimic this, however, with apparent disorientation. Careful examination of the mental state is likely to reveal suggestive discrepancies; for example, disorientation for person may be much more marked than for time, or may be bizarre to an excessive extent. A patient is described in the next chapter who lived in Birmingham, UK but found himself after a hysterical fugue in Montreal. Although apparently disorientated, he actually showed an abnormality of memory–a dissociative state.

References

American Psychiatric Association (1980) *Diagnostic and Statistical Manual of Mental Disorders*, 3rd Edn (DSM III). Washington: American Psychiatric Association.

Critchley M (1962) Periodic hypersomnia and megaphagia in adolescent males. *Brain 85*, 627–656.

Dickens C (1837) The Posthumous Papers of the Pickwick Club.

Fenwick P (1986) Murdering while asleep. *British Medical Journal 293*, 574.

Freud S (1976) *The Interpretation of Dreams* (transl. Strachey J). Pelican Freud Library. Harmondsworth: Penguin.

Jovanovic UJ (1978) Sleep profile and ultradian sleep periodicity in neurotic patients compared with the corresponding parameters in healthy human subjects. *Waking and Sleeping 2*, 47–55.

Kramer M, Hlasny R, Jacobs G and Roth T (1976) Do dreams have meaning? An empirical enquiry. *American Journal of Psychiatry 133*, 778–781.

Kräupl Taylor F (1983) Descriptive and developmental phenomena. In Shepherd M and Zangwill OL (eds) *Handbook of Psychiatry Volume I*. Cambridge: Cambridge University Press.

Lishman WA (1978) *Organic Psychiatry*. Oxford: Blackwell Scientific.

Marcuse FL (1959) *Hypnosis: Fact and Fiction*. Harmondsworth: Penguin.

Merskey H (1979) *The Analysis of Hysteria*. London: Baillière Tindall.

Oswald I (1980) *Sleep*. 4th Edn. Harmondsworth: Penguin.

Oswald I (1981) Assessment of insomnia. *British Medical Journal 283*, 874–5.

Scharfetter C (1980) *General Psychopathology: An Introduction*. Cambridge: Cambridge University Press.

Waxman D (1984) *Psychological Influences and Illness: Hypnosis and Medicine*. London: Macmillan.

— 4

Disturbance of Memory

Memory declares that I did this; I could have done this, says my pride; and memory loses the day.   Nietzsche (1889)

That memory disturbance was a specific feature following head injury and other conditions was recognized in neuropsychiatric writings in the mid-nineteenth century. Hughlings Jackson (1887) recognized it to be part of deterioration in organic mental functioning. The earliest detailed study of disordered memory from a psychological standpoint was by Ribot (1881). Later, Korsakov (1890) described his eponymous condition, pointing out that gross disorder of memory may occur in patients in whom other intellectual functions and judgement are preserved.

Mechanisms of memory

One of the major justifications for using psychopathology in the description of memory disturbance is that there exists no good analogue of memory in animals (Gray, 1982). Conventionally, disturbance of memory is described in terms of the length of time information has been retained. It is in fact quite arbitrary to make a distinction between memory and perception as they are both stages in information processing (Weinman, 1981). *Storage* is organized in three ways:

Immediate memory (sensory store). Information is held for less than a second in the form in which it was perceived. Visual (iconic) and auditory (echoic) storage is separate, and information is not processed in semantic form. This level is not usually affected in organic disorders. It is, of course, closely related to attention.

Short-term memory (primary memory). This is limited to approximately 15–20 seconds unless the material is rehearsed, and usually only about six or seven items can be stored–as new items are added, previous ones are lost. Verbal items may be retained as sounds rather than meanings. There is some evidence for separate mechanisms for visual and verbal mechanisms located in the right and left hemispheres respectively. The *digit span* is used to examine this function. The rate of forgetting in short-term memory has been measured experimentally by Milner (1972), and the performance of the task in remembering deteriorated after about 30 seconds.

Long-term memory (secondary memory). Duration is for most of life and capacity is very large. Information is stored in coded form, either semantically or by association. Forgetting may be by loss of information or failure of retrieval. Language and personal events (episodes) may be stored by different mechanisms (Tulving, 1973). Storage in, and also retrieval from, the long-term memory is impaired in the *dysamnestic syndromes*. Information is stored in reorganized and sometimes distorted form.

Description of the functions of memory is chiefly referable to long-term memory and can be subdivided *phenomenologically* into the following five categories:

1   *Registration* is the capacity to add new materials to the memory store. This takes place either by a process of learning in which there is repeated presentation of material, or registration on a single presentation.
2   *Retention* is the ability to store knowledge which can subsequently be returned to consciousness.
3   *Retrieval* is the capacity to obtain stored material from the memory; its loss denotes an organic impairment.
4   *Recall* is the return of stored, remembered information into consciousness at a chosen moment.
5   *Recognition* is the feeling of familiarity which accompanies the return of stored material to consciousness. It is therefore not strictly part of the process of memory but is intimately connected.

Abnormality of memory may occur in any of these areas. Disturbance of memory affects: (a) the reliability of the material recalled (is it a faithful reproduction of what was observed and registered?), (b) duration of memory — there is a differential loss of disturbance of short-term as opposed to long-term memory, (c) accessibility of memory. Information needs to be readily accessible when required, and available in a form which is useful for thinking and planning. The rate of forgetting differs in the various disturbances of function.

Organic impairment of memory

Memory disturbances can be separated into those that are psychogenic, sometimes occurring in healthy people; and those that are organic, associated with disease of the brain. These latter are referred to as *organic* or *true* amnesia, and can be described in terms of the different functions of memory.

IMPAIRMENT OF REGISTRATION

Adequate perception, comprehension and response to the material presented is a prerequisite for the learning involved in memory (Welford, 1951).

Apperception is the ability to understand perceptions in their context; to interpret them appropriately; to connect them with each other and form associations; and to incorporate them into total experience. This is grossly disturbed in states of disturbed consciousness and, therefore, registration cannot take place either. Failure of apperception is a symptom *par excellence* in acute confusional psychoses, and this partly explains the occurrence of the various perceptual disturbances.

Two examples of failure of registration are the anterograde amnesia following head injury and the *palimpsest* or alcoholic amnesia (so-called 'alcoholic black-out'), an early sign of established alcohol dependence. In this state, the heavy drinker may be acting and talking relatively normally whilst continuing drinking. His state of consciousness is not grossly abnormal and he interacts with people and co-ordinates his behaviour without obvious defect. However, the next day he may have no recollection of the latter part of the evening's happenings at all. When reminded, he still has no memory; even when told of what he himself said or did: there is complete failure of registration. An alcoholic patient was terrified on waking up in the morning when his girlfriend said 'What did you get up to last night, Arthur?' He had no idea what he had been doing!

IMPAIRMENT OF RETENTION

Retention can be divided into immediate, recent and remote memory. After temporal lobectomy the degree of defect of recent memory varies in proportion to the extent of bilateral hippocampal damage (Scoville and Milner, 1957). Remote memory is left intact. Defect of memory does not occur following unilateral operations unless there was pre-existing damage to the other lobe. Impairment of recent memory is usually an early finding in dementias both senile and (Alzheimer's type) and multi-infarct dementia (arteriosclerotic), as well as other, less common, presenile causes. The discrepancy between the clarity of remote memory and the defect of recent memory is strikingly highlighted by Pratt's elderly patient who described the village where she had spent her childhood: 'I can remember it as clearly as if I had seen it yesterday'—in fact, she had.

Disturbance of recent memory storage occurs, for example, in the *retrograde amnesia* of cerebral trauma. So, perceptions which reached the sensorium just before the accident in which the patient suffered a head injury, are removed entirely. Retrograde amnesia lasts for no longer than a few minutes before the injury, and the term should not be used for other types of amnesia. Hypnosis and intravenous barbiturates have been successfully used to increase memory for events immediately preceding head injury.

IMPAIRMENT OF RETRIEVAL

Zangwill (1983) has developed the case for there being two quite distinct types of amnesia: *diencephalic* (typically occurring in the Korsakov syndrome) and *hippocampal* (as in post-encephalitic states or after bilateral operation on the temporal lobes). In the Korsakov syndrome, which term should be reserved for memory disorder alone, there is severe amnesia, lack of insight, denial of disability and confabulation. In the hippocampal type, there is amnesia of equal severity, but insight and judgement are well preserved and there is no confabulation. In both types of amnesic syndrome there is a relatively pure retrieval deficit (Weizkrantz, 1978).

The degree of amnesia, and also the quite considerable residual learning capacity, is similar in these two conditions; however, in the hippocampal (temporal lobe type) storage capacity is diminished and forgetting accelerated, whilst in Korsakov syndrome the defect is predominantly in the retrieval of recently acquired information. Experimental evidence for this has been collected by Piercy (1977).

IMPAIRMENT OF RECALL

Failure of recall is characteristic of psychological failures of memory; for example, in hysterical fugue or acute anxiety or during an interview for a job in a healthy person. Recall may be tested in laboratory experiments and in clinical interview. This function is discussed further in the section on psychogenic disturbance of memory below.

Recollection is the reintegration of a complete event from a variety of different ones: it is a function of recall. It may be possible to recall a complete, learned poem from memory store. To remember the events of a complex series of events or a complete day–for instance, a wedding day or the circumstances proving that you were not involved in a crime–requires recalling a number of separate items of information by exploring many different avenues. This is the area of memory investigated in psychoanalytic treatment. Impairments of recall and recognition are not found in pure form in organic disorders but are characteristic of psychogenic disturbance and probably reflect integration, at a high level, of several psychological functions.

IMPAIRMENT OF RECOGNITION

Recognition is primarily affective in nature: a feeling of familiarity, rather than cognitive. This was first realised by Claparède (1911) observing patients with Korsakov syndrome who, seeing their doctor every day but not acknowledging any familiarity, still treated him as if he were not a stranger. He demonstrated that such patients still had some residual capacity for retention and hence for learning new habits even though the patient described no memory for the event nor feeling of familiarity for the task. Thus recognition has been disturbed even though there is still some capacity for retention and retrieval. Disorders of recognition, although affective in quality, often have a largely organic basis.

Miscellaneous disturbances of memory

DÉJÀ VU AND RELATED PHENOMENA (IDENTIFYING PARAMNESIA)

Recognition was described as an abnormality of the affect associated with memory. Déjà vu is not primarily a memory disorder, but a disturbance in which the associated feeling of familiarity that normally occurs with previously experienced events, occurs when the event is experienced for the first time. In jamais vu, an experience which the patient knows he has experienced before is not associated with the appropriate feeling of familiarity. The patient may have the feeling that some important memory is about to be recalled, although it does not actually arrive.

Déjà vu and jamais vu are common normal experiences but may also be significant symptoms of temporal lobe epilepsy. An epileptic patient said: 'I feel that I've done something terribly wrong'. However, these experiences on their own, or associated only with vague feelings of depersonalization, should not be accepted as evidence of temporal lobe epilepsy as these symptoms are frequently experienced both in neurotic patients and in normal individuals (Lishman, 1978).

CONFABULATION

This is a falsification of memory occurring in clear consciousness in association with an organically derived amnesia (Berlyne, 1972). Bonhoeffer (1901) observed that confabulation in the Korsakov syndrome could take two forms:

1   Confabulation of *embarrassment*, which was a direct result of the memory loss and depended for its presence on a certain attentiveness and activity. The patient tries to cover an exposed memory gap by an ad hoc confabulated excuse relating to his recent behaviour.
2   In other cases, confabulation exceeded the needs of the memory impairment; the patient describes spontaneously adventurous experiences of a *fantastic* nature. Such memory disturbance may occur with organic deterioration following alcohol abuse and also with *presbyophrenia*, where there is intellectual impairment, especially gross memory disturbance and disorder of behaviour in the elderly.

Suggestibility is a prominent feature of the confabulating patient and was considered by Pick (1921) to be dependent on clouding of consciousness, weakened judgement and the interplay of fantasy; and may, in fact, closely resemble day-dreams. The confabulating patient may produce mutually contradictory statements consecutively and not make any attempt to correct them. Confabulation has been considered to be commonest at the beginning of the Korsakov syndrome, and it gradually disappears as the patient deteriorates in intellectual function. Personality traits and social habits tend to be accentuated with Korsakov syndrome. An alcoholic proprietress of a club confabulated with effortless aplomb. Her social graces and friendliness made her very popular, even though she believed she was in hospital having just been delivered of her baby (in fact, now a daughter aged 12).

The material of confabulations has been likened to dreams (Scheid, 1934). It has also be explained, in terms of memory disturbance, that confabulations are actual experiences taken out of their chronological order (Van der Horst, 1932); that the individual's wishes and interests guide confabulation in the same way as in dreams and fantasy. It seems probable that confabulation is related to the normal mechanisms of recollection. The owners of a certain make of car were asked by the police, as part of a large-scale murder hunt, what they were doing on a particular Monday about nine months previously. To answer this question, an individual would have no recollection for that particular Monday; so he would recreate a typical programme with regular movements and times of appointments for a Monday from about that period. It would seem that the mechanism of *social confabulation* is of that order. To the question, 'What did you do yesterday?', the confabulating patient mentioned above said, 'I pushed my baby in the pram down to the office to see my old workmates there'. This could indeed have happened 12 years previously when she had resigned her job in that office during her pregnancy. The *fantastic* type of confabulation is also directly associated with memory. Normally one has a clear memory of which sensations and events were experienced and which were fantasized; yet with confabulation it is probable that distant fantasies are remembered, but it is not remembered that they were fantasy rather than reality. Such confabulations, like the *momentary* type are autobiographical. The momentary or embarrassment confabulation is very much more common than the fantastic type, and is a true memory displaced in its time context (Berlyne, 1972). Confabulation occurs in dementia and other organic states, as well as in the Korsakov syndrome. Marked suggestibility is a feature of all types of confabulation.

Fantastic confabulation with persecutory content has been described by Roth and Myers (1969). This is a falsification of memory occurring in clear consciousness. Typically, the patient believes others are stealing his money or trying to defraud him. Memory falsifications of various types occur in schizophrenia, depressive illness, asocial personality disorder and obsessional states. The more definite fantastic and gap-filling features of organic confabulation are always associated with memory defect.

PERSEVERATION

Perseveration usually occurs in association with disturbance of memory and is a sign of organic brain disease—perhaps the only pathognomonic sign in psychiatry. It occurs with clouding of consciousness and is particularly useful in distinguishing this from hysterical abnormalities (Allison, 1962). Perseveration is defined as a response that was appropriate to a first stimulus being given inappropriately to a second, different stimulus. This may be demonstrated verbally or in motor activity. The interviewer, while conducting the mental state examination, asks: 'What is the capital of Italy?'–'Rome'; and then subsequently, 'What is the object that you wear which tells you the time?'–'Rome'. Alternatively, the examiner asks the patient to put his right hand on his left shoulder, which he does correctly; and then, on asking him to put his left hand on his left knee, he again puts his right hand on his left shoulder.

MEMORY DISTURBANCE AND ELECTROCONVULSIVE THERAPY (ECT)

There is always some memory disturbance after electroconvulsive therapy (ECT). Memory may be lost for events preceding ECT (retrograde amnesia); initially for some time, but rapidly shortening to a few seconds (Williams, 1977). There is also some anterograde amnesia, with difficulty in retention for some hours after treatment. Defect of memory for current events may persist for a few weeks after completing a course of treatment. This memory disturbance is similar to other organic amnesic states.

The retention defect is related to the strength and duration of electrical stimulation and to the duration of the seizure. Confusion and memory disturbance have been claimed to be less after unilateral, non-dominant ECT. There is no evidence for loss of the ability to acquire new patterns of behaviour or execute established ones, even after a long course of ECT.

Using a very wide-ranging battery of tests to examine all areas of cognitive function, Weeks *et al.* (1981) state that ECT does not produce lasting impairment when used in everyday clinical circumstances. Memory functions tested included recall, releasing rate, and recognition in the auditory-verbal and visuo-spatial modalities. Similarly Fraser (1982) considers that the memory loss that follows ECT is minimal and can only be detected for a few hours after treatment. Amnesia is both retrograde and anterograde with delayed recall of material learned soon after ECT most affected. Unilateral placement of electrodes accelerates post-ictal recovery and shortens the duration of amnesia (Fraser).

TEMPORAL LOBE DISORDER

It is useful to summarize at this stage the psychopathological phenomena of temporal lobe dysfunction: disturbance of memory, perception and affect. Disorder of memory includes the hippocampal defects of diminished storage and accelerated forgetting; déjà vu and jamais vu also occur, as described above. There may be altered states of consciousness such as a fugue, with impaired registration. Panoramic recall, in which the patient may feel that he is rapidly re-enacting long periods of his life, is also described.

Perceptual disturbance of temporal lobe dysfunction occur with all the major abnormalities described in Chapter 6, but especially visual, olfactory, gustatory, visceral and auditory hallucinations. Disturbance of speech and behaviour, as described in Chapter 2, may occur. Abnormal affect, associated with the attack but not accounted for by external circumstances, include rage, terror or marked suspiciousness.

Affective disorder of memory

Memory is not only disturbed by organic damage to the brain itself; it is also affected by emotion. This is certainly true of normal, healthy people, in whom the affective state strongly influences the processes of remembering and forgetting. It is also true of affective and schizophrenic psychoses, and of neuroses and personality disorders. The predominant mood in these disorders results in *selective forgetting* and *falsification* of the history: schizophrenic patients are prone to give histories containing delusions; anxious patients give anxious histories; depressed patients give sad histories. The history is inevitably modulated by the mental state. Context of memory is important for affective aspects; for instance, many people remember their quite trivial activities at the time they heard of John Kennedy's assassination.

SELECTIVE FORGETTING

Alternatively, memory can be considered as a process of *selective forgetting*; it is not a simple filing and retrieval mechanism. Forgetting is subject to the influence of affect: which sensations are registered; what is retained and for how long; what information is available for recall. *Falsification* always occurs to some extent due to this interplay of memory with affect. This is demonstrated in the quotation from Nietzche at the beginning of this chapter. Certain catastrophic events which lowered self-esteem are remembered remarkably vividly, with the attendant feelings of embarrassment and humiliation. These, especially with anankastic or paranoid personality types, are prone to become affect-laden complexes associated with the development of emotional symptoms.

Usually, however, there is a tendency for painful and embarrassing events to be obliterated and distorted by memory in time. The event itself may be accurately remembered but the craven attitude of the subject may be distorted so that he remembers his part in the drama to be one of unadulterated heroism.

The selective nature of forgetting is produced as evidence of the existence of the *unconscious*. It is important evidence for the psychodynamic concept of *ego defence mechanism*. Descriptive psychopathology neither explains phenomena in terms of defence mechanisms nor denies their existence. As the theoretical supposition is that they are unconscious functions of the self, description can only be made when they are manifested in conscious experience or behaviour. Pleasant experiences we remember better than unpleasant ones, and unpleasant better than emotionally neutral experiences.

There appears to be a reciprocal relationship between depression and cognition, forming a vicious cycle which will perpetuate and intensify depression (Teasdale, 1983). From the associative network theory, changes occur in depression in the accessibility of memories, current events and symptoms gaining consciousness. This results in negative interpretations of experience cognitively, which are then themselves remembered selectively. Thus, unhappy experiences and the unfortunate side of neutral events become the basis in depression for negative attitudes towards self and capacity for coping. These negative affects are then remembered to form the memories of failure for future interpretations of experience.

FALSIFICATION OF MEMORY

In *pseudologia fantastica*–fluent plausible lying–the untruthful statements are often grandiose and extreme. Questions are answered with fluency and the story appears to be believed implicitly by the pseudologic himself. This usually occurs with an associated personality disorder of hysterical (histrionic) or asocial type, and often when the individual is experiencing a major life crisis, such as facing criminal proceedings. Often the picture is of a very isolated person, without family or friends, drifting into the Accident and Emergency department of a large hospital in a strange city late at night, with stories of his own exploits and importance and the unfortunate vicissitudes he has experienced. There is overlap with the so-called Munchausen syndrome (Chapter 13). With personality disorders, especially at times of heightened affect, memory is falsified and distorted; events and circumstances are misrepresented. The advice of doctors may be grossly misconstrued. An opthalmic surgeon examined a depressed patient's eyes and informed her that her visual acuity was satisfactory and no treatment was required. She told her psychiatrist that her 'eyesight would be bad for evermore and the surgeon has told me that nothing can be done about it.'

Memory impairment is a regular feature of organic states. When there is a defect of reasoning and judgement, falsification occurs. So the grandiose delusions and memory disturbance of *general paralysis of the insane* may result in falsification and distortion of events remembered. Similarly, confabulation as in the Korsakov state is commonly associated with falsification.

In schizophrenia, remembered circumstances often take on a new meaning: 'I remember last week three red cars were following me at the traffic lights in Stafford... I realized that I have become involved in politics.' This was stated by a health visitor who had quite suddenly come to believe that all her actions were being observed and, subsequently, her behaviour controlled. Memory is accurate, but its significance is distorted. A distinction should be made between delusional memories in which the primary delusional experience is described as a memory, and delusional retrospective falsifications. This is a backdating of delusions to a time before the patient was ill, based on an admixture of remembered true events and delusional interpretations of the meaning of those events. A person who believed that she was 'much more of a genious than Albert Einstein' considered that her powers to heal people had started as a child, because her hands had sometimes been shiny.

There is sometimes difficulty in deciding whether events have actually occurred or whether they were dreamt. This occurs in normal people and also in Korsakov states, and has been suggested as the explanation of the fantastic type of confabulation. The same feeling of familiarity that the circumstances have been previously experienced occurs whether it is memory for an actual event or for a dream. In déjà vu and jamais vu experiences, the falsification relates to this feeling of familiarity (recognition, recollection).

Inaccuracy of recall is sometimes called *paramnesia*. As well as occurring in the normal state and in personality disorders, it is a prominent feature of affective disturbances. A woman with depression falsified the events of her life: 'I am not married. My children are illegitimate. We do not own this house. We are bankrupt' (see Chapter 16). All these statements were untrue and the falsification of her memory occurred because of her depressive mood. Memory itself was accurate, but on remonstrating on any particular point of fact, further depressive explanations of events would be given. For instance, the marriage licence was described as a forgery, and complicated legal explanations were given as to why the house did not belong to her and her husband. In mania, unacceptable events or opinions may be brushed aside as not having occurred, and unrealistic goals pursued as though there were nothing to prevent their attainment.

While a clear-cut, organic disturbance of retention occurs in dementia; more subtle, and not necessarily pathological, disturbances of memory are found as part of the normal ageing process. Ribot's law of memory regression (1882) formulates the finding that memory for recent events is lost before memory for more remote events. Earlier periods of life are remembered best and one reason for the predilection for reminiscence of an old person is the sense of security this engenders in talking about facts that are well remembered, rather than discussing areas where he is afraid that his defective memory will let him down so that he makes a fool of himself. As he dements, a multi-lingual person will forget the later attained foreign languages to a much greater extent than his original mother tongue. More recently acquired words are lost first, so that words like 'velocipede', 'wireless' and 'gramophone' will be used rather than 'bicycle', 'radio' and 'record player'.

PSYCHOGENIC DISTURBANCE OF MEMORY

Cryptamnesia is the experience of not remembering that one is remembering. A person makes a witty remark, writes a haunting melody, without realising that he is quoting (plagiarizing) rather than producing something original. The process is seen when words or phrases come into popular usage for a few months or years by some process of mass spread, in which people using the expression believe they are introducing a new idea.

Generally, unpleasant and uncomfortable experiences are not remembered accurately or completely–'forgetting of the disagreeable'. This is a defect of recall which can be seen as a successful *defence mechanism*; it helps to maintain the integrity of the person. However, in the *affect of hopelessness*, reactivation of memories of previous failures is a frequent reason for perpetuating neurotic behaviour (Engel, 1968). Psychogenic amnesia may appear without any organic disease present, but the presentation of organic brain disease is always modified by psychogenic factors (Pratt, 1977).

Misnaming objects and momentary loss of memory for words in healthy subjects may result from faulty retrieval from short and long-term memory stores, rather than from the psychoanalytic explanation of repression. Such errors may be categorized as acoustic or semantic: acoustic tending to occur in short-term stores up to 30 seconds, and semantic in long-term after more than 5 minutes (Shallice & McGill, 1977).

Hysterical fugue

The symptoms pertaining to hysteria in the International Classification of Diseases (World Health Organization, 1977) are of two types: conversion and dissociation. In dissociation, there is a narrowing of the field of consciousness with subsequent amnesia for the episode. In many ways dissociative symptoms represent a layman's impression of 'madness'. In hysterical fugue states, there is narrowing of consciousness, wandering away from normal surroundings and subsequent amnesia. The person appears to be in good contact with his environment and usually behaves appropriately, although he sometimes displays disinhibition. There is quite often loss of identity or assumption of another, false identity. The duration of the episode can be very variable, from a few hours to several weeks; and the subject may travel considerable distances. A citizen of Birmingham, UK described a state in which he 'came to' in a city he did not recognize, and where people were speaking French. As he walked about the streets, he found he was near an airport terminal and, to his surprise, he discovered that he was in Montreal. Germane to his adventure was the history of the breakdown of his marriage just before he took off. In such a state, there is no 'organic brain disease but a narrowing of the field of consciousness which may be limited to one circumscribed area of experience, in relation to which behaviour seems outwardly consistent and often directed to a goal within that area' (Office of Population, Censuses & Surveys, 1968).

Ganser state

The original paper by Ganser (1898) has been much misunderstood. In it he described four criminals who showed:
(i) *vorbeigehen (to pass by)* or approximate answers, described by Ganser: 'In the choice of answers the patient appears to pass over deliberately the indicated correct answer and to select a false one, which any child could recognize as such';
(ii) clouding of consciousness with disorientation;
(iii) 'hysterical' stigmata;
(iv) recent history of head injury, typhus or severe emotional stress;
(v) 'hallucinations', auditory and visual (from his description they sound like pseudohallucinations); and,
(vi) amnesia for the period during which the above symptoms were manifest.
The Ganser state is very rarely seen in English prisons but, when it does occur, it is more likely in those awaiting trial than those already sentenced.

There has been considerable argument whether the condition is primarily hysteria or an organic psychosis, with different authors supporting each contention (Latcham *et al.*, 1978). A case that illustrated both the hysterical and organic elements was a female university student, aged 20, who experienced head injury with concussion when in Italy. Her premorbid personality was markedly histrionic and theatrical, and she had developed hysterical inability to walk at the age of 13 for a few weeks. After transfer from the Italian hospital to Britain, she demonstrated approximate answers thus: *question*–'What is the capital of Italy?'; *answer*–'Naples.'; *question*–'How many legs has a centipede?'; *answer*–'seven'. This was accompanied by interference in the treatment of other patients, flirtatious behaviour, lability of mood and a facetious manner. On serial testing of intellectual function on the Wechsler Adult Intelligence Scale, initial testing twelve days after head injury had to be abandoned; after one month there was marked impairment, worse for *performance* than *verbal* items. Intellectual function had eventually returned to a superior level by nine months. Whitlock (1967) considers the distinction between Ganser state and pseudodementia to lie in disturbed consciousness; present in the former and not the latter. However, sometimes, clouding of consciousness in an organic state cannot be distinguished from the altered mental state of hysteria, in the absence of other organic signs.

Enoch and Trethowan (1979) have regarded the four main features of the Ganser syndrome: (i) approximate answers; (ii) clouding of consciousness; (iii) somatic conversion features; and, (iv) pseudohallucinations (not always present). They regard the syndrome as an hysterical dissociative reaction and have pointed out the similarity of features with those exhibited by normal people asked to simulate mental disorder: the difference being that the Ganser subjects were subsequently amnesic for their abnormal behaviour.

Multiple personality

This is described in more detail in Chapter 9. There is considerable doubt about the authenticity of multiple personality, often being considered iatrogenic, created by the medical interest shown in the case; or simulated, used by the patient during criminal proceedings. However, in supposed bona fide cases, there is often complete amnesia subsequently for one or more of the personalities: one personality may claim not to know of the existence of another personality (with a different name) within the same person.

It is important to realize that phenomenologically there is only an arbitrary distinction between memory and perception on the one hand, and memory and fantasy on the other. When I describe what I perceive in the present, I rely on my memory for percepts and their names to do so. When I remember objects and events, this is dependent upon my previous capacity for perception. At what point in time the distinction is made between perception and memory is variable in different situations. Similarly, when I 'remember' a past event or object, I am actually imagining it or recreating it in fantasy.

References

Allison RS (1962) *The Senile Brain.* London: Edward Arnold.
Berlyne N (1972) Confabulation. *British Journal of Psychiatry 120*, 31–9.

Bonhoeffer K (1901) *Die akuten Geisteskrankheiten der Gewohnheitstrinker.* Jena: Gustav Fischer. Cited by Berlyne N. (1972)

Claparède E (1911) Recognition et moiité. *Archives Psychologiques (Genève) 11,* 79–90.

Engel GL (1968) A life setting conducive to illness: the giving up–given up complex. *Annals of Internal Medicine 69,* 293–300.

Enoch MD & Trethowan WH (1979) *Uncommon Psychiatric Syndromes.* Bristol: John Wright.

Fraser M (1982) *ECT: A Clinical Guide.* Chichester: John Wiley.

Ganser SJM (1898) A peculiar hysterical state *Arch. Psychiat. Rerr. Krankh 30,* 633. Trans. Schorer CE (1965) *British Journal of Criminology 5,* 120–126.

Gray JA (1982) The Neurobiology of the Hippocampus.

Jackson J (1887) Remarks on evolution and dissolution of the nervous system. In Taylor J (ed.) (1931) *Selected Writings of John Hughlings Jackson, Vol. 2.* London: Hodder & Stoughton.

Korsakov SS (1890) Eine psych. Storung combiniert mit multipler Neuritis. *Allg. Zeitschr. f. Psych. Vol. 46*

Latcham RW, White AC & Sims ACP (1978) Ganser Syndrome: the aetiological argument. *Journal of Neurology, Neurosurgery & Psychiatry 41,* 851–4.

Lishman WA (1978) *Organic Psychiatry: The Psychological Consequences of Cerebral Disorder.* Oxford: Blackwell Scientific.

Milner B (1972) Disorders of learning and memory after temporal lobe lesions in man. *Clinical Neurosurgery 19,* 421–46.

Nietzsche F (1889) Twilight of the Idols. transl. Hollingdale, RS (1968). Harmondsworth: Penguin.

Office of Population Censuses & Surveys (1968) A Glossary of Mental Disorders. *Studies on Medical & Population Subjects No. 22.* London: HMSO.

Pick A (1921) Neues Zur Psychologie der Konfabulation Msschr. *Psychiat. Neurol. 49,* 314–21. Cited by Berlyne N (1972).

Piercy MF (1977) Experimental studies of the organic amnesia syndrome. In Whitty CWM & Zangwill OL (eds) *Amnesia: Clinical, Psychological & Medicolegal Aspects.* London: Butterworth.

Pratt RTC (1977) Psychogenic loss of memory. In Whitty CWM & Zangwill OL (eds) *Amnesia: Clinical, Psychological & Medicolegal Aspects.* London: Butterworths.

Ribot E (1882) *Diseases of Memory: An Essay in the Positive Psychology.* London: Kegal Paul, Trench.

Roth M & Myers DH (1969) The diagnosis of dementia. *British Journal of Hospital Medicine 2,* 705–17.

Scheid W (1934) Zur Pathopsychologie des Korsakow Syndroms. *Z. Neurol. Psychiat. 151,* 346–69 Cited by Berlyne N (1972).

Scoville WB & Milner B (1957) Loss of recent memory after bilateral hippocampal lesions. *Journal of Neurology, Neurosurgery & Psychiatry 20,* 11–21.

Shallice T & McGill J (1977) Attention & Purpose. In Requin J & Bertelson P (eds) *The Origins of Mixed Errors.* New York: Academic Press.

Teasdale JD (1983) Negative thinking in depression: cause, effect, or reciprocal relationship? *Advances in Behavioural Research and Therapy 5,* 3–25.

Tulving E (1973) Episodic & semantic memory In *Organization of Memory.* New York: Academic Press.

Van der Horst L (1932) Ueber die Psychologie des Korsakowsyndroms. *Msschr. Psychiat. Neurol. 83,* 65–84

Weeks D, Freeman CPL & Kendell RE (1981) Does ECT produce enduring cognitive deficits? In Palmer RL (ed.) *Electroconvulsive Therapy: An Appraisal.* Oxford: Oxford University Press.

Weinman J (1981) *An Outline of Psychology as applied to Medicine.* Bristol: John Wright.

Weizkrantz L (1978) A comparison of hippocampal pathology in man and other animals. In CIBA Foundation *Functions of the Septo-Hippocampal System* Amsterdam: Elsevier.

Welford AT (1951) *Skill & Age — An Experimental Approach.* London: Oxford University Press.

Whitlock FA (1967) The Ganser syndrome. *British Journal of Psychiatry 113,* 19–29.

Williams M (1977) Memory disorders associated with electroconvulsive therapy. In Whitty CWM & Zangwill OL (eds) *Amnesia: Clinical, Psychological & Medicolegal Aspects,* pp. 134–139. London: Butterworths.

World Health Organization (1977) *International Classification of Diseases.* 9th Revision. Geneva: World Health Organization.

Zangwill OL (1983) *Disorders of memory.* In Shepherd M & Zangwill OL (eds) *Handbook of Psychiatry, Vol. 1: General Psychopathology,* pp. 97–113. Cambridge: Cambridge University Press.

— 5

Disorder of Time

There are men I know who can wake themselves at any time to the minute. They say to themselves literally, as they lay their heads upon the pillow, 'Four-thirty,' 'Four-forty-five', or 'Five-fifteen,' as the case may be; and as the clock strikes they open their eyes. It is very wonderful this; the more one dwells upon it, the greater the mystery grows. Some Ego within us, acting quite independently of our conscious self, must be capable of counting the hours while we sleep. Unaided by clock or sun, or any other medium known to our five senses, it keeps watch through the darkness. At the exact moment it whispers 'time!' and we awake. The work of an old riverside fellow I once talked with called him to be out of bed each morning half an hour before high tide. He told me that never once had he overslept himself by a minute. Latterly, he never even troubled to work out the tide for himself. He would lie down tired, and sleep a dreamless sleep, and each morning at a different hour this ghostly watchman, true as the tide itself, would silently call him.   Jerome K Jerome (1900)

Space and time are always present in sensory processes. They are not primary objects themselves but they invest all objectivity. Kant calls them 'forms of intuition'. They are universal. No sensation, no sensible object, no image is exempt from them. Everything in the world that is presented to us comes to us in space and time and we experience it only in these terms.   Jaspers (1962)

This is how Jaspers, the philosopher, looks at human subjective experience. He continues: 'If we want to bring these primary things home to ourselves in some neat phraseology we may say that they both represent the sundered existence of Being, separated from itself. Space is extended being (the side-by-side) and time is sequential being (the one-after-the-other).'

CLOCK TIME AND PERSONAL TIME

An important distinction is that between *clock time* and *personal time.* Clock time–chronological, physical or historical time–is objective, quantitative, independent of the emotional self. Personal time is subjective–the experience of the way time seems to be passing, circumscribed by the individual's existence. Both these perceptions of time may be altered with psychiatric illnesses. Clock or objective time may be altered so that the knowledge of time intervals is disturbed. Personal or subjective time is altered by the affective state and by circumstances in the way a defined period of objective time is experienced: 'it felt as if it would never end.' With reference to daily or circadian rhythms and assessment of time, the association with mental illness has been reviewed by Sampson and Jenner (1975).

The experience of the passage of time is well known to vary in different, normal circumstances. When a person is happy or engrossed time seems to dash by excessively fast; when sad, bored, idle, or waiting for some important event, time drags. Chronic psychiatric patients, although having few events in their daily programme, rarely complain of boredom (Morgan, 1977). It has been claimed that the body clock normally runs a little slower than a twenty-four hour cycle–nearer to twenty-five hours (Wever, 1979). Everyday indications of this include: we tend to go to bed and get up as late as we conveniently can; given a rare opportunity, we will make both even later; when we extend the day, for instance with electric light, we do so preferentially in the late evening and not the early morning.

BIOLOGICAL RHYTHMS AND TIME

Although our units of time are to some extent arbitrary, natural and biological time occurs in definite periods. The four which have the most relevance to mental illness are: circadian rhythms (about twenty-four hours–night and day); monthly cycles; seasonal variation; and life epochs–from birth to death. All these rhythms are important for the mental state in times of health, and form the basis for such stereotypes as early morning depression; premenstrual tension; midsummer madness; and involutional melancholia. Many of these biological rhythms with variation of mood are mediated biochemically–through the endocrine system.

Personal time (and also, to a lesser extent, clock time) is often described in relation to these biological rhythms. Our whole notion of the progression of time is closely related to processes of physical function: birth, growth and decay.

Disorder of time sense

An ability to separate events into past, present and future, even if limited; capacity to estimate duration; and the ability to put events in sequence, is necessary for intellectual processes to be carried out. Disorder of time sense is closely associated with disturbance of consciousness, attention and memory.

DISORIENTATION IN TIME AND ORGANIC DISTURBANCE

The abnormality elicited in testing for disorientation in time has two components, and these need not occur together. The first is *memory disorder*, in which the person does not remember what has occurred in the intervening period since a distant remembered event; and so this event is reckoned to be in the immediate past. This is demonstrated in testing for knowledge of the date, when the patient with organic brain disease will either give the correct date or one in the past; never in the future. The other abnormality is impairment of the ability to assess the *duration of time*, and this is disturbed in organic states.

In *Korsakov syndrome*, in which there is severe amnesia associated with confabulation, the two abnormalities of disorientation in time, memory disorder and assessment of duration, may not both occur. It has been demonstrated experimentally with such subjects that they can be hypnotized and told to carry out an action after a fixed duration of time. They have been able to comply quite accurately; that is, the estimation of time is well preserved.

In organic states there may be disturbance in the perception of the passage of time, and also disorientation for the time of day, date and even year. In the milder organic states, of any cause, there is an overestimate of the progress of time–a similar abnormality is described with hypothermia. Abnormalities for the assessment of time span have occurred with temporal lobe lesions and post-encephalitic states.

DISORIENTATION IN SCHIZOPHRENIA

Age disorientation, defined as a five-year discrepancy between true and subjective age, has been considered to correlate clinically with intellectual impairment in chronic schizophrenia (Crow & Stevens, 1978). Such patients were much less able than chronic schizophrenic patients without age disorientation to answer questions about date and the duration of time. They systematically underestimated the present year and the duration of their stay in hospital, and sometimes their own age.

This gives quantitative support to the observation that for some chronic patients 'time stands still': they remain in the cultural set of the time when they developed their illness. Such patients tend to use the idiomatic language; sing the popular songs; wear the modish clothes; and tell the characteristic jokes of the time before their illness became established. It is a mistake to believe that they are indulging in nostalgia; their cultural life is still firmly fixed within that particular period. Not only in the back ward of an old-fashioned mental hospital, but also in a hostel in the community, they live in their own time capsule with invisible, but impregnable, walls.

PASSIVITY OF TIME

A particular situation of loss of awareness of time is that of the schizophrenic patient who may describe a shrinking of time in which he believes that time has been removed or compressed. This is experienced as a form of *passivity*, in that the appreciation of time appears to be influenced from outside the self. There may be time-related disturbance of the continuity and identity of self (see Chapter 11).

Passivity experience, or delusion of control, is not the only form in which time sense is disturbed in schizophrenia. There is a more generalized disintegration in sense of time and space, analogous to the dislocation of thinking processes that occur in other types of schizophrenic thought disorder. A schizophrenic in-patient described: 'I had no cigarettes. I was down in the gymnasium looking at the clock like the earth's face. When looking at one spot I would be above it. I didn't know how many million billion miles. The records kept going on. I couldn't alter the noise element' (the latter two words being a *stock phrase* with idiosyncratic meaning).

Affective disturbance of time

Time, as a modality of personal experience, is disturbed with mood disorders. Lewis (1967) quotes a patient with *affective functional psychosis:* 'Everything seems very much longer. I should have said it was afternoon, though they say it is midday. They always tell me it is earlier than I think... and it looks as if I'm wrong and I can't help feeling I'm right... I cannot see any end to anything, only end to the world....' Another of his patients said: 'I never know any moment what is going to happen. It's the most terrible outlook I've ever had to look to. It's all perpetual. I've got to suffer perpetually'.

This last sentence is perhaps the key to the abnormal psychopathology. Objective assessment of the duration of time in such depressed patients is quite accurate. It is the abnormal mood associated with time sense that is significant. In depression 'real time' seems to the patient to be passing very quickly, but this is associated with the unpleasant affect of boredom and of suffering. This is well illustrated by the Biblical writer Job: 'My days are swifter than a weaver's shuttle and they come to an end without hope' (Job 7:6). Correspondingly, the manic patient feels he has a capacity for more rapid and effective thought than other people (not borne out in practice), and feels real outside time is passing slowly.

The disturbance of time in affective disorders is closely associated with the feeling of familiarity which is upset in both depersonalization and déjà vu experiences. A depressed patient said that 'it always seems to be the same time of day... quarter to seven'. Yet she was able to work out by looking at the November sky and remembering what meals she had eaten that it was, in practice, much earlier. When offered a new novel by a nurse, she complained, 'you always give me the same book'; again, a type of déjà vu experience.

Discontinuity of time is described. The patient feels that time is standing still, that in some way everything temporal has come to an end. This is described not uncommonly with psychotic depression. A patient says, 'I have stopped being, I have just stopped, everything else has just stopped as well'. The incessant sequential march of events no longer impresses the person with its inevitability.

This feeling of time standing still may also be experienced in ecstacy states, where the person feels he is existing in the past, the present and the future all at the same time. Such states may occur with mania, with some neurotic conditions or in normal people undergoing an exceptional psychic experience.

DEPERSONALIZATION AND DEREALIZATION

Loss of the feeling of reality for time experience is a type of depersonalization. The person can assess time spans quite accurately and there is no loss of memory. However, he has no feeling that things are happening or time is passing. Time itself takes on a feeling of unreality and he feels unable to function.

An awareness of the future is usually assumed by the person as part of his total sensory process of time. He remembers the past, albeit selectively; he can estimate the length of time span in the present; and he has a feeling of continuity extending into the future. This awareness of the future may be lost, for example in LSD intoxication, when there is a sensation of living only in the present: 'There is no future, just now'.

Appreciation of the smooth passage of life, with the past becoming the present and leading to a future for which plans can be made in anticipation, may be disturbed in the state of reactive depression described by Engel (1967) as the *affect of hopelessness* or the *giving up–given up complex*. The sense of continuity of the past, through the present into the future, is lost and the person feels that there is no point in going on, there is nothing worth trying to achieve. The sense of the future may also be lost in psychotic depression, 'it will never exist'.

An appreciation of movement involves the sensory experience of both time and space. Abnormality may result in an inability to assess speed or even to assess that objects are moving at all.

DÉJÀ VU IN TIME DISORDER

The time disturbance in déjà vu is an alteration of the feeling of familiarity that invests objects. This feeling of familiarity, or its lack, is a constant experience normally taken for granted: previously experienced people, places or events are invested with a feeling of familiarity which is absent for new experience. Déjà vu is the experience of this feeling of familiarity for objects that have not been visually perceived before (and by derivation, although strictly the term 'déjà vécu' should be used, a feeling of familiarity with circumstances that have not been experienced before). Jamais vu is the absence of this feeling of familiarity for objects that have been seen before.

Déjà vu occurs in the normal state and in pathological conditions. The composer Ralph Vaughan Williams, in describing his first hearing of the tune used in *'Dives and Lazarus'*, explained: 'I had that sense of recognition–here's something which I have known all my life, only I didn't know it' (Kennedy, 1964). Most people can recall similar déjà vu experiences. It is also commonly associated with temporal lobe epilepsy. A patient described his aura before a fit experienced in hospital: 'I went into the kitchen. The window looked as if I'd seen it before. I felt very peculiar'. Déjà vu and jamais vu are quite often described in schizophrenia.

Déjà vu has been produced with brain stimulation. Penfield and Kristiensen (1951) were able to reproduce familiar sensation with stimulation of a brain electrode of epileptic patients. This stimulation clearly produced an abnormality of the feeling of familiarity, not an abnormality of memory. It was a disturbance of the feeling of recognition that accompanies recall in the process of memory. Janet considered déjà vu to be a form of loss of reality or negation of the present; whilst Freud (1901) regarded it as being associated with the recall of unconscious fantasies.

NEUROTIC DISTURBANCE OF TIME SENSE

Neurotic patients frequently describe symptoms in which time features prominently. Anxious patients may describe pressure of time: the feeling that 'time deadlines are closing in and I shall not be able to cope'. This is often more closely related to personality and the presence of an acute neurotic reaction than actual objective pressures on time.

In depressive neurosis there is frequently considerable distress over wasted time that is lost for ever: 'Remember the years that the locusts have eaten'. This is experienced in the affect of hopelessness (see above) in which there is a reactivation of memories of past failure and shame.

Obsessive-compulsive neurosis reveals a time component in that one form, more common in men than women, is typified by agonizing slowness in completing any task. A man who set his alarm for 5 am 'in order to get myself organized for the day' took until 5 pm to be dressed and downstairs.

Biological rhythms and their relation to psychiatry

Biological clocks, that is, physiological or chemical mechanisms that act in regular periodic cycles, have important associations with the mental state and its disturbance. However, there is still a great deal of ignorance about the connections with different mental illnesses. Brief reference is here made to daily, monthly and annual rhythms, and also to the association with the stage of life.

CIRCADIAN RHYTHMS

On comparison of internal with clock time, repeated estimates of fixed time spans shows a gradual increase in time of the estimate, suggesting that there is a slowing of the internal clock. Subjects were asked repeatedly to guess a fixed duration of time: their estimate started by being slightly longer than actual time and became progressively longer. The intrinsic period of the circadian rhythm in humans is approximately twenty-five hours, but this is usually modified by external cues such as daylight (Wher & Goodwin, 1983). This has been likened to the finding in vigilance experiments, where there is a gradual decrease of efficiency. There was also found to be a greater overestimation of fixed intervals in the morning, as compared with the afternoon; and this was found to be correlated with body temperature. The internal clock accelerates when the body temperature is raised.

There is considerable circumstantial, but little direct, evidence that circadian rhythms are causally associated with affective disorders (Thompson, 1984). Early morning wakening and diurnal variation in mood, with the mood most depressed in the early morning, are considered as biological symptoms of depression and have been postulated as a *phase advance* of the sleep–wake cycle; that is, each point of the rhythm occurs earlier than usual relative to the light–dark cycle. There is a change in depression in that rapid eye movement (REM) sleep occurs earlier, rather than later, in the night and this also may point to phase advance of the circadian rhythm. There has also been work carried out on the use of sleep deprivation in the treatment of depression (Vogel et al, 1980).

In depression, changes of body temperature and cortisol levels over the twenty-four hours have also been interpreted as phase advance of the circadian rhythm, but results are equivocal. The action of antidepressant drugs has been investigated in terms of their effect upon the rhythm by lengthening the intrinsic cycles of rest, temperature and sleep; but again the evidence is not clear. Corroboration studies of air travellers crossing time zones have suggested that travel from east to west is more likely to be associated with depression, and west to east with hypomania (Jauhar & Weller, 1982). However, physiological studies of jet lag would not support such an association (Arendt & Marks, 1982), and the original findings have not yet been repeated elsewhere.

It has been suggested that there may be a shortened rhythm, of less than twenty-four hours, in chronic schizophrenics. Abnormalities of circadian rhythm have also been described, but not fully substantiated, in anorexia nervosa and with neurotic personality.

MONTHLY CYCLES

Clearly, the most obvious human biological rhythm to recur monthly is the menstrual cycle; and this has been linked with changes in the mental state. Similar psychological mood swings with a monthly cycle have been sought, but not convincingly found, in the male. Estimates for the frequency of *premenstrual*

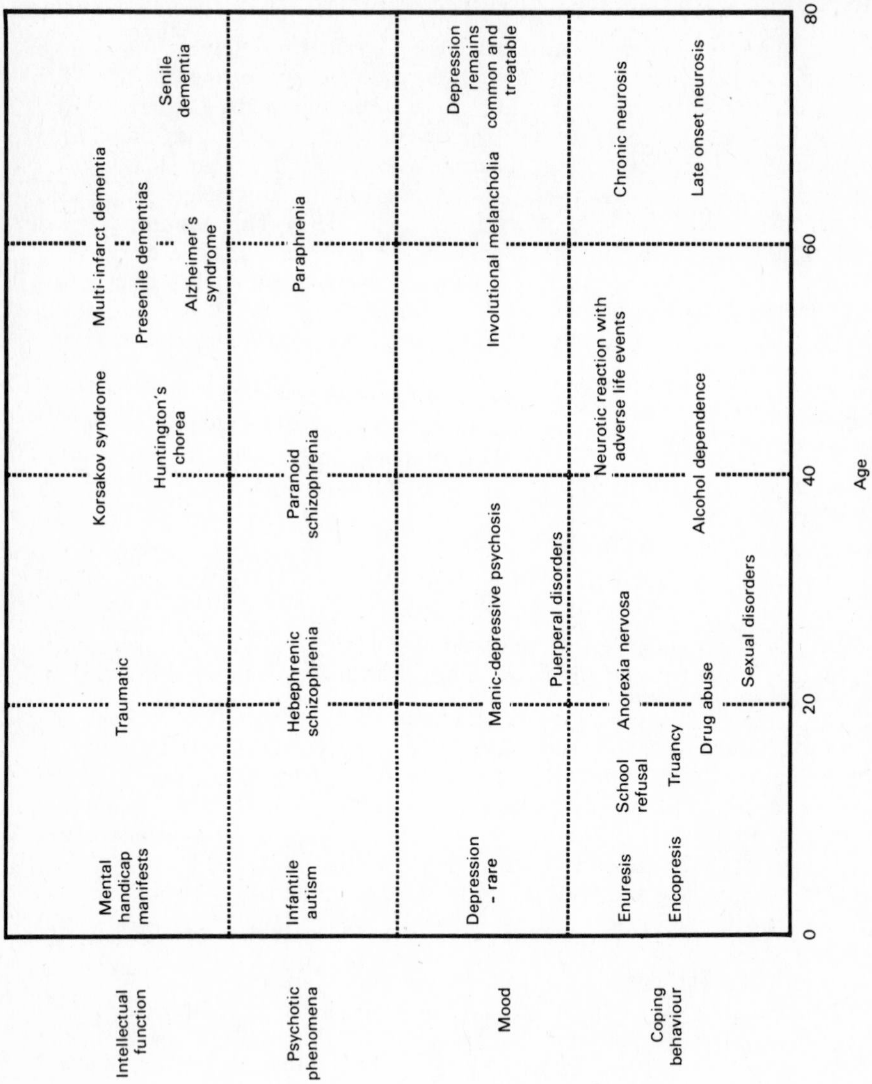

Figure 5.1 Psychiatric disturbance and life epoch

tension have varied in the general population between 30% and 80% of women of reproductive age (Clare, 1982). Psychological symptoms include lethargy, anxiety, irritability and depression.

Much numerical data have been provided by Dalton (1984) to support the contention that there is increased psychopathology of various types during the eight days of the premenstruum and the menstrual period itself, relative to the rest of the cycle. She states that 46% of emergency psychiatric admissions, 53% of attempted suicides, 47% of admissions for depression and 47% of admissions for schizophrenia of women of reproductive age occur during these stages. However, these figures require substantiation. Premenstrual syndrome is the recurrence of symptoms in the premenstruum with absence in the postmenstruum. Disabling tension has been described, as have mood swings of severe proportion and sudden onset; varying from genial equanimity to murderous irritability, suicidal depression and incapacitating lethargy.

SEASONAL VARIATION

Season of the year has been invoked for the onset of episodes of many psychiatric illnesses. Understandably, this is more pronounced at increasingly higher latitudes in the northern hemisphere. Similar associations of illness with summer or winter have been observed in the southern hemisphere.

In schizophrenia, patients show an excess of birth dates in the winter months in northern and southern hemispheres (Hare, 1982). There is a higher rate for admission to psychiatric hospital during the summer months.

For every decade since 1921–30, suicide rates in England and Wales have been highest in the months of April, May and June (Morgan, 1979). There appears to be no association between season of birth and affective illness; however, the onset of depressive illness and the administration of electroconvulsive therapy both become more common in spring and autumn (Rawnsley, 1982). Symonds and Williams (1976) found a peak for the admission of female manic patients in August and September.

LIFE EPOCHS

Virtually the whole of psychopathology is mediated through, and influenced by, changes in situation and life epoch. It is important to take into account the relative preponderance of different factors: biological change; pressure of social context; and individual perception of life situation. It is outside the scope of this book to chart these associations in detail, but an impressionistic sketch is offered in Figure 5.1. The psychological effects of important life changes have been studied in primary care situations: birth of the first child (Jewell, 1984); starting school (Pitt & Browne, 1984); puberty (Howe & Page, 1984); leaving school (Brown, 1984).

References

Arendt J & Marks V (1982) Physiological changes underlying jet lag. *British Medical Journal 284*, 144–6.
Brown A (1984) Leaving school. *British Medical Journal 288*, 1884–6.

Clare AW (1982) Psychiatric aspects of premenstrual complaint. *Journal of Psychosomatic Obstetrics & Gynaecology 1*, 22–31.

Crowe TJ & Stevens M (1978) Age disorientation in chronic schizophrenics: the nature of the cognitive deficit. *British Journal of Psychiatry 133*, 137–42.

Dalton K (1984) *The Premenstrual Syndrome and Progesterone Therapy*. 2nd Ed. London: Heinemann.

Engel GL (1967) A psychological setting of somatic disease. The giving-up-given-up complex. *Proceedings of the Royal Society of Medicine 60*, 553–555.

Freud S (1901) The psychopathology of everyday life. In *Standard Edition of the Complete Works of Sigmond Freud*, Vol. VI, 151 (transl. Stanley J, 1960). London: The Hogarth Press.

Hare E (1982) The epidemiology of schizophrenia. In Wing JK & Wing L (eds) *Handbook of Psychiatry 3: Psychoses of Uncertain Aetiology*, 42–48. Cambridge: Cambridge University Press.

Howe C & Page C (1984) Puberty. *British Medical Journal 288*, 1809–11.

Jaspers K (1959) *General Psychopathology* (transl. Hoenig J & Hamilton MW, 1963). Manchester: Manchester University Press.

Jauhar P & Weller MPI (1982) Psychiatric morbidity and time zone changes: A study of patients from Heathrow Airport. *British Journal of Psychiatry 140*, 231–53.

Jerome JK (1900) *Three Men on the Bummel*. Gloucester: Alan Sutton.

Jewell MD (1984) Birth of the first child. *British Medical Journal 288*, 1584–6.

Kennedy M (1964) *The Works of Ralph Vaughan Williams*. London: Oxford University Press.

Lewis A (1967) The experience of time in mental disorder. In *Inquiries in Psychiatry*, 3–15. London: Routledge & Kegan Paul.

Morgan HG (1979) *Death Wishes? The Understanding and Management of Deliberate Self-Harm*. Chichester: John Wiley.

Morgan R (1977) Three weeks in isolation with two chronic schizophrenic patients. *British Journal of Psychiatry 131*, 504–13.

Penfield W & Kristiensen K (1951) *Epileptic Seizure Patients*. Springfield, Illinois: Thomas.

Pitt G & Browne MJ (1984) Starting School. *British Medical Journal 288*, 1655–7.

Rawnsley K (1982) *Epidemiology of affective psychoses*. In Wing JK & Wing L (eds) *Handbook of Psychiatry 3: Psychoses of Uncertain Aetiology*, 129–133. Cambridge: Cambridge University Press.

Sampson GA & Jenner FA (1975) Circadian rhythms of mental illness. *Psychological Medicine 5*, 4–8.

Symonds RL & Williams P (1976) Seasonal variations in the incidence of mania. *British Journal of Psychiatry 129*, 45–8.

Taylor WS (1947) Pierre Janet 1859–1947. *American Journal of Psychology 60*, 637–645.

Thompson C (1984) Circadian rhythms and psychiatry. *British Journal of Psychiatry 145*, 204–206.

Vogel DW, Vogel F, McAbee RS & Thurmond AJ (1980) Improvement depression by REM sleep deprivation. *Archives of General Psychiatry 37*, 247–253.

Wever RA (1979) *The Circadian System of Man*. New York: Springer-Verlag.

Wher TA & Goodwin FK (1983) *Circadian Rhythm in Psychiatry*. Pacific Grove, California: The Boxwood Press.

6

Pathology of Perception

The consciousness of particular material things present to sense is nowadays called perception...if we look at an isolated printed word and repeat it long enough, it ends by assuming an entirely unnatural aspect. Let the reader try this with any word on this page. He will soon begin to wonder if it can possibly be the word he has been using all his life with that meaning. It stares at him from the past like a glass eye, with no speculation in it. Its body is indeed there, but its soul is flesh. It is reduced, by this new way of attending to it, to its essential nudity.... We apprehended it, in short, with a cloud of associates, and thus perceiving it, we felt it quite otherwise than as we feel it now divested and alone.

William James (1890)

SENSATION AND PERCEPTION

Sensation is only the first stage in receiving information from outside the self. For visual stimuli to be perceived, they must be made meaningful; and this is a process of eliminating the irrelevant, and associating what is seen with other important data to form a *percept:* some of what is received visually is perceived, but most of the visual field is not.

The distinction from sensation has been clarified by Kräupl Taylor (1966) who identifies three increasingly sophisticated stages of *perception:*

1 'A sensation by itself can never form the content of an existential experience, only a *field of sensations* can do that.' When I am aware of my surroundings, it is not a single sensation but several different sensations of which I am aware at the same time. I see the print of this book; I also see the book itself; and I hear the door banging downstairs; and I am aware of the hardness of my chair. I am never aware of one solitary sensation. They all have their effect with varying intensity to produce a *field of sensations.*

2 A *sensory percept* is experienced as 'a sensory configuration without recognition.' Whilst I look at the picture on the far wall, I am also dimly aware of what I know to be a filing cabinet on my right. I am concentrating on the picture and so the cabinet, although perceived as a sensation, is not meaningful.

3 A *meaningful percept* is an entity that is recognized as something familiar. In the example given above, I move my head. Now I am looking at the filing cabinet and I know immediately what it is. I recognize it as a grey filing cabinet and nothing else.

THE REQUIREMENTS FOR PERCEPTION

What is required for perception to take place? First, to be able to perceive, I must be able to hold myself distinct and in opposition to the object of perception. As discussed in Chapter 11, I know what is me and what is the object that I am perceiving. I can make an absolute distinction between 'me' and 'it', and I am in no doubt as to which is which.

Secondly, I and the object are held together by movement of myself towards the object. The movement may be literal, physical movement: I go nearer to it in order to hear the noise that comes from it. It may be movement in thought: when I investigate the object, my thinking is moved from another area of contemplation *towards* the object, and so the object and I become coupled–object and perceiver of that object.

Thirdly, the object must hold some challenge to be explored. It is only the fact that the object is different from the other possible objects of perception which touch it in time or space that makes it definite, and therefore a possible object of perception. The self can be, of course, both the perceiver and the object of perception. We are concerned in this chapter with abnormalities of perception in which there are disorders in the subjective awareness of experience.

SENSE PERCEPTION AND IMAGERY

Our awareness of objects is of two kinds, *sense perception* and *imagery* (Trethowan & Sims, 1983). A person normally has no difficulty in distinguishing between the two: immediately and with absolute certainty he knows whether he is perceiving real objects or imagining them. Sense perception is experienced as being real and therefore to be acted on; imagery (= *fantasy*) is created voluntarily by himself and is not real in the sense of external perception. I can create an elaborate fantasy of an enjoyable meal, even to the extent of making myself salivate. However, I do not have the slightest difficulty in knowing that the meal is not there and my feelings after letting the fantasy go are not at all like the feelings of having a real meal removed before eating it. Other subjective experiences of sensory objects are assessed according to how they approximate to these two and this is shown in Figure 6.1.

On introspecting we distinguish between sense perception and fantasy. However, in everyday life the two are mixed. Intrinsic to our 'world' is a

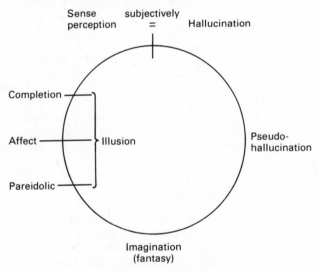

Figure 6.1 Modes of perception

mixture of fantasy and fact. When we buy an airline ticket, we not only 'buy' a passport to travel, we also 'buy' an image of the aeroplane and sundrenched Mediterranean beaches. Our actions are founded on this combination of percept and imagery.

Fantasy: imagery

William James (1890) described 'the stream of consciousness' in his book *The Principles of Psychology*. This describes the highly complex experience which we have when direct perception is mixed with the interpretation of these perceptions: intrusion of associated memories; fantasies; evanescent sights, sounds, smells; and so on. Thus *fantasy* is an essential part of a person's ongoing mental activity. Fantasy very frequently involves the five senses, especially vision. However, 'an important part of human thought involves anticipating sets of intentions which themselves are not ordinarily reflected in direct images' (Singer, 1981). People vary considerably in their capacity for day-dreams and also in their predominant content. Normative data would suggest that, in general, a richness of fantasy life is associated more with satisfaction with life and success, rather than neuroticism.

When somebody describes a sensory experience in the past, the implication is that the following steps have taken place: at the time, he perceived the sensation as meaningful and recorded it; and then the act of memorizing that allows him to reproduce the perception–the ability to take this image from stored data into full pictorial consciousness–is, in phenomenological terms, fantasy. That is, subjectively fantasy and memory of percepts are identical. This is not the only route by which fantasy occurs. Some events are recorded without being perceived as meaningful. The subject matter of dreams may sometimes be based on the memory of such sensations.

Fantasy is volitional: the subject is able to collect different reproduced perceptions in different sensory modalities and from different times, and create a single composite present fantasy experience; that is, day-dreaming. Even at the time when the initial perception is formed, one of the things that distinguishes perception from sensation is the fact that perception is always admixed with fantasy. The prisoner 'notices' the hole in the floorboard because of his fear that rats may infest the cell at night. Sensory perceptions and fantasy can therefore never be completely separated.

Abnormal perception

We will now divide abnormal perception into *sensory distortions*, where a real perceptual object is perceived distorted; and *false perceptions*, where a new perception occurs which may or may not be in response to an external stimulus. Under false perceptions will be included *illusions, hallucinations* and *pseudo-hallucinations*. There is also, of course, the possibility of a neurological deficit affecting perception.

Subjectively, *hallucination* is similar to sense perception: it is experienced as a *normal* perception, and it can be distinguished from the fantasy elements that invest it. In *vivid imagery* the whole perception is imaginary. *Pseudohallucination* has a close affinity to imagery but also has some aspects which are characteristic of sense perception or hallucination: vividness, definition, constancy and apparent independence from volition. In the experiences of *illusion, fantasy (imagery)* makes a significant contribution. We will now discuss sensory distortions, including: changes in intensity and quality of perception; changes in the concomitants of perception; changes in various other properties of perception; and split perceptions.

SENSORY DISTORTIONS

Disturbance of the mental state, with or without organic brain pathology, may cause sensory distortion. The *intensity* of perception may be altered so that it is either heightened or diminished. For example, heightening in the auditory modality is called *hyperacusis:* a symptom in which the patient complains of everything sounding abnormally loud–'I can't bear noise.' Ordinary conversation may sound intolerably noisy, and even whispering at a distance may be found uncomfortable. There is, of course, no true improvement of auditory perception but simply a lowering of the threshold at which noise becomes unpleasant. The symptom occurs in depression, migraine and some toxic states, for example, the *hangover* following acute alcohol excess. *Visual hyperaesthesia* occurs: colours look more intense or vivid. This may be associated with ecstacy experiences, and may occur in the organic psychosyndrome caused by *lysergic acid diethylamide* (LSD) administration, in functional psychoses especially mania, and occasionally with epileptic aura.

Intensity and quality of perception

Intensity of perception may be lowered in depression: 'Everything looks black.' Complaint may be made that all food tastes the same; sounds are muffled, quiet, monotonous. It is an alteration of perception, but not an impairment of the sense organs. For example, the patient who saw everything 'black' was still able to tell the colour of objects and carry out colour matching accurately. Intensity may be described as painful, as in hyperacusis; or the normal pain threshold of sensation may be lost so that pain is *not* felt.

There may be alteration in the quality of perception. Changes in the colour of perceived objects may be described with mescaline, or with digitalis poisoning. A change of perceived shape is sometimes described with parietal lobe lesions. In *microsia*, objects seem smaller than their real size; in *macropsia*, larger; and in *dysmegalopsia*, larger on one side than the other. These conditions occur in acute organic states; epilepsy; very rarely in acute schizophrenia; and occasionally with neuroses. With mescalin, parts of the body may appear severed or detached in space.

Changes in the feeling associated with perception

Perception is accompanied by affect, which may be a feeling of familiarity, of enjoyment, of involvement, or of proximity. This is usually appropriate, and so ignored. However, changes in these feelings may present as symptoms: 'Everything looks clear but it all looks miles away.' 'I feel in seclusion. It is like looking through the wrong end of a telescope.' These, and many other feelings, are described in *derealization* (Chapter 12). There is a feeling of unreality in the perceptual field; an alteration in the feelings associated with the objects of perception.

The affective concomitants of perception in schizophrenic patients were investigated by Cutting (1981). He showed that a group of acute schizophrenic patients disagreed significantly with chronic schizophrenics, depressed patients, and those with neuroses or personality disorders, in judging which of two faces in photographs was the more friendly. On a control task of judging colours there was no difference between the groups. In a further experiment, acute schizophrenics disagreed with patients of other diagnostic groups in judging friendliness and meanness of faces, but agreed with them in judging the ages of the faces. This would suggest that the disturbance in schizophrenics is with the meaning and association of perception, rather than in the physical capacity to perceive.

The underlying *mood state* profoundly affects perception. For example, a depressed patient said, 'The freshness is all gone. Things no longer appear enjoyable... I am dead. Life around me has absolutely no meaning'. In *ecstasy states* a quite ordinary perception may be transformed to become absorbingly beautiful. A boy who had taken LSD did not experience delusions or hallucinations and was not markedly altered in mood; however, he gazed abstractedly at where the dull dirty pink of the hospital wall merged with the dull dirty cream of the hospital ceiling, quite absorbed by the beautiful contrast of colours!

Splitting of perception

This rather rare phenomenon is described sometimes in organic states, and also in schizophrenia: the patient is unable to form the usual assumed links between two or more perceptions. A patient watching television experienced a feeling of competition between the visual and auditory perceptions. She felt that the two were not coming from the same source but were competing for her attention and conveying opposite messages. *Splitting of perception* occurs when the links between different sensory modalities fail to be made, and so the sensations themselves, although in fact associated, appear to be quite separate and even in conflict.

FALSE PERCEPTION

Now we turn from the altered perception of real objects to consider the perception of objects which are not there: in fact, *new perceptions*, which include illusion, hallucination and pseudohallucination. Illusions were separated phenomenonologically from hallucinations by Esquirol (1838). He described them as transformations of perceptions, coming about by a mixing of the reproduced perceptions of the subject's fantasy with natural perceptions.

Illusion

Three types of illusion are normally described: *completion illusion, affect illusion* and *pareidolic illusion*. Completion illusions depend on inattention for their

VIᵥ/ALDI

VW/AUDI

VIVALDI

Figure 6.2 Illusion

occurence. The faded lettering of an advertisement outside a garage is represented in Figure 6.2. Being more interested in music than cars, the author regularly misreads this as 'Vivaldi'. We commonly miss the misprints in a newspaper because we read the words as if they were written correctly. Immediately our attention is drawn to the mistake, our perception alters. An incomplete perception that is meaningless of itself, is filled in by a process of extrapolation from previous experience to produce significance.

Completion illusion demonstrates the principle of *closure* in gestalt psychology (see Chapter 9): there is a human tendency to complete a familiar but not quite finished pattern (Beveridge, 1985). It is necessary for us to make sense of our environment; when the sensory cues are nonsensical, we alter them slightly with remembered or fantasy material, so that the whole perceptual experience becomes meaningful.

When *illusion* arises through *affect*, perception of everyday objects is changed. The illusion can only be understood in the context of the prevailing mood state. A child who is frightened of the dark, wakes up in the half light and mistakes a towel hanging by the wall for a person moving. The experience only lasts a short time and disappears when the intense fear goes: the illusion is banished by attention. Of course, there is no absolute distinction between these different types of illusion. The degree of completion, or of affect involved, is variable. For example, a man looking through advertisements for a post, found a job that he liked and misread the written word '*suitable*' for the illusional word '*superior*... applicant is required'. Clearly this was both an affective and a completion illusion. Similarly, in the stage of *searching* that occurs following bereavement, momentary recognition of the dead person may occur for someone in a crowd. Close observation of the individual immediately dispels the feeling of familiarity.

Pareidolia occurs in a considerable proportion of normal people. It may also be provoked by psychomimetic drugs. Typically, images are seen from shapes in pareidolic illusion. For example, the author used to see the head of a spaniel in a chip on the first paving stone of the path leading to the house where he lived as a child: not just a dog, but definitely a spaniel.

Pareidolic illusions are created out of sensory percepts by an admixture with imagination. The percept takes on a full and detailed appearance–'a Victorian lady with a crinoline and frilled bloomers'. The person experiencing it, like someone seeing a photograph, knows that it is not truly there, that it is pictorial, but he cannot dismiss what he sees. Completion and affect illusions occur during inattention; they are banished by attention, which will, if anything, increase the intensity of pareidolic illusions as they become more intricate and detailed.

Pareidolic illusion occurs in children more than adults. It must be distinguished from the following:

1 *Perceptual misinterpretation*, that is simply making a mistake as to the nature of perception without that perception being particularly influenced by emotion mixed with fantasy.
2 *Functional hallucination*, which occurs when a certain percept is necessary for the production of an hallucination, but the hallucination is not a transformation of that perception. For example, the patient hears voices when the tap is turned on; he hears voices in the water, but the voices and the noise of water are quite distinct and can be heard separately and synchronously like any other voice that is heard against a background noise. The perception of hearing running water is necessary to produce the hallucination but the hallucination is not a transformation of that perception (see p.78).
3 *Fantastic interpretations* or elaborate *day-dreaming* can be very similar to pareidolic illusions and, as we have already discussed, there is a large admixture of fantasy in such illusions.

Hallucination

Hallucinations are, phenomenonologically, the most significant type of false perception. Here are four definitions of hallucination:

1 A perception without an object (Esquirol, 1838).
2 Hallucinations proper are actual false perceptions which are not in any way distortions of real perceptions but spring up on their own as something quite new and occur simultaneously with and alongside real perception (Jaspers, 1962).
3 An hallucination is an exteroceptive or interoceptive percept which does not correspond to an actual object (Smythies, 1956).
4 According to Slade (1976a) three criteria are essential for an operational definition: (i) percept-like experience in the absence of an external stimulus; (ii) percept-like experience which has the full force and impact of a real perception; and (iii) percept-like experience which is unwilled, occurs spontaneously and cannot be readily controlled by the percipient.

One of the simplest facts about hallucinations is often one of the most difficult to comprehend. That is, to the patient, what the doctor calls an hallucination is a *normal sensory experience.* Subjectively, therefore, an hallucination is indisting-uishable from a normal percept. The only clue to the sufferer that he might be hallucinated is that there is no corroborative evidence for the percept in other modalities. A woman hears voices giving a commentary on her activity: 'She is going to the sink. She is putting the coffee on'. She sees no-one else in the room but recognizes the voices of her neighbours. She cannot understand how she can be hearing them, but she is so convinced by the reality of the voices that she draws the curtains and takes the mirrors off the walls. There is some conflict in her mind: she hears voices but can see no person to account for them. However, she resolves this conflict in what is a rational way, assuming that she believes implicitly in the genuineness of the perception: 'Someone must have fixed a device or altered my sense of hearing.' She does not doubt the percept.

Horovitz (1975) has investigated hallucinations using a cognitive approach, looking at each of the following four constructs in terms of coding, appraising and transforming information: 'Hallucinations are mental images that (1) occur in the form of images, (2) are derived from internal sources of information, (3) are appraised incorrectly as if from external sources of information, and (4) usually occur intrusively. Each of these four constructs refers to a separate set of psychological processes, although together they comprise a holistic experience.' This provides a conceptual framework for investigating the phenomena of hallucination.

Hallucinations can take place at the same time as normal sensory stimuli are received. In this way they are unlike dreams, which in fact have more of the characteristics of illusions. Hallucinations are like normal percepts, of which several can be perceived simultaneously or in rapid succession. Thus, the patient can hear hallucinatory voices at the same time as he is seeing his interviewer and listening to him speak. Hallucination is like *after-image, pareidolia* or the observation of a normal sensory object, in that attention will not remove it.

The sense of reality experienced by patients when they hallucinate has been studied by Aggernaes (1972), developing the concepts of Rasmussen. He pointed out six qualities of which normal people can be aware when they experience a sensation, which also occurred in over 90% of a series of hallucinations:

(1) With normal sensation we are able to distinguish *perceiving* with our sense organs from *imagining* the same objects; hallucinations similarly are experienced as *sensation* and not *thought* or *fantasy*.
(2) When a subject experiences something, he realizes its possible *relevance* for his own emotions, needs or actions; hallucinations also have this quality of behavioural relevance.
(3) Normal sensation has a quality of *objectivity* in that the experiencer feels that under favourable circumstances, he would be able to experience the same something with another modality of sensation; this is also the experience of the hallucinator.
(4) An object is considered to *exist* if the observer feels certain that it still exists even though nobody else is experiencing it at that time; perceived objects and hallucinations share this quality.
(5) Experience of object perception and hallucination are *involuntary* in that the experiencer feels that it is impossible or extremely difficult to alter or dismiss the experience simply by wishing to do so.

(6) Normally the experiencer is aware, or through simple questioning becomes aware, that his experience is not simply the result of being in an unusual mental state; this quality of *independence* is present with normal perception and with hallucination.

One further quality of normal object perception was found to be absent more often than not with hallucination. This is the quality of *publicness:* the experiencer is aware that anybody else with normal sensory faculties would be able to perceive this something. Often the hallucinator does not believe that others could share his experience (delusional explanation may be found for this).

AUDITORY HALLUCINATION

Hallucinations can occur in any of the areas of the five special senses and also with somatic sensation. We will start by discussing *auditory hallucinations*, as they are most often of supreme diagnostic significance. In acute organic states, the auditory hallucinations are usually unstructured sounds–*elementary hallucinations*; for example, the patient hears whirring noises or rattles, whistling, machinery or music. Often the noise is experienced as very unpleasant and frightening.

Hearing voices is, of course, characteristic of schizophrenia, but also occurs in other conditions; for example, *chronic alcoholic hallucinosis* or *affective psychoses* occasionally. These voices are sometimes called *phonemes* (confusion exists, unfortunately, because the word is used with a totally different meaning in linguistics, where phonemes are the unit of speech-sound from which words are made). Usually in *organic states* the phonemes are simple words or short sentences, often spoken to the patient in the second person either as peremptory orders or abusive remarks. These abusive or imperative phonemes also occur in schizophrenia, but other more complicated speech is also heard: the voices may be single or multiple; male or female, or both; people known and recognized by the patient, or not known. They are experienced as coming from outside his mind or his self. The voice is clear, objective and definite, and is assumed by the patient to be a normal percept which at the same time may be baffling and incomprehensible in its import. Particularly characteristic of schizophrenia are voices which say the patient's *own thoughts out loud*, which give a *running commentary* on the patient's actions or voices, which *argue* or *discuss* vigorously *with each other*. They refer to the patient in the third person (Schneider, 1959).

Auditory hallucinations in schizophrenia are generally private events, but several early writers observed vocalizations which corresponded with the content of the voices taking place at the same time as the hallucinations. Green and Preston (1981) increased the audibility of the whispers of such a patient to an intelligible level using auditory feedback, and they considered it important to investigate the relationships further between abnormal whispered speech and hallucinatory experience.

Patient's descriptions of their phonemes vary greatly. Sometimes patients talk openly and quite blandly about their 'voices'. Not uncommonly, a patient may deny voices but assert that he hears 'spoken messages' or 'transmissions', or some other spoken sound; and it may be very difficult to decide whether this is a real perception or an auditory hallucination. The phonemes may be so insistent, compelling and interesting that ordinary conversation with the doctor is found boring, and even unreal, in comparison. The voices may form an insistent background to life, so ensuring that a large part of the patient's speech and behaviour is occupied in answering and obeying the voices. Psychiatric nursing staff often observe that the auditory hallucinations described by patients are as real to them as any other remembered conversations; and both hallucinatory and real auditory perception form the memories on which patients base their life and behaviour in the present.

Auditory hallucinations occur when there is a combination of vivid mental imagery and poor reality testing in the auditory modality (Slade, 1976b). This has been investigated using a battery of tests including the *verbal transformation effect*. The word TRESS was repeated on a tape recorder to the subjects for ten minutes. After a time, subjects began to hear other words and syllables. Normal subjects and schizophrenics who were not auditorily hallucinated usually heard words that were phonetically linked to the original monosyllable; but psychotic patients who were auditorily hallucinated heard words that were quite different phonetically as often as those that were linked. The difference between this group of patients and the other two groups was statistically significant.

It appears that auditory hallucinations are dependent upon the meaningfulness of sensory input. When various types of auditory input were presented to schizophrenic patients with hallucinations, it was found that it was not the degree of external stimulation that was required to diminish hallucinations but the structure of the stimulus and the degree to which it was attended to. When active monitoring of material was required by the subject reading aloud a prose passage and deciding the content afterwards, this produced a greater decrease of hallucinatory experience than any of the conditions in which sounds were played to the subject through earphones (Margo *et al.*, 1981). Morley (1987) reported the psychological treatment of a thirty-year-old man with auditory hallucinations. Distraction by means of music presented by a portable cassette produced transient reduction in the frequency and clarity of hallucinations. Subsequently, these hallucinations were totally abolished by the unilateral placement of a wax earplug: attention was considered more effective than distraction. The patient located the hallucination 'about a foot away from my right ear', and the plug was only effective in the right ear.

Schizophrenic patients experiencing auditory hallucinations were found to be impaired in cognitive processing in the aspects of tolerance of ambiguity and availability of alternative meanings. *Tolerance of ambiguity* was tested by asking the patient to recognize a spoken word, which was obscured by a masking noise of people reading. The masking noise was gradually reduced in volume until recognition occurred. *Alternative meanings* tests the subject's knowledge of less familiar meanings of words. These two processes reduced the quality of perception (resulting in hallucination) by introducing errors of premature judgement without the safeguard of subsequently considered alternatives (Heilbrun & Blum, 1984).

The mechanisms used by chronic schizophrenics to cope with persistent auditory hallucinations were discussed by Falloon and Talbot (1981). The strategies used to cope with intrusive voices could be classified as changes in behaviour, in sensory/affective state, and in cognition. Changes in behaviour included alteration of posture, such as lying down or seeking out the company of others. Physiological arousal was altered to cope with hallucinations through relaxation or physical exercise such as jogging. Cognitive methods included control of attention or active suppression of hallucinations. These authors believe that the commonest application of strategies used by patients can be beneficial in the control of these distressing symptoms.

VISUAL HALLUCINATION

Visual hallucinations characteristically occur in *organic states* rather than in the functional psychoses. It is often difficult to decide whether the full criteria for the presence of an hallucination have been fulfilled in the visual modality. Distortion of visual percepts, based on either sensation of external stimuli or internal interference with the visual pathway, may produce disturbances which are similar to those occurring with entirely new perceptions. Sometimes the account of his experience given by the patient sounds like a sensory transformation rather than an hallucination, but the bizarre and complex nature of the experience renders phenomenonological description difficult.

Visual hallucinations occur with *occipital lobe tumours* involving the visual cortex; especially when the temporal and parietal lobes are also involved. Hallucinations and other visual disturbances may occur with other physical lesions such as: *loss of colour vision; homonymous hemianopia* (loss of half of the field of vision; the same half in both eyes); *dyslexia* (inability to read at a level appropriate to the individual's age and intelligence) and *alexia* in a dominant hemisphere lesion; and *cortical blindness* (blindness due to a lesion of the cortical visual centre). They may, as in delirium tremens, be associated with an affect of terror, or with an affect of hilarious absurdity. Similar visual hallucinations, illusions and changes in mood occur in other forms of delirium. Visual hallucinations also occur in the *post-concussional state*, in *epileptic twilight states* and in metabolic disturbances; for example, *hepatic failure*. They have been described in *glue* and *petrol-sniffing*. The drugs *mescaline* and *lysergic acid diethylamide* (LSD) are potent causes of visual perceptual change. Visual hallucinations are infinitely variable in their content. They range from quite crudely formed flashes of light or colour, through more organized patterns and shapes to complex, full, visual perceptions of people and scenes. Visual and auditory hallucinations may occur synchronously in organic states; for example, in *temporal lobe epilepsy*, a visual hallucination of a human figure was also heard to speak.

With psychomimetic drugs, there are alterations in spatial perception, in the perception of movement and in the appreciation of colour. Visual illusions and hallucinations occur. *Synaesthesiae* also occur with LSD and similar drugs, although only rarely (Anderson & Rawnsley, 1954); that is, a sensory stimulus in one modality is perceived as a sensation in another modality. One mescaline subject 'felt, saw, tasted and smelled the noise of the trumpet'.

Visual hallucinations are very uncommon in schizophrenia (although some of the earlier writers used the term 'hallucination' for other visual abnormalities that occurred), and are not reckoned to occur in uncomplicated affective psychoses. It is common in schizophrenia for the patient to describe auditory hallucinations associated with visual *pseudohallucinations*. Although the phonemes are complete, and appear to have all the characteristics subjectively of a normal percept, the visual experiences are often inferred on the basis of the auditory hallucinations and of contemporaneous delusions. It is possible to see, in most instances, how psychotically disordered fantasy accounts for the content of the visual experiences. Vivid elaborate scenic hallucinations have been described in *oneiroid* states of schizophrenia. In these states there is also an altered state of consciousness.

Delirium tremens

The alcoholic withdrawal syndrome of delirium tremens is a specific form of acute organic syndrome, and is characterized by gross changes in perception, mood and conscious state (see Chapter 2). Pareidolic or affective illusions are often prodromal in delirium tremens, and these are followed by visual and haptic Lilliputian hallucinations, which are often of little animals or diminutive men. There is a bizarre intermingling of affect so that the patient experiences stark terror and, at the same time, a sort of crazy comicalness especially common with these disorders.

The hallucinations in delirium tremens may change so rapidly that the patient has difficulty in describing them. Illusions are frequently associated, especially affective illusions, in which, through the predominant mood state of terror, cracks in the wall of the ward, or curtains moving in the breeze may be misinterpreted in a frightening way. At the same time such patients are highly suggestible and can form abnormal visual experiences as a result of suggestion.

HALLUCINATION OF BODILY SENSATION

Hallucinations of bodily sensation may be *superficial, kinaesthetic* or *visceral*. Superficial hallucinations may be *thermic:* an abnormal perception of heat and cold–'my feet on fire'; *haptic:* of touch–'a dead hand touched me'; or *hygric:* a perception of fluid–'all my blood has dropped into my legs and I can feel a water level in my chest.' *Paraesthesiae* is the term describing the sensation of tingling or 'pins and needles'. These may be delusionally ascribed, although of course

Figure 6.3 The experience of delirium tremens

they are often organically mediated; for example, ulnar nerve compression causing pins and needles in the forearm.

Kinaesthetic hallucinations are those of muscle or joint sense. The patient feels that his limbs are being bent or twisted, or his muscles squeezed. Such hallucinations in schizophrenia are often linked with bizarre somatic delusions. A schizophrenic man described 'I thought my life was outside my feet and made them vibrate': he experienced kinaesthetic hallucinations of vibration. Kinaesthetic hallucinations may occur in organic states: 'a feeling of being rocked about'. Abnormal kinaesthetic perceptions have also been described in the withdrawal state from benzodiazepine drugs (Schopf, 1983). A man, after recovery, described his episode of delirium tremens: 'I felt as if I was floating in the air about fifty feet above the ground'. He illustrated this feeling with the picture in Figure 6.3.

Visceral hallucinations are false perceptions of the inner organs. There is only a limited range of possible visceral sensation; for example, pain, heaviness, stretching or distension, palpitation and various combinations of these such as throbbing. However, the possible range of bizarre schizophrenic false perceptions and interpretations is limitless. One man believed that he could feel semen travelling up his vertebral column into his brain where it became laid out in sheets.

Hallucinations of bodily sensation are quite common in schizophrenia and are almost always delusionally elaborated, often *delusions of control* (Chapters 7 and 8). Haptic hallucinations may be experienced as touch–'like a hand stroking me'; or painful–'knives stabbing my neck'. A patient believed that the smoke sensor in the ward was an infra-red camera 'because I feel it warm on my neck'. Another patient described a haptic hallucination in which she experienced genital stimulation which she ascribed to having sexual intercourse simultaneously with 'both Kennedy brothers all the time'. It is important to realize that there is both a hallucinatory and delusional component in such experiences. One particularly unpleasant form of haptic hallucination is called *formication* (Latin, *formica* = ant)–the sensation of little animals or insects crawling over the body or just under the skin. This is especially associated with some drug states and withdrawal symptoms; for example, cocaine addiction and alcohol withdrawal. It is often associated with *delusions of infestation*, but the latter may occur without hallucination.

OLFACTORY AND GUSTATORY HALLUCINATION

Olfactory hallucinations

Olfactory hallucinations occur in schizophrenia, epilepsy and in some other *organic* states. The patient has an hallucination of smell. The smell may or may not be unpleasant, but it usually has a special and personal significance; for example, it may be associated with the belief that people are pumping a poisonous or anaesthetic gas into the house which the patient alone can smell. Sometimes patients have an olfactory hallucination relating to themselves: 'I smell repulsive, unbearable–like a corpse, like faeces'. This particular patient killed himself. He felt that he created such a stench that he was intolerable in any reasonable society. Sometimes patients misinterpret and *over-value* normal body odours. A delusion of a patient believing himself to smell malodorously without an accompanying olfactory hallucination is quite common in schizophrenia and related paranoid states.

Olfactory hallucinations occur in epilepsy, especially in association with a temporal lobe focus, and commonly form the aura (or earliest phase) of such fits. A patient described a smell of burning rubber regularly just before he became unconscious. Visual, auditory, gustatory and visceral hallucinations also occur in temporal lobe epilepsy.

Gustatory hallucinations

Gustatory hallucinations (of taste) occur in various conditions. In schizophrenia they sometimes occur with delusions of being poisoned. There may be a persistent taste; for example, 'onions', 'metallic', or some more bizarre type of taste. In depression and in schizophrenia the flavour of food may disappear altogether or become unpleasant. Changes in gustatory perception may occur with some organic states, such as temporal lobe epilepsy; and also with some psychotropic drugs, for example, lithium carbonate or disulfiram. It is often difficult to describe how this disturbance of taste is mediated and, therefore, whether it is hallucinatory or not.

Differentiation of hallucinations

Before deciding that a patient is hallucinated, the possibility of other perceptual experiences must be considered. These are not necessarily of pathological significance. The differential diagnosis of hallucination includes illusion, pseudohallucination, hypnagogic and hypnopompic images and, of course, normal perception.

Pseudohallucination

Kandinsky (1885) described *pseudohallucination* as a separate form of perception from true hallucination. The characteristics of pseudohallucinations are summarised in Table 6.1. Pseudohallucinations can be identified in the visual, auditory or tactile modalities; in general they are recognized by the subject as having no external correlate.

Pseudohallucinations are considered to be absolutely different from normal sense perception (and therefore also subjectively from hallucination), in that the experience is figurative, not concrete or 'real', and is located in inner subjective space (seen with the 'inner eye'). In other characteristics pseudohallucinations are more like sense perceptions (or true hallucinations) than fantasy. So the image seems to have definite edges, to be vivid, coloured, constant over some time and not created voluntarily. Jaspers stresses that there is a gradation from the more fully formed pseudohallucination to vivid imagery, but that there is an absolute distinction between hallucination and pseudohallucination because of the first two characteristics of Table 6.1. Pseudohallucinations are always located in *subjective* space and perceived with the inner eye (or ear). It is important to distinguish pseudohallucinations from hallucinations, although sometimes both may occur in the same patient and be described by the patient as a single experience.

Table 6.1 The nature of pseudohallucinations (partly derived from Jaspers and from Aggernaes)

Perception=Hallucination		Pseudo-hallucination	Fantasy=Imagery
1 Experience	is concrete, tangible, objective, real	'inner eye' →	pictorial subjective
2 Location in	outer objective space	→	inner subjective space
3 Definition	definite outlines, complete sound	←	indefinite, incomplete only individual details
4 Vividness	full, fresh, bright	←	most elements are dim or neutral
5 Constancy	retained	←	evanescent
6 Independence from volition	cannot be dismissed, recalled or changed at will	←	requires voluntary creation
7 Insight	has quality of perception – no distinction made between perception and hallucinations	→	fantasy has quality of idea
8 Behavioural relevance	relevant to emotions, needs, actions	←	not relevant
9 Sensory modality	could experience object in another modality	→	could not experience this object in another modality
10 Existence	object exists independent of observer	→	depends on observer for existence
11 Known to be dependent on 'my abnormal state'	Independent	←	Dependent

Part of the confusion over the meaning of the term pseudohallucination has arisen because it is used in two different and mutually contradictory ways according to Kräupl Taylor (1981). It has been used to refer to self-recognized hallucinations (either exterocepted or introcepted) (Hare, 1973), or to introspected images of great vividness–the view held by Kandinsky and, later, Jaspers. Kräupl Taylor quotes Jaspers: 'It is a fact that one cannot have experiences in both perceptual and imagined spaces at the same time. There is no transition from one space view to the other, only a jump'. Thus, the latter would consider pseudohallucinations, despite their vividness, as being ultimately a variant of fantasy and therefore not carrying the diagnostic implications of true hallucinations. The difficulty arises in the patient's own observations upon his experience: he may wrongly ascribe internal experience to outside reality because the phenomenon is obtrusive, undesired and vivid. When he is relying on memory to describe the experience, what was actually imagined may be judged as having been perceived. For these reasons it is mistakenly thought that there are transitional stages between pseudohallucinations and true hallucination.

Hare (1973) has given as an example of pseudohallucination the voice heard by an obsessional or depressed person. It is described by the patient as a voice, but is actually recognized as his own thoughts. Pseudohallucinations are not pathognomonic of any particular mental illness. A patient with hysterical personality disorder saw a robed figure at the foot of her bed lifting his index finger to his mouth to caution her to silence. The image was sharp and vivid but was recognized as being seen with the inner eye. The patient knew that the figure was not at the foot of the bed and that other people in the room could not see him. When she tried to relate the figure in space to the background of her field of vision, in this case the walls and curtains of the room, she realized that she could not do so; it had no definite location in outer space, that is, outside herself.

A further example of pseudohallucination was the experience of a man aged 31 who was 'depressed' following his wife's death in Australia. He wished to return to Australia and so stowed away on a ship, but then he leapt into the sea and was discovered: 'Nothing could stop me remembering my wife that night. I believed I could see her in the water beckoning to me. So certain was I that I got two lifebelts and dived into the sea. I began to search for my wife. The water was ice cold and I saw the light of the ship disappearing.' After ten hours in the sea he was rescued.

One could argue that his belief was delusional: a secondary delusion precipitated by depressive mood. However, the perception was vivid and compelling, unlike fantasy. It was regarded as being different from a normal perception in its emotional concomitants and, therefore, also different from an hallucination. Although acted on, it was in some way symbolic: he was unhappy and wanted to die, rather than actually believing his wife was alive and well and living in the sea!

Pseudohallucination is perhaps the most likely phenomenonological form to describe the apocalyptic experience of *visions*; although, of course, these may also occur in dreams and as vivid imagery. Unlike hallucinations which are, apart from those associated with sleeping and waking, pathological, pseudohallucinations occur in people without mental illness at times of life crisis. For example, pseudohallucinations of bereavement are well recognized, and a particularly dramatic one has been described above. In more usual circumstances the widow hears her deceased husband's voice; she hears the characteristic thump of his boots on the floor as she prepares for bed; she sees him in his armchair scraping his pipe; she thinks she saw him walking along the street and looking into the newsagent's window 'with his characteristic quizzical look'. These experiences have been described as *hallucinations of widowhood*, but I would take issue from a psychopathological standpoint and reckon them usually to be pseudohallucinations.

Nearly half of a population of widows and widowers from mid-Wales interviewed by Rees (1971) were found to have abnormal perceptual experiences relating to the dead spouse within the first ten years of widowhood. Unless the visual, auditory, or tactile experience, or the sense of presence of the dead spouse was considered *real* it was excluded from the number; dreams of the spouse were also excluded. He looked at the circumstances in which these perceptions occurred and found them to be most characteristic of normal, stable people of higher social class, especially after a long and happy marriage and parenthood. They were generally experienced by the subject as reassuring and helpful rather than disturbing. It was unusual for these experiences to have been disclosed, even to close friends or relatives. The description of their form would suggest pseudohallucination.

Other abnormalities of perception

AUTOSCOPY

Autoscopy is the experience of *seeing* oneself and knowing that it is oneself. It is sometimes called the *phantom mirror image*. It is one of the abnormalities of unity of self as described in Chapter 11; but in *autoscopy* the experience is necessarily visual. Autoscopy may take the form of a pseudohallucination; for instance, a person sees himself distinctly and vividly; the image lasts for some time and did not seem to be conjured up voluntarily. The phenomenon is considered to be in the subject's 'mind's eye' rather than in precisely located external space. Schizophrenic patients may have such pseudohallucinations, but it also occurs in organic states such as temporal lobe epilepsy and parietal lobe lesions. On occasions autoscopy may take the form of true visual hallucination, this is likely to be associated with an organic state.

Various abnormalities of body image of a perceptual nature occur in organic states in which the person may see himself or part of himself replicated. Autoscopy is quite different from the *Capgras syndrome*, which is not an abnormality of perception at all but a delusional misidentification of a person or people close to the patient. *Negative autoscopy* has also been described in which, for instance, the patient looks in the mirror and sees no image at all.

EXTRACAMPINE HALLUCINATION (CONCRETE AWARENESS)

'I know that there is someone behind me on the right all the time; he moves when I move'; 'I keep on hearing them talking about my disease down in the post office' (half a mile away): these hallucinations are experienced outside the limits of the sensory field; outside the visual field or beyond the range of audibility. They are not of diagnostic importance as they occur in schizophrenia, epilepsy, other organic states and also as *hypnagogic hallucinations* in healthy people. The phenomenon is quite definitely experienced as a perception by the patient, and not just as a belief or idea.

HYPNAGOGIC AND HYPNOPOMPIC HALLUCINATION

These are perceptions which occur whilst going to sleep (*hypnagogic*), and on waking (hypnopompic). According to Zilboorg and Henry (1941), hypnagogic hallucinations were first mentioned by Aristotle. It is known that the conscious level fluctuates considerably in different stages of sleep, and both types of abnormal perception probably occur in a phase of increasing drowsiness: the structure of thought, feelings, perceptions and fantasies and, ultimately, self-awareness, becomes blurred and merged into oblivion. These experiences occur in many people in good health. They are also described with *narcolepsy, cataplexy* and *sleep paralysis* to form a characteristic tetrad of symptoms. *Toxic states*, for example glue-sniffing; acute fevers, especially in children; post-infective *depressive states*; and *phobic anxiety* neuroses are other conditions that may be associated.

The perception may be visual, auditory or tactile. It is sudden in occurrence and the subject believes that it woke him up; for example, a loud voice in the street below saying 'world war!'; a feeling of someone pushing him over the bed;

or seeing a man coming across the bedroom. The importance of these phenomena in psychopathology is to recognize their existence and realize that they are not necessarily abnormal, even though they be truly hallucinatory.

FUNCTIONAL HALLUCINATION

This is the strange phenomenon in which an external stimulus is necessary to provoke hallucination, but the normal perception of the stimulus and the hallucination in the same modality are experienced simultaneously. A *schizophrenic* patient heard hallucinatory voices only when water was running through the pipes of his ward. He heard no phonemes for most of the time, but when he heard water rushing through the pipes along the wall, he became very distressed by voices that told him to damage himself. He was terrified of the content of these voices because he was afraid he might act on them. He could readily separate the noise of water from the voices, and the latter never occurred apart from the former; but both perceptions were recognized as distinct and *real*. Another patient heard voices when the radio or television was switched on; he had persecutory delusions that these activities were carried out deliberately to upset him and he became very distressed, and at times violent, as a result.

REFLEX HALLUCINATION

As a doctor was writing in his case notes during his interview of a female patient, she said 'I can feel you writing in my stomach.' The patient saw and heard the act of writing and was quite sure that it accounted for the tactile sensation in her abdomen. A stimulus in one sensory modality producing an hallucination in another is called a *reflex hallucination*. This is, in fact, an hallucinatory form of *synaesthesia*, mentioned earlier as the experience of a stimulus image in one sense modality producing an image in another; for example, the feeling of discomfort caused by seeing and hearing somebody scratch a blackboard with their fingernails. Another reflex hallucination occurred in a woman who experienced pain whenever certain words were mentioned. Functional and reflex hallucinations are not themselves of great diagnostic or theoretical significance, but they require mentioning for completeness, and recognition in order to identify other more important symptoms with confidence.

ABNORMAL IMAGERY

Some of the abnormalities of imagery in which fantasy is admixed in various perceptual disturbances have already been described. Sometimes there is a failure of the capacity for imagery. The patient may complain that he cannot imagine what things look like—a depressed patient said that he could not remember anyone's face. Memory, in this context, is subjectively the same as fantasy. With failure of imagery, although the person complains that he cannot create the image of a person he tries to remember enough to enable him to see the person in his mind's eye, he is able to describe the characteristics of the person quite accurately. So there is no true failure of memory and the defect is in the concomitant feelings associated with fantasy, rather than with the actual ability to fantasize.

Alongside the recognized symptoms of definitive mental illnesses, there are sometimes bizarre experiences described which may throw doubt on the diagnosis. A middle-aged man demonstrated symptoms of a depressive illness; the depression was indisputable. However, he also described, on several occasions, seeing yellow and green snakes inside his head, wriggling and attempting to descend the nerves. His interviewers disagreed whether this was a complex visual hallucination or an exercise in deliberately misleading the doctor. As he improved on treatment, this visual experience did not recur, but he was quite able to remember it accurately and said that it had been associated with his feelings of guilt. Visual imagery is more likely in people who describe vivid imagination and dreams premorbidly, and also in those of more histrionic personality. It is usually associated with the emotional peaks and troughs rather than the humdrum plateaux of ordinary experience.

SENSORY DEPRIVATION

Continuing perception is necessary for consciousness. The field of sensation varies all the time as individual sensations in different modalities from the outside world and from inside oneself compete for attention. *Consciousness* consists of the integration of this changing field to form a composite awareness of oneself in one's environment. The essential nature of sensation is perhaps best realized by studying its absence as revealed by research on the effects of sensory deprivation (Zubek, 1969).

Sensory deprivation was studied using Canadian college students as volunteers (Bexton *et al.*, 1954). The subjects lay on a bed wearing gloves with cardboard cuffs and translucent goggles in a light, but partially soundproof room; there was a continual background noise. This experience was found to be extremely unpleasant and, despite being paid, subjects were not prepared to remain in this state for more than three days.

This technique has been refined subsequently to blot out external sensations more completely. Various perceptual abnormalities are experienced. Visual hallucinations of varying complexity were described, but further study of these perceptual changes resulted in their being considered, more cautiously, to be 'reported visual sensations' and 'reported auditory sensations' (Zuckermann). These were classified into 'meaningless sensations' and 'meaningful integrated sensations'. Some of the latter are more like hallucinatory experiences. Depending on the completeness of deprivation of other sensations, abnormal perception occurs in modalities other than vision. Subjects show an altered affective state: they become panicky, restless, irritable; or, alternatively, bored and apathetic.

The distinction has been made between *sensory deprivation* and *perceptual deprivation*. This latter is achieved by rendering the sensations patternless and meaningless, rather than by preventing sensations, using such devices as translucent goggles and continuous 'white' noise. The deleterious effects of sensory deprivation have been considered by Slade (1984) as:

1   inability to tolerate the situation;
2   perceptual changes;
3   intellectual and cognitive impairments;
4   psychomotor effects;
5   physiological changes in terms of the electroencephalograph and galvanic skin response measures.

Fantasy is often used as a means of reducing the unpleasant affective component of sensory deprivation. The subject may become disorientated, and show increasing difficulty with problem solving and concentration. For perception and maintenance of the normal state of consciousness, it is necessary to have a variety of sensory stimuli available and for these stimuli to be changeable. If the objects of perception do not themselves change, the observer will move his point of observation in order to create change.

References

Aggernaes A (1972) The experienced reality of hallucinations and other psychological phenomena. *Acta Psychiatrica Scandinavica 48*, 220–38.

Anderson EW & Rawnsley K (1954) Clinical studies of lysergic acid diethylamide. *Monatsschrift für Psychiatrie und Neurologie 28*, 38–55.

Bexton WH, Heron W & Scott, TH (1954) Effects of decreased variation in the sensory environment. *Canadian Journal of Psychology 8*, 70–76.

Burton R (1621) *The Anatomy of Melancholy*. Reprinted in Everyman's Library, 1932. London: Dent.

Beveridge A (1985) Language Disorder in Schizophrenia. Thesis for the Degree of M.Phil. University of Edinburgh.

Cutting J (1981) Judgement of emotional expression in schizophrenics. *British Journal of Psychiatry 139*, 1–6.

Esquirol JED (1838) *Les Maladies mentales*. Paris: Baillière.

Falloon IRH & Talbot RE (1981) Persistent auditory hallucinations: coping mechanisms and implications for management. *Psychological Medicine 11*, 329–40.

Fish F (1967) *Clinical Psychopathology*. Bristol: John Wright.

Green P & Preston M (1981) Reinforcement of vocal correlates of auditory hallucinations by auditory feedback: A case study. *British Journal of Psychiatry 139*, 204–8.

Hare EH (1973) A short note on pseudohallucinations. *British Journal of Psychiatry 122*, 469–76.

Heilbrun AB & Blum NA (1984) Cognitive vulnerability to auditory hallucinations: Impaired perception of memory. *British Journal of Psychiatry 144*, 508–12.

Horowitz MJ (1975) A cognitive model of hallucinations. *American Journal of Psychiatry 132*, 789–95.

James W (1890) *The Principles of Psychology* (reprinted 1950). London: Dover Publications.

Jaspers K (1962) *General Psychopathology* (transl. Hoenig J & Hamilton MW). Manchester: Manchester University Press.

Kandinsky V (1885) *Kritische und klinische*. Betrachtungen im Gebiete der Sinnestanschangen.

Kräupl Taylor F (1966) *Psychopathology: Its Causes and Symptoms*. London: Butterworth.

Kräupl Taylor F (1981) On pseudohallucinations. *Psychological Medicine 11*, 265–72.

Margo A, Hemsley DR & Slade PD (1981) The effects of varying auditory input on schizophrenic hallucinations. *British Journal of Psychiatry 139*, 122–7.

Morley S (1987) Psychological modification of auditory hallucinations: Distraction versus attention. *Behavioural Psychotherapy 15* (in press).

Rees WD (1971) The hallucinations of widowhood. *British Medical Journal 4*, 37–41.

Schneider K (1959) *Clinical Psychopathology*, 5th Edn (transl. Hamilton MW). New York & London: Grune & Stratton.

Schopf F (1983) Withdrawal phenomena after long-term administration of benzodiazepines: A review of recent investigations. *Pharmacopsychiatry 16*, 1–8.

Singer JL (1981) *Daydreaming and Fantasy*. Oxford: Oxford University Press.

Slade PD (1976a) Hallucinations. *Psychological Medicine 6*, 7–13.

Slade PD (1976b) An investigation of psychological factors involved in the predisposition to auditory hallucinations. *Psychological Medicine 6*, 123–32.

Slade PD (1984) Sensory deprivation and clinical psychiatry. *British Journal of Hospital Medicine 32*, 256–60.

Smythies JR (1956) A logical and cultural analysis of hallucinatory sense-experience. *Journal of Mental Science 102*, 336.

Trethowan WH & Sims ACP (1983) *Psychiatry* (Concise Medical Textbooks). London: Baillière Tindall.
Zilboorg G & Henry GW (1941) *A History of Medical Psychology*. New York: Norton.
Zubek JP (1969) *Sensory Deprivation: Fifteen Years of Research*. New York: Appleton-Centry-Crofts.
Zuckermann M (1969) In Zubek JP (ed.) *Sensory Deprivation: Fifteen Years of Research*, pp. 47–84. New York: Appleton-Centry-Crofts.

7

Delusions and Other Erroneous Ideas

Psychiatry is too quickly satisfied when it throws light on the general structures of delusions and does not seek to comprehend the individual, concrete content of the psychoses (why this man believes himself to be that particular historical personality rather than some other; why his compensatory delusion is satisfied with specifically these ideas of grandeur instead of others).
Sartre (1943)

The *phenomenological* or *empathic* method is useful in that it enables the doctor to understand his individual patient. *False beliefs* include primary and secondary delusions, overvalued ideas and sensitive ideas of reference.

Ideas, beliefs and delusions

Very rarely does anyone claim to be deluded; what the patient thought was a delusion does not usually prove to be so. *A delusion is a false, unshakeable idea or belief which is out of keeping with the patient's educational, cultural and social background; it is held with extraordinary conviction and subjective certainty.* Subjectively or phenomenologically it is indistinguishable from a true belief. A man who is a Bachelor of Medicine of the University of London holds a delusion that he is being used as 'an envoy from Mars'. He believes that he is both a doctor and an envoy, and neither thought seems to him to be delusional or imaginary. He likes to imagine himself a rich man with an estate in Gloucestershire. He has not the slightest difficulty in identifying this latter idea as fantasy. To the man himself, a delusion is much closer to a true belief than imagination, and the reasons enlisted to support its veracity are produced in the same way that a person would prove any belief on which he was challenged. Normally, fantasy is easily distinguished from reality, although the subject may show great reluctance in accepting his aspirations as 'mere fantasy'. Similarly, there is usually very little difficulty for the observer in deciding whether a false belief is a misinterpretation of the facts based on false reasoning, or a delusion.

MEANING OF DELUSION

The delusions of the mad are not well received by the sane. At best they have been treated as harmless and humorous; but often they have been regarded as deliberate attempts to deceive, or as evidence of demonism. The English word *delude* comes, of course, from Latin and implies playing or mocking, defrauding or cheating. The German equivalent *Wahn* is a whim, false opinion, or fancy, and makes no more comment than English upon the subjective experience. The

82

French equivalent, *délire* is more empathic; it implies the ploughshare jumping out of the furrow (*lira*), perhaps a similar metaphor to the ironical 'unhinged' (Hope, 1985, pers. comm.).

Delusions and insanity in law

Delusion has been considered in law to be the fundamental feature of *insanity*. 'Delusions therefore, when there is no frenzy or raving madness, is the true character of insanity', stated Lord Erskine defending Hadfield, who, when clearly mentally ill, fired at King George III in 1800 (West & Walk, 1977).

The special verdict of *not guilty by reason of insanity* can only be brought in English law when the degree of insanity satisfies the *Rules laid down by Judges*, generally called the *McNaughton Rules*. These rules were drawn up in the mid-nineteenth century by judges in the House of Lords as definitive guidance following the attempted assassination of the Prime Minister, by McNaughton. They state: 'To establish a defence on the ground of insanity it must be clearly proved that, at the time of committing the act, the party accused was labouring under such a defect of reason from disease of the mind, as not to know the nature and quality of the act he was doing was wrong'. The rules would be fulfilled by a man who bisects his victim with a meat cleaver believing the latter to be a carcass of beef; or by someone who shoots another person believing them to be an enemy assassin and himself to be the Queen's personal bodyguard. These McNaughton Rules are restricted and exclude many defendants who are undoubtedly psychotic. They are now rarely employed, the plea of *diminished responsibility* being more frequently used in defence for homicide; but the Rules remain the basis for the concept of legal insanity.

There are two major flaws in using the McNaughton Rules. To ask a psychiatrist to comment on what was going on in a person's mind, perhaps months ago, at the time of homicide is difficult; to make a precise causal connection between the act and the state of mind is often impossible. The so-called Napoleonic principle is more expedient: 'If at the time of the act, the accused was suffering from madness, there is no crime'. The psychiatrist must then testify that at the time of the act, the accused was severely mentally ill. The Butler Committee (Department of Health and Social Security, 1976) proposed, although this was not implemented, the legal definition for severe mental illness to be (my italics):

A mental illness is severe when it has one or more of the following characteristics

(a) Lasting impairment of intellectual functions shown by failure of memory, orientation, comprehension and learning capacity.
(b) Lasting alteration of mood of such degree as to give rise to *delusional appraisal* of the patient's situation, his past or his future, or that of others, or to lack of any appraisal.
(c) *Delusional beliefs, persecutory, jealous or grandiose.*
(d) Abnormal perceptions associated with *delusional misinterpretation* of events.
(e) Thinking so disordered as to prevent reasonable appraisal of the patient's situation or reasonable communication with others.

Delusion is a prominent feature of three of these five characteristics.

Definition of delusion

The decision to call a belief *delusional* is not made by the person holding the belief, but by an external observer. There can be no phenomenological definition of delusion, because the patient is likely to hold this belief with the same conviction and intensity as he holds other non-delusional beliefs about himself; or as anyone else holds intensely personal non-delusional beliefs. Subjectively, a delusion is simply a belief. Stoddart's definition of a delusion (1908), 'a judgement which cannot be accepted by people of the same class, education, race and period of life as the person who experiences it', has some advantages. However, it could include as delusional, falling-in-love with a person others regard as unsuitable; a minority religious belief; or holding any unusual idea without acknowledging reasonable argument to the contrary.

The judgement the patient makes may be culturally acceptable, or even true, and yet clearly delusional because of the *evidence* evinced for holding the belief, for instance, a man who believed his wife was unfaithful to him *because* the fifth lamp-post along on the left was unlit. Jaspers (1959) regarded a delusion as a perverted view of reality, incorrigibly held. So delusions have three components:

1　They are held with unusual conviction.
2　They are not amenable to logic.
3　The absurdity or erroneousness of their content is manifest to other people.
Hamilton (1978) defined delusion as: 'A false unshakeable belief which arises from internal morbid processes. It is easily recognisable when it is out of keeping with the person's educational and cultural background'.

Delusions are entirely different from thought disorder, which is considered in Chapter 8. Delusions are ideas that the patient believes to be true but an observer considers false. Formal thought disorder is the alteration from normal that the patient himself describes subjectively in his thinking processes.

Primary and secondary delusions

The confusing subject of primary and secondary delusions requires some explanation. It is probably most meaningful to use the term *primary* to imply that delusion is not occurring in response to another psychopathological form such as mood disorder. *Secondary* delusion is used in the sense that the false belief is understandable in present circumstances–because of the persuasive mood state or because of the cultural content.

Gruhle (1915) considered that a primary delusion was a disturbance of symbolic meaning, not an alteration in sensory perception, apperception or intelligence. Primary delusions occur in schizophrenia and not in other conditions; they include both delusional perception and delusional intuition (Cutting, 1985). However, intuition, notion or idea is not pathognomonic of schizophrenia; because in any individual case there is too much scope for arguing whether this delusion is indeed *primary*, that is, ultimately un-understandable, or *secondary* in nature. Secondary delusions occur in many conditions other than schizophrenia and can be understood in terms of the person's background culture or emotional state.

Wernicke (1906) formulated the concept of an *autochthonous idea*: an idea which is 'native to the soil', aboriginal, arising without external cause. The trouble with finding supposed autochthonous or primary delusions is that it can be disputed whether they are truly autochthonous. For this reason they are not considered of *first rank* in Schneider's (1957) classification of symptoms. It is too difficult to decide in many cases whether a delusion is autochthonous. Several writers have claimed that all delusions are understandable if one knows enough about the patient.

The ultimately un-understandable

Jaspers' concepts of the *un-understandable*, and of *meaningful connections*, is helpful here. If we ask an offender to describe the psychic world in which he lives–his attitudes, his feelings and how these developed through his childhood until now–we may be able to understand his sexual cruelty which at first seemed quite incomprehensible: the behaviour becomes meaningful in the context of his parent's abuse. However, when we consider the middle-aged schizophrenic spinster who believes that men unlock the door of her flat, anaesthetize her and interfere with her sexually, we find an experience that is ultimately not understandable. We can understand, on obtaining more details of the history, how her disturbance centres on sexual experience; why she should be distrustful of men; her doubts about her femininity; and her feelings of social isolation. However, the *delusion*, her absolute conviction that these things are happening to her, that they are true, is not understandable. The best we can do is to try and understand externally, without really being able to feel ourselves into her position (*genetic empathy*, Chapter 1), what she is thinking and how she experiences it. We cannot understand how such a situation could have developed.

This is the core of the primary or autochthonous delusion; it is *ultimately un-understandable*. The patient described above also believed the police were using rays to observe her. One does not have to try and find which delusion came first, the anaesthesia or the observation by rays, to decide which is primary; *primary* is not dependent on temporal relationships. In that both delusions are not ultimately understandable, they are both primary delusions. A delusion can still be primary in this, Jaspers', sense, although it arises upon the basis of a memory, an atmosphere or a perception.

How ideas and delusions are initiated

A delusion is a belief, an idea, a thought, a notion, or an intuition, and it arises in the same type of setting as any other idea: in the context of a perception, a memory, or an atmosphere; or it may be autochthonous, appearing to occur spontaneously.

1   An example of an idea occurring on the basis of a percept, is: I smell food cooking and then form the idea that I will go and eat.
2   Ideas may follow *memory*: I remember listening to a string quartet, and form the idea of playing a gramophone record.
3   Ideas may arise out of an *atmosphere* or mood state. I already feel irritable, and when I collect my car from the garage and it makes an unexplained noise I

become unreasonably angry and blame the mechanic for not repairing it satisfactorily.

4   An idea may be *autochthonous*. I visit a ward of the hospital on an afternoon when I never normally go there. Although I accept that all behaviour has an explanation for its occurrence, I do not know why on this particular occasion I did this. Theoretical explanations may be given as to where such ideas come from, for example, the *unconscious*, but subjectively they seem to have occurred *de novo*. Delusions occur in similar settings on the basis of percept, memory, atmosphere, or *de novo*–'out of the blue'.

SECONDARY DELUSION

Primary delusions differ from secondary delusions in that the former are ultimately not understandable. Secondary delusions are understandable when a detailed psychiatric history and examination is available. That is, they are understandable in terms of the patient's mood state and life history. A manic patient claimed to be Mary Queen of Scots. She accepted that the Queen in question lived and died centuries ago, but claimed descent from her and felt fully entitled to say that she was she. The belief could be understood in terms of her elated and expansive mood, and disappeared as her affective state subsided. A depressed patient believed that he had committed the 'unforgivable sin'. Discussion and persuasion, even with a person whose religious views he respected, was of no avail in giving him relief. The belief could be seen as an integral part of his depressed mood. Depressive delusions may remain after treatment has resulted in improvement from retardation, and account for suicide occasionally occurring in the recovery phase of depression. A secondary delusion may become understandable when the patient's social background is known and the doctor knows the beliefs of the sub-culture from which he comes. It has been suggested that there may be a decline in the prevalence of delusion occurring with depressive illness, but Eagles (1983) studying admissions to hospital in Edinburgh from 1892 to 1982 considers there to be no genuine reduction.

Secondary delusions (*delusion-like ideas*) can be traced for their origins to the circumstances of that person's life; to his current mood state; to the beliefs of his peer group; and to his personality. They are understandable and often transient. There is no *subjective* distinction between a secondary delusion and an overvalued idea; for the distinction between the two can only be reliably made on the evidence given for holding them. A delusion, whether primary or secondary in nature, is based on delusional *evidence*: the reason the patient gives for holding his belief is like the belief itself, false, unacceptable and incorrigible.

Types of primary delusion

Kurt Schneider discusses the dilemma of primary symptoms in schizophrenia extremely lucidly by giving six different possible meanings for the term *primary*, but he still leaves us in doubt as to whether the belief is primary or not. He makes it clear, however, that primary symptoms are not the same as *first-rank symptoms* of schizophrenia. Primary symptoms are those that arise without understandable cause in the context of the psychotic illness. They are therefore the necessary manifestations of the underlying psychopathology, in the same way that swelling and redness is a necessary consequence of physical trauma. First-rank symptoms, on the other hand, are simply a useful empirical list of symptoms that are found commonly in schizophrenia and not in other conditions. Describing their presence makes no claim as to how they arose.

True delusions or *delusions proper* are distinguished by Jaspers from *delusion-like ideas*. *True* delusions become, therefore, synonymous with primary delusions, and delusion-like ideas with secondary delusions. Delusion-like ideas can be seen to *emerge* understandably from the patient's internal and external environment, especially from his mood state. True delusions cannot be so explained; they are psychologically irreducible. They have the following types: (1) autochthonous delusion (delusional intuition); (2) delusional percept; (3) delusional atmosphere; (4) delusional memory.

AUTOCHTHONOUS DELUSION (DELUSIONAL INTUITION)

These are delusions which appear to arise suddenly, 'out of the blue'; they are phenomenologically indistinguishable from the sudden arrival of a normal idea. The patient gropes for explanations for the occurrence of his delusion in answering the interviewer's question, in the same way that a healthy person would find it difficult to account for the arrival of any idea if he were asked to explain it. The difference lies in the ability of the observer to empathize with, to understand a non-delusional idea even though it may be bizarre and destructive; but he cannot understand how a person can have come to believe his delusion.

Schneider regarded the term *delusional idea* as based on outmoded psychology and he felt it should therefore be abandoned. It is often confused with *delusion-like idea* even in some text books and this is another good reason for abandoning it. *Delusional intuition* is perhaps the most satisfactory translation of the German *Wahneinfall*. Delusional intuition occurs as a single stage, unlike *delusional perception* which occurs in two stages: perception and then false interpretation. Like delusional perceptions, delusional intuitions are self-referent and usually of momentous import to the patient.

DELUSIONAL PERCEPT

This is present when the patient receives a normal perception which is interpreted with delusional meaning, and has immense personal significance. It is a *first rank symptom of schizophrenia*. Jaspers delineated the concept of delusional percept; and Gruhle used this description to cover almost all delusions—he minimized the importance of delusional intuition. Schneider (1949) considered the essence of delusional perception to be the abnormal significance attached to a real percept without any cause that is understandable in rational or emotional terms; it is self-referent, momentous, urgent, of overwhelming personal significance and, of course, false.

It is often difficult to decide whether a delusion is truly a delusional percept or is being used to explain the significance of certain objects of perception within a delusional system. A woman said, 'every night blood is being injected out of my arms' (*sic*). When asked for her evidence she explained that she had little brown spots on her arms and therefore knew that she was being injected. The interviewer looked at the spots on her arms, rolled up his sleeve and showed her spots identical in appearance on his own arm. He said that they had been on his arm as long as he could remember and were called 'freckles'. She agreed that both sets of spots looked similar and accepted his explanation of his own spots, but still insisted that her freckles proved that she was being injected in her sleep. This was a delusional percept.

Another patient, who had other delusional symptoms, believed that many of the patients in the hospital were well-known citizens cunningly disguised with wigs, make-up and false beards. She recognized that they did not look like the people whom she presumed them to be but considered this to be part of a gigantic hoax, in which she was herself involved, to 'help people spiritually'. Although her percepts were normal and her interpretations delusional, this was not considered to be a delusional percept but a misinterpretation. All the circumstances in her life were explained in terms of an immensely complicated delusional system, and these perceptions had no immediate personal significance beyond the significance which she found in all the objects and events around her.

In a delusional percept there is a direct experience of meaning for this particular normal percept; it is not simply an interpretation of this percept to fit in with other established delusional beliefs. Delusional perception is, therefore, a direct experience of meaning which the patient did not have previously. Objects or persons take on new personal significance which is delusional in nature, even though the perception itself remains unchanged. This is different from a delusional misinterpretation in which the delusional system affects all aspects of the patient's life, and so every event or perception is interpreted as being involved with that delusion. A patient sees that a doorknob is missing: this is not the precipitant of immediate *new* personal significance of a delusional nature; rather it further confirms the belief he already held that people are trying to trap him and subject him to vivisection.

Perception, when considering delusional percept, can be understood in quite a wide sense. There is no difference, in subjective experience, between perceiving an object by means of a sense organ and perceiving or understanding the sense of written or spoken messages, although the perceptual routes are different. Thus delusional perception includes delusional significance attached to words and sentences as well as to purely sensory objects. For example, an in-patient at Rubery Hill Hospital walked to an entrance of the hospital and saw a dilapidated notice–'R U B E...ILL'. She suddenly realized that this was a concealed message, just for her–'Are you be(ing) ill?'; that people were concerned to help her and that she would get better. The delusional interpretation was attached to the meaning of the letters of the notice.

There are two distinct stages in delusional perception: (1) the object becomes meaningful within a field of sensations, and is perceived; (2) that object becomes invested with delusional significance. These two stages need not be simultaneous for the experience to be a delusional percept. On occasions they have been separated by an interval of years. A patient believed that his mind was being jammed by an electronic device. He claimed that this had started when, five years before, he had lifted the telephone receiver and heard an unusual clicking noise. The delusional belief he had only held for a few months.

DELUSIONAL ATMOSPHERE

For the patient experiencing delusional atmosphere, his world has been subtly altered: 'Something funny is going on'. He experiences everything around him as sinister, portentous, uncanny, peculiar in an indefinable way. He knows that he personally is involved but cannot tell how. He has a feeling of anticipation, sometimes even of excitement, that soon all the separate parts of his experience will fit together to reveal something immensely significant. This is in fact what usually happens, as delusional atmosphere is part of the underlying process and, often, the first symptom of schizophrenia and the context in which a fully formed delusional percept or intuition arises. The mood of the atmosphere is very important and this experience is often referred to as *delusional mood*. The patient feels profoundly uncomfortable, often extremely perplexed and apprehensive. When the delusion becomes fully formed, he often appears to accept it with a feeling of relief from the previous unbearable tension of the *atmosphere*.

A middle-aged man presented initially as a psychiatric out-patient with apparent obsessional symptoms. He kept checking that his neighbours could not hear what he was saying in his home. He had resigned from several jobs because he believed that his employers would not accept his religious beliefs. He felt that people around him were hostile and implacably opposed to him, although he could not define quite how: he just 'felt it'. He kept moving house, but the feeling stayed with him. This continued for several years and he then arrived at a Casualty Department claiming that his neighbours were talking about his actions and controlling his thoughts. The atmosphere had developed insidiously over years and eventually he manifested *auditory hallucinations* and *passivity of thought* (see Chapter 8).

DELUSIONAL MEMORY

This is the symptom when the patient recalls as 'remembered' an event or idea that is clearly delusional in nature; that is, the delusion is retrojected in time. These are sometimes called *retrospective delusions*. An event that occurred in the past is explained in a delusional way. A man of 50 whose mental illness had lasted for about two years claimed that his health had been permanently affected since the age of 16 when he had had 'an operation to implant a golden convolvulus' in his bowels. A delusional memory is likely to have the characteristics of either a delusional intuition or a delusional percept, but to be remembered from the past rather than happening in the present.

If delusional meaning is attached to a normal percept which is remembered, this then becomes a *delusional percept*. It has the two components that were described as being necessary for delusional percept: the image of the remembered percept, and the attachment to this percept of delusional significance. A married woman remembered years previously seeing a man standing in a pub 'with a sad look on his face.' She 'realized,' at the start of her schizophrenic illness two weeks before admission to hospital, that he had been in love with her then, and she tried to locate his name in the telephone directory and make contact again, feeling that they were involved in a special relationship.

Of course, it is a mistake to expect phenomenological symptoms to reveal themselves tidily from the patient's conversation. There is no absolute demarcation between delusional memory and delusional percept or intuition. The patient describes a delusion. Did this occur one hour, one week, or ten years ago? At what point will this be delusional memory, not delusional intuition? Similarly, there is no absolute distinction between a normal event, perception or idea that occurred in the past and is remembered with a delusional interpretation; and a delusional event, perception or idea that occurred in the past and is also remembered with a delusional interpretation. Both these are delusional memories and it is not possible to know how much of the event was factual and how much delusional. A schizophrenic woman, aged 34, described twelve years ago picking up a telephone to ring a man she liked very much: 'God moved my arm and made me put the telephone back'. It was not possible to decide exactly what part of this experience was factual and what delusional, and at what time the delusion occurred.

Fine distinctions are sometimes imposed upon the classification of primary delusions, but are more collector's items than features of useful clinical significance. *Delusional awareness* is an experience which is not sensory in nature, in which ideas or events take on an extreme vividness as if they had additional reality. *Delusional significance* is the second stage of the occurrence of delusional perception. Objects and persons are perceived normally, but take on a special significance which cannot be rationally explained by the patient.

The origins of delusion

Those affected believe their delusions but do not always act on them. A patient knows himself to be a supernatural messenger and yet is quite prepared to make a tray in Occupational Therapy. We are able in our own experience of our thinking to distinguish between reality and imagination (fantasy). I know whether I am a Test cricketer or just imagining myself to be. The distinction between reality and fantasy is assumed as being obvious, and it is unusual to have difficulty deciding which form of experience we have. That is not to say that we do not act on our fantasies. Jaspers considered that our concrete perception of reality is a primary event not determined by sense organs. *Reality* lies in the interpretation of, or the significance attached to, the event. When a man shakes hands with his future father-in-law it is not the event itself, the physical contact, that matters. It is the significance of the event. In all events and experiences, it is the significance associated with it that invests it with reality. Loss of significance makes the event seem unreal.

Fish (1967) has made a useful précis of the earlier German theories of the origins of delusion: Conrad suggested that in a primary delusional experience, a psychological event takes on a new meaning and this is called *apophany*. Gruhle considered *delusional perception* to be the most significant form of delusion; a normal percept taking on a new meaning. This results in a disturbed relationship of the understanding of events. Matussek considered that with delusional perception there is a change either in the significance of the words used or in the actual nature of the perception itself. These writers, and also Schneider, regard *delusional perception* as the key to understanding the nature of delusional experience.

Hagen regarded *delusional atmosphere* as primary, arising for reasons unknown, and resulting in a rearrangement of meanings in the world around the patient, who gropes for an answer to this problem of understanding and finds it in creating a delusion. It is easier to bear the certainty of a delusion than the uncertain foreboding of the atmosphere. Jaspers considered that there is a subtle change of personality due to the illness itself; and this creates the condition for the development of the delusional atmosphere in which the delusional intuition arises.

All these theories assume that the delusion is *primary* and *ultimately not understandable* in the same sense that Jaspers considers the experience of reality to be primary. Experience holds a symbolic implication beyond the fact of the event itself; for example, the doctor writing a prescription for his patient in the consulting room means much more to the latter than if the doctor were doodling on his prescription block. (A patient in North Africa in the nineteenth century ate the prescription his doctor gave him, so great was his confidence in, and veneration for, the doctor (Sims, 1972)). It seems that the symbolic belief attached to events and perceptions is altered in delusion, and this is why the patient does not necessarily act on his delusions. The delusional atmosphere is not an essential prerequisite for a delusional intuition as the latter may occur apparently *de novo*.

Some writers have not tried to explain delusions because they find them totally incomprehensible and they consider that they are directly due to abnormality of the brain (Schneider, 1949). Bleuler concentrated on the *alteration in affect* as primary rather than delusional atmosphere or perception. He considered that heightened affect loosens the capacity to form associations and thus facilitates the arrival of a delusion. At the beginning of his schizophrenic illness there is extreme affect, perhaps in the form of anxiety or ambivalence, which the patient cannot express.

Kretschmer (1927) stressed the importance of the underlying personality. He described the *sensitive premorbid personality* occurring in a person who retains *affect-laden complexes* and has a limited capacity for emotional self-expression. Such a person is driven painfully by, for example, powerful sexual feelings, but has great difficulty in communicating his passion and relating to other people. He is very much aware of social constraints and is rigidly controlled by his superego. Such a person, somewhat rigid, narrow-minded and suspicious in his views, readily forms *sensitive ideas of reference*. A key experience may occur in his life circumstances and quite suddenly these ideas become structured as *delusions of reference*.

A girl was always shy, reticent and sensitive at school. Quite often she was unable to force herself to go to school. She was meticulous in her attention to personal neatness and cleanliness. After leaving school she remembered vividly several occasions as a child when she had felt humiliated. At the age of 18, when she was working in a factory, she was in the women's cloakroom brooding because her boyfriend had told her that he was leaving her for someone else. She heard one of the other women say, 'Ugh, doesn't she smell?' Immediately she applied the statement to herself, and to explain her boyfriend's behaviour. From then onwards she was convinced that she smelt unpleasant all the time, although she could smell nothing herself. This delusion dominated her life, prevented her mixing and caused her great distress. This development of a delusion (*Sensitiver Beziehungswahn*) from sensitive ideas of reference, as the sequel to a *key experience*, is sometimes seen at the onset of schizophrenia but is not common. The key experience as demonstrated in this case has two important qualities.

First, it has particular appropriateness to the patient's areas of conflict as sensitive ideas of reference. Secondly, it occurs at a time of marked emotional turmoil and distress, so that the psychic ground is prepared for a catastrophic event.

Attempts have been made to find all delusions understandable in terms of the person's internal experience or social background. Westphal considered that if one knew all about the patient, the change in his view of himself and the belief that he had become noticeable in some way, would explain the delusion (Fish, 1967). Freud's (1907) theories on the development of delusions also attempted to make them ultimately understandable through the mechanisms of denial, projection and so on. Other authors have claimed that delusions are understandable in a social context. Laing (1961) considered the flight into madness as a necessary defence against a highly destructive family: not only understandable, but admirable, and even worth emulating.

When four different psychological theories were appraised to explain paranoid phenomena, a basis of *shame-humiliation* was found to be the most consistent (Colby, 1977). Winters and Neale (1983) consider existing theories of delusional thinking develop two main themes: *motivational* and *defect*. The motivational theme explains the arrival of a delusion to explain unusual perceptual experience or to reduce uncomfortable psychic states. Defect implies some fundamental cognitive-attentional deficit resulting in delusion.

Erroneous ideation

OVERVALUED IDEA

An overvalued idea is an acceptable, comprehensible idea pursued by the patient beyond the bounds of reason. It is usually associated with abnormal personality. Disorders associated with overvalued ideas have been reviewed by McKenna (1984) whose definition of overvalued idea 'refers to a solitary, abnormal belief that is neither delusional nor obsessional in nature, but which is preoccupying to the extent of dominating the sufferer's life'. It is *overvalued* in the sense that it causes disturbed functioning or suffering to the person himself or to others. The background evidence on which an overvalued idea is held is not necessarily unreasonable or false. It becomes so dominant that all other ideas are secondary and relate to it: the patient's whole life comes to revolve around this one idea. It is usually associated with very strong affect which the person, because of his temperament, has great difficulty in expressing.

According to McKenna, the term was introduced by Wernicke (1909), who distinguished it from obsession, in that it was not experienced subjectively as 'senseless', and from delusion. Jaspers considered that delusion is qualitatively different from normal belief with a radical transformation of the meaning attached to events and incorrigible to an extent quite unlike normal belief. An overvalued idea, on the contrary, is an isolated notion associated with strong affect and abnormal personality, and similar in quality to passionate political, religious or ethical conviction. Fish, considered there was frequently a discrepancy between the degree of conviction and the extent to which the belief directed action. But the patient with an overvalued idea invariably acted on it, determinedly and repeatedly; it is almost carried out with the drive of an instinct, like nest-building.

Table 7.1 Disorders with overvalued ideas (after McKenna, 1984)

Content of disorder	Abnormality of personality	Reference
Paranoid state – querulous or litiginous type		Kraepelin (1905) Jaspers (1959)
Morbid jealousy		Ey (1954) Shepherd (1961)
Hypochondriasis		Pilowsky (1970) Merskey (1979)
Dysmorphophobia	Abnormality of personality is usually present with overvalued ideas in all these conditions	Hay (1970) Munro (1980)
Parasitophobia (Ekbom's syndrome)		Hopkinson (1973)
Anorexia nervosa		Dally (1979) Crisp (1980)
Transsexualism		Huxley, Kenna and Brandon (1981)

McKenna lists the disorders of content commonly associated with the form of overvalued idea. These are represented in Table 7.1. Not in all cases of each of these conditions is the psychopathology an overvalued idea: for instance, morbid jealousy may be delusional; hypochondriasis may occur secondary to depressed mood. However, when found it is almost invariably associated with abnormal personality.

Morbid jealousy is often manifested as an overvalued idea. A husband was terrified that his wife was being unfaithful to him. He checked on her every movement; interrogated her repeatedly; examined her underwear; employed detectives to follow her; and misinterpreted any innocent contact she had with other men. On examination, he was not deluded but the importance he attached to investigating and maintaining his wife's fidelity, and the time taken to do this, was excessive and destroyed his family life and lost him his job. The form of the abnormal idea in many of the disturbances of body image, for example, *dysmorphophobia* and *transsexualism*, is usually an overvalued idea. A person with *paranoid personality* disorder became involved in a protracted law suit because a farmer ploughed across a public right of way. It is reasonable that hikers get annoyed when a footpath is destroyed, but this person took reasonable irritation to extreme lengths and constructed a man-trap to eliminate the farmer. His enthusiasm for footpaths had become an overvalued idea.

PARANOID IDEAS AND SYNDROMES

The word *paranoid* means in psychiatry 'self-referent' and is not limited to *persecutory*; all delusions are delusions of reference in that they relate to the patient himself. A person will not form a delusional belief concerning six-inch men on Mars, unless he himself is significantly implicated in some way. So a paranoid delusion is a delusion of self-reference, not necessarily persecutory in nature. A paranoid personality disorder is that type of abnormal personality in which the person's reaction to other people is unduly self-referent; paranoid states include those mental states in which self-referent phenomena are conspicuous, that is, *delusions, delusion-like ideas of reference*, or *overvalued ideas* predominate. A patient, all of whose delusions are grandiose in nature and none of them persecutory, may still be suffering from *paranoid* schizophrenia.

Although primary delusions are characteristic of schizophrenia, secondary delusions (delusion-like ideas) occur in a number of conditions; for example, manic–depressive psychosis in both manic and depressive phases; epilepsy and other organic psychosyndromes; acute drug intoxication; various alcoholic states; and, of course, in schizophrenia. The term *paranoia* originally was synonymous with delusional insanity. Kraepelin (1905) used the term more specifically to describe the condition where there are delusions but no hallucinations. The personality, mood state and volition of the patient, in Kraepelin's description, are well preserved.

Overvalued ideas are commonly found associated with personality disorders of paranoid or anankastic type. So *paranoid state* is a collective term for a number of conditions where the *content* is unduly self-referent, but the *form* of the idea has not been precisely delineated. If the bizarre idea is a primary delusion (and there would normally be first-rank symptoms also present to corroborate this), then the patient is probably suffering from paranoid schizophrenia. If the delusion is secondary in nature, another psychosis is the likely diagnosis. If the form of the idea is not delusional, but better described as an overvalued idea, the paranoid symptoms are probably arising on the basis of personality disorder. Clarification of the *form* is necessary for adequate diagnosis, which in its turn is useful for assessment of prognosis and planning appropriate treatment.

Content of delusions

Delusions are, of course, infinitely variable in their content but certain general characteristics commonly occur. Unlike the form which is dictated by the type of illness, the content is determined by the emotional, social and cultural background of the patient: Napoleons are now rare in mental hospitals; schizophrenics in primitive tribes describe their thoughts as being interfered with by the spirits of their ancestors rather than by television.

DELUSIONS OF PERSECUTION

This is the most common content of delusion. It was separated from other types of delusion and from other forms of melancholia by Lasègue (1852). People who believe delusionally that their lives are being interfered with from outside more often feel this to be harmful than beneficial. A variant on the usual beliefs of persecution or malevolent intent are *delusions of prejudice*: the patient/victim believes that he is being slighted, overlooked, passed over in favour of someone else. The interfering agent in delusions of persecution may be animate or inanimate–other people or machines; may be systems, organizations or institutions more frequently than individuals. Sometimes the patient experiences persecution as a vague influence without knowing who is responsible.

Persecutory delusions occur in many different conditions: in schizophrenia; in affective psychoses of manic and depressive type; in organic states both acute and chronic. The affect associated with the belief of persecution may vary from an inappropriate indifference and apathy in schizophrenia to stark terror, as commonly seen in delirium tremens. Manic patients with persecutory delusions show gross overactivity and flight of ideas in attempting to express and deal with their beliefs. In depression, the persecutory delusions take on the characteristic colouring of the dominant state. Persecutory overvalued ideas are a prominent facet of the *litiginous* type of paranoid personality disorder.

MORBID JEALOUSY

This disorder of content, described by Ey (1950), may be manifested in various forms; for example, delusion, overvalued idea, depressive affect, anxiety state. The feeling of jealousy, coupled with a sense that the loved object 'belongs to me', is part of normal human experience; it is of social value in marital relationships for preserving the family. Various terms have been used to describe abnormal, morbid or malignant jealousy. Kraepelin used the term 'sexual jealousy'. Enoch and Trethowan (1979) have considered it important to distinguish psychotic jealousy from other types; and this is dependent on the demonstration of a *delusion of infidelity*. It is sometimes difficult to distinguish understandable jealousy from that which is clearly delusional.

An undisputed delusion of being the victim of infidelity without other psychotic symptoms has been described (Todd & Dewhurst, 1955). This is identifiably delusional when the belief of the spouse is based on delusional evidence. Such delusions are resistant to treatment and do not change with time. A patient was very concerned that his wife was being unfaithful with numerous people, including his boss, her general practitioner and others. Four years later, despite various treatments, his belief was unchanged, but he said, 'I don't blame her now. She is much younger than I am and everyone does that sort of thing'. Delusions of jealousy are common in alcoholism; for instance, Shrestha *et al*. (1985) found sexual jealousy to be present in 35% of alcoholic men and 31% of women. As jealousy appeared to be justified in some cases, *morbid jealousy* was considered to be present in 27% of men and 15% of women. Delusional jealousy also occurs in some organic states, for example the punch-drunk syndrome of boxers following multiple contra-coup contusion. Quite frequently, the spouse, wearied by continued accusations of infidelity, does form another sexual involvement, which may result in an acute exacerbation in the mental state of the patient and further marital conflict.

The sexual content of the delusion is obvious and all-important. Jealousy is directed towards the sexual partner. The deluded person is very attached to, and often emotionally utterly dependent upon, the other; he may have a sense of owning her completely. The victim is often much more sexually attractive than the deluded partner; for instance, a young wife or a sociable and popular husband. The deluded person may have been promiscuous in the past and therefore resignedly expects his spouse to show similar behaviour. He may have become impotent and projected the blame for his failure onto her. He may have homosexual fantasies directed towards the men with whom he claims his wife is consorting. Morbid jealousy arises with the belief that there is a threat to the exclusive possession of his wife, but this is just as likely to occur from conflicts inside himself–his own inability to love or his sexual interest directed towards someone else–as from changing circumstances in his environment or his wife's behaviour. Husbands or wives may show sexual jealousy; as may cohabitees and homosexual pairs. Jealousy is particularly prominent in these latter two types of relationship, since the insecurity of a liaison not condoned by law is especially likely to germinate suspicion. Crimes of violence are more frequently associated with morbid jealousy than with any other psychopathology.

DELUSIONS OF LOVE

The delusions associated with loving and being loved are quite different from the behavioural and affective abnormalities of *nymphomania*, the situation of a woman characterized by morbid or uncontrolled sexual desire, and *satyriasis*, the male equivalent of excessive sexual activity. Both these latter conditions exist initially in the opinion of an external commentator–the doctor.

Approximately twice as many schizophrenic patients had sexual preoccupations in the mid-twentieth century as compared with the mid-nineteenth century (Klaf & Hamilton, 1961). *Erotomania* was described by Sir Alexander Morrison (1848) as being 'characterized by delusions...the patient's love is of the sentimental kind, he is wholly occupied by the object of his adoration, whom, if he approach it is with respect...the fixed and permanent delusions attending erotomania sometimes prompt those labouring under it to destroy themselves or others, for although in general tranquil and peaceful, the patient sometimes becomes irritable, passionate and jealous'. Erotomania is commoner in women than men and a variety has been called by Hart (1921) 'Old Maids' Insanity', in which persecutory delusions often develop. These have sometimes been classified as paranoia, rather than paranoid schizophrenia; these delusional symptoms sometimes occur in the context of a manic-depressive psychosis (Guirguis, 1981). Trethowan (1967) demonstrated the social characteristics of erotomania, relating the patient's previous difficulties in parental relationships to the present erotomania.

A variation of erotomania was described by, and retains the name of, *de Clérambault* (1942). Typically, a woman believes a man, who is older and of higher social status than she, is in love with her. The victim has usually done nothing to deserve her attention and may be quite unaware of her existence: sometimes he is a well-known public figure quite remote from the patient. In a case of ours, the victim was a previous employer of the patient. She believed that he was the father of her child (although at another time she agreed that there had been no sexual relationship with her employer). She also believed that he was sending her money and she would write letters thanking him for his generosity and affirming her gratitude for the evidence of his love (Sims & White, 1973).

DELUSIONAL MISIDENTIFICATION

In the *Capgras syndrome* (Capgras & Reboul-Lachaux, 1923) the patient believes that someone close to him has been replaced by an impostor pretending to be that person; the abnormality is delusional and not hallucinatory. According to Christodoulou and Malliara-Loulakaki (1981), the psychopathological term *delusional misidentification* is applied to four, rare, closely related syndromes:

1   the Capgras syndrome;
2   the syndrome of Frégoli (Courbon & Fail, 1927), in which the false identification of familiar people occurs in strangers;

3 the syndrome of intermetamorphosis (Courbon & Tusques, 1932), characterized by the patient claiming that the familiar person (usually regarded as a persecutor) and the misidentified stranger share physical similarities as well as psychological;
4 the syndrome of subjective doubles (Christodoulou, 1978), in which the patient believes that another person has been physically transformed into his own self.

The Capgras syndrome is regarded by Enoch and Trethowan as 'a rare, colourful syndrome in which the person believes that a person, usually closely related to him, has been replaced by an exact double'. It is a specific delusional misidentification of a person with whom the subject usually has close emotional ties and towards whom there is a feeling of *ambivalence* at the time of onset. The belief, in Capgras syndrome, has the full characteristics of delusion (Enoch & Trethowan). Similarly, the syndrome of intermetamorphosis is a delusion in which the patient believes that an individual has been transformed both psychologically and physically into another person: it is not a misperception.

A female in-patient asked about her husband: 'Who is that person who drives my family up to the hospital every evening? It is a cheek. He stays at home and opens all my husband's letters. Anyway at least he pays the bills... He does look very like my husband only perhaps a little fatter'. Although being unable to describe any perceptual difference between this man and her husband she was utterly convinced that the former was an impostor masquerading for some subtle purpose as her husband. Most patients show definite schizophrenic symptoms and there is no alteration of perception but a delusional misidentification in which the delusion reflects a subtle change of the ambience in the patient's feelings for the victim. The ambivalence of the relationship prior to the development of the delusion was exemplified by a patient's mother who was believed to be an impostor; she was her only close relation but the patient felt irritated by and excessively dependent upon her.

In the cases reviewed by Berson (1983), 55% (seventy cases) were unquestionably diagnosed as schizophrenic, and a further eight patients (totalling 61%) were probably schizophrenic; 13% were suffering from manic-depressive psychosis; and 24% were considered to have an organic diagnosis. Of 133 cases, 57% were female; the age range was from 12 to 78 with a mean of 42.8 years. Majority opinion would not favour denoting this as a separate disease, but rather as a symptom which colours the clinical state and dominates the symptomatology. The four different varieties of delusional misidentification have in common psychopathologically the *form* of a delusion. The Capgras syndrome, when it occurs in schizophrenia, is thus a delusional percept (Sims, 1986). In the Capgras syndrome there is no outward change in the appearance of the object, and there is no false perception, for the patient admits that the double exactly resembles the original (Enoch & Trethowan, 1979).

The ambivalence towards the object of misidentification, may be expressed in the history with a clear account of both negative emotions, such as hostility, fear or contempt, and affection and dependence. On those few occasions when an object, rather than a person, is wrongly identified, that object has important emotional connotations for the patient; for example, home or a letter from a relative. The objects of misidentification in Berson's review of 133 patients comprised: sixty spouses and two lovers; on twenty-nine occasions a child or children; forty parents; twenty-four siblings; thirteen therapists; four grandparents; three in-laws; two neighbours; two domestics; and one each of fiancé, cousin, stepson, employer and priest. On eight occasions, the self was misidentified either solely or with other evidence of the syndrome; on two occasions animals were, and eight times inanimate objects. Thus, for 31% of occasions, the delusional misidentification refers to a marital partner, and for 46% to a first-degree relative: in only 4% was the misidentification of the patient him or herself.

GRANDIOSE DELUSIONS

Primary grandiose delusions occur in schizophrenia. The patient may believe himself to be a famous celebrity or to have supernatural powers. He may believe himself to be involved in some very special and secret mission about which he has not yet been fully briefed but, in anticipation of which he is waiting with excitement for the dénouement. Beliefs of this sort are sometimes called *delusions of special purpose*, and are of the form of delusional intuition.

Expansive or grandiose delusional beliefs may extend to objects. So, sometimes a psychotic patient demonstrates delusions of invention, in which, for example, he builds a machine which he believes to have special capabilities, considering himself to be a creative prodigy. Secondary grandiose delusions, or delusion-like ideas, occur in manic states. A patient said that there was no life on Mars because 'if there had been I would have been able to get in touch by telepathy using my great genius'. He evinced no evidence of true passivity experiences. A manic patient, mentioned above, believed that she was descended from the Royal Stuart line, and therefore was actually in some way Mary Queen of Scots. She invited the Queen and the Prime Minister to a party in her student flat because she thought they would be honoured to be invited: 'It is only fair that they should have an invitation'. The expansive affect of mania can be very clearly seen to render this delusion understandable.

RELIGIOUS DELUSIONS

Religious delusions are common. However, they formed a higher proportion of all delusions in the nineteenth than the twentieth century: three times as many schizophrenic patients of both sexes had religious preoccupation in the nineteenth century (Klaf & Hamilton, 1961). Decision as to whether beliefs are delusional or not must rest on the principles described above: that is, on the way the belief is held and the evidence produced in its support. Because a religious belief is very bizarre and at variance with those held by the interviewer, it does not necessarily make it a delusion. Religious delusions may be grandiose in nature: for example, a patient who believed that she was an emissary of God to the Birmingham Housing Department. They may also be secondary to depressive mood as in the patient of Emil Kraepelin (1904) quoted at the beginning of Chapter 16: 'I cannot live and I cannot die, because I have failed so much, I shall bring my husband and children to hell.'

The religious nature of the delusion is seen as a disorder of *content* dependent on the patient's social background, interests and peer group. The *form* of the delusion is dependent on the nature of the illness. So religious delusions are not caused by excessive religious belief, nor by the wrongdoing which the patient attributes as cause, but they simply accentuate that when a person becomes mentally ill his delusions reflect, in their content, his predominant interests and concerns.

DELUSIONS OF GUILT AND UNWORTHINESS

Such delusions are common in depressive illness. They often lead to suicide and, rarely, to homicide, when the killing of a close relative may be followed by the patient's suicide (see Chapters 16 and 19).

The beliefs about guilt may totally dominate the patient's thinking. An elderly woman spent the day rushing round the house wringing her hands and telling her worried family that she was wretched, worthless and only deserved to die. She told her married daughters that they were illegitimate, that the house she lived in was not hers but stolen and she told her husband of thirty years standing that they were not legally married. When it was suggested to her that she came into hospital, she assumed that she would be killed on arrival and she asked whether this could take place there and then, so that she could receive her just desserts.

DELUSIONS OF POVERTY AND NIHILISTIC DELUSIONS

Delusions of poverty are common in depression. *Cotard's syndrome* contains features typical of psychotic depression in the elderly: nihilistic and hypochondriacal delusions which are often bizarre, dramatic and tinged with grandiosity; a mood depressed with either agitation or retardation; and a completely negative attitude. According to Griesinger (1845), 'the patient confuses the subjective change in his own attitude to outside things...the real world seems to the patient to have disappeared completely, or to be dead'. This is graphically depicted by Cotard (1882):

> I would tentatively suggest the name 'nihilistic delusions' (délire de negations) to describe the condition of the patients to whom Griesinger was referring, in whom the tendency towards negation is carried to its extreme. If they are asked their name or age, they have neither–where were they born? They were not born. Who were their father and mother? They have no father, mother, wife or children. Have they a headache or pain in the stomach, or any other part of the body? They have no head or stomach and some even have no body. If one shows them an object, a rose or some other flower they answer, 'that is not a rose, not a flower at all'. In some cases negation is total. Nothing exists any longer, not even themselves.

Sometimes delusions of persecution and negation coexist; and the more prominent are the nihilistic delusions, the more severe is the depression. In general, nihilistic delusions are a depressive form of self-blame, whilst in persecutory delusions the blame is cast elsewhere. Nihilistic delusions are the reverse of grandiose delusions where oneself, objects or situations are expansive and enriched. Feelings of guilt and hypochondriacal ideas are developed to their most extreme, depressive form in nihilistic delusions.

HYPOCHONDRIACAL DELUSIONS

A very depressed man said that he was full of water, that there was nothing else inside him, that he could not pass water, but that if he did that would be the end of him. He could not drink or the water would flood the room. Other less striking hypochondriacal beliefs and delusions occur in depression, and Schneider (1970) has considered that locating the experience of depression as a sensation in a bodily organ is equivalent to a first-rank symptom of depressive psychosis (Chapter 16). An elderly woman with depression, who had had a mitral valve replacement for rheumatic heart disease, said that she felt worthless and hopeless, and described her physical functions as 'nothing is working'.

Hypochondriacal delusions may also occur in schizophrenia and have the characteristics of other schizophrenic ideas. They are more likely to be given a persecutory than a nihilistic explanation. Thus, a patient believed that his bodily functions were being interfered with by rays emitted from a planet and that this was part of a plot to control his thoughts and behaviour. Hypochondriacal delusions are discussed in association with hypochondriasis in Chapter 13. Facial pain is described in Chapter 14, and other delusion-like ideas and overvalued ideas of the body in Chapter 13. Delusions concerning the patient's origins are described and have some affinity to hypochondriacal delusion. The patient believes, on delusional evidence, that he is not his parent's child; perhaps, that he is of royal birth, part animal or supernatural. Alternatively, he may believe that he does not exist and was never born.

An unusual type of hypochondriacal delusion is the condition of *koro* (Lapierre, 1972). The three features of this condition are: (1) the definite belief that the penis is shrinking into the abdomen; (2) the belief that when the penis disappears into the abdomen death will follow; (3) extreme anxiety accompanying this delusional idea. Yap (1965) describes this as a culture-bound depersonalization syndrome and considers it to be a manifestation of acute anxiety associated with folk beliefs concerning sexual exhaustion. It has occurred in epidemic proportions amongst Malays in Singapore (Gwee, 1963), but has also been described in individual cases in a French Canadian (Lapierre), in a West Indian and a Greek Cypriot (Ang & Weller, 1984), and in an Englishman (Berrios & Morley, 1984).

DELUSIONS OF INFESTATION

These have been described by Hopkinson (1970). In *Ekbom's syndrome* (Ekbom, 1938) the patient believes that he is infested with small but macroscopic organisms. The patient's experience may take the form of a tactile hallucinatory state, a delusion or an overvalued idea. The aetiology is also variable. It is probably most common as a symptom of circumscribed hypochondriasis in affective psychosis, along with other depressive symptoms, but also occurs in paranoid schizophrenia, monosymptomatic hypochondriacal psychosis, in organic brain syndromes or with neurotically determined conditions. A more recent review of this subject will be found in Berrios (1985).

Patients have believed that they had a spider in their hair, worms and lice beneath the skin, or infestation with various insects. The delusion may be accompanied by other depressive delusions or overvalued ideas of being dirty, guilty, unworthy or ill. These delusions may also occur in schizophrenia, in which condition they characteristically take on a bizarre character and are accompanied by other schizophrenic symptoms. A 49-year old mother of four children, one of whose sons had developed a schizophrenic illness, complained of recurrent pain in her vagina which she explained as being caused by a parasite which had migrated from her stomach, where it had been responsible for epigastric pain, diagnosed earlier as hiatus hernia (McLaughlin & Sims, 1984). She described the parasite as wandering through her blood stream, and as having been responsible for various aches and pains she had experienced in the past. She related having passed multiple small red worms and worm-casts in her faeces and, on one occasion, a two-inch green frog!

Delusions of infestation may occur in organic states with tactile hallucinations: in delirium tremens during alcohol withdrawal, and in cocaine addiction. They are described in cerebrovascular disease, in senile dementia and in other brain disease, and have been ascribed to disorder of the thalamus. Overvalued ideas and delusion-like ideas of infestation sometimes occur in people with personality disorder of anankastic or paranoid type with no psychotic illness.

Characteristically these ideas occur in patients aged over fifty. Typically those with delusions of infestation have always been concerned with personal cleanliness. Sometimes the condition is precipitated by a skin disease and becomes a delusional elaboration of existing tactile symptoms. It has been suggested that the symptom develops in stages: first abnormal cutaneous sensation; then an illusion develops; and, finally, the fully-formed delusion of infestation occurs.

COMMUNICATED INSANITY

Lasègue and Falret (1877) described 'la folie à deux (ou folie communiquée)'. Occasionally a delusion (delusional intuition) is transferred from a psychotic person to one or more others with whom they have been in close association, so that the recipient shares the false belief: the *Principal* acquires the delusion first and is dominant; the *Associate* becomes deluded through association with the Principal. This situation, where partners accept, support and share each others beliefs, has been called the *psychosis of association*. The Associate is usually socially deprived or disadvantaged, mentally or physically.

Gralnick (1942) in a review of the English literature on folie á deux subdivided the condition into four possible relationships between Principal and Associate:

(1) in *folie imposée* the delusions of a mentally ill person are transferred to someone who was not previously mentally ill, although characteristically the victim has some social disadvantage. Separation of the pair is often followed by remission of symptoms in the Associate.

(2) *Folie communiquée* occurs when a normal person suffers a contagion of his ideas after resisting them for a long time. Once he acquires these beliefs he maintains them despite separation.

(3) In *folie induite* a person who is already psychotic adds the delusions of a closely associated person to his own.

(4) *Folie simultanée* describes a situation in which two or more people become psychotic and share the same delusional system simultaneously. It has been considered that the Principal is always psychotic (Soni & Rockley, 1974), but the Associate may or may not be psychotic.

In a case report of a family affected with folie à quatre (Sims *et al.*, 1979), the initially referred patient believed that a large industrial concern had put 'bugging' devices in the walls of his brother's house. He claimed that employees of the firm had been following him everywhere and interfering with his own house. His wife believed this story initially and produced supposedly corroborative evidence. A year later following his in-patient treatment, she no longer accepted the plot and believed her husband to be mad. She was a very anxious person who had previously received psychiatric treatment and came from a family in which three members had suffered from Huntington's Chorea. When the patient's brother was visited at home, it was found that he, and the sister who lived with him, both believed in the plot and were both currently receiving treatment for a schizophrenic illness in which first-rank symptoms were present.

Folie à deux is an interesting condition which demonstrates how the content of belief is dictated by social and environmental circumstances, but the precise form of the symptoms varies according to the nature of the illness. Thus the non-psychotic victim of folie imposée will show delusion-like ideas, overvalued ideas or misinterpretations, but will not show 'true' delusions or delusional percept.

DELUSIONS OF CONTROL

These delusions, otherwise known as *passivity* or *made experiences*, are discussed with disorder of thinking in Chapter 8.

Reality of delusions

It cannot be stressed too often that patients believe their delusions literally. Subjectively, delusions are completely different from fantasy. Patients do not describe them 'as if' they existed. Their reality is 'known' with the unconcerned certainty that the undeluded person assumes for the concrete events and ideas of his own life, such as the floor being solid. Delusions arrive in the minds of the mad in the same way as ideas arrive in the minds of the creative: the two are subjectively indistinguishable. Although they have heard this said, it is difficult for those coming new to psychiatry to grasp this simple but important fact. Schizophrenics do not always act on their delusions, but quite frequently they do so act. A man who believed that American battleships were sailing down the main street of Birmingham, UK (100 miles from the sea), had the refined social conscience to report this to the police! Persons holding delusions of morbid jealousy are potentially very dangerous: extreme physical violence and murder not uncommonly occur in this context. The patient with depressive delusions of guilt and unworthiness may well act on them by killing himself.

Delusions are not alterable by persuasion. Although schizophrenic delusions do not always respond to treatment with psychotropic drugs, gratifyingly they do frequently clear. As the patient gets better he retains full memory for the time when he was deluded, and he may give various explanations for the remission of his symptoms: 'The people in the flat above were undoubtedly using mirrors to watch me before I came into hospital but they have stopped entirely since I came home'. A woman believed that she was being influenced by an 'atmosphere' all around that emanated from a neighbouring suburb and was making her ill. As she improved she described this 'atmosphere' as geographically moving away, so that at first she no longer experienced it in her own house and garden; later it left the street. As the delusions fade, the patient may gain insight and regard them as false beliefs 'due to the illness'. Such a person needs help in accepting himself as a fit repository for his own self-confidence once more. He may feel himself to be damaged, vulnerable and untrustworthy and suffer a massive loss of self-esteem.

References

Ang PC & Weller MPI (1984) Koro and psychosis. *British Journal of Psychiatry 145*, 335.

Berrios GE (1985) Delusional parasitosis and physical disease. *Comprehensive Psychiatry 26*, 395–403.

Berrios GE & Morley SJ (1984) Koro-like symptoms in a non-Chinese subject. *British Journal of Psychiatry 145*, 331–4.

Berson RJ (1983) Capgras' syndrome. *American Journal of Psychiatry 140*, 969–78.

Capgras J & Reboul-Lachaux J (1923) L'illusion des sosies dans un délire systematique chronique. *Bulletin de la Societé Clinique de Médecine Mentale 11*, 6–16.

Christodoulou GN (1978) Syndrome of subjective doubles. *American Journal of Psychiatry 135*, 249–51.

Christodoulou GN, Malliara-Loulakaki S (1981) Delusional misidentification syndromes and cerebral 'dysrhythmia'. *Psychiatrica Clinica 14*, 245–51.

Colby KM (1977) Appraisal of four psychological theories of paranoid phenomena. *Journal of Abnormal Psychology 86*, 54–9.

Cotard J (1882) Nihilistic delusions. In Hirsch SR & Shepherd M (eds) *Themes & Variations in European Psychiatry, 1974* (transl. Rohde M, pp. 353–374). Bristol: John Wright.

Courbon P & Fail G (1927) Syndrome d'illusion de Frégoli et schizophrenie. *Bulletin de la Societé Clinique de Médecine Mentale 15*, 121–4.

Courbon P & Tusques J (1932) Illusion d'intermétamorphose et de charme. *Annals médico-psychologique 90*, 401–5.

Crisp AH (1980) *Anorexia Nervosa: Let Me Be*. London: Academic Press.

Cutting J (1985) *The Psychology of Schizophrenia*. Edinburgh: Churchill Livingstone.

Dally P (1969) *Anorexia Nervosa*. London: Heinemann.

De Clérambault GG (1942) *Les psychoses passionelles Oeuvre psychiatrique*. Paris: Presses Universitaire.

Department of Health & Social Security (1976) *A Review of the Mental Health Act, 1959*. London: HMSO.

Eagles JM (1983) Delusional depressive in-patients, 1892-1982. *British Journal of Psychiatry 143*, 558–63.

Ekbom K (1938) Praeseniler Dermat-zooenwahn. *Acta Psychiatrica Scandinavica 13*, 227–59.

Enoch MD & Trethowan WH (1979) *Uncommon Psychiatric Syndromes*, 2nd Edn. Bristol: John Wright.

Ey H (1950) Jalousie morbide. In *Etudes Psychiatriques Vol II*. Paris: de Bronwen.

Ey H (1954) *Etudes Psychiatriques Vol II*. Paris: Desclée.

Fish (1967) *Clinical Psychopathology*. Bristol: John Wright.

Freud S (1907) Delusions and Dreams in Jensen's Gradiva Volume IX. In the *Standard Edition of the Complete Psychological Works* (transl. Strachey J 1959). London: The Hogarth Press.

Gralnick A (1942) Folie à deux: the psychosis of association. A review of 103 cases and the entire English literature. *Psychiatric Quarterly 16*, 230–63.

Griesinger W (1845) *Pathologie und Therapie der psychischen Krankheiten*.

Gruhle HW (1915) Self-description and empathy. *Z. ges. Neurol. Psychiat. 28*, 148.

Guirguis WR (1981) Pure erotomania in manic-depressive psychosis. *British Journal of Psychiatry 138*, 139–40.

Gwee AL (1963) Koro–a cultural disease. *Singapore Medical Journal 4*, 119–22.

Hamilton M (1978) *Fish's Outline of Psychiatry*, 3rd Edn. Bristol: John Wright.

Hart B (1921) *The Psychology of Insanity*. Cambridge: Cambridge University Press.

Hay GG (1970) Dysmorphophobia. *British Journal of Psychiatry 116*, 399–406.

Hopkinson G (1970) Delusions of infestation. *Acta psychiatrica Scandinavica 46*, 111–119.

Hopkinson G (1973) The psychiatric syndrome of infestation. *Psychiatrica Clinica 6*, 330–45.

Huxley PJ, Kenna JC & Brandon SC (1981) Partnership in transsexualism Part II. The nature of the partnership. *Archives of Sexual Behaviour 10*, 143–60.

Jaspers K (1959) *General Psychopathology.* (transl. Hoenig J & Hamilton MW 1963). Manchester: Manchester University Press.

Klaf FS & Hamilton JG (1961) Schizophrenia: a hundred years ago and today. *Journal of Mental Science 107*, 819–827.

Kraepelin E (1905) *Lectures on Clinical Psychiatry.* 3rd Edn (transl. Johnstone, T 1917). New York: W. Wood.

Kretschmer E (1927) The sensitive delusion of reference (transl. Candy J). In Hirsch SR & Shepherd M (eds). *Themes & Variations in European Psychiatry, 1974.* Bristol: John Wright.

Laing RD (1961) *The Self and Others.* London: Tavistock.

Lapierre YD (1972) Koro in a French Canadian. *Canadian Psychiatric Association Journal 17*, 333–4.

Lasègue C (1852) cited by Cotard J (1882), Du délire des négations. *Arch Neurol Paris 4*, 152–170 & 282–296.

Lesègue C & Falret J (1877) La folie à deux (ou folie communiquée) *Annales médico-psychologique 18*, 321 (transl. Michaud R, 1964), supplement to *American Journal of Psychiatry 121*, 4.

McKenna PJ (1984) Disorders with overvalued ideas. *British Journal of Psychiatry 145*, 579–85.

McLaughlin JA & Sims ACP (1984) Co-existence of Capgras & Ekbom syndromes. *British Journal of Psychiatry 145*, 439–41.

Merskey H (1979) *The Analysis of Hysteria.* London: Baillière Tindall.

Morrison A (1848) *Cases of Mental Disease.* London: Longman & Co. & S. Highley.

Munro A (1980) Monosymptomatic hypochondriacal psychosis. *British Journal of Hospital Medicine 24*, 34–8.

Pilowsky I (1967) Dimensions of hypochondriasis. *British Journal of Psychiatry 113*, 89–93.

Sartre JP (1943) *Being and Nothingness.* (transl. Barnes HE 1958). London: Methuen.

Schneider K (1949) The concept of delusion 'Zum Begriff des Wahns' *Fortschr. Neurol. Psychiat. 17*, 26–31 (transl. Marshall H). In Hirsch SR & Shepherd M (eds) *Themes and Variations in European Psychiatry 1974.* Bristol: John Wright.

Schneider K (1957) Primary and secondary symptoms in schizophrenia. *Fortschr. Neurol. Psychiatr. 25*, 487–90. (transl. Marshall H). In Hirsch SR & Shepherd M (eds) *Themes and variations in European Psychiatry*, 1974. Bristol: John Wright.

Shepherd M (1961) Morbid jealousy: some clinical and social aspects of a psychiatric symptom. *Journal of Mental Science 107*, 687–753.

Shrestha K, Rees DW, Rix KJB, Hore BD & Faraghere B (1985) Sexual jealousy in alcoholics. *Acta Psychiatrica Scandinavica 72*, 283–90.

Sims ACP (1972) The English Hospital, Tangier 1883-1908. *Medical History 16*, 285–90.

Sims ACP (1986) The psychopathology of schizophrenia with special reference to delusional misidentification. In Christodoulou GM (ed.) *The Delusional Misidentification Syndromes.* Basel: Karger.

Sims ACP & White AC (1973) Co-existence of the Capgras and de Clérambault Syndromes–A case history. *British Journal of Psychiatry 123*, 635–8.

Sims ACP, Salmons PH & Humphreys P (1977) Folie à quatre. *British Journal of Psychiatry 130*, 134–8.

Soni SD & Rockley GJ (1974) Socio-clinical substrates of folie à deux. *British Journal of Psychiatry 125*, 230–5.

Stoddart WHB (1908) *Mind and its Disorders.* London: Lewis.

Todd J & Dewhurst K (1955) The Othello syndrome. *Journal of nervous and mental diseases 122*, 367–74.

Trethowan WH (1967) Erotomania–An old disorder reconsidered. *Alta No. 2*, 79–86.

Wernicke C (1906) *Fundamentals of Psychiatry.* Leipzig: Thieme.

West DJ & Walk A (1977) *Daniel McNaughton: His Trial and the Aftermath.* Ashford: Headley Brothers.

Winters KL & Neale JM (1983) Delusions and delusional thinking in psychotics: A review of the literature. *Clinical psychology Review 3*, 227–53.

Yap PM (1965) Koro–a culture-bound depersonalization syndrome. *British Journal of Psychiatry III*, 43–50.

8

Disorder of the Thinking Process

Inferior Schools!
Inferior Schools!
Preferably Dr. Sims?,
   Your tablets have been a miserable failure.
I have had to sit with these mad surgeries.
With regard to these tablets it will depend what the Lord wants.
   With these women it is certainly destiny humph.

Mrs Sylvia Burt.

This letter to me was clearly intended to convey a message. However, this message was considerably weakened by its partial incomprehensibility. Thinking cannot be separated from other mental functions, from everything else that is going on.

This chapter is concerned with disorder of thinking, and the following chapter with disorders of language. Thinking is the process which results in a product–thought. It is difficult to study the subjective aspects of thinking, and mostly one is concerned with objective phenomena of psychic life; what Jaspers (1959) calls 'performance'. Accuracy, form and quantity are of importance in considering the performance of thinking. The *accuracy* of thinking is essential in the correct perception of shape; in assessment of duration of time; or in recall of an event. *Form* of thinking can vary; for example, from perception to the abstract solution of a mathematical problem, to undirected fantasy thinking. *Quantitative* aspects of thinking include the speed of association, the amount of work done, the extent of memory, and so on.

There are always two distinct aspects in studying disorder of thinking (Anderson & Trethowan, 1973). These are the patient's subjective awareness of his own disturbed thinking patterns, and the manifestation of abnormal thinking he betrays in his speech (Chapter 9). This latter is the expression of thought, and determines what the observer may deduce about the patient's thinking. We need to know also about the experience of thinking in the patient's description of his subjective psychic events. *Formal thought disorder*, from the subjective, phenomenological standpoint, is abnormality in the mechanism of thinking described by the patient introspecting into his own processes of thought.

Types of thinking

The process of thinking has been arbitrarily divided by Fish (1967) into the following three types: (1) *undirected fantasy thinking* = dereistic = autistic thinking; (2) *imaginative thinking*; and (3) *rational* or conceptual *thinking*. The implications of these types of thinking for psychopathology are discussed in more detail. They can be considered as *functions* of thinking; that is, they are the necessary mechanisms for thinking to take place, but are not themselves manifest in the phenomena. We can contrast those phenomena which are the products of the *performance* of thinking, the percept or the idea, with the functions which do not become explicit.

FANTASY THINKING

This may be of short duration; for example, the day-dream before going to sleep; or it may become an established way of life. Jaspers quotes Montaigne: 'Plutarch says of people who waste their feelings on guinea-pigs and pet dogs, that the love element in all of us, if deprived of any adequate object, will seek out something trivial and false rather than let itself stay unengaged. So the psyche in its passions prefers to deceive itself or even in spite of itself invent some nonsensical object rather than give up all drive or aim'.

Fantasy allows the person to escape from, or deny, reality; or, alternatively, convert reality into something more tolerable and less requiring of corrective action. A girl, aged 20, who had a very deprived childhood and walked the city streets at night as a prostitute, listened to a vicar broadcasting on local radio. She started to send him and his wife flowers and cards, made contact with them and began to call them 'Mum' and 'Dad'. When questioned by the police one night she gave their names as next of kin and said they really were her parents.

Shy, reserved people, not suffering from mental illness, may use dereistic thinking to compensate for the disappointments of life. Bleuler (1911) saw this isolation from the real world into autistic thinking as characteristic of the schizophrenic: 'The very common preoccupation of young hebephrenics with "the deepest questions" is nothing but an autistic manifestation'. Fantasy may develop from the stage of being deliberate and sporadic into an established mode: the person comes to believe the contents of his fantasy, which becomes subjectively real and accepted as fact. Freud realized this was so in some of the accounts he received from women of an incestuous relationship with their father during childhood (Jones, 1962). Various types of experience come into this category, such as: *pathological lying* (pseudologia fantastica), *hysterical conversion* and *dissociation* (somatic and psychological hysterical symptoms), and the *delusion-like ideas* occurring in affective psychoses. These latter can be understood as arising from the patient's affective and social setting.

Fantasy is usually understood, in its positive sense, as the creation of images or ideas which have no external reality. However, fantasy thinking may also reveal itself in the denial of external events. The observations on which the psychodynamic explanation of *ego defence mechanisms* have been described are relevant in this context. The slip of the tongue, or the 'forgetting' of the emotionally laden word is not accidental: it is a form of self-deception. The obvious, significant, but unpleasant, object of perception may be 'over-looked', and this often reveals fantasy denial. Fantasy thinking denies unpleasant reality, even though the fantasy itself may also be unpleasant. This rearranging or transformation of reality is shown by neurotic patients habitually, and all people occasionally.

IMAGINATIVE THINKING

This is the harnessed use of fantasy and memory to generate plans for everyday life and utilize the succession of ideas that fills consciousness. It does not go beyond the rational or the possible, but is not necessarily confined to solving immediate problems. De Bono's concept (1967) of *lateral thinking* is relevant here. Associations occur freely but the *determining tendency* (see below) of the thought process is strong and sustained. Fantasy is enlisted in a constructive manner.

RATIONAL OR CONCEPTUAL THINKING

This is the use of logic, without intermingling of fantasy, to solve problems. It is a very complex matter to recognize and classify a problem so that reason can be applied to find a solution. In practice, of course, these three types of thinking, fantasy thinking, imaginative thinking and rational thinking are not discrete but constantly intermixed.

The processes of disordered thinking

A model of associations based upon Jaspers

In this model of thinking (psychic performance), thoughts (psychic events) can be seen to flow in an uninterrupted sequence so that one or more *associations*, with resulting further psychic events, may arise from each thought. The sequence of thoughts with the associations linking them forms the framework of this model, which is represented diagrammatically in Figure 8.1.

The mass of possible associations resulting from a psychic event is called a *constellation*. There is an enormous number of possible associations, but

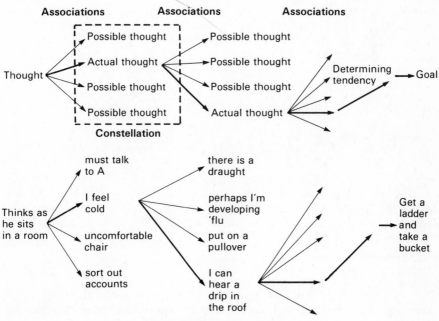

Figure 8.1 Model of association

thinking usually proceeds in a definite direction for various immediate and compelling reasons. This consistent flow of thinking towards its goal is ascribed to the *determining tendency* (Jaspers). The idea of *associations* is not intended to imply that one psychic event evokes another by an automatic, unintelligent, non-verbal reflex, but that the thought, which may be expressed verbally or not, is a concept which results in the formation of a number of other concepts; one of which is given prominence by operation of the determining tendency. This model is conjectural but has some value in allowing description of the abnormalities of thinking and speech which occur in mental illness.

We are subjectively aware of our thought process being a stream or a flow. To develop the metaphor: thoughts are capable of acceleration and slowing, of eddies and calms, of precipitous falls, of increased volume of flow, of blockages. This analogy should not be taken too far, as it is without neurophysiological basis, but it is useful for examining certain abnormalities and is based on subjective experience.

ACCELERATION OF THINKING

Acceleration of flow of thinking occurs as a *flight of ideas*. In this there are logical bridges between each of two sequential ideas expressed. However, the goal of thinking is not maintained for long. It is continuously changing because of the effect of frivolous affect and a very high degree of distractibility. The determining tendency is weakened, but associations are still formed normally. The speed of forming such associations, and therefore of the pattern of thought, is grossly accelerated. This is demonstrated in Figure 8.2.

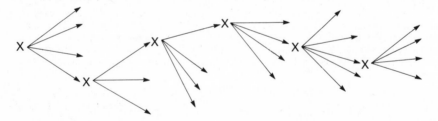

Figure 8.2 Abnormal flow of thinking: flight of ideas

Here is an example of such flight of ideas from a female manic patient, aged 45. She said: 'They thought I was in the pantry at home...Peekaboo...there's a magic box. Poor darling Catherine, you know, Catherine the Great, the fire grate, I'm always up the chimney. I want to scream with joy...Hallelujah!' Discussing the transcript of this conversation when her mental state had improved, the patient found it quite easy to point out the logical bridges in her thinking between each pair of statements, but there was no sense of building up an argument from the first to the final statement.

RETARDATION

In retardation (such as occurs in depression), thinking, although goal-directed, proceeds so slowly, with such morbid preoccupation with gloomy thoughts, that the person may fail to achieve those goals. The patient is likely to show little initiative, and to begin neither planning nor spontaneous activity. When asked a question he will ponder over it, but as no thought comes to him he makes no response. Eventually, after considerable delay, the answer usually comes. He has difficulty in making decisions, and in concentration; there is loss of clarity of thought; and poor registration of those events he needs to remember. In terms of the model of the flow of thinking, there is, in retardation, a poverty in the formation of associations as shown in Figure 8.3.

Figure 8.3 Retardation

Retardation of thought, although usually associated with *depression*, may occur with *agitation* of mood: there may be a complex situation with impaired concentration from retardation and a subjective experience of restless, anxious thoughts. Thus, Sutherland (1976), a middle-aged psychologist describing his own mental illness said:

> I contemplated throwing myself off the cross-Channel ferry,...We arrived in Naples...and my friends...were upset by my condition whilst feeling powerless to help...whilst the others sat at table I rolled around moaning in the dust.
> I revisited many of the places I had once loved; the Museo Nazionale with its magnificent mosaics pillaged from Pompeii, Pompeii itself and Capri. None of them evoked a spark of interest–I stared listlessly and uncomprehendingly at the pictures in the museum with harrowing thoughts still racing in my mind. I could not guide the children round Pompeii, since I could not concentrate sufficiently to follow the plan. Capri had lost its beauty and charm. I could not even giggle at the vulgarity of the interior of Axel Munthe's villa though the beauty of the formal garden and the magnificent view of the island and the sea from the belvedere evoked a slight response. The phrase 'see Naples and die' echoed through my mind: I was convinced I would never return alive to England, let alone ever revisit Naples.

This possible combination of depressed affect and accelerated activity can be seen to conform quite readily with Kraepelin's (1904) description of *mixed affective states*.

CIRCUMSTANTIALITY OF THINKING

In both flight of ideas and retardation, affect influences the speed of thinking: it dictates which idea takes precedence, and can also distort judgement. In circumstantiality, the slow stream of thought is not impeded by affect, but by a defect of intellectual grasp, a failure of differentiation of the *figure ground*. This is the disorder of perception in which the most distinct percept–the *figure*–cannot be clearly separated from the least distinct–the *ground*. Characteristically, this occurs in epileptic patients, and is seen in other organic states and in subnormality. A somewhat similar process occurs with obsessional personality, but here the excess of detail is introduced anxiously to avoid any possible omissions: *i*s are dotted, *t*s crossed to such an extent that the process of reaching a goal is substantially impaired.

On being asked a question, circumstantiality is shown by the patient in a reply which contains a great welter of unnecessary detail; obscuring and

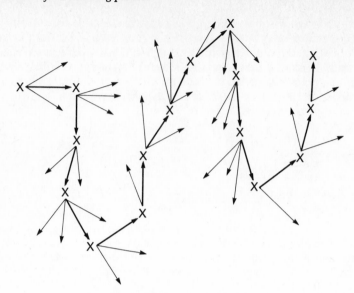

Figure 8.4 Model of circumstantiality

impeding the answer to the question. All sorts of unnecessary associations are explored exhaustively before the person returns to the point. His whole conversation becomes a mass of parentheses and subsidiary clauses. He even has to explain and apologize for these digressions before he can get back to moving towards the goal. However, the determining tendency remains, and he does eventually answer the question. Circumstantiality is represented diagrammatically in Figure 8.4.

INTERRUPTION TO THE FLOW OF THOUGHT

There are many ways in which the continuity of flow of thinking may be disturbed. Carl Schneider (1930) has described some of these abnormalities: *verschmelzung–fusion*, literally melting; *faseln–muddling*; *entgleiten–snapping off*; *entgleisen–derailment*. These processes (and others) occur together to give the patient a feeling of confusion and bewilderment. He is likely to complain of feeling bemused; to be lacking in concentration; and to be slightly apprehensive of he knows not what. He cannot precisely describe his altered thinking and consequent changes in speech.

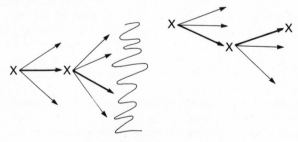

Figure 8.5 Model of derailment

In *derailment* there is a breakdown in association, so that there appears to be an interpolation of thought bearing no understandable connection with the chain of thoughts: 'The traffic is rumbling along the main road. They are going to the north. Why do girls always play pantomime heroes'. Such an excerpt from the speech of a schizophrenic contains no meaningful connections, even to the patient himself. With derailment, the subject is unable to link the ideas and describes a change in his direction of thinking.

With *fusion* there is some preservation of the normal chain of associations, but there is a bringing together of heterogeneous elements. These form links which cannot be seen as a logical progression from their constituent origins towards the goal of thought. A female schizophrenic patient, aged 38, wrote as follows:

> Two men are controlling the brain through telethapy (*sic*) or by means of ways of the spirit who open and closes the back channels of my brain releasing words and holding back the truth, by no means will I speak but will answer only to written questions by means of writing, knowing full well the channels of my brain is filtering and only half of what is the truth, also I knowing I am being read not only by a few but many very clever people but not at all acceptable they make people believe that I am some kind of miracle which I am not, I only hold the name Holyland which came to me by marrying Alfred Holyland, only by doing this do they wish to make some false stories of me coming from some special place which I have not.

Fusion is demonstrated at the beginning of this excerpt where she says that the brain is controlled 'by means' and then this word becomes associated with 'ways'. 'Telethapy'–not the same as telepathy–is a neologism. There are also examples of passivity. 'Channels' and 'means' are used as stock words; that is, they are used more often in her conversation than their normal meaning could suggest, and they take on for her a greater range of meaning than normal. It is difficult to represent this diagrammatically, and I hope the result in Figure 8.6 is not misleading.

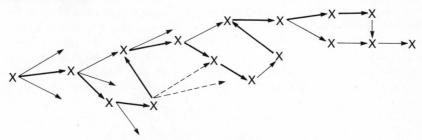

Figure 8.6 Model of fusion

Schneider's *mixing* or *muddling* is a grossly disordered amalgam of the constituent parts of a single thought process and represents extreme degrees of fusion and derailment. The resultant speech disorder is called *drivelling*.

Thought blocking

Snapping off is the experience a schizophrenic patient has of his chain of thought, quite unexpectedly and unintentionally, breaking off. It may occur in the middle of sorting out a problem or even in mid-sentence. It is not caused by distraction by other thoughts and, on introspecting, the patient can give no

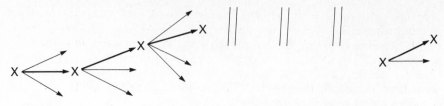

Figure 8.7 Model of thought blocking

adequate explanation for it: it simply occurs. It is otherwise described as *thought blocking*, a somewhat misleading term. The patient may explain it in terms of *thought withdrawal*: 'My thinking stopped because the thoughts were suddenly taken out of my head'. Figure 8.7 shows a model of thought blocking.

CHANGES IN THE FLOW OF THINKING

Here are two further abnormalities of the flow of thought: *Crowding of thought* and *perseveration*.

Crowding of thought occurs in schizophrenia. The patient describes his thoughts as being passively concentrated and compressed in his head. The associations are experienced as being excessive in amount, too fast, inexplicable and outside the person's control. The patient may even locate his thinking anatomically as being 'crowded into the back of my head' or elsewhere. It becomes a headlong chase or dance of thoughts and has some of the characteristics of flight of ideas, but also shows a schizophrenic quality of passivity.

Perseveration (Chapter 4) is mentioned here as a disturbance of the flow of thinking. It is characteristically an organic symptom. The patient retains a constellation of ideas long after they have become inappropriate. An idea from that constellation which occurred in a previous sequence of thought is given in answer to a different question. In perseveration, a correct response is given by the patient to the first stimulus, for example: 'Where do you live?', 'Rowley Regis'. However, any subsequent stimuli which demand different responses may get this same inappropriate first response, for instance: 'What is the capital of France?', 'Rowley Regis'. 'Who lives at home with you?', 'Rowley...my son and his wife'.

Disturbance of judgement

A *judgement* is a thought which expresses a view of reality. The word is used here in the sense: 'in my judgement such and such takes place'. To assess whether it is disturbed or not, one needs to measure it against objective fact. This can be difficult, perhaps requiring consultation with an expert in the same field as the patient. Assessment of faulty judgement is not made solely on the basis of that particular belief or argument, but on taking the whole of the person's behaviour and opinions into account: a man's claims to be a figure of royalty persecuted by the Marxists could, in fact, be true. But the opinion that his judgement was disturbed would be confirmed if he had suddenly become convinced about his royalty when a psychiatric nurse had said to him, 'You have tattoos on your arm', or if he were also found to be hoarding pebbles and dead spiders in an old tobacco tin. Delusions are, of course, a disturbance of judgement. Various forms of thought disorder and intellectual deficit may also result in disturbance of judgement.

DISTURBANCE OF JUDGEMENT AND DELUSION

Primary delusions are not synonymous with incorrigible false beliefs, because individuals or groups of people may hold such latter ideas within the context of their culture: some people were prepared to burn others for believing that the earth was round. It is necessary to look at the nature of the belief, and the evidence for believing it. How is it that such a demonstrably false idea should be believed, without even the rational doubtings that accompany the abstract convictions of a normal person?

The thinking or 'psychic performance' required to produce a delusion is quite independent of intelligence. It occurs in clear consciousness with no signs of physical disturbance of the brain. Judgement in other areas of life apart from the delusion can be preserved, and the very ingeniousness the patient uses to explain and defend his delusional belief demonstrates that his essential capacity to think logically is intact. A schizophrenic delusion is not a simple defect of reasoning; its development cannot be understood solely in terms of the patient's real life experience. For instance, not all those with delusions of persecution have any first-hand experience of being persecuted. It is an assumption about the world the patient inhabits, which he does not create by a process of logical conscious thought from premises distorted by emotion. The starting points of his thinking are already 'deluded' and his logic elaborates from this basis.

We can understand why the belief should be within the particular context (associated with his mother; related to interplanetary travel) but we cannot explain how the *form* of a primary delusion should have occurred. This is a fundamental distinction from delusion-like ideas (secondary delusions) which occur, for example, in affective psychoses. In these latter we can see the *content* being progressively influenced by the changing mood state so that, eventually, the false belief becomes a logical development from the extreme abnormality of mood.

'True' or primary delusions are not understandable in this way and, therefore, it is not acceptable to classify delusions within thought disorder as a disorder of content, as some authors have done. The whole process of thought in primary delusion is disordered, not just the content. If an idea were formed on delusional grounds–'I knew that my wife was unfaithful immediately I saw the bulb had gone out' (Chapter 7)–but the notion itself was not false nor unacceptable to the person's peer group (his wife subsequently admitted to being unfaithful), it would still be a delusion, although it could hardly be considered a disorder of content. There is a difference between *delusion* and *overvalued ideas* in that, although both may be held with absolute conviction, the latter is a reasonable, possibly even true belief, but is dominating conscious thought to an unreasonable extent.

CONCRETE THINKING

Abnormal processes of thinking in schizophrenia and organic states may result in a literalness of expression and understanding. Abstractions and symbols are interpreted superficially without tact or finesse: the patient is unable to free himself from what the words literally mean, excluding the more abstract ideas that are also conveyed. This abnormality is described as *concrete thinking*. It is difficult to devise psychological tests to demonstrate and measure concreteness. However, it is recognizable clinically, often quite dramatically. For example, a female schizophrenic patient came into the room for interview and promptly took her shoes off, saying, 'I always like to keep my feet on the ground when I'm talking'. Another chronic schizophrenic patient was observed by his doctor walking sideways along the hospital corridor. When asked why he was walking like that, he said that it was 'because of the side effects'.

Concreteness is important in making the psychopathological distinction between the disturbed thinking of the schizophrenic patient and the description of internal experience of a person with strong religious beliefs. Watson (1982) has regarded some religious experiences as being similar in nature to the symptoms of schizophrenia. There do also appear to be some important differences (Sims, 1986):

1 Religious experiences are usually regarded by the believer as being metaphorical or 'spiritual'; the physical boundaries of self are not invaded. In fact, the paradox the Christian describes is that he is a 'freer' person, more independent of external influences than previously when Christ 'lives in him'.
2 Religious experiences provoke sustained meaningful, goal-directed activity, whereas the behaviour that results from schizophrenic experience is often unreasonable in that it does not follow logically from the experience; is bizarre in flouting popular customs; is concrete in making spiritual values physical; and tends to trivialize the sublime. A schizophrenic patient read 'if thy right hand offend thee, cut it off', and attempted just that producing a long and permanent scar on his wrist.
3 Schizophrenic delusions and hallucinations are associated with a loss of ego boundaries and are based upon delusional evidence, but there is no change in the boundaries of self in other areas of his experience for the religious believer, and his belief is based upon his source of religious authority.
4 Religious beliefs are held alongside the possibility of religious doubts; in this they are like other abstract concepts. Schizophrenic delusions and hallucinations are accepted without doubt, reminiscent of concrete reality: one does not have doubts about the existence of the chair one sits on.

PSYCHOLOGICAL THEORIES OF SCHIZOPHRENIC THINKING

Disturbance of intelligence is clearly an important cause of defect of judgement. This is discussed further in Chapter 10. Intelligence and the ability to form concepts are closely connected.

It is the task of thinking to make sense of a world in which sensations compete for attention; conflict in their message; and may, in fact, convey no clear meaning. Making sense of the outside world or *conceptualization* is disturbed in various ways.

Over-inclusive thinking

The difference between the concrete thinking of organic psychosyndromes and that occurring in schizophrenia was described by Cameron (1944) who considered that the schizophrenic is unable to preserve conceptual boundaries. This he called *over-inclusive thinking*: ideas which are only remotely related to the concept under consideration become incorporated within it in the patient's thinking. Thus when asked, 'What of the following are essential parts of a room; walls, chairs, floor, a window?', the over-inclusive schizophrenic might include 'chair'. This feature of over-inclusiveness can be seen in many aspects of the schizophrenic's thinking, and questionnaires have been devised to test for it. The lack of adequate connection between two consecutive thoughts is called *asyndesis*.

The concrete thinking of schizophrenia, however, could not be distinguished from that of other psychotic and neurotic patients (Payne *et al.*, 1970), and it was found to be associated with intelligence. Over-inclusive thinking only occurred in about half of the schizophrenic patients tested, usually those who were more acutely ill. The other half, usually more chronic schizophrenics, showed much more marked *retardation*. McGhie (1969) found that Payne's tests of over-inclusiveness did not select schizophrenics from some other diagnoses, for example, those with obsessional or manic thought disorder; and Gathercole (1965) considered these tests demonstrated *fluency of association* rather than over-inclusive thinking.

A young man, who had suffered from schizophrenia for several years, was known to have been abusing drugs recently. To the doctor's enquiry, 'What drugs have you been using', he replied, 'LSD, health foods and marijuana'. This is a clear example of over-inclusive thinking. However, it was volunteered spontaneously; he might well have given an entirely correct response to a formal questionnaire that did not touch upon significant areas of his experience.

Personal construct theory

Formal thought disorder implies a disorder of conceptual, abstract thinking, a disorder of the form of thinking; and this occurs in organic states and in schizophrenia. Bannister and Salmon (1966) have developed a method of investigating schizophrenic thought disorder based on *Personal Construct Theory* which was originally described by Kelly (1955). In Kelly's description thinking could be considered as a series of construct systems in which each construct has a different and limited *range of convenience*. To simplify, a *construct* is generally an adjective in nature, whilst an *element* is a noun. So a dichotomous *construct*, *tufted–smooth* can be introduced. Its *range of convenience* includes carpets, chins and birds. These three nouns are *elements*. Its range of convenience does not include feelings on meeting people, post cards, Tuesdays, and so on; that is, it is unusable for these elements. The different words a person uses can be shown to be associated and correlated in meaning in a way which is specific for that person but is, to some extent, predictable.

Personal construct theory can be investigated experimentally using the *Repertory Grid* (see Figure 8.8). This is a technique for demonstrating the relationships between concepts when they are measured and represented quantitatively. Thus the relationship between elements, and between constructs, and between each other, may be calculated mathematically. The resulting interrelationships can be plotted in two-dimensional form to demonstrate graphically the connections between individual elements and constructs in *semantic space:* that is, where these words exist inside the world of the individual person who is being investigated.

In schizophrenia, the thought disorder is widespread, affecting many areas and aspects of thinking. To apply personal construct theory, the schizophrenic construes people and things in a loose and unpredictable way. There is a process of *serial invalidation*, in that the behaviour of elements against constructs should predict the behaviour of subsequent elements presented to the patient, but this does not occur reliably in the thinking of schizophrenics, in whom the relationship between elements and constructs is disturbed. For example, if with the element *Uncle Bill* the construct *generous* is scored positively, then the construct *kind* for that element would be likely to be positive also, but the construct *hostile* would be negative. Serial invalidation implies that the link between the elements and constructs, which would allow prediction of subsequent elements, is destroyed; Bannister and Salmon consider that this arises from the schizophrenic's doubts about the consistency of the elements themselves. In the example above, Uncle Bill might be construed therefore as both generous and hostile. Bannister and Salmon consider that the schizophrenic adapts to his situation of doubt by making constructs less clearly formulated and, therefore, rendering them less prone to invalidation. On carrying out experiments with a repertory grid test, schizophrenics were found to construe less reliably than normal people and this was more marked for construing people than objects. The thought disorder did not affect all areas of thinking equally, but was significantly worse in the interpersonal realm.

Figure 8.8 is a repertory grid of a middle-aged woman suffering from chronic paranoid schizophrenia. She misidentified her son Nigel, believing on occasions

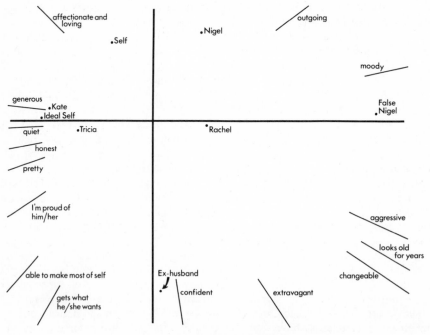

Figure 8.8 Repertory grid: delusional misidentification

that he was replaced by an impostor who looked like him but was aggressive in behaviour. The repertory grid reveals very clearly the ambivalence which is so prominently displayed towards the victim of the *Capgras syndrome* (delusional misidentification, Chapter 7).

Positive and negative symptoms of schizophrenia

Another approach to investigating cognitive disorder in schizophrenia is to compare abnormalities of schizophrenics with positive symptoms (hallucinations, delusions and thought disorder) with those suffering from negative symptoms (muteness, withdrawal, apathy and anergia). The distinction between positive and negative symptoms was originally introduced by Reynolds (1828-1896) and carried no theoretical implications (Berrios, 1985). Frith (1977) considered those with negative symptoms to have an extreme lack of persistence in activity, and this prevents them continuing very far with testing. One does not know what results they would have achieved if they had been able to carry out more elaborate tasks. Those patients with positive symptoms showed normal persistence but abnormal responses. This was demonstrated in selecting likenesses in a series of schematic faces.

The *positive* symptoms are most prominent in *acute* schizophrenia. Diagnosis is usually made on their presence and the effectiveness of treatment with, for example, phenothiazine or butyrophenone drugs, is assessed by the extent of their elimination. *Negative* symptoms are conspicuous in *chronic* schizophrenia and they are largely responsible for the extreme difficulties in rehabilitation that occur.

More recently Crow (1980) has considered that there are two different schizophrenic syndromes with different mechanisms of organic aetiology typified by *positive* or *negative* symptoms respectively. This is represented in terms of psychopathology; course of treatment; response to neuroleptic treatment; and postulated aetiology in Table 8.1.

Table 8.1 Two syndromes in schizophrenia (after Crow, 1980)

	Type 1	*Type 2*
Characteristic symptoms	Hallucinations Delusions } positive symptoms Thought disorder	Affective flattening } Negative symptoms Poverty of speech Loss of drive
Type of illness	Acute schizophrenia	Chronic schizophrenia
Response to neuroleptics	Good	Poor
Outcome	Reversible	?Irreversible
Intellectual impairment	Absent	Sometimes present
Postulated organic aetiology	Increased dopamine receptors	Cell loss and structural changes in brain

Schizophrenic inattention

McGhie has concentrated on the disturbance in the function of *attention* in schizophrenic patients: that they are unable to filter and discount sensory data irrelevant to the task being performed. He showed that the performance of schizophrenic patients was very poor compared with normal subjects, but they were not prone to distraction by auditory or visual external stimuli in the way that normal people were. Hebephrenic patients especially showed less distraction, and also poor perception and recall of visual information. Hebephrenics were considered to have an:

> inability to sweep out irrelevant extraneous information...especially where the situation demanded the rapid processing and short term storage of information. This experience is described subjectively: 'When people talk to me now it's like a different kind of language. It's too much to hold at once. My head is overloaded and I can't understand what they say. It makes you forget what you've just heard because you can't get hearing it long enough. It's all in different bits that you have to put together in your head–just words in the air unless you can figure it out from their faces'.

The effect of this inattention in ordinary social life is well observed by Morgan (1977), in his description of three weeks lived in close proximity to two chronic schizophrenics:

> In the case of Vine our relationship remained just the same, but I did perhaps come to understand his disabilities a little better, and this helped. He would keep 'losing his thread', to some extent in talk but even more noticeably in action. For example, although we went through the sequence of routine tests over 500 times together, he never once completed a sequence without having to be reminded of what came next and what remained to be done each time. Vine's other main trouble was a curious one. I would say to him, for example, 'Let's do the tests first and then I'd like you to get on with the washing up', and I would be surprised when his response to this was to dash off to the sink and start clattering the plates. Eventually I made out that he had some defect of attention. He would often jump like a startled rabbit when he realized he was being addressed anyway, and I think that by the time he had recovered and collected himself from that, the first half of my sentence had gone and all he heard was the second half. Certainly I found that by inserting a little preliminary padding, I got a more competent response.

Disorder of control of thinking

Under this heading we could discuss three different patterns of thinking: passivity of thought, or delusions of control of thinking; obsessions and compulsions, in which the unacceptable thoughts are accepted by the patient as being under his control but are resisted; and the rigid control of thought and intolerance for variation that becomes habitual with the anankastic or obsessional personality. The latter two will be considered in Chapter 17.

DELUSIONS OF THE CONTROL OF THOUGHT

Control of thinking may be disorganized in that the patient ascribes his thought processes to outside influences. The subjective disturbance in thinking in schizophrenia is experienced as *passivity*. The schizophrenic experiences his thoughts as foreign or alien; not emanating from himself and not within his control. There is a breakdown in the way he thinks of the boundary between himself and the outside world so that he can no longer accurately discriminate between the two. He may describe passivity of thought, thought withdrawal, thought insertion and/or thought broadcasting; these are *first-rank symptoms* of *schizophrenia* (Schneider, 1959). In Table 8.2 the first rank symptoms are listed.

Table 8.2 First-rank symptoms of schizophrenia (Schneider) and symptoms from the Present State Examination (Wing *et al.*, 1974)

First-rank symptoms	*Equivalent symptom from present state examination*
Delusion	
1 Delusional percept	Primary delusion
Auditory hallucinations	
2 Audible thoughts	Thought echo or commentary
3 Voices arguing or discussing	Voices about the patient
4 Voices commenting on the patient's action	Voices about the patient
Thought disorder: Passivity of thought	
5 Thought withdrawal	Thought block or withdrawal
6 Thought insertion	Thought insertion
7 Thought broadcasting (diffusion of thought)	Thought broadcast or thought sharing
Passivity experiences: Delusion of control	
8 Passivity of affect ('made' feelings)	Delusions of control
9 Passivity of impulse ('made' drives)	Delusions of control
10 Passivity of volition ('made' volitional acts)	Delusions of control
11 Somatic passivity (influence playing on the body)	Delusions of alien penetration

Various forms of thought passivity are described. The patient may describe sharing his thoughts with other people: his thoughts being controlled or influenced from outside himself. These *delusions of control* are often associated with delusional explanations of how his thinking could be controlled; for example, electronic devices, computers, telepathy. *Thought insertion* is described in which he believes that his thoughts have been placed there from outside himself. Correspondingly he may describe his thoughts being taken away from himself against his will: *thought withdrawal*. This may be given as explanation for thought blocking when the thoughts stop and the mind suddenly goes completely blank. Thought insertion and withdrawal are first-rank symptoms of schizophrenia. *Thought blocking* is not, as it is difficult to decide whether it is truly thought blocking, or some form of retardation or other difficulty with thinking; and blocking is subjectively similar to epileptic absences. *Thought broadcasting* occurs in schizophrenia when the patient describes his thoughts as leaving himself and being diffused widely out of his control. It also is a passivity experience, and of first rank.

A further subjective symptom associated with thought, of first-rank importance, is the experience of *audible thoughts*: hearing one's own thoughts out loud. The patient knows that they are his thoughts, yet he hears them audibly either while he is thinking them, just before; or just after. This is of course a disorder of perception: an auditory hallucination (Chapter 6).

We have discussed earlier in the chapter fusion, mixing, derailment and crowding of thought; all of which occur in schizophrenia. The resultant confusion causes a loss of ability to think clearly, often described in terms of passivity. The patient may feel that his brain is replaced by cotton wool or convoluted rubber. His thoughts are jumbled, muzzy, vague, blurred: 'I try to part my way through them but they are like treacle and keep on coming back and making me stick'.

First-rank symptoms of schizophrenia

British psychiatry has increasingly based its diagnosis of schizophrenia on the empirical list of first-rank symptoms, and these have proved useful in other cultures, for example, Sri Lanka (Chandrasena & Rodrigo, 1979). According to Schneider, the presence of one or more first-rank symptoms in the absence of organic disease can be used as positive evidence for schizophrenia. These symptoms of first rank are not a comprehensive list of the clinical features of schizophrenia; for the changes in affect, volition and motor activity that may occur in the condition are not included at all, and many other sorts of delusion, hallucination and disorder of thinking occur in schizophrenia. For a symptom to be regarded as of first rank it must have the following characteristics:

1   It must occur with reasonable frequency in schizophrenia.
2   It must generally not occur in conditions other than schizophrenia.
3   It must not be too difficult to decide if the symptom is or is not present.

There are some symptoms which only occur in schizophrenia but occur too rarely to be of practical use as first-rank symptoms. There are many features which are characteristic of schizophrenia but may also occur in other conditions, for example, unspecified auditory hallucinations, poverty of affect, over-inclusive thinking. There are some symptoms which only occur in schizophrenia but there is too much scope for argument as to whether it is, or is not, this precise symptom for it to be valued as of first rank. An example of this is a *primary delusion*. Some clinicians may regard a particular belief of the patient as primary delusion, while others do not.

First-rank symptoms cannot be used as a diagnostic check-list. A patient who shows seven of them is not more schizophrenic than someone who shows three. To elicit them requires considerable clinical experience; they cannot be collected quantitatively by riding past the patient on a bicycle! For a psychiatrist to use them clinically, he must first know them. Secondly, he must know how this person from this social and racial background is likely to describe any particular first-rank symptom ('my thoughts are controlled by...television...the spirits of my dead ancestors'). Thirdly, he must ask the appropriate direct questions skilfully, without putting words in his patient's mouth. Fourthly, he must be able to interpret the patient's answers and decide whether a first-rank symptom is being described. The whole process requires a dexterous use of the phenomenological method as described in Chapter 1.

There are many practising psychiatrists whose comment at this stage of the discussion of first rank symptoms would be, 'Why bother?' They would also agree that it is often difficult to diagnose schizophrenia; that it is important not to give this unfortunate label to people who do not suffer from the illness; and that it is equally important to treat those who do suffer from it appropriately, effectively and as early in the course of illness as possible.

In clinical practice, the eliciting of first-rank symptoms could best be seen as a means of deciding the degree of certainty that may be attached to the diagnosis. In a patient who shows the general features of schizophrenia (delusion, hallucination, thought disorder, disordered affect, volition, motor activity, behaviour, social relationships, life history) the diagnosis is made but some doubts remain. If first-rank symptoms are found, then, in the absence of clear organic pathology, one can reckon that the diagnosis has been confirmed. Some of the first-rank symptoms are found to be less reliable at follow-up than others as indicators of schizophrenia, for example, *voices heard arguing* (Mellor *et al.*, 1981). One of the advantages of first-rank symptoms as a diagnostic tool is that, because of their emphasis on form rather than content, a person who is feigning mental illness is unlikely to produce them. They therefore have a subsidiary use as a method of distinguishing between true and simulated psychosis, for example, in prisoners.

Examples of first-rank symptoms

The only type of *delusion* which is regarded as of first rank is a *delusional perception*; that is a normal perception delusionally interpreted and regarded as being highly significant to the patient (Chapter 7). Examples of delusional percept, and of other first-rank symptoms as follows are cited by Mellor (1970). Delusional percept is exemplified in the following account:

> A young Irishman was at breakfast with two fellow-lodgers. He felt a sense of unease, that something frightening was going to happen. One of the lodgers pushed the salt cellar towards him (he appreciated at the same time that this was an ordinary salt cellar and his friend's intention was innocent). Almost before the salt cellar reached him he knew he must return home, 'to greet the Pope, who is visiting Ireland to see his family and to reward them... because Our Lord is going to be born again to one of the women... And because of this they (all the women) are all born different with their private parts back to front'.

Three types of auditory hallucinations are regarded as being of first rank. These are: *audible thoughts, voices heard arguing* and *voices giving a running commentary*. By *audible thoughts* is meant the patient's experience of hearing his own thoughts said out loud. In English usage the symptom often carries its German name, *Gedankenlautwerden*, or its French, *echo de pensées*. The patient may hear people repeating his thoughts out loud just after he has thought them; answering his thoughts; talking about them having said them audibly; or saying aloud what he is about to think so that his thoughts repeat the voices. He often becomes very upset at the gross intrusion into his privacy and concerned that he cannot maintain control of any part of himself, not even his thoughts:

> A 35 years old painter heard a quiet voice with 'an Oxford accent', which he attributed to the BBC. The volume was slightly lower than that of normal conversation and could be heard equally well with either ear. He could locate its source at the right mastoid process. The voice would say, 'I can't stand that man, the way he holds his hand he looks life a poof'... He immediately experienced whatever the voice was saying as his own thoughts, to the exclusion of all other thoughts. When he read the newspaper the voice would speak aloud whatever his eyes fell on. He had not time to think of what he was reading before it was uttered aloud.
>
> (Mellor, 1970)

Voices heard arguing with each other implies two or more hallucinatory voices quarrelling or discussing with each other. The patient usually features in the third person in the content of these arguing voices. The symptom is not likely to be volunteered spontaneously in this form: the patient does not actually say, 'I hear voices that argue or discuss with each other'. So the symptom has to be cautiously and subtly enquired for.

> A 24 year old male patient reported hearing voices coming from the nurse's office. One voice, deep in pitch and roughly spoken, repeatedly said, 'G.T. is a bloody paradox', and another,

higher in pitch, said, 'He is that, he should be locked up'. A female voice occasionally interrupted, saying 'He is not, he is a lovely man'.   (Mellor, 1970)

Hallucinatory *voices giving a running commentary* on the patient's activities occur and are of first rank. The time sequence of the commentary may be such that it takes place just before, during or after the patient's activities. Again the symptom is not volunteered spontaneously but may quite often be inferred from the patient's complaints against his voices. For the interviewer there is always the problem of asking questions in such a way that he is 'let in on the inside'. He is asking questions about perceptions that are quite obvious to the patient. The patient does not know that he is unique; that other people do not share his perceptual experience. So the interviewer has the difficulty of asking questions about something of which he has no personal experience; the patient has to answer questions which, because of his situation, seem to have no point. The abnormal thing about *voices commenting* is that they should be experienced as perceptions and as coming from outside the self; many normal people have thoughts, recognized as their own, commenting on their actions:

> A 41 year old housewife heard a voice coming from the house across the road... The voice went on incessantly in a flat monotone describing everything she was doing, with an admixture of critical comments. 'She is peeling potatoes, got hold of the peeler, she does not want that potato, she is putting it back, because she thinks it has a knobble like a penis, she has a dirty mind, she is peeling potatoes, now she is washing them...   (Mellor, 1970)

Passivity experiences are those events in the realm of sensation, feeling, drive and volition which are experienced as *made* or influenced by others. They have been well described as delusions of control, because the patient's experience of the event being made to occur takes the form of a delusion. The terms *disorders of passivity, made experiences, delusions of control* and *disorders of personal activity* are, in practice, synonymous and interchangeable. The event is experienced as alien by the patient in that it is not experienced by the patient as his own, but inserted into the self from outside. Passivity experiences of thinking occur as thought withdrawal, thought insertion or thought broadcasting. In *thought withdrawal* it is believed by the patient that his thoughts are in some way being taken out of his mind; he has some feeling of loss resulting from this process. It may be coupled with other thought passivity experiences:

> A 22 year old woman said, 'I am thinking about my mother, and suddenly my thoughts are sucked out of my mind by a phrenological vacuum extractor, and there is nothing in my mind, it is empty...'   (Mellor, 1970)

In *thought insertion*, he experiences thoughts that do not have the feeling of familiarity, of being his own, but he feels that they have been put in his mind without his volition, from outside himself. As in thought withdrawal, there is clearly a disturbance in the self-image, and especially in the boundary between what is self and what is not self; thoughts which have in fact arisen inside himself are considered to have been inserted into his thinking from outside:

> A 29 year old housewife said, 'I look out of the window and I think the garden looks nice and the grass looks cool, but the thoughts of Eamonn Andrews comes into my mind. There are no other thoughts there, only his... He treats my mind like a screen and flashes his thoughts onto it like you flash a picture.'   (Mellor, 1970)

In *thought broadcasting* the patient experiences his thoughts withdrawn from his mind and then, in some way, made public and projected over a wide area. The explanation he gives for how this can occur will, as usual for the content of a delusion, depend on his background culture and predominant interests:

> A 21 year old student said, 'As I think, my thoughts leave my head on a type of mental ticker-tape. Everyone around has only to pass the tape through their mind and they know my thoughts.'
>
> (Mellor, 1970)

Obviously, careful enquiry must be made about the nature of 'influence' or 'control'. There is a phenomenological world of difference between the statements, 'My thinking is influenced by my parents inasmuch as my thoughts are crowded from the back into the front of my head'–a passivity experience; and 'what I do is influenced by my father in that I ponder what he would do in the circumstances and then do the same' (or, 'do the opposite')–not passivity. All passivity experiences are regarded as first-rank symptoms. It is not really very important to decide which type of passivity is described; whether it is, for example, passivity of impulse or of volition; but it is very important to decide whether it is a passivity experience or not. *Passivity of emotion* occurs when the affect that the patient experiences does not seem to him to be his own. He believes that he has been *made* to feel it:

> A 23 year old female patient reported, 'I cry, tears roll down my cheeks and I look unhappy, but inside I have a cold anger because they are using me in this way, and it is not me who is unhappy, but they are projecting unhappiness onto my brain. They project upon me laughter, for no reason, and you have no idea how terrible it is to laugh and look happy and know it is not your, but their reaction.'
>
> (Mellor, 1970)

In *passivity of impulse*, the patient experiences a drive, which he feels is alien, to carry out some motor activity. The impulse may be experienced without the subject carrying out the behaviour. A Jewish woman, aged 55, suffering from schizophrenia said: 'I feel my hand going up to salute, and my lips saying "Heil Hitler"... I don't actually say it... I have to try very hard to stop my arm from going up... they put drugs in my food; that is what makes it happen'. If carried out, the *action* is admitted to be the patient's own, but he feels the *impulse* which precipitated him into doing it was not his own:

> A 26 year old engineer emptied the contents of a urine bottle over the ward dinner trolly. He said, 'The sudden impulse came over me and I must do it. It was not my feeling, it came into me from the X-ray department, that was why I was sent there for implants yesterday. It was nothing to do with me, they wanted it done. So I picked up the bottle and poured it in. It seemed all I could do.'
>
> (Mellor, 1970)

Similarly with *passivity of volition*, the patient feels that it is not his will that carried out the action:

> A 29 year old shorthand typist described her actions as follows, 'when I reach my hand for the comb it is my hand and arm which move, and my fingers pick up the pen, but I don't control them... I sit there wanting them to move, and they are quite independent, what they do is nothing to do with me... I am just a puppet who is manipulated by cosmic strings. When the strings are pulled my body moves and I can't prevent it.'
>
> (Mellor, 1970)

Somatic passivity is the belief that outside influences are playing on the body. It is not the same as haptic hallucination, but it is a delusional belief that the body is being influenced from outside the self. It may occur in association with various somatic hallucinations. For example, a kinaesthetic hallucination occurred, with a passivity experience given as explanation in the patient who felt that his hand was being drawn up to his face. He could feel it moving although, in fact, it was motionless. Somatic passivity may also occur in association with a normal percept; these experiences are quite common in schizophrenia:

> A 38 year old man had jumped from a bedroom window, injuring his right knee which was very painful. He described his physical experience as, 'The sun-rays are directed by U.S. army satellites in an intense beam which I can feel entering the centre of my knee and then radiating outwards causing the pain.'   (Mellor, 1970)

First rank symptoms are of general use in clinical practice and they have also been adapted for psychiatric research. The method of ascertaining and measuring schizophrenic symptoms, amongst other symptoms, developed by Wing, Cooper and Sartorius (1974) in their 'Present State Examination' uses first-rank symptoms as a basis for diagnosing schizophrenia. The Present State Examination provides the clinician with a means of ascertaining which symptoms and syndromes are present.

Koehler (1979), in a review of the way different authors describe the presence of first-rank symptoms in the English literature, considered that they were sometimes used in a very narrow and sometimes a very wide sense. He makes the distinction between *alienation* of thought and *influence* of thought, and makes a plea for clear statements on the boundary criteria for first-rank symptoms and the nosological bias attached to the phenomena. From the quoted examples of Mellor above, alienation is necessary; that is, a delusion of control and not just an experience of influence of thought. Similarly, thought broadcasting would be regarded as of first rank when the patient describes this as having occurred outside his control, irrespective of whether these thoughts are shared with others. Thus this chapter is recommending a narrow view of first-rank symptoms. First-rank symptoms have been used to establish the diagnosis; they are not necessarily useful prognostically (Bland & Orn, 1980).

This difference between alienation or experience of control and influence can be exemplified by the schizophrenic symptom of *thought insertion*. Thought insertion is more concrete than the insertion of an idea into one's thinking. A normal person may say: 'my mother gave me the idea' or even 'the idea was put into my head by my mother'. Neither of these are thought insertion. The patient experiencing passivity believes that by some concrete process the boundaries of his self involving thinking is so invaded that his mother is actually putting thoughts into his head; so that he thinks her thoughts, or perhaps she is thinking inside him.

References

Anderson EW & Trethowan WH (1973) *Psychiatry*, 2nd Edn. London: Baillière Tindall.

Bannister D & Salmon P (1966) Schizophrenic thought disorder: specific or diffuse? *British Journal of Medical Psychology 39*, 215–19.

Berrios GE (1985) Positive and negative symptoms and Jackson: A conceptual history. *Archives of General Psychiatry 42*, 95–7.

Bland RC & Orn H (1980) Schizophrenia: Schneider's first-rank symptoms and outcome. *British Journal of Psychiatry 137*, 63–8.

Bleuler E (1911) *Dementia Praecox or the Group of Schizophrenias* (transl. Zinkin J, 1950). New York: International Universities Press.

Cameron N (1944) Experimental analysis of schizophrenic thinking. In Kasanin, JJ (ed.) *Language & Thought in Schizophrenia*. Berkeley: University of California Press.

Chandrasena R & Rodrigo A (1979) Schneider's first rank syndromes: their prevalence and diagnostic implication in an Asian population. *British Journal of Psychiatry 135*, 348–51.

Cooper J & Kelleher M (1973) The Leyton Obsessional Inventory: a principal components analysis on normal subjects. *Psychological Medicine 3*, 204–8.

Crow TJ (1980) Molecular pathology of schizophrenia; more than one disease process? *British Medical Journal 280*, 66–8.

De Bono E (1967) *The Use of Lateral Thinking*. Harmondsworth: Penguin.

Fish F (1967) *Clinical Psychopathology*. Bristol: John Wright.

Frith CD (1977) Two kinds of cognitive deficit associated with chronic schizophrenia. *Psychological Medicine 7*, 171–73.

Gathercole (1965) A note on some tests of over-inclusive thinking. *British Journal of Medical Psychology 38*, 59–62.

Jaspers K (1962) *General Psychopathology* (transl. Hoenig J & Hamilton MW). Manchester: Manchester University Press.

Jones E (1962) *The Life and Work of Sigmund Freud*. Harmondsworth: Penguin.

Kelly GA (1955) *The Psychology of Personal Constructs*. New York: Norton.

Koehler K (1979) First rank symptoms of schizophrenia: questions concerning clinical boundaries. *British Journal of Psychiatry 134*, 236–48.

Kraepelin E (1904) *Lectures on Clinical Psychiatry*. (transl. Johnston ET). New York: Hafner.

McGhie A (1969) *Pathology of Attention*. Harmondsworth: Penguin.

Mellor CS (1970) First-rank symptoms of schizophrenia. *British Journal of Psychiatry 117*, 15–23.

Mellor CS, Sims ACP & Cope RV (1981) Changes of diagnosis in schizophrenia and first rank symptoms: An 8 year follow-up. *Comprehensive Psychiatry 22*, 184–8.

Morgan R (1977) Three weeks in isolation with two chronic schizophrenic patients. *British Journal of Psychiatry 131*, 504–13.

Payne RW, Hochberg AC & Hawks DV (1970) Dichotic stimulation as a method of assessing the disorder of attention of an overinclusive schizophrenic patient. *Journal of Abnormal Psychology 76*, 185–93.

Schneider C (1930) *Psychologie der Schizophrenie*. Leipzig.

Schneider K (1959) *Clinical Psychopathology*, 5th Edn (transl. Hamilton MW). New York & London: Grune & Stratton.

Sims ACP (1985) Neurotic illness: Conserving a threatened concept. *British Journal of Clinical Pharmacology 19*, 95–155.

Sims ACP (1986) Demon Possession: medical perspective in a Western culture. In Palmer B (ed) *Medicine and The Bible*. Exeter: Paternoster.

Sutherland NS (1976) *Breakdown: A Personal Crisis and a Medical Dilemma*. London: Weidenfeld & Nicolson.

Watson JP (1982) Aspects of personal meaning in schizophrenia. In Shepherd E & Watson JP (eds) *Personal Meanings*. Chichester: John Wiley.

Wing JK, Cooper JE & Sartorius N (1974) *The Measurement and Classification of Psychiatric Symptoms: An Instruction Manual for the PSE & Catego Program*. Cambridge: Cambridge University Press.

9

Language and Speech Disorders

...conceptualizing the relationship between language and thought. The model might be likened to a typist copying from a script before her. Her copy may appear to be distorted because the script is distorted although the communication channel of the typist's eye and hand are functioning correctly. Alternatively, the original script may be perfect, but the typist may be unskilled, making typing errors in the copy and thus distorting it. Finally, it is possible for an inefficient typist to add errors to an already incoherent script. Unfortunately, the psychopathologist can observe only the copy (language utterances): he cannot examine the script (the thought). In general most theorists concerned with schizophrenic language have accepted the first of the three alternatives, namely that a good typist is transcribing a deviant script. The patient is correctly reporting a set of disordered thoughts. As Critchley put it: 'Any considerable aberration of thought or personality will be mirrored in the various levels of articulate speech–phonetic, phonemic, semantic, syntactic and pragmatic'. The language is a mirror of the thought.

Maher (1972)

It is very obvious that the functions of thinking and speaking overlap and cannot be readily separated from each other; at the same time they are different.

The contents of this chapter cannot be considered in isolation from its predecessor, although it is considering speech and language from a different perspective. On this subject, theory has been prone to run ahead of factual information but the emphasis here is on the abnormalities that occur rather than on explaining them.

The model proposed by Maher above, attempts to demonstrate the link between thinking and the behaviour of speech in language. The script is likened to thought and the typist to speech. Most clinicians have taken the view that language closely mirrors thought and see the primary abnormality as the thinking disorder (Beveridge, 1985). Disordered language is then seen as merely a reflection of this underlying disturbance with diagnosis of thought disorder only possible on the basis of what the patient says. Some of the more recent linguistic theories used for the analysis of schizophrenic speech challenge this primacy of thinking.

The relationship between thinking and language is equally complicated for organic disorders. Here there can be quite marked disturbance in the use of language with no apparent thought disorder. This is revealed in the rare isolated abnormalities of specific function of language described below. An understanding of how the healthy person expresses thoughts in language can only be achieved by study of the normal development of language and speech. This is outside the scope of this book, but is discussed in relation to perception in Carterette and Friedman (1976).

PSYCHOGENIC ABNORMALITIES

There is no specific abnormality of language in affective psychosis or the neurotic disorders. However, the prevalent mood influences the former and neurotic thinking is manifested in the latter, perhaps by greater emphasis in speech upon the first person singular.

Manic speech has been analysed and the speech and number of associations demonstrated in *flight of ideas* and *pressure of talk* is seen in the greater number of *cohesive links* (p.138) occurring in manic speech. The content of depressive speech is, of course, influenced by the mood state and so also is the choice of words. Sentences tend to be short and have simple associations with *retardation*.

Hysterical mutism may occur as an abnormal reaction to stress. A man aged 35 had been unable to tolerate the continual nagging from his wife and her two sisters who lived with them. One day, after heavy drinking the previous evening, he smashed his wife's furniture at home and then became mute for twenty-four hours. He was eventually referred from the Accident and Emergency Department to the Psychiatric Ward, and speech returned gradually over the next two to three days without other treatment.

With the phenomenon of *approximate answers* (Chapter 13) the patient just avoids giving a correct answer to a simple question: 'How many legs has a sheep?', 'Five'. This is, according to Anderson and Mallinson (1941): 'a false response to the examiner's question where the answer, although wrong, indicates that the question had been grasped'. This symptom occurs in a number of conditions, including hebephrenic schizophrenia, where it is often associated with fatuous mood, so called hysterical pseudodementia (before making such a diagnosis the wise psychiatrist thoroughly excludes an organic cause); in the Ganser syndrome; and in other organic conditions.

Paraphasia is the evocation of an inappropriate sound in place of a word or phrase. It may be caused by an organic disturbance of speech, but is closely mimicked in the situation when the patient produces a sound, deliberately or unconsciously, to change the topic of conversation. This may be used to avoid a certain subject, or because the patient is so preoccupied by internal or external experiences that other questions seem irrelevant.

Pseudologia fantastica is the condition of fluent plausible lying, often associated with hysterical or asocial personality disorders. The patient appears to believe in the fantastic statements. The characteristic picture is of a very isolated person, without family or friends, drifting into the Casualty Department of a large hospital in a strange city late at night with stories of his own importance and exploits, and the unfortunate vicissitudes these have engendered resulting in his need for help; there is considerable overlap with the *Munchausen syndrome* (Chapter 20).

Eccentric and pedantic use of words may sometimes be seen in those of *anankastic personality*; obsessionality obtrudes into the choice of words and construction of sentences.

Speech disturbances

This subject is dealt with in textbooks of neurology and is only summarized here. Many abnormalities such as paraphasia (above) have both organic and psychogenic causes; sometimes these can be distinguished only with considerable difficulty.

APHONIA AND DYSPHONIA

Aphonia is a loss of the ability to vocalize, the patient talks only in a whisper. *Dysphonia* denotes impairment with hoarseness, but without complete loss of function. It occurs with paralysis of the ninth cranial nerve or with disease of the vocal cords. Aphonia may also occur without organic disease in *hysterical* aphonia, a quite common presentation to the Ear, Nose and Throat Out-Patient Department. Such a patient may speak in a 'stage whisper'; phonation may fluctuate according to the response of those the person is addressing

DYSARTHRIA

Disorders of articulation may be caused by lesions of the brain stem such as bulbar and pseudo-bulbar palsy. It may also occur with structural or muscular disorders of the mouth, pharynx, larynx and thorax. Idiosyncratic disorders of articulation are sometimes seen in schizophrenia and also, perhaps consciously produced, with personality disorders.

STUTTERING AND STAMMERING

These have in the past been enquired about under neurotic disturbances of childhood with such behaviour as nail-biting. However, psychogenic aetiology has certainly not been proved, and any association with neuroticism may well be secondary to the barriers in communication that stuttering causes.

LOGOCLONIA

This describes the spastic repetition of syllables that occurs with Parkinsonism (Scharfetter, 1980). The patient may get stuck using a particular word.

ECHOLALIA

The patient repeats words or parts of sentences that are spoken to him or in his presence. There is usually no understanding of the meaning of the words. It is most often demonstrated in excited schizophrenic states, in mental handicap and with organic states such as dementia, especially if dysphasia is also present.

CHANGES IN THE VOLUME AND INTONATION OF SPEECH

Usually, depressed patients speak very quietly with a monotonous voice. Manic patients often speak loudly and excitably with much variation of pitch. Excited schizophrenics may also speak loudly; intonation and stresses on words may be idiosyncratic and inappropriate. None of these modes of behaviour have diagnostic significance. The speed and flow of talk mirrors that of thought and has been dealt with in Chapter 8.

UNINTELLIGIBLE SPEECH

Speech may be unintelligible for several reasons and most of the abnormalities described here, if taken to extremes, will result in incomprehensibility:

1 *Dysphasia* may be so profound that, although syllables are produced, speech is unintelligible;

2 *Paragrammatism* (disorder of grammatical construction) and *incoherence of syntax* may occur in several disorders. Recognizable words may be so deranged in their sentences as to be meaningless–*word salad* as occurs in schizophrenia.

In mania, the speed of association may be so rapid as to disrupt sentence structure completely and render it meaningless; while in depression, retardation may so inhibit speech that only unintelligible syllables, often of a moaning nature, are produced.

3 Private symbolism may occur in schizophrenia with the use of: (i) new words with an idiosyncratic meaning–*neologisms*; (ii) *stock words* and *phrases* in which existing words are used with special individual symbolic meaning; or (iii) a private language, which may be spoken (*cryptolalia*), or written (*cryptographia*).

Organic disorders of language

Dysphasic symptoms are probably more useful clinically than any other cognitive defect in indicating the approximate site of brain pathology (Lishman, 1978). However, the auditory, visual and motor mechanisms of speech are spread through several different parts of the brain–often several functions are affected and lesions are usually diffuse, and thus precise brain localization is not often possible. Ninety per cent of right-handed people without any brain damage have speech located in the left hemisphere and 10% have right-hemisphere speech. Amongst those who are left-handed or ambidextrous, 64% have left hemisphere speech, 20% right hemisphere and 16% bilateral speech representation.

Two current theories of language are those of Brain (1965) and Geschwind (1967). Brain's theory is psychological and physiological in nature; word recognition is based on *schemata*, which are retained as permanent standards for comparison at an unconscious level. Learning the concepts attached to names becomes increasingly precise from early childhood as the essential elements are recognized and abstracted. There must be *word* and *sentence schemata*, and recognition must take place both visually and auditorily; there must also be schemata for the production of speech. Thus, before speech takes place, a rapid schema of speech is called up unconsciously as the person thinks or selects the words and phrases 'inside his head'. Geschwind's contribution is more anatomical in nature: *naming* occurs when an object stimulates the visual association cortex and thence produces associations in the auditory cortex (Wernicke's area). Information is then transmitted to the motor association cortex (Broca's area) for processing in preparation for speech. The essential coding processes in addition to transmission of data are *comprehension* and *repetition*.

SENSORY APHASIA

The terms aphasia and dysphasia are often used interchangeably. However, aphasia implies the loss of language altogether and dysphasia impairment of, or difficulty with, language. Dysphasia is conventionally divided for classification

Table 9.1 Impairment of language function with different types of dysphasia (after Lishman, 1978); compr.n = comprehension

Type	Spontaneous Speech-fluent	Comprehension	Repetition	Naming	Reading	Writing
Pure word-deafness	+	−	−	+	+	+ not to dictation
Pure word-blindness	+	+	+	+	−	+
Primary sensory dysphasia	+	−	−	±	−	−
Conduction dysphasia	+	+	−	±	Aloud − Compr.n +	−
Nominal dysphasia	+	+	+	−	±	±
Pure word-dumbness	−	+	−	±	+	+
Pure agraphia	+	+	+	+	+	−
Primary motor dysphasia	−	+	−	±	Aloud − Compr.n ±	−
Alexia with agraphia	+	+	+	−	−	−
Isolated speech area	−	−	+	−	−	−
Transcortical motor dysphasia	−	+	+	−	Aloud − Compr.n +	−
Transcortical sensory dysphasia	+	−	+	−	−	−

into *sensory* (receptive) and *motor* (expressive) types. Very frequently there is a global impairment of language with evidence of impairment of both elements. Table 9.1 summarizes some of the abnormalities that occur with the different aspects of language that are impaired.

Pure word-deafness (subcortical auditory dysphasia)

Such a patient can speak, read and write fluently, correctly and with comprehension. He cannot understand speech, even though hearing is unimpaired for other sounds; he hears words as sounds, but cannot recognize the meaning even though he knows that they are words. This is therefore a form of *agnosia* (lack of recognition) for the spoken word. The neuropsychiatric implications of this and other symptoms is not dealt with in this account; the reader is referred to Lishman.

Pure word-blindness (subcortical visual aphasia)

This patient can speak normally and understand the spoken word; he can write spontaneously, and to dictation, but cannot read with understanding (*alexia*). The condition is therefore *agnosic alexia without dysgraphia*. He may have more difficulty with printed than written script. Such a patient will also suffer a right homonymous hemianopia (loss of the right half of the field of vision in both eyes) and an inability to *name* colours even though they can be perceived.

Primary sensory dysphasia (receptive dysphasia)

These patients are unable to understand spoken speech, with loss of comprehension of the meaning of words and of the significance of grammar. Hearing, otherwise, is not impaired. Consequent upon this deficit in the auditory association cortex (*Wernicke's area*) there is also impairment of speech, writing and reading. Speech is fluent, with no appreciation of the many errors in the use of words, syntax and grammar.

Conduction dysphasia could be considered to be a type of sensory dysphasia in which sensory reception of speech and writing are impaired, in that the patient cannot repeat the message, although he can speak and write. If he is questioned on the message, he is able to give 'yes' and 'no' answers correctly, thus demonstrating comprehension. There are marked errors of grammar and syntax (*syntactical dysphasia*).

Nominal dysphasia

The patient is unable to produce names and sounds at will. The patient may be able to describe the object and its function and recognize the name when presented: a patient described a watch as a 'clock vessel'. Typically, 'empty' words such as 'thing' and 'object' are used frequently and nouns rarely. Speech is flat, structure of sentences generally correct, and understanding unimpaired.

Jargon aphasia

Speech is fluent but there is such gross disturbance to words and syntax that it is unintelligible. The intonation and rhythm of speech are retained. This is considered a severe type of sensory dysphasia; there is failure to evaluate the patients' own speech in that patients are not emotionally disturbed when listening to recordings of their own grossly impaired speech.

MOTOR APHASIA

Pure word-dumbness

The patient understands spoken speech and writing and can respond to comments. Writing is preserved but speech is indistinct and cannot be produced at will. There is no local disturbance of muscles required in speaking and the disability is an *apraxia* limited to movements required for speech.

Pure agraphia

An isolated inability to write may also occur with unimpaired speech (*agraphia without alexia*); there is normal understanding of written and spoken material. This is the equivalent for writing of pure word-dumbness in speech.

Primary motor dysphasia

There is disturbance to the processes of selecting words, constructing sentences and expressing them. Speech and writing are both affected, and there is difficulty in carrying out complex instructions, even though understanding for both speech and writing may be preserved. The patient finds it difficult to choose and pronounce words, and speech is hesitant and slow; he recognizes his errors, tries to correct them and is clearly upset. Gesture may be used to replace verbal communication. Speech is attempted and recognized as spoken words, but words are omitted, sentences shortened and perseveration occurs.

Alexia with agraphia

Visual aspects of language are construed as being more complex than auditory in that visual schemata are required–'seeing the written word inside his head'–*in addition* to auditory–'hearing the words in one's head'. In alexia with agraphia, the patient is unable to read or write, but speaking and understanding speech is preserved. Alexia in this condition is similar to that of pure word-blindness: the patient cannot understand words that are spelled out aloud, showing that he is illiterate because of disturbance of the visual symbolism of language.

Isolated speech area

Impaired comprehension may occur with slow, hesitant speech in an abnormality in which it is assumed that the anatomical Wernicke's and Broca's areas and the connections between them are intact, but connections from other parts of the cortex with this language system are disturbed. Two types, expressive and receptive are described: *transcortical motor dysphasia* and *transcortical sensory dysphasia*.

Most frequently, of course, with dysphasia, there is a mixture of expressive and receptive elements and the clear syndromes cannot be demonstrated; but their significance is partly theoretical in demonstrating the range of anatomical lesions and the specificity of resultant symptoms. It is important to distinguish the phenomena of dysphasia, perhaps with neologisms and defects of syntax, from the *word salad* of schizophrenia with superficially similar defects of language. *Verbigeration* describes the repetition of words or syllables that expressive aphasic patients may use while desperately searching for the correct word.

MUTISM

Mutism–refraining from speech during consciousness–is an important sign in psychiatric illness because of the problems of differential diagnosis. Eliciting the history and mental state becomes impossible in a mute patient. All the major categories of psychiatric disorder may manifest mutism: mental handicap; organic brain disease; functional psychosis; and neurosis and personality disorder. Some more specific causes include depressive illness; catatonic schizophrenia; and conversion hysteria. Mutism occurs as an essential element of stupor (Chapter 2), and it is necessary to assess the level of consciousness as part of a full neurological examination for all cases with this sign. If there is no lowering of consciousness, as in functional psychoses and neuroses, it is likely that the mute patient will be understanding everything that is said around him. As well as specific brain disorders, the causes of stupor include general metabolic disorders that also affect the brain; such as, hepatic failure, uraemia, hypothyroidism and hypoglycaemia.

Schizophrenic language disorder

This subject has been reviewed by Beveridge and his framework is followed here. It is generally acknowledged that the schizophrenic patient's use of language and words is different from a normal person's, and that this difference is not just caused by delusional beliefs or the interruption of thinking caused by auditory hallucinations. However, the precise nature of this abnormality has so

Table 9.2 Models for investigating language disorder in schizophrenia (after Beveridge, 1985)

Model of Language	Technique Employed
Concept of thought disorder	Psychiatric: clinical description of schizophrenic speech
Behavioural – learning theory	Word association test, multiple choice vocabulary test
Statistical	The Cloze technique, type–token ratio
Linguistic	Analysis of syntax, cohesion or propositions

far defied clarification and this account is provisional: it describes the way some of the phenomena have been viewed but cannot yet fit this into a single explanatory theory. Investigation into language disorder can be ascribed to one of the four models of Table 9.2.

CLINICAL DESCRIPTION AND THOUGHT DISORDER

The only unequivocal demonstration of disorder of thinking can be through language. Thought disorder may be revealed in the flow of talk (as in Chapter 8), disturbed content and use of words and grammar, and in the inability to conceptualize appropriately. Critchley (1964) considered that the 'causation of schizophrenic speech affection lies in an underlying thought disorder, rather than in a linguistic inaccessibility'. Some of the ways in which clinicians have categorized schizophrenic thought disorder manifesting in speech are linked in Table 9.3.

Table 9.3 Categorization of thought disorder in speech

Clinician	Categorization
Kraepelin	Akataphasia
Bleuler	Loosening of associations
Gardner	Form of regression
Cameron	Asyndesis
Goldstein	Concrete thinking
Von Domarus	Defect of deductive reasoning
Schneider	Derailment, substitution, omission, fusion, and drivelling

Kraepelin (1919) defined *akataphasia* as a disorder in the expression of thought in speech. *Loss of the continuity of associations*, which implied incompleteness in the development of ideas, was the first of the simple functions included amongst the fundamental symptoms of schizophrenia by Bleuler (1911). Gardner (1931) considered thought disorder to be a form of *regression*.

Cameron (1944), in describing *asyndesis*, considered there to be an inability to preserve conceptual boundaries and a marked paucity of genuinely causal links. He gave the example of a patient who completed the sentence 'I get warm when I run because...' with all the words: 'quickness, blood, heart of deer, length, driven power, motorized cylinder, strength'. The patient was prone to use imprecise expressions–*metonyms*–and–*over-inclusive thinking* because of interpenetration of associations.

Concrete thinking due to an inability to think abstractly was proposed by Goldstein (1944), but this has been challenged by Payne, Matussek and George (1959). Allen (1984) considers that speech-disordered schizophrenics produce evidence of concrete thinking, thinking without inferring and restricted to what is explicitly stated, whilst non-speech-disordered schizophrenics do not. When the thematic organization of speech was analysed for schizophrenic patients with positive speech disorder (incoherence of speech) or negative speech disorder (poverty of speech), there was no difference found: speech disordered schizophrenics, positive as well as negative, showed cognitive restriction and produced fewer inferences than non-speech-disordered patients.

A deficiency in the logic of *deductive reasoning* in schizophrenia was suggested by Von Domarus (1944). Some of the abnormalities of thinking expressed in speech observed by Schneider have been discussed in Chapter 8.

An attempt has been made by Andreasen (1979) to classify description of patients' cognitive and linguistic behaviour upon the phenomena demonstrated, without making inferences for concepts of 'global' thought disorder, which occurs both in mania and schizophrenia. Some types of thought disorder, such as *neologism* and *blocking*, occurred too infrequently to have diagnostic significance. However, she found high reliability between raters with many types of thought disorder and also discrimination between different psychotic illnesses. Derailment, loss of goal, poverty of content of speech, tangentiality, and illogicality were particularly characteristic of schizophrenia.

Derailment implies loosening of association so that ideas slip onto either an obliquely related, or totally unrelated, theme. *Loss of goal* is the failure to follow a chain of thought through to its natural conclusion. *Poverty of content of speech* includes poverty of thought, empty speech, alogia, verbigeration and negative formal thought disorder; patients' statements convey little information, and tend to be vague, over-abstract, over-concrete, repetitive and stereotyped. *Tangentiality* means replying to a question in an oblique or even irrelevant manner. *Illogicality* implies drawing conclusions from a premise by inference which cannot be seen as logical.

Misuse of words and phrases

The schizophrenic shows misuse of words in that he has, in the terminology of Kleist (1914), a defect of word storage. He has a restricted vocabulary and so uses words idiosyncratically to cover a greater range of meaning than they usually encompass. These are called *stock words or phrases* and their use will sometimes become obvious in a longer conversation where an unusual word or expression may be used several times. For example, a patient used 'dispassionate' as a stock word, and used it frequently with a bizarre and idiosyncratic meaning in the course of a few minutes' speech. A woman who was delusionally concerned that the police were intruding into her private affairs interspersed her conversation, often bizarrely, with the expression 'confidentially speaking'.

This abnormality appears partly to reflect a poverty of words and syntax, and also an active tendency for words or syllables by association to intrude into thoughts, and therefore speech, soon after utterance. In the sample of speech in Chapter 8, p.111, the following words could be seen as stimuli and responses, by intrusion: 'means'–'ways'; 'opens'–'closed'; 'holding back the truth'–'by no means will I speak;' 'written questions'–'by means of writing;' 'miracle'–'Holyland.'

Words carry a *semantic halo*; that is, their constellation of associations is greater than just the meaning of the word. A boy aged 16 steals an apple. If I call him 'a trespasser', it has Biblical associations; 'a criminal' suggests a greater degree of viciousness than the action merits; 'a delinquent' is readily associated with his youthfulness because of the phrase 'juvenile delinquent'. The constellations of associations in schizophrenics are disordered in that they often make apparently irrelevant associations. These may be explained by misperception of auditory stimuli with specific inattention; the actual mediation of associations in schizophrenics may be similar to normal people. This comes some way to explaining why the associations seem appropriate subjectively to the schizophrenic patient himself, as he does not realize that he has misperceived the cue: it seems reasonable to him but is quite irrelevant to the interviewer. To quote Maher, 'What seems to be bizarre is not the nature of the associations that intrude into the utterance, but the fact that they intrude at all'.

Amongst the disorders of words, *neologism* is well recognized. This creation of a new word becomes necessary for the schizophrenic to fill a semantic gap. A patient believed that his thoughts were influenced from outside himself by a process of 'telegony'; although such a word does actually exist the patient had no notion of this, nor what it meant. He created the word to describe a unique experience of his for which no adequate word existed. A 47-year-old male schizophrenic of expansive mood described himself: 'I am the triplicate actimetric kilophilic telepathic multibillion million genius'.

The unintentional puns of schizophrenics have been explained by Chapman, Chapman & Miller (1964). If a word has more than one meaning, it is likely that one usage is *dominant*. For example, the majority of people would be more likely to use the word 'bay' to refer to an inlet of the sea than to a tree, the noise a hound makes, the colour of a horse, an opening in a wall, the second branch of a stag's horn, an uncomfortable place at which to stand, or even, phonetically, a Turkish governor! There is a marked tendency for schizophrenics to show *intrusion* of the dominant meaning when the context demands the use of a less common meaning. Chapman *et al.* (1964) used a sentence such as, 'the tennis player left the court because he was tired' and asked schizophrenic patients to interpret its meaning with one of three different explanations: one referring to a tennis court, one to a court of law and one altogether irrelevant. An analysis of responses shows that dominant meanings, here a court of law, intrude into the responses of schizophrenics quite frequently, but intrusion of minor meanings are less frequent.

Maher has described disorder of schizophrenic language in which intrusion occurs through *clang associations* with the initial syllable of a previous word, 'the *sub*terfuge and the mistaken planned *sub*stitutions....' This is unlike the clang associations which occur normally in poetry and in humour, and also in manic speech, where the *clang* occurs on terminal syllables. The repetitiveness of speech disorder is also thought to be associated with the intrusion of associations: the normal process of eliminating irrelevant associations does not take place so that a word in a clause will provoke associations by pun, clang and ideational similarity. When that clause is completed, a syntactically correct clause may then be inserted disrupting meaning but demonstrably associated with that previous word or idea.

Maher considers that an inability to maintain attention may account for the language disturbances seen in some schizophrenic patients. Disturbed attention allows irrelevant associations to intrude into speech similar to the disturbance affecting the filtering of sensory input. In this theory, normal coherent speech is seen as the progressive and instantaneous inhibition of irrelevant associations to each utterance, and so the determining tendency proceeds with the active elimination of those associations that are not goal-directed.

Destruction of words and grammar

Alogia is a term used to describe negative thought disorder, or poverty of thoughts when expressed in words. Correspondingly, *paralogia* is used to describe positive thought disorder, or the intrusion of irrelevant or bizarre thought. *Paraphasia*, (see p.127) is a destruction of words with interpolation of more or less garbled sounds. Although the patient is only able to produce this non-verbal sound, it clearly has significance or meaning to him. *Literal paraphasia* is gross misuse of the meaning of words to such an extent that statements no longer make any sense. *Verbal paraphasia* describes the loss of the appropriate word but the statements are still meaningful; for example, a patient described a chair as 'a four-legged sit up'.

Disturbances in the words and their meanings are much more common in schizophrenia than disturbance of grammar and syntax. However, grammar is sometimes disturbed: the loss of parts of speech is described as *agrammatism*. Adverbs are occasionally lost, to result in coarsening and poverty of sentences, a form of *telegramese*. For example, 'rich table is worn; the woman is rich to write; son is also lamentation'. This, as well as showing a *stock* word, shows loss of parts of speech; for example, the indefinite article. The meaning is more disjointed than the grammar. *Paragrammatism* occurs when there are a mass of complicated clauses which make no sense in achieving the goal of thought. However, the individual phrases are quite comprehensible.

It seems probable that the rules of syntax are preserved in schizophrenia long after a marked disturbance in the use of words. So that, if in the preceding sentence an intrusive association were to replace the word *rules*, the word used would probably, correctly, be a noun. For instance the patient above might say 'the *lamentations* of syntax are...'.

BEHAVIOURAL CONCEPTS OF LANGUAGE DISORDER

Language can be seen as *learned behaviour* in terms of the use of individual words in response to a stimulus of previous association. This is exemplified in the *word association test*, in which it was considered that schizophrenics gave more unusual responses to stimulus words than normal controls. This has been refuted in a review by Schwartz (1978) who considered that their associations were less unusual than college students'! Chapman *et al.* (1964 & 1976) considered that schizophrenics responded to a word's dominant meaning regardless of context. Thus, as above, the word 'court' would be intruded in the sense of 'law court' even though the context clearly referred to 'tennis court'.

Such behavioural models have been criticized for taking a simplistic view of language, concentrating on the meaning of individual words rather than its structure and complexity as actually used. Such criticism has been expressed by Miller (1965): 'One might argue that psycho-linguists should confine their attention to the significance of isolated words and avoid the complexities of sentences altogether... Unfortunately language is not so simple: a venetian blind is not the same thing as a blind Venetian'.

STATISTICAL MODEL OF LANGUAGE

The *Cloze* procedure involves deleting words from the transcripts of speech and assessing whether the omitted word can be guessed. Maher considered that, in schizophrenia, the greater the severity of the illness, the greater is the degree of unpredictability of the utterance of language. In normal speech, a large part of every sentence could be omitted without losing the meaning. For example, if the words 'a ...part...could be...the' were omitted from the last sentence, the meaning would still be obvious; if letters were omitted from words, for instance, *nrml spech*, the meaning is still clear. *Predictability* is the ability to predict accurately the missing words; in this sense schizophrenics are unpredictable in their speech. They are likely to use unexpected words and phrases. In the perception of language the schizophrenic is less able to gain information from the redundancies, both semantic and syntactic, in everyday speech.

Schizophrenic speech is considered less predictable than normal speech, and lack of predictability is more marked with clinically manifest thought disorder (Manschreck *et al.*, 1979). An experiment was carried out on the Cloze procedure in which raters were asked to assess passages of schizophrenic or normal speech with the fourth or fifth word deleted. With fifth-word deletion, thought-disordered schizophrenic speech was significantly less predictable than normal or non-thought-disordered schizophrenic speech; this latter was no less predictable than normal speech.

Whether schizophrenic speech is really less redundant than normal has been questioned by Rutter (1979) who was able to demonstrate no difference. The view that schizophrenic language can be reduced to such simple mathematical rules has been rejected by Mandelbrote (1963).

The *type-token ratio* is a measure of the number of different words as compared with the total number of words (Zipf, 1935). Maher concluded that the type-token ratio of schizophrenics was lower than for normals. The tendency of schizophrenic patients to repeat certain words and use them in an idiosyncratic way is referred to as the use of *stock words*.

LINGUISTIC APPROACHES TO SCHIZOPHRENIA

Various linguistic theories have been applied to schizophrenia. Chomsky (1959) has proposed that humans are able to use strings and combinations of words they have never heard before through use of a limited set of integrative processes and generalized patterns. However, Moore and Carling (1982) have labelled

Chomskyan linguistics a *container* view of language; separated from the real way users of language apply it to their own meanings and contexts. Individual case studies have used tape-recorded interviews with schizophrenic patients to demonstrate distinctive abnormalities. However, on closer analysis such abnormalities are often found to occur in the speech of normal people, although less frequently. A further study of bilingual patients showed psychotic symptoms to be present in their native language but absent in their second language. The problem of individual studies is, of course, the extent to which they can be generalized to all schizophrenic patients.

Syntactical analysis

In two studies of speech analysed by computer, compared with manic and normal controls, schizophrenics showed less complex speech, fewer well-formed sentences, more semantic and syntactic errors, and less fluency. Such studies do not, of course, justify the conclusion that differences are due directly to the disease or to thought disorder, nor does it take into account the social context or emotional aspects. However, marked differences are of interest when one considers that the majority of schizophrenic patients do not show overt disorder of language (Beveridge, 1985).

Cohesion analysis

A method of examination of schizophrenic speech has been developed by Rochester and Martin (1979) looking at the links between sentences that occur in discourse. These links are called *cohesive ties*. Schizophrenics use less of these cohesive ties, and of the five types of tie described, they use less *reference* ties (connection through meaning) and more *lexical* ties (connected words). For instance, in the two sentences:

1 'A commuter and a skier are in a ski lift and *he* looks completely unconcerned'.
2 'Mother needed *independence* she was always *dependent* on my father.'

Sentence 1 shows an *unclear reference* in that this schizophrenic fails to guide the listener as to whom he is describing. In sentence 2, *independence* and *dependent* are lexically tied because of similar derivation. This type of tie is a weaker bond between sentences, and the result of these abnormalities is that they make it more difficult for a listener to follow what the patient is saying. However, even in the most severe group of schizophrenic speakers, 80% of their speech was still normal. Studies with manic patients have shown more ties than for schizophrenics, but also some disruption. Cohesion analysis does not explain all the abnormalities of schizophrenic speech; appropriate ties would still leave much material that is abnormal.

Propositional analysis

This is a form of textual analysis in which the text is broken down into its component propositions and these are then represented diagrammatically to show the mental geometry (Hoffman *et al.*, 1982). Normal speech is considered to proceed as in a single tree diagram with all branches leading from a single key proposition; but psychotic speech more often breaks the 'rules' of propositional relationships.

Beveridge, in his critical account of propositional analysis, found the method of deciding upon the relationships between propositions unclear; it forces the observer into making intuitive judgements of potentially deviant language in a way similar to the standard clinical interview. The arrangement of the tree diagram is also somewhat arbitrary and may result in the discourse being made to make more sense than it did when spoken. There is also a problem of context, in that oral discourse requires implicit propositions at twice the rate of written speech, and ambiguously placed propositions occur ten times as frequently. Hoffman's method attempts to deal 'with the highly complex and ill-defined relationship between thought and language. A wholly objective method cannot enter into this area whereas a wholly subjective method is not readily available to testing' (Beveridge).

These methods of analysis of schizophrenic language are tentative and do not yet cover the range of abnormalities occurring in the condition. However, the patient's use of language and syntax does enable a quantitative method of evaluating the mental state and subjective experience to be developed. Study of language disorder should be an area in which descriptive psychopathology can contribute to psychiatric research.

References

Allen HA (1984) Positive and negative symptoms and the thematic organisation of schizophrenic speech. *British Journal of Psychiatry 144*, 611–7.

Anderson EW & Mallinson WP (1941) Psychogenic episodes in the course of major psychoses. *Journal of Mental Science 87*, 383–96.

Andreasen NC (1979) Thought, language and communication disorder. *Archives of General Psychiatry 36*, 1315–30.

Beveridge A (1985) Language Disorder in Schizophrenia. Thesis for the Degree of M.Phil., University of Edinburgh.

Bleuler E (1911) *Dementia Praecox: Or the Group of Schizophrenias*. New York: International University Press.

Brain WR (1965) *Speech Disorders: Aphasia, Apraxia and Agnosia*, 2nd Edn. London: Butterworth.

Cameron N (1944) Experimental analysis of schizophrenic thinking. In Kasanin J (ed.) *Language and Thought in Schizophrenia*. Berkeley: University of California Press.

Carterette G & Friedman MP (1976) *Handbook of Perception Volume VIII, Language and Speech*. New York: Academic Press.

Chapman LJ, Chapman JP & Daut RL (1976) Schizophrenic inability to disattend from strong aspects of meaning. *Journal of Abnormal Psychology 85*, 35–40.

Chapman LJ, Chapman JP & Miller GA (1964) A theory of verbal behaviour in schizophrenia. In *Progress in Experimental Personality Research Vol. 1*

Chomsky N (1959) Review of Skinner. *Language 35*, 26–58.

Critchley M (1964) The neurology of psychotic speech. *British Journal of Psychiatry 110*, 353–64.

Gardner GE (1931) The measurement of psychotic age: A preliminary report. *American Journal of Psychiatry 10*, 963–75.

Geschwind N (1967) Neurological foundations of language. In Myklebust HR (ed.) *Progress in Learning Disabilities*. New York: Grune & Stratton.

Goldstein K (1944) Methodological approach to the study of schizophrenic thought disorder. In Kasanin JS (ed.) *Language and Thought in Schizophrenia*. Berkeley: University of California Press.

Hoffman RE, Kirstein L, Stopek S & Cicchetti DV (1982) Apprehending schizophrenic discourse: a structural analysis of the listener's task. *Brain & Language 15*, 207–33.

Kleist K (1914) Aphasie und Geisteskrankheit. Munchener Medizinische Wochenschrift 61, 8.

Kraepelin E (1919) *Dementia Praecox & Paraphasia*. (transl. Barclay). Edinburgh: Livingstone.

Lishman WA (1978) *Organic Psychiatry: The Psychological Consequences of Cerebral Disorder.* Oxford: Blackwell Scientific.

Maher BA (1972) The language of schizophrenia: A review and interpretation. *British Journal of Psychiatry 120*, 3–17.

Manschreck TC, Maher BA, Rucklos ME & White MT (1979) The predictability of thought-disordered speech in schizophrenic patients. *British Journal of Psychiatry 134*, 595–601.

Miller GA (1965) Some preliminaries to psycholinguistics. *American Psychologist 20*, 15–20.

Moore T & Carling C (1982) *Understanding Language: Towards a Post-Chomskyan Linguistics.* London: Macmillan.

Payne RW, Matussek P & George EI (1959) An experimental study of schizophrenic thought disorder. *Journal of Mental Science 105*, 627–52.

Rochester S & Martin J (1979) *Crazy Talk. A Study of the Discourse of Schizophrenic Speakers.* New York: Plenum Press.

Rutter DR (1979) The reconstruction of schizophrenic speech. *British Journal of Psychiatry 134*, 356–9.

Scharfetter (1980) *General Psychopathology: An Introduction.* Cambridge: Cambridge University Press.

Schwartz S (1978) *Language and Cognition in Schizophrenia.* New Jersey: Lawrence Erlbaum.

Von Domarus E (1944) The specific laws of logic in schizophrenia In Kasanin JS (ed.) *Language and Thought in Schizophrenia.* Berkeley: University of California Press.

Zipf GK (1935) *The Psychobiology of Language.* Boston: Houghton Mifflin.

─10──────────

Disorder of Intellectual Performance

Save in the case of a few illiterates–high or low, it makes no matter–by whom no difference in quality is perceptible, what brings men together is not a community of views but a consanguinity of minds.   Proust (1913)

What is intelligence

Intellectual performance is an absolute prerequisite for reasonable functioning in all human activities. *Intelligence* is a word, used in both everyday and technical conversation, which everyone understands but finds difficult to define; and it conveys various nuances of meaning for different people and in differing contexts. Binet, in introducing his method of measuring human abilities, considered that intelligence was a general capacity for judgement, comprehension and reasoning that could be manifest in many different ways (Binet & Simon, 1905). Other psychologists, such as Thurstone (1938), considered that intelligence comprises several specific abilities that are mutually independent; and a method was introduced for testing these separate *primary abilities*.

Thinking involves the use of rational, problem-solving mental activity: the application of intelligence. Defective intellect is found in mental subnormality (mental handicap), and in organic mental states, especially in the progressive intellectual impairment of dementia. A person's intelligence is his *permanent* capacity for psychic performance, 'the individual's totality of abilities, those instruments of performance and purpose available to him for adaptation to life' (Jaspers, 1963).

Perception; registration and retention of memory; mental alertness and physical health; adequate motor functions such as speech and writing; are all prerequisites for the expression of intelligence. Thus sensory functioning; full consciousness and orientation; the capacity for attention; and concentration all contribute. For intellectual performance, motivation, drive and the appropriate affective set are necessary. Different thought processes occur as components of intelligence, including apperception; abstraction; forming associations and combining them; judgement; and logical deduction.

In dementia, there are defects in these qualities which directly and necessarily impair intellectual function. However, the defect is not fundamentally one of intelligence, which may have been normal or above average before the illness; but lies in *intellectual function*, with the sensory apparatus, with registration, retention of memory, or with the motor aspects of speech.

Lack of knowledge is not the same as low intelligence, although the two are often found together. Sometimes quite a detailed range of knowledge in a small field of interest is compatible with subnormal intelligence (*idiot savant*). On the contrary, those who come new to interviewing and assessing the mental state often expect much more general knowledge and information from those of *normal* intelligence than is actually possessed.

Since the concept of intelligence was defined by Binet, there has been argument as to whether intelligence is a unitary factor or a constellation of related abilities such as mathematical ability, verbal facility, quick grasp of situations, aptitude for abstract reasoning, a faculty for extracting the essential elements of a problem, a facility for turning events to one's own advantage, and so on. What these skills and abilities have in common is the capacity of the person to think in a purposeful way so that he adapts to new elements in his environment. This adaptation and skill in learning could be applied equally to pearl diving or playing chess. Intelligence, then, implies the capacity to lead one's life, to cope with and to master the external environment. This is much broader than the score on a psychometric test.

General capacity for understanding and reasoning may be contrasted with *primary abilities*. These latter would include, according to Thurstone, verbal comprehension, word fluency, number, space, memory, perceptual speech and reasoning. However, there does seem to be a unitary general factor of intelligence (*g*), as proposed by Spearman (1927), in addition to these specific abilities. *Creativity* is a different type of ability requiring *divergent* thinking and this requires, to some extent, different tests for its measurement.

INHERITANCE AND INTELLIGENCE

From studies of different degrees of relationships, it is clear that genetic determinants are important for intelligence. The mean correlation between the intelligence measurement as intelligence quotient (IQ) of parents and their biological children is 0.50; between identical twins, 0.90; and between parents and adopted children, 0.25. Although the influence of heredity is very strong, the environment may also play a part.

There is also a hereditary basis for many of the specific causes of mental handicap (Heaton-Ward & Wiley, 1984), such as chromosomal abnormalities and those related to individual genes. Chromosomal abnormalities include disorder of both autosomes, for instance, Down's syndrome which most commonly shows trisomy 21-22, and of the sex chromosomes such as Klinefelter's syndrome (XXY), Turner's syndrome (XO, in this condition mental handicap is rare) and so on. Amongst abnormality of the genes associated with mental handicap, inheritance of the abnormal gene may be dominant, such as tuberous sclerosis (epiloia), recessive such as microcephaly; or X-linked such as some forms of hydrocephalus. Further consideration of the genetics of mental handicap is outside the scope of this book.

MEASUREMENT OF INTELLIGENCE

Examination for human ability includes *aptitude tests*, which ascertain the capacity to learn; and *achievement tests* which measure skills, ability and knowledge already acquired. Tests of intelligence have demanded satisfactory levels of *validity*, that is, evidence that they are truly measuring the type of ability of interest to the tester; and *reliability*, that is, they are consistent over time.

Intelligence testing previously concentrated on the concept of *mental age* but now emphasizes the *intelligence quotient*. Tests such as the Wechsler Adult Intelligence Scale (WAIS) and the Wechsler Intelligence Scale for Children (WISC) have both *verbal* and *performance* scales. Discrepancy between the abilities tested by these two scales is of importance clinically–organic psychosyndromes tend to deplete the performance to a significantly greater extent than verbal score, as the former is more sensitive to deterioration through brain damage. The IQ remains relatively stable in healthy people after the age of six. Psychologists are now very cautious in using the results of intelligence testing to predict future performance in life activities.

In addition to global assessment of intelligence, psychometry is useful in looking for specific defects in learning or intellectual grasp suggestive of localized lesions; or, at a cruder level, discrepancy between verbal and performance abilities suggesting intellectual impairment due to a global organic process. O'Connor (1976) has discussed whether the intellectual failure in mental handicap is developed hierarchically; for example, lack of language resulting in poor thinking and abstracting capacity. He considers that experimental evidence tends to support such theories but is too complex for straightforward interpretation.

Impaired intellectual performance

The broad categories of cause of impaired intellectual performance are shown in Table 10.1. Only with irreversible disturbance of brain structure or function is

Table 10.1 Causes of impaired intellectual performance

Disturbance		Examples
Disturbance of cerebral structure or function }	– congenital – acquired	Mental handicap Dementia
Lack of sensory experience		Blindness, deafness, sensory deprivation
Disturbed contact with reality		Psychosis
Disturbance of affect impairing perception, attention and motivation		Depressive illness

the impairment permanent. Other causes are potentially reversible, and it therefore becomes vitally important to distinguish them from mental handicap or dementia.

CONGENITAL DISTURBANCE OF CEREBRAL STRUCTURE AND FUNCTION

Mental handicap of any degree of severity will result in impaired social competence. Brain pathology is demonstrable in most of those with severe mental handicap, and is associated with marked effects upon memory, language and intellectual performance. The descriptive terms used for the degree of handicap have traditionally been linked to levels of the intelligence quotient, and these are summarized in Table 10.2. The diagnostic categories are not based entirely upon measures of intelligence but also take account of social and other handicaps; this is especially true for milder degrees of retardation.

Intellectual incapacity is the hallmark of mental handicap. However, other psychiatric symptoms occur in different conditions and these other symptoms are modified, especially in their expression, by the impairment in intelligence and consequent lack of verbal fluency. This is especially so for symptoms such as, thought disorder; ideas and experiences of influence and passivity; hallucinations; delusions, especially of complex and systematized content; and

Table 10.2 Mental retardation: international classification of diseases – ICD 317-319
(after World Health Organization, 1977)

ICD number	ICD title	Obsolete terms	Retardation range	IQ level
			Dull, normal	85–99
			Borderline	70–84
317	Mild mental retardation	Feeble-minded; high-grade defect; mild mental subnormality; moron	Mild	50–69
318.0	Moderate mental retardation	Imbecile; moderate mental subnormality	Moderate	35–49
318.1	Severe mental retardation	Severe mental subnormality	Severe	20–34
318.2	Profound mental retardation	Idiocy; profound mental subnormality	Profound	0–19

ambivalence arising from complex unconscious conflict (Reid, 1982). Abnormalities of mood such as elation, depression, anxiety and panic, are ascertainable over a broad range of intellectual impairment, but are often poorly sustained and subject, in the presence of brain damage, to lability and excitability. With profound retardation no psychiatric phenomena can be elicited. Abnormalities of behaviour such as hysterical conversion symptoms; self-injury of various types; and repetitive acts such as echolalia and stereotypic rituals, are relatively common. Impaired attention concentration and memory, and also disorientation are frequent. Many 'symptoms' which would be construed as evidence for psychiatric morbidity in those not handicapped do not have the same implications for those who are. One cannot rely on verbal descriptions for the presence of symptoms and this makes accurate serial observations over time of behaviour, posture, gesture, facial expression, social expressiveness and level of activity, relatively more important.

The brain pathology of different syndromes may account for additional psychiatric symptoms. For example, in Down's syndrome there is a strong vulnerability to premature dementia of Alzheimer type; these patients are also more liable to develop affective disorders in adult life. There is no clear evidence that symptoms of schizophrenic or catatonic type are associated with specific forms of handicap. Epilepsy is especially common, occurring in up to 43% of severely and profoundly retarded adults in hospital (Reid *et al.*, 1978), but this was not found to correlate with other behavioural symptoms.

ACQUIRED DISTURBANCE OF CEREBRAL STRUCTURE AND FUNCTION

The clinical picture common to different causes of *dementia* is a progressive disintegration of intellect, memory and personality. From the practical aspect, it is important to distinguish *primary* dementias which are progressive and untreatable, from those which are *secondary* to some other disease and may therefore be treatable, at least to the extent of arresting further deterioration (for example, myxoedema, frontal meningioma). It is usually impossible to diagnose the cause of dementia from signs and symptoms, although they do differ in the speed of onset and progression.

Most commonly, the onset of dementia is insidious, with gradual impairment of memory or other deterioration of intelligence. A previously punctual, efficient and tidy man in his late fifties started arriving late for appointments; created muddles at work; became forgetful of current details; and began to look dishevelled in dress. Occasionally, of course, dementia may be sudden; for instance, following unconsciousness from head injury or brain surgery. Deterioration of personality may be the presenting feature with quite unexpected social blunders from a person of previously impeccable behaviour; for instance, an elderly politician who, quite out of character, made a risqué remark to a younger colleague's wife. Sometimes depressive symptoms are the first noticeable sign superimposed upon an intellectual deterioration that is already quite marked. On occasions, circumstances such as the death of the patient's spouse, by giving access to the home to the doctor or social worker, reveals the patient's severely impaired intellectual function.

LACK OF EXPERIENCE

Lack of exposure to appropriate opportunities for learning will result in impaired intellectual performance (Casey & Bradley, 1982). This will chiefly be due to psychosocial or sensory deprivation. *Critical periods* are important for acquiring specific skills, and if learning has not taken place by the end of that time, it may not be possible to obtain the skill later. Sensory handicaps for learning would include congenital deafness or blindness. In such situations there is, of course, no defect of intelligence, but some aspects of intellectual performance may be permanently restricted if the sensory defect is not corrected at an early stage or adequate early compensatory training given.

The effect of psychosocial deprivation upon intellectual performance is demonstrated in the highly contentious issue of relative IQ levels of different ethnic groups in the same society. Children from a socially deprived group, when adopted into more privileged families may show a 15 point higher mean IQ than children from their original social milieu (Scarr & Weinburg, 1976).

The intellectual deterioration of dementia is shown in loss of interest in work or hobbies; inability to make decisions; loss of application to the current task; incapacity for persistence; and loss of intellectual grasp in complex social situations. Attention and concentration are impaired, and there is a poverty of associations of thought with inability to produce new ideas; the patient is distractible and tires easily. He may react to the challenges of the outside world by either keeping rigidly to an absolutely fixed routine of life (*organic over-orderliness*), or by reducing his range of activities (*shrinkage of the milieu*), or even by an explosion of anger or intense anxiety (*catastrophic reaction*).

Intellectual flexibility is lost with difficulty in shifting from one frame of reference to another (Lishman, 1978). As there is no capacity to change frames, he is limited by the most immediate and recent stimulus. He is unable to grasp the essentials of an argument or situation and cannot exclude from his consideration the inessentials: he is submerged by the detail of circumstances. *Concretization* takes place in that abstract ideas are interpreted in a concrete way. Judgement is often faulty and there is limited insight into the nature of his own illness.

There is now a lot of evidence linking environmental factors, especially the harmful effects of social deprivation, with intelligence; enriched environments have been shown to overcome handicap. For example, low and persistent impairment of intelligence was associated with abuse in thirty-four patients with *abuse dwarfism* (Money *et al.*, 1983). Rescue from this situation resulted in gradual, progressive improvement in IQ over several years.

DISTURBED CONTACT WITH REALITY

Disturbed contact with reality, as with psychotic illnesses, will necessarily impair intellectual performance. This is often very obvious with schizophrenia; quite often marked with depressive illness; and less apparent with mania. In psychiatric illness, the impairment of performance is a direct effect of the psychotic disturbances in reality judgement–because of the predominant psychotic thinking the subject no longer finds it important to answer questions correctly or carry out procedures testing skill to the best of his ability. In illnesses which show complete recovery from the psychosis, there is contemporaneously a complete return of full intellectual performance. Permanent intellectual impairment may occur in some patients with chronic schizophrenia.

DISTURBANCE OF AFFECT

Disturbance of affect may impair perception, attention and motivation; and thereby result in apparent deterioration of intellectual performance. This is exemplified by depressive illness. Depressed patients who have previously undergone psychometry, for instance with the WAIS, even though able to give answers on testing, may show considerable diminution of score with marked retardation in completing tasks. On recovery there is a full return to premorbid intellectual performance.

The quality of intellectual appraisal may be substantially altered by disorder of mood, in that disturbed mood may impair the ability to interpret situations. The effect of maternal depression upon the cognitive development of the child is an important facet of the association between mood and intelligence. For instance, in a study of ninety-four women and their first-born children, cognitive functioning of the children was carried out at the age of four (Cogill *et al.*, 1986). Significant intellectual deficits were found in those children whose mothers had suffered with depression in the child's first year; marital conflict and a history of psychiatric problems in the father were also linked with lower test scores.

Subjective feeling of incapacity with impaired intellect

A feeling of capacity for performing their normal activities is developed in people successful in any sphere. They form an accurate assessment of what is within their capability to achieve and can gauge what is outside; they attempt and achieve the possible, and rarely have accidents. The feeling of capacity forms a customary association with normal behaviour, in the same way that feelings of familiarity invest the objects of perception. The ordinary events and circumstances of each day are tackled with the sense that it will be possible to deal with them. Placed in an entirely new situation, for example, a new job in a different town, a person who is normally confident and competent may become anxious, slow and indecisive. His gradual return of efficient action is based on familiarity with the new circumstances, memory of previous coping, and the ability to form problem-solving associations. It is characteristic of mental subnormality that there is a subjective lack of this feeling of capacity.

What does it feel like to be subnormal? What is the phenomenology of mental handicap? There can be no direct answer to these questions as the person so afflicted does not usually have the words to express himself, and has no experience of normal competence with which to compare his state. However, those who do have language show evidence of a need for esteem and self-esteem; for example, the frequent defence by a patient that she is 'high grade' (Kirman & Bicknell, 1975).

The patient does not have the ability to analyse his feelings and their causes. Timidity and withdrawal is characteristic of many people with mental handicap; this timidity often alternates with heedless boldness. He is shy with new people and frightened of new experiences; even of ordinary childhood activities like going on a swing or sharing a room with a kitten. At the same time, he is fearless to a reckless extent in other areas of life, for instance, playing with bonfires or near busy roads. Both abnormalities of behaviour, timidity and recklessness, can arise from defect in the feeling of capacity.

A number of other aspects of attitude and behaviour in mental handicap are associated with this lack of feeling of capacity for normal activities. There is a fear of change, and uncertainty which may manifest itself in apparent obsessional tidiness. It is, of course, not obsessional in a phenomenological sense of the word, in that there is no resistance. The person demands the curtains to be drawn to exactly the same place; he insists on sitting in the same chair; he gets very anxious if members of the family are away from home; he intensely dislikes weeks with bank holidays when the routine of his daily activities is disturbed; if the traffic system is changed he may be involved in an accident, because he insists on walking along the road in the way he always has.

The concept of mental age is fallacious, because the handicapped person does not function like an inquisitive but inexperienced child. His regressed and childlike behaviour, for example sucking his thumb at the age of 12, is not so much a manifestation of infancy as expressing overtly, and without awareness of the social context, the sort of occasional regressive feeling of any 12-year-old. The normal 12-year-old would usually conceal these wishes for social reasons; his intellectual grasp of his environment and the social reinforcements he receives from his peers all prevent him from expressing regressive childish behaviour. More attention to the subjective experience of those who are handicapped is likely to result in improvements in training and in the quality of their life.

References

Binet A & Simon T (1905) New methods for the diagnosis of the intellectual level of subnormals. *Annals of Psychology 11*, 191.

Casey PH & Bradley RH (1982) The impact of the home environment on children's development: Clinical relevance for the pediatrician. *Journal of Developmental and Behavioural Pediatrics 3*, 146–52.

Cogill SR, Caplan HL, Alexandra H, Robson KM & Kumar R (1986) Impact of maternal postnatal depression on cognitive development of young children. *British Medical Journal 292*, 1165–7.

Heaton-Ward WA & Wiley Y (1984) *Mental Handicap*, 5th edn. Bristol: John Wright.

Jaspers K (1959) *General Psychopathology*, 7th edn. (transl. Hoenig J & Hamilton MW, 1963). Manchester: Manchester University Press.

Kirman B & Bicknell S (1975) *Mental Handicap*. Edinburgh: Churchill Livingstone.

Lishman WA (1978) *Organic Psychiatry: The Psychological Consequences of Cerebral Disorder*. Oxford: Blackwell.

Money J, Annecillo C & Kelley JF (1983) Growth of intelligence: failure and catchup associated respectively with abuse and rescue in the syndrome of abuse dwarfism. *Psychoneuroendocrinology 8*, 309–19.

O'Connor N (1976) The psychopathology of cognitive deficit. *British Journal of Psychiatry 128*, 36–43.

Proust M (1919) *Within a Budding Grove*. (transl. Scott Moncrief CK & Martin T, 1981). Harmondsworth: Penguin.

Reid AH (1982) *The Psychiatry of Mental Handicap*. Oxford: Blackwell Scientific.

Reid AH, Ballinger BR & Heather BB (1978) Behavioural syndromes identified by cluster analysis in a sample of 100 severely and profoundly retarded adults. *Psychological Medicine 8*, 399–412.

Scarr S & Weinburg RA (1976) IQ test performance of black children adopted by white families. *American Psychologist 31*, 726–39.

Spearman CE (1927) The Abilities of Man: Their Nature and Measurement. London: Macmillan.

Thurstone LL (1938) *Primary mental abilities. Psychometric Monographs No. 1*. Chicago: University of Chicago Press.

World Health Organization (1977) *International Classification of Diseases*. 9th Revision. Geneva: World Health Organization.

─11─
The Disordered Self

Often, when I was alone, I sat down on this stone, and then began an imaginary game that went something like this: 'I am sitting on top of this stone and it is underneath.' But the stone also could say 'I' and think: 'I am lying here on this slope and he is sitting on top of me.' The question then arose: 'Am I the one who is sitting on the stone, or am I the stone on which *he* is sitting?' This question always perplexed me, and I would stand up, wondering who was what now.   Jung (1963)

EGO AND SELF

In all psychiatric conditions there is some disturbance in the way one thinks about and estimates oneself; this differs according to the nature of the illness. *Ego* and *self* are used more or less interchangeably in this chapter. *Ego* has the advantage of being a technical term and therefore more circumscribed in its meaning; this is also a disadvantage when it is simply oneself as usually understood that is being referred to.

Freud's use of the word *ego* echoes Nietzsche (1901): '...of *reason*. It is *this* which sees everywhere deed and doer; this which believes in will as cause in general; this which believes in the "ego", in the ego as being, in the ego as substance, and which *projects* its belief in the ego-substance on to all things'. Freud (1933) described ego as standing 'for reason and good sense while the id stands for the untamed passions'. The ego 'has been modified by the proximity of the external world with its threat of danger... The poor ego has to serve three severe masters and does what it can to bring their claims and demands into harmony with one another. These demands are always divergent and often seem incompatible. No wonder that the ego so often fails in this task. Its three tyrannical masters are the external world, the super-ego and the id'.

SELF-CONCEPT AND BODY IMAGE

The body is unique in that it is experienced both *inside* and *outside*; is both *self* and *object*. For most of the time we are not aware of our body but, for example, in extreme anxiety, pain and sexual excitement, there is an awareness of physiological systems or organs as objects: 'my heart banging, my finger throbbing'. For the rest of the time, we assume the parts of the body to be integrated within a 'self' of which we are not separately aware, and which we take for granted. It is through our body that we have contact with the world outside our self: movements of the body relate us to external space.

Many different terms are used to describe the way a person conceptualizes himself. Neurologists, neuropsychiatrists, psychoanalysts and psychologists have used variously the terms *body schema, body concept, body cathexis, body image* and *perceived body*. They describe approximately the same thing, but with different nuances. For example, *self-concept* tends to refer to the fully conscious

149

and abstract awareness of oneself; whilst *body image* is more concerned with unconscious and physical aspects. The *body schema* is more than, and usually bigger than, the body itself. For instance, if you imagine yourself on your way to work, automatically included within your schema of yourself are your clothes and your spectacles, if worn. The body schema changes with changing circumstances. When I drive my car I incorporate within my concept of my physical size the width of my car, so that I am unlikely to attempt to drive through a doorway or up a flight of steps. Spectacles, a cigar, the carpenter's screwdriver, the blind man's stick all contribute to that person's concept of his *self*. *Cathexis* implies the notion of power—perhaps analogous to electrical charge.

Social aspects are obviously important. A man with shoulder-length hair is not usually so endowed through neglect; more likely it represents a deliberate choice—how he sees himself in his social setting. It accords with his chosen peer group and also distinguishes him from those from whom he would wish to disassociate. Critchley (1950) has commented on 'that curious emotional state usually known as being in love' where there is 'a compulsive trend in two body-images of opposite sex towards propinquity and contiguity, eventually culminating in a total fusion or merger'. As a phenomenologist, one could take exception to Critchley's misuse of the term *compulsive*. According to Schilder (1935) body images are never isolated; they are always encircled by the body images of others. Body images are more closely bound together in the erogenic zones, and are social in nature. Our body image and the way other people see us are not dependent on each other; that is, a person sees himself and forms his self image in a social setting. He sees himself in relation to other people, but his view

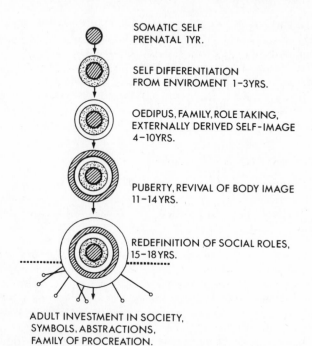

SOMATIC SELF
PRENATAL 1YR.

SELF DIFFERENTIATION
FROM ENVIROMENT 1–3YRS.

OEDIPUS, FAMILY, ROLE TAKING,
EXTERNALLY DERIVED SELF-IMAGE
4–10YRS.

PUBERTY, REVIVAL OF BODY IMAGE
11–14YRS.

REDEFINITION OF SOCIAL ROLES,
15–18YRS.

ADULT INVESTMENT IN SOCIETY,
SYMBOLS, ABSTRACTIONS,
FAMILY OF PROCREATION.

Figure 11.1 Developmental phases of the self image (after Bahnson)

of himself is not actually dependent upon how another individual sees him, but much more on how he *believes* that the person might see him.

The development of body image has been neatly summarized diagrammatically by Bahnson (1969). He considers that self-image is changeable and amorphous. At any one time the individual only perceives a small sample from a gallery of possible self-images. In Figure 11.1 the manner which '*phenomenological selves* are superimposed on each other like the layers of an onion' is demonstrated. Different aspects of self-image develop as the person increases the scope and complexity of his relationships. The term *ego* is not phenomenologically describable and there has been argument that the self cannot observe itself; that is, a thing and what observes that thing cannot be the same. However, it is the nature of *self* or *ego* to be experienced as either subject or object: a small nuisance like a mouth ulcer can make me feel uncomfortable (subjectively); I can describe what a person with a mouth ulcer experiences (objectively).

SELF-IMAGE AND NON-VERBAL COMMUNICATION

In social relationships a person expresses views he has about himself: his words, and the way he says them, convey how he views his relationship with the other person and also how he sees himself; for example, the shopkeeper 'talking down' to a child. Probably more important than this verbal manner of expressing, often unconscious, views on how we see ourselves is *non-verbal communication*. All gestures and postures, movements of the face and pauses in our conversation convey meaning to the person we are talking to; partly, this is also a comment on the way we see ourselves.

'The central core of self image consists for a person of his name, his bodily feelings, body image, sex and age. For a man the job will be central–unless he is suffering from job alienation. For a woman, her family and her husband's job may also be important' (Argyle, 1975). Non-verbal aspects of communication are important in sending and receiving information about the personality. The role in society one has adopted and the group with which one identifies are intentionally conveyed and therefore display self-image. These include 'age, sex, race, social class, rank, occupation, school or college attended, nationality, regional origins, religious group and family connections'. These attributes of the person are often deliberately displayed, but there are other characteristics which will be received non-verbally by observers even when the person has no intention of revealing them; for example, temperament, personality traits such as introversion, intellect, beliefs and values, past experiences.

Non-verbal communication expresses the attitudes of a person according to Argyle, for the following reasons:

1 There is in some areas of human concern a lack of language or 'verbal coding.' For example, shape is more readily expressed with the hands than verbally. Describing personality, our own or another's, or commenting on personal relationships, is more easily done non-verbally. A person will attempt to communicate non-verbally his or her own physical attractiveness, role and attitude towards the other person.
2 Non-verbal signals are more powerful; actions speak louder than words. For a school teacher, beckoning is more likely to result in action than a verbal order.

3   Non-verbal signals are less censored and therefore more likely to be genuine. If conflicting messages are given verbally and non-verbally, the non-verbal signal is accepted as truthful.

4   Some messages, because of social censorship, cannot be made explicit in a social setting and therefore cannot be verbalized but can be conveyed non-verbally by appropriate postures, gesture and movement in space. For example, by facial expression and turning away, a person might suggest without making it explicit, 'I do not like you and am bored with speaking to you'.

5   Verbal messages are punctuated and emphasized non-verbally; for example, the pause at the end of a phrase or the cadence of voice used. These embellishments add meaning to the actual words used.

A person interacts with others by the use of language. However, non-verbal signals are also important in expressing meaning and conveying feelings. The *ego* talks with the body as well as with words.

AWARENESS OF THE BODY

We have an awareness of our self and an awareness, which overlaps with this but is slightly different, of our bodies. What is this sense of body image or awareness? According to Head and Holmes (1911), the body schema is formed as the composite experience of sensations. Schilder developed further the importance of perceiving sensations in forming the body schema, 'the picture of our own body which we form in our mind, that is to say, the way in which the body appears to ourselves'. Freud also was concerned with body image in the development of personality: 'the ego is firstly the body ego'. Clearly abnormality of body image may be the result of abnormal sensations, but this is not always so. For instance, the abnormality of body image of an amputee is directly due to the physical damage; but a hypochondriacal patient may have no abnormal sensations, yet believe he has cancer. In transsexualism, a person will have a normal sensory experience of his body but says that he hates his body and especially his penis; he may feel tht he is actually a woman trapped inside a male body (Morris, 1974). His disturbed body image is not a result of disturbed sensation; there is a conflict between ego (the way he experiences himself and the gender he ascribes to it) and body image. The distinction made for convenience between this chapter and Chapter 14, between self-awareness and awareness of the body is artificial.

The body image can be altered through enhancement, diminution (or ablation), or distortion. It incorporates more than just the body, except perhaps for those few occasions when a person is both unclothed and conceptualizing himself as naked: tailors have long tried to persuade us that 'clothes make the man'. Certainly, they are an effective means of non-verbal communication. Clothes give us some insight into the way a person sees himself (or herself), and also into the way they intend to interact with other people. A person complements his mood and his social role of the moment in his choice of clothes. He wears clothes, as a ship hoists a flag, for signalling, and particular clothes are worn to convey a message to someone who can read it. A medical student wears a suit for an oral examination; a woman undoes the top button of her blouse on leaving the office for lunch. As the patient comes into a doctor's consulting room, he starts to give information about himself from his appearance before either of them utters a word. A person whose clothes are chosen for him, as in mental hospitals in the past, presents a peculiarly bleak and meaningless appearance; this aspect of his body image is expressionless and conveys nothing of himself.

Disorders of self

In descriptive psychopathology, one uses the term *ego disorders* or *disorders of self* to describe the abnormal inner experiences of *I-ness* and *my-ness* which occur in psychiatric illness. These may occur in the patient's state of *inner awareness* irrespective of any changes he may show in his attitude to, or experience of, the world outside himself. Jaspers (1962), with characteristic clarity, described self-awareness, that is the ability to distinguish *I* from *not I*, as having four formal characteristics.

1 *The feeling of awareness of activity*. Carrying out any function or activity gives opportunity for the sense of self awareness; if there is neither physical nor mental activity, there can be no awareness of the self.
2 *An awareness of unity*. At any given moment I know that I am one person.
3 *Awareness of identity*. There is continuity; I have been the same person all the time.
4 *Awareness of the boundaries of self*. I can distinguish what is *myself* from the *outside world*, and all that is not the self.

The disorders of inner experience in which these characteristics are disturbed are now explored in more detail. We will deal with these four functions described by Jaspers in order; although Scharfetter (1981) would add a fifth dimension of *ego-vitality* to the list. This aspect is, in fact, included in the first characteristic above–the awareness of activity which subsumes 'being' and 'existing' with other present participles.

DISORDER OF ACTIVITY

I do something and know that I am doing it. Everything I do, in everything I experience, through every event, I am aware that the experience has the unique quality of *being mine*. 'It was incredible. I pinched myself to make sure it was really happening to me' expresses the relationship we experience between awareness of reality and activity.

Being: the patient's experience of his very existence may be altered, 'I do not exist; there is nothing here'. This is the core experience of *nihilistic delusions* which may occur in affective psychoses (Chapter 16). Less pronounced nihilistic ideas (not delusions) are experienced as *depersonalization*: an alteration of the way one experiences oneself which is accompanied by a feeling of an alteration, or loss of significance for self–'I feel unreal, a bit woozy, as though I can't be quite certain of myself any more'.

Perceiving may be altered; abnormality of perception has been considered elsewhere, but the patient's experience of himself perceiving may become different: 'it does not seem to be me hearing (seeing); it is like being in a dream'. A patient with endogenous depression combined these features of abnormality of being and perceiving as follows: 'I do not feel alive; my eyes stare like out of a corpse; I am as if I am nowhere'.

Moving may show abnormality. A characteristic schizophrenic passivity experience was described: 'my arm is being moved by someone else'. This is a *psychotic* description of the awareness of movement, demonstrating a delusion of control. This function of self can also be disturbed in a non-psychotic or neurotic way. Thus, a housebound housewife suffering from a phobic neurosis said: 'if I am in the street on my own, I panic. I feel as if I am falling over'. Note the characteristic neurotic description of an *as if* experience.

Memorizing and *imagining* may be changed in that the patient with depression feels he is unable to initiate the act of memory or fantasy; or, alternatively, a schizophrenic feels that this activity when it occurs is not initiated by him but from outside himself. A depressed patient said, 'my memory has gone, I have no thoughts, I cannot think at all'.

Loss of feeling occurs as a common symptom in depression. The patient's experience of severe dysphoria is to *feel a loss of feeling*. He or she finds this very distressing and bewildering: 'I cannot love my husband. Nothing has happened to us. I have just lost my feelings for him'.

Willing may be altered; for example, the schizophrenic patient who no longer experiences his will as being his own. Commonly, neurotic patients describe an inability to initiate activity, a feeling of powerlessness in the face of life's vicissitudes.

Some of these abnormalities of experience of one's own activities are closely associated with mood; for example, the *nihilistic delusions* of the depressed patient who believes that he does not exist: the alteration of self-concept is directly linked to the mood state. Sometimes, however, it is not the affect associated with the change of activity, but the belief about the initiation of the activity which is changed. These are the passivity experiences (made experiences) which are discussed in more detail with other first-rank symptoms of schizophrenia in Chapter 9.

DISORDER OF SINGLENESS

In health, a person is integrated in his thinking and behaviour, so that he does not have to be aware of his feeling of unity. He just assumes that he is one person, and he knows his limitations and capabilities. This assumption of unity may be lost in some conditions. In *dreams* one sometimes sees oneself, even perhaps with some surprise, in the drama. In some forms of transcendental meditation, by carrying out repetitive monotonous acts, the subject enters a *self-induced trance* in which he can observe himself carrying out the behaviour. 'Self' is both the observer and also the object of observation.

Multiple personality

In hysterical dissociative states, dual and multiple personalities have been described (Prince, 1905; McDougall, 1911; Abse, 1982). Slater and Roth (1969) comment: 'A girl who is by turns "May" and "Margaret", may be quiet, studious and obedient as May, and unaware of Margaret's existence. When she becomes Margaret, however, she may be gay, headstrong and wilful, and refer to May in contemptuous terms. It seems that these multiple personalities are always artificial productions, the product of the medical attention that they arouse'.

So many of the terms used in psychiatry are not precise points on the map of semantic space but indefinite smudges, not well localized. Several of these vague descriptions with different names may partly overlap and coalesce. An example of this is seen in the terms *dual personality, autoscopy (heautoscopy), phantom mirror image* and *doppelgänger*. To attempt to clarify these diverse terms, *dual personality* is not a phenomenological description but simply implies that the outside observer (doctor) sees more than one 'personality' manifested at different times by the same person (patient). The patient may appear to be quite a different person at different times, and each 'person' claims to have no knowledge of, nor memory for, the other. Changing roles with alternating personalities is commonly quite conscious and deliberate as a game with children; an 8-year-old girl said: 'I like to talk to myself when I play the piano and then I am the teacher and the little girl'. However, this experience of two personalities is very rare as an hysterical and apparently unconscious state in adults.

Abse states that 'one-way amnesia' is usual for multiple personality: that is, personality *A* is amnesic for the other personality *B*; but the second, *B*, can discuss the experiences of *A*. Usually *A* is inhibited and depressed, and *B* is freer and more elated. The forms of multiple personality seen in practice are usually:

1 simultaneous partial personalities;
2 successive well-defined partial personalities;
3 clustered multiple partial personalities.

When such patients have been treated in psychotherapy, ingenious explanations are often given by patient and by therapist for the appearance of the additional personalities.

Autoscopy (heautoscopy)

Autoscopy and *phantom mirror image* are synonymous. According to Fish (1967): 'in this strange experience the patient sees himself and knows that it is he. It is not just a visual hallucination because kinaesthetic and somatic sensation must also be present to give the subject the impression that the hallucination is he'. This very rare perceptual experience may involve several of the modalities of sensation; for example, vision and touch. The loss of *feeling of familiarity* for oneself is prominent; 'self' is viewed quite dispassionately and objectively. In autoscopy, the abnormal perceptual experience is especially associated with disorders of the *parietal lobe*. A patient who had a lesion of the brain occasionally 'saw' himself standing at his left side and felt 'crowded' by this person. Lukianowicz (1958) has defined it thus: 'Autoscopy is a complex psychosensorial hallucinatory perception of one's own body image projected into the external visual space'.

In practice, these phenomena can be extremely difficult to identify. The following description by a 37-year-old, intelligent man with a history of epilepsy, receiving treatment with phenobarbitone, is considered an example of autoscopic pseudohallucination. The patient held his head rigidly with apparent torticollis to the right. If he rotated it to the left there was marked head nodding, but not if he turned it further to the right:

I'm standing outside myself on the left hand side but only when I'm sitting down...it comes in short episodes for about 30 seconds...my true self loses all its senses as all the senses are in my hallucinatory self...the true self is just a shell without any senses...the hallucinatory self can see the true self and the whole surroundings, and it seems to me as though the hallucinatory self is looking at me and at other things in the room from a position standing to the left hand side of me, and everything is in the right perspective. If it was occurring now, the hallucinatory self would see you more full face and from higher up than I see you now because it is standing... I can't see it or hear it but it can see the side of my head. It seems to be there. I know that it isn't me as such. It's like having a dream and you know that it is a dream. I thought it was a dream but it has occurred when I am fully waking. It seems as clear as a nightmare at the time but I know afterwards that it is a figment like a very vivid dream but more real than a dream. I would not see a fleck of dust on my cheek or something like that. The other one is not a different personality.

When this experience occurred the patient felt all sensation was in the 'hallucinatory self' including hearing, seeing, and feeling cold: 'I felt cold on the back of the hallucinatory self'. There had been no experience of taste or smell. There had been an experience of affect: 'I was talking to a representative. The hallucinatory self felt sorry for this man because he looked abnormal. It had no feelings for the real self. He looked abnormal because I had stopped talking and a glazed expression had come into my eye'.

A bizarre example of autoscopy was reported by Ames (1984)–self-shooting of a phantom head. This patient was suffering from schizophrenia. He described seeing and hearing a voice from another head that was set on his own shoulders, attached to his body and trying to dominate his own head. He described himself as having two heads but believed that the other head was actually that of his wife's gynaecologist whom he believed to be having an affair with her. The voice from the second head was that of the gynaecologist and there were also the voices of Jesus and Abraham around him, conversing with each other and talking about his having two heads. The patient tried to remove the other head by shooting six shots at it and through his own palate, causing extensive damage to his brain. Ames labelled this condition the 'phenomenon of perceptual delusional bicephaly'.

It is important to reserve autoscopy for a perceptual disturbance of self-image: 'seeing one's self' (Lukianowicz). In a comprehensive review, Damas Mora, Jenner and Eacott (1980) widen the definition considerably to 'the experience of duplication of one's real self'. However, this would include three forms: heautoscopic depersonalization, which is similar to the doppelgänger or experience of the double described below; heautoscopic hallucination (specular hallucination), which is the form described above; and, heautoscopic delusion, a rare form when the subject has a fixed delusional belief in his separate concrete existence but has no complementary perceptual experience. It is considered best to retain the word 'autoscopy' (heautoscopy) to refer to the perceptual form of heautoscopic hallucination. However, as Damas Mora *et al.* have pointed out, many subjects clearly have doubts about the reality of their vision and it may then be a visual pseudohallucination. Heautoscopic depersonalization, awareness of one's self, is now described under the term 'doppelgänger'.

Doppelgänger

The *Doppelgänger* phenomenon is an *awareness* of oneself as being both outside alongside, and inside onself: the subjective phenomenon of *doubling*. It is cognitive and ideational, rather than being necessarily *perceptual*. However, it may also have a perceptual *component*. It has nothing in common phenomenologically with the *Capgras syndrome* (Chapter 8), which is a delusional misidentification, in which the patient believes that someone he knows well has been replaced by an impostor who looks identical. The delusion in Capgras syndrome is that, although he agrees that the person looks exactly like the person he purports to be, he is actually an impostor falsely simulating the real person.

Having an awareness of one's double may be perceptual, delusional or, more commonly, a variety of *depersonalization*. There is a common North European myth that someone may see his *double* ('wraith', 'fetch') shortly before his death, and it has therefore become a sinister omen (Todd & Dewhurst, 1962). These authors present interesting historical material to substantiate the link between perceptual doppelgänger and death. The usual legend is that, as the person lies dying, his wraith floats before his eyes and he sees himself performing all the most disreputable and reprehensible actions of his life: they are paraded before him as he expires.

As a clear hallucination, *seeing* one's double is rare, but the vague feeling of being beside oneself, alongside oneself or having another self (the soul-double) is quite common. Patients describe experiencing their 'true' self and their 'other' self: their *self* as, unfortunately and realistically, they have to accept themselves; and their *ideal self* that they would wish to be; their reticent and submissive self which suffers, and a hostile self which derides and punishes them. This contrast is a popular literary subject, and it then becomes richly embellished by fantasy. Unlike a psychotic experience, one easily identifies with the victim of his own double; for example, Dostoevsky's Golyadkin in *The Double* (1846). This double is not clearly described in perceptual terms; he just exists, and the story describes his exploits. This symptom appears to be neurotically produced, in that the sufferer is unable to resolve the conflicting claims of different parts of his own personality; and, rather than accepting that he contains within himself opposed forces, he personifies these aspects and sees himself as having two or more different selves. A patient described thinking of himself quite vividly as two different people: 'an international self' and 'a little boy who couldn't make up his mind'. Using the application of repertory grid technique described by Ryle (1975), these selves may be represented as in Figure 11.2.

In this representation of semantic space, the patient, a barrister aged 45, experiences himself as two quite different selves: an 'international self' who is very like his 'ideal self' and also similar to a 'judge' whom he admires, respects and envies but does not know very well–this self is 'happy', 'interesting' and 'bright'; a 'little boy self', who is rather like the 'real self' he knows himself to be, lacking in confidence–described as 'takes things personally', and 'makes one feel guilty'. This patient's father died when he was a small child. The three important women in his life–his mother, his wife and his sister–are seen to be at right angles to the main axis of his conflict and are described as 'worrier' and 'tolerant' (Sims, 1985).

This neurotic conflict of the double has also been extensively used in literature where the two aspects of one personality may be portrayed as different, but closely related, people who become very involved with each other in a destructive way: for example, the brothers James and Henry in Robert

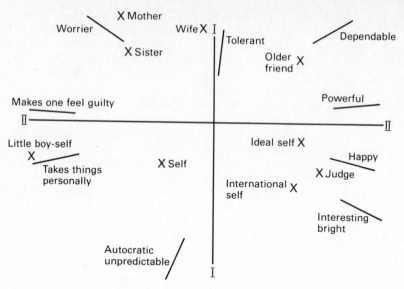

Figure 11.2 Repertory grid of two selves

Louis Stevenson's *The Master of Ballantrae* (1889). In this story, as in real life, the *victim* is generally conscientious, inhibited, quiet, consistent and moral. He is often respected but unpopular with acquaintances; faithful but dull in the eyes of women. The *double* (what he feels lies inside himself and wishes he could express) is usually domineering, ruthless, volatile and amoral. In the fantasy of the inhibited subject, this second self is immediately popular with women; but his behaviour soon precipitates calamities which frequently rebound upon the victim.

It is of course the anticipation of these disasters that inhibits the real person from acting upon his fantasies. The conflicts of an anxious obsessional, with profligate fantasies never to be realized, are given expression in these contrasted characters. He wants to break out of the mundane constraints of his orderly life and act in a liberated way, but he feels totally inhibited by the anticipated censure of other people.

Lability in the awareness of personality

The loss of unity of self in schizophrenia was exemplified by a patient who described how, every night, he became a horse and trotted down Whitehall. At the same time as this was happening in his mind, he also believed he was in Whitehall watching the horse. This type of symptom has been called *lability in the awareness of personality*, and was described by Bonhoeffer (1907) as occurring in paranoid psychosis.

DISORDER OF IDENTITY

A person who feels threatened in his job and is afraid of redundancy is not likely to function well because of his feeling of impermanence. A *feeling of continuity* for oneself and one's role is a fundamental assumption of life without which competent behaviour cannot take place. In health, we have no doubts about the continuity of ourself from our past into our present. However, schizophrenic patients sometimes deny that they have always been the same person. Characteristically, this takes the form of a *passivity experience* and the patient claims that at some time in the past he *has been* completely changed from being one person to another, whom he now is. This complete alteration in the sense of identity is exclusively psychotic; there is a break in the sense of identity of self, and there is a subjective experience of someone completely different, although still described as oneself, 'taking over'.

A feeling of loss of continuity, which is, however, of lesser intensity than the psychotic change described above and without its element of passivity, may be experienced in health, and in neuroses and personality disorders. The person knows that both are truly himself, but he feels very altered from what he was. This may occur following an overwhelmingly important life situation, or during emotional development without an outside event. For example, an adolescent may quite suddenly feel in the course of a week 'as if' he is quite a different person. It should be stressed that the sense of reality is never lost to the extent that he actually believes himself to be a different person. In the non-psychotic it is more that thoughts do not seem to be in keeping with himself as he has come to accept himself.

The feeling of loss of continuity contributes to the inertia of the schizophrenic, and the apathy of the depressive. Lack of a clear sense of identity from the past continuing into the future is a strong disincentive to concerted activity. The schizophrenic, as part of disturbance of passivity, may have doubts about his continuity from the past to the present; the depressive, secondary to disorder of mood, often sees no continuation into the future.

DISORDER OF THE BOUNDARIES OF SELF

By this is meant the disturbance in knowing where *I* ends and *not I* begins. Abnormality is not confined to schizophrenia. For example, in LSD intoxication the feeling of impending ego-dissolution associated with the feeling of self 'slipping away' with considerable anxiety has been described (Anderson & Rawnsley, 1954). One subject put this as: 'I was being disorganised...the world around was looking very distorted indeed...things were pretty rocky so I decided to sit back quietly for a moment and reassure myself by returning to my own private inner world. As soon as I introspected in this manner I felt to my dismay that "I" myself was somehow disturbed. The central core of the personality, the ego, the sense of personal identity, was itself fluctuating and, for want of a better phrase, dissolving'. Another subject said: 'If anyone present went out of the room it felt as though I were being deprived of something. I became smaller–definitely felt vulnerable'.

Boundaries of self in schizophrenia

In schizophrenia, the sense of invasion of self appears to be fundamental to the nature of the condition as it is experienced. There is a merging between *self* and *not self*; this is clearly portrayed in Figure 11.3, painted by a young schizophrenic patient. The patient is not aware of the disturbance being one of

Figure 11.3 Picture by a young schizophrenic patient (Louis Burley)

ego boundaries; he describes a problem only inasmuch as 'other people are doing things to me, events are taking place outside myself'. The external observer finds a blurring or loss of the boundaries of self which is not apparent to the patient himself.

All *passivity experiences* falsely attribute functions to *not self* influences from outside, which are actually coming from inside the self. The experience of *auditory hallucinations* are confidently ascribed by the patient to sensory stimuli outside the self whereas, in fact, they arise inside self. These auditory hallucinations comment upon the patient in the *third person*, which also demonstrates his confusion with the boundaries of self. Usually I think of myself in the first person singular. Occasionally I address myself, in my thoughts, in the second person, but I do not think about myself nor comment on my actions in the third person; this would reveal a considerable disturbance of the boundaries of self. Similarly, *hearing one's own thoughts out loud* implies locating one's innermost core experiences in distant space, and this is a massive disturbance of the boundaries of self. Once again, however, it is the interviewer identifying an ego disturbance of disorder of the patient's experience of self; the patient himself complains of the upsetting content, not of the disordered form of self-experience.

Much of the confusion of role and of self-image in schizophrenia appears to show this loss or inconsistency of boundaries, sometimes described in directly physical and concrete terms. A patient described the difficulty he had in thinking as being caused by 'a vibration an inch in front of my toes'.

Passivity, *delusion of control*, is discussed in Chapter 9. The subjective experience of passivity is a disorder of the distinction between what is and what is not *self*. Sensations, emotions, impulses and actions that in objective reality come from inside the self are ascribed to *not self*. The auditory hallucinations of schizophrenia and *delusional percept* are intensely personal and self-referent, and these symptoms seem to be very much an invasion into the integrity of the self. The disturbance of self-image, with disorder of the boundaries of self, is thus fundamental in all the *first-rank symptoms* of schizophrenia.

Other alterations to boundaries

In states of *ecstasy* there are also disturbances in the boundaries of self (Chapter 16). The participant describes feeling at one with the universe; merging with Nirvana; experiencing unity with the saints; identity with the trees and flowers; a oneness with God. Ecstasy states occur in normal people and in those with personality disorder, as well as in sufferers from psychoses. This alteration in awareness of the boundaries of self is different from that of schizophrenia described above. In ecstasy it is an *as if* experience, and it is mediated affectively.

The phenomenon described by Jung in himself with which this chapter begins is a lack of definition of the boundaries of self. However, there was no loss of reality judgement; it was a game and Jung did in fact know what was himself and what was the stone. In psychosis, this ability to discriminate is lost. A schizophrenic patient said: 'I am invaded day and night. I have no more privacy since television came inside me'. Another patient believed that whilst he was in a hospital ward, he was helping other patients because he permeated the medical staff and thereby assisted them in their work.

Clinical range of disorders of self

Alterations in the awareness of oneself occur over a very wide spectrum of states of mind and mental illness. They occur in normal people in certain normal life experiences; for example, in association with exhaustion; hunger; thirst; ecstasy; acute but appropriate anxiety; sexual arousal; hypnagogic states and dreams. They also occur in normal people in abnormal circumstances; for example, in divers or pilots exposed to abnormal effects of gravity, in sensory deprivation and during hypnosis. Normal people taking drugs may also experience changes in self-awareness. Some degree of alteration amounting to mild *depersonalization* is very common with many drugs, for example tricyclic antidepressants, but more marked changes occur with cannabis, mescalin and lysergic acid.

In abnormal mental states, there are many conditions in which awareness of self is changed. In almost all neurotic conditions and related disorders complaints about self-awareness occur. For example, in acute anxiety neurosis, hypochondriacal neurosis, hysteria with conversion symptoms and anorexia nervosa, disturbance of self-image is prominent. In psychosis, self is disturbed as part of the loss of reality judgement. For instance, a depressed patient may describe nihilistic delusions in which he believes 'everything is finished', and he ascribes the perceptions he has about himself to those beliefs–'I am dead'. Schizophrenic patients are likely to show misinterpretation or alteration of self-perceptions with delusional elaboration. There is a very wide range of abnormality of perception both of the self and of parts of the body occurring with organic states (Chapter 13).

It is, of course, an arbitrary distinction we make between *self-image* and *body image*, as the self is perceived as the body, and *my own body* is experienced as altogether different from *body in general*. The subjective experience of disturbance in self-image is called depersonalization; this is extremely variable in its nature, and its form is related to the underlying psychiatric condition. It is discussed in Chapter 12.

SELF-IMAGE IN NEUROSIS

The neurotic, irrespective of type of neurosis, is very concerned with himself and how others see him. He often feels extremely vulnerable to the harmful effects of his bad relationships with others, to exaggerated symptoms in his own body and to the destructive effects of his own neurotic thinking. This results in an all-pervading sense of subjective anxiety that influences all his planning and all his contacts with people. He feels very much alone and different; he feels threatened by 'them' whom he regards as being able to cope normally. This leads him to think of himself as being absolutely unique and this uniqueness demands all his attention so that he has great difficulty in thinking of the well-being of others.

This concern with self-image is akin to the idea of *narcissism*; it has the three qualities of total absorption with self, an all-pervading fear of loss of self, and an anxiety in relationships which leads to a withdrawal from close personal contact. This disturbance of the thinking of the neurotic is not intellectual nor perceptual; it is restricted to the cognitive realm of self-image and evaluation of personal relationships.

Panic attacks occur in situations either when the individual is stressed in terms of his personal resources to meet threatening objects or circumstances, or when tested in his competence to establish human relationships as an equal. Panic then becomes a withdrawal from this challenge and a demonstration of lack of capacity to cope. Pathological anxiety is very frequent in all neurotic disorders, not only anxiety states.

The cognitive aspects of neurosis can be investigated using Personal Construct Theory (Kelly, 1955; Bannister & Fransella, 1971). This is an investigation of the subjective semantic world in which the patient lives; in which he tries to make his internal world, and the internal screen on which the external world is projected, meaningful. This is well demonstrated by the repertory grid technique, establishing a quantitative relationship between elements and constructs (see Chapter 9, p.115).

Ryle has described the characteristics of neurotics revealed by the repertory grid. There is often a very wide discrepancy or distance in semantic space between 'self' as the subject sees it and 'ideal self'. More of the variation is accounted for by the first two principal components; there is a tendency for neurotics to see their world and the people in it very much in black and white. This inability to make fine distinction between people, their failure to read accurately those around them, makes them poor in making judgements about people and therefore makes it more likely that they enter into inappropriate and unrewarding relationships. It arises from their feeling of lack of competence in human relationships based upon self-doubting.

References

Abse W (1982) Multiple personality. In Roy, A (ed.) *Hysteria*. Chichester: John Wiley.

Ames D (1984) Self-shooting of a phantom head. *British Journal of Psychiatry 145*, 193–4.

Anderson EW & Rawnsley K (1954) Clinical studies of lysergic diethylamide. *Mschr. Psychiatr. Neurol. 128*, 38–55.

Argyle M (1975) *Bodily Communication*. London: Methuen.

Bahnson CB (1969) Body and self-images associated with audio-visual self-confrontation. *Journal of Nervous & Mental Disease 148*, 262–80.

Bannister D & Fransella F (1971) *Inquiring Man*. Harmondsworth: Penguin.

Bonhoeffer K (1907) Klinische Beiträge zur Lehre von den Degenerationspsychosen. Alt's Samml. Vol. 7, Halle.

Critchley M (1950) The body image in neurology. *Lancet 1*, 335–41.

Damas Mora JMR, Jenner FA & Eacott SE (1980) On heautoscopy or the phenomenon of the double: case presentation and review of the literature. *British Journal of Medical Psychology 53*, 75–83.

Dostoevsky F (1846) *The Double* (transl. Garnett C, 1913). London: Heinemann.

Fish FJ (1967) *Clinical Psychopathology*. Bristol: John Wright.

Freud S (1933) *New Introductory Lectures on Psychoanalysis*. (transl. Strachey J) Standard Edition of the Complete Works of Sigmund Freud, 1964, Vol XXII. London: Hogarth Press.

Head H & Holmes G (1911) Sensory disturbances from cerebral lesions. *Brain 34*, 102–254.

Jaspers K (1959) *General Psychopathology*. (transl. Hoenig J & Hamilton MW from the German 7th Edn, 1963). Manchester: Manchester University Press.

Jung CG (1963) *Memories, Dreams, Reflections*. London: Collins & Routledge & Kegan Paul.

Kelly GA (1955) *The Psychology of Personal Constructs*. New York: Norton.

Lukianowicz N (1958) Autoscopic phenomena. *Archives of Neurology and Psychiatry 80*, 199–220.

McDougall W (1911) *Suggestion*. Encyclopaedia Britannica.

Morris J (1974) *Conundrum*. London: Faber & Faber.

Nietzsche F (1901) *The Will to Power* (transl. Kaufmann W & Hollingdale RJ, 1968). New York: Vintage Books.

Prince M (1905) *The Dissociation of a Personality*. New York: Longman.

Ryle A (1975) *Frames and Cages*. London: Sussex University Press.

Scharfetter C (1981) Ego-psychopathology: the concept and its empirical evaluation. *Psychological Medicine 11*, 273–80.

Schilder P (1935) *The Image & Appearance of the Human Body; Studies in the Constructive Energies of the Psyche*. London: Kegan Paul.

Sims ACP (1985) Neurotic illness: Conserving a threatened concept. *British Journal of Clinical Pharmacology 19*, 95–155.

Slater E & Roth M (1969) *Clinical Psychiatry: Mayer Gross, Slater & Roth*; 3rd Edn. London: Baillière Tindall & Cassell.

Stevenson RLB (1889) *The Master of Ballantrae*. London and Glasgow: Collins.

Todd J & Dewhurst K (1962) The significance of the Doppelgänger (hallucinatory double) in folk-lore and neuropsychiatry. *Practitioner 188*, 377–82.

—12——

Depersonalization

But could you lift his blue, thick gaze and pass
Behind, you would walk a stage where endlessly
Phantoms rehearse unactable tragedy.

'In free air captive, in full day benighted,
I am as one for ever out of his element
Transparently enwombed, who from a bathysphere
Observes, wistful, amazed, but more affrighted,
Gay fluent forms of life weaving around,
And dares not break the bubble and be drowned.'

C Day Lewis (1948)

Definitions and descriptions

Depersonalization is the term used to designate a peculiar change in the awareness of self, in which the individual feels as if he is unreal (Sedman, 1972). It is best to reserve the use of the word to this *as if* feeling rather than the experience of certainty of unreality that occurs in psychosis. This *as if* experience is extremely common occurring, for example, on careful enquiry in 30% of all new consecutive psychiatric out-patient referrals in an unpublished series of mine.

Frequently it is accompanied by the symptom of *derealization*, a term used by Mapother (1935) to denote a similar change in the awareness of the external world. Depersonalization and derealization go together because the ego and its environment are really experienced as one. The less a patient takes himself for granted, the more unfamiliar and alien does the world around him become (Scharfetter, 1980). A young female patient said: 'I felt as if I didn't fit into the world... When I saw the moon, I felt I couldn't cope. One day it wasn't there and the next it was. I saw it and it upset me and I went to pieces... I felt I did not want to be alive because I was not related to anything. I just seemed totally out of everything and I started to cry. I couldn't cope with the hurt and the pain. I felt I never would feel part of anything'.

There is one particular feature described by patients, and not occurring in the depersonalization, that healthy people, especially children, may experience spontaneously in states of fatigue, after prolonged sleep deprivation or under sensory deprivation. This is the patient's description of the experience being intensely unpleasant (Ackner, 1954). It may be subjectively much the worst symptom in an affective neurotic illness. A young married woman said: 'I feel very weird in my head. I have a great deal of torment. My mind will not leave me alone. It's the surroundings; I cannot get my mind to myself. I felt as though I was going to fall over. I feel as if I'm lost in a fog. I just feel as if I'm not in my head. I feel numb'.

The symptom is described in a number of different ways and it is often

164

impossible to make a distinction between depersonalization and derealization: 'everything seemed to be going away from me'. The four qualities of the experience of self described in Chapter 11 may each be involved in the description of symptoms, although always with this *as if* character: activity; singleness; identity (continuity); and boundaries or definition. There is virtually always other evidence of disturbance of mood present—depression or anxiety, or both. Coupled with this is a feeling of loss of self-esteem as a very prominent symptom: 'I feel unreal, flat, not properly there, less of a person, as though I can't go and get stuck in'; that is, the feeling of unreality about oneself or one's environment has implications for lack of competence in relationships. The patient not only feels unreal but also 'detached'; there is a barrier to normal communication.

Some other symptoms are sometimes included with a description of depersonalization but, for the sake of clarity, should be separated and regarded as different phenomena. Thus disturbances of body image or schema, disorder of subjective time sense, hypochondriacal preoccupation, déjà vu phenomena, metamorphopsia (the distortion of visually perceived objects) or autoscopy may be described by the same individual. However, these are not symptoms within the description of depersonalization. It is also better to avoid Langfeldt's (1960) inclusion of schizophrenic passivity experiences within the term depersonalization.

SUBJECTIVE EXPERIENCE OF DEPERSONALIZATION

Depersonalization is difficult for the doctor to portray; it is extraordinarily difficult also for the patient to describe. He often prefaces his attempts at description by embarrassed statements such as, 'sometimes I think I must be going mad' or 'you will think me very peculiar when I tell you this doctor, but....' Then follows a halting and perplexed list of disjointed, unpleasant experiences which the patient feels to be unique, and for which he is unable to construe metaphors that satisfy him. Because of his failure in description, he believes that others will find these symptoms either bogus or clear evidence of imminent madness; so he omits them from his initial account even though such symptoms are very common amongst psychiatric patients. Depersonalization is the symptom the patient has when he experiences himself as being altered or deficient within his inner space; derealization is its equivalent in his outer space, with regard to things outside himself. Because there is no definite and easily ascertained boundary containing self, it is not always easy to decide whether the disorder is depersonalization or derealization. Neither is this important; they merge and overlap and are often simply included within the term *depersonalization*.

There is always a change in mood with depersonalization; the patient loses the *feeling* of familiarity he has for himself or for the world outside himself. He may describe himself as feeling like a puppet; hollow, detached, strange; on the outside; uninvolved with life; not himself; like a ghost—not solid, a stranger to himself. Similarly, with derealization he may describe his environment as flat, dim in colour, smaller, distant, cloudy, dream-like, still, 'nothing to do with me'.

Depersonalization is so common, and to the patient so obscure and unpleasant, that, whenever the description of symptoms is interrupted by the patient's baffled hesitancy, he should be questioned with possible depersonalization symptoms in mind. His relief at finding someone prepared to listen, and even perhaps understand, is often enormous. Schilder (1935) has described these symptoms: 'In a case of depersonalization the individual feels completely changed from what he was previously. This change is present in the ego (self) as well as in the outside world and the individual does not recognize himself as a personality. His actions appear to him as automatic. He observes his actions and behaviour from the point of view of a spectator. The outside world is foreign and new to him and is not as real as before'. This awareness of self and of the environment is experienced as being intensely unpleasant.

The localization of this symptom to an individual organ is called *desomatization*. There are many different possible alterations in the awareness of different organs: changes of size or quality; for example, feeling large, or tiny, or empty, or detached, or filled with water or foam. The patient may have a feeling of his legs being weightless, of floating, or of simply being unfamiliar. Change of feeling concerning the body or depersonalization may be associated with distortion of time; the passage of time appears altered in some way. People with depersonalization are in doubt about just what is troubling them and they may preface their description with '*as if*', and it is this element of uncertainty that occurs in the depersonalization of healthy people and neurotics, and differentiates them from the delusions about the self occurring in psychoses. *De-affectualization* has been used to describe a sense of the loss of the capacity to feel emotion, so that the person seems unable to cry, love or hate (*British Medical Journal*, 1972).

A patient says 'I am going mad inside my head'; on further questioning, he is describing finding his own mental processes to be strange: the feeling of familiarity that occurs when a person perceives previously known objects (opening the front door at home and looking inside), also occurs when one introspects into one's own thinking (remembering or *fantasizing* my front hall). I know what is there in my thoughts; I know what I will think about any particular object because it is unlikely to be very different from what I thought about it last time. I also know, in general terms, what I will think about myself because of past experience. The loss of familiarity of oneself occurring in depersonalization, or of outside self in derealization, is similar to the abnormality of the feeling of familiarity occurring in jamais vu (where there is no sense of previously having seen a well-known object) and its opposite, déjà vu (where an unfamiliar object or experience seems to be familiar).

Another variation of experience, which should not be regarded as depersonalization, is the experience of seeing oneself in other people. A neurotic female patient was crippled with multiple hypochondriacal complaints and loss of self-esteem. She was normally diffident and polite in her relationships. However, she was very rude and sometimes physically violent towards her twin sister who irritated her, because her twin's passive, dependent behaviour reminded her of herself. There was no true misidentification here, but an unpleasant feeling of familiarity occurred. Seeing herself in someone else seemed a nasty invasion of her privacy.

Like other aspects of self-perception, depersonalization has a social aspect. Frequently, the person feels that he is less able to accept himself, his personality, his behaviour than other people accept their own. He considers that his feelings about himself, his loss of reality is unique. This is a barrier to his giving an account of his symptoms and this in its turn is a barrier to communication in all areas of life. He feels himself to be different, isolated and ostracized. Depersonalization is an experience of an individual, but it has considerable social consequences.

It frequently occurs in attacks which may be of any duration from seconds to months, but most commonly last for minutes or hours. Improvement is usually first manifested in a gradual increase in time free from symptoms, rather than a reduction in the symptoms themselves when present. Onset may be insidious and with no known initiating cause or it may be in response to provocation. A middle-aged man who described his depersonalization 'like something supernatural—my body separated from me—a lost feeling', vividly recalled his first attack at the age of 11 when undergoing anaesthesia for the reduction of a fracture. Subsequent attacks felt similar despite the absence of provocation. He had also experienced attacks of sleep paralysis since the age of 25 and had discovered that by keeping himself awake until very tired he would fall asleep more quickly and thus avoid it.

Self-induced episodes of depersonalization, as an unpleasant symptom, have been recorded following particular patterns of behaviour. Thus Kennedy (1976) described self-induced depersonalization persisting as a complaint after transcendental meditation and yoga.

Organic and psychological theories

Theories accounting for the occurrence of depersonalization, including organic, psychological, psychoanalytic and schizophrenic, were carefully reviewed by Sedman (1970). Depersonalization is regularly cited as a common symptom associated with organic states, especially temporal lobe epilepsy (Sedman & Kenna, 1965). This is based upon the contention of Mayer-Gross (1935) that depersonalization is a *pre-formed functional response* of the brain; that is, a non-specific mechanism resulting from many different influences upon the brain, occurring in an idiosyncratic way in individuals in a similar manner to epileptic fits or delirium. He was in this following the neurophysiological hierarchical concepts of Hughlings Jackson (1884), who considered that the highest levels of cerebral function were lost first, leaving uninterrupted the activity of lower levels.

Organic theories purporting to account for depersonalization would suggest that alteration of consciousness acts as a release mechanism. However, Sedman (1970), in reviewing the literature, showed that, even in various forms of organic psychosyndromes, the incidence of depersonalization phenomena was similar to that found in normal populations, at between 25 and 50 per cent; in more severe chronic organic psychosis the rate was lower. From a variety of studies no quantitative relationship had been demonstrated between the degree of *torpor* (that is, the stage on the continuum from full alertness to unconsciousness) and the development of depersonalization. On studying the performance of depersonalized subjects on psychosomatic tests, there did not appear to be evidence to support a specific relationship between clouding of consciousness and depersonalization. There appeared to be many individuals who, despite any type of assault upon their brains, never developed depersonalization.

From this information Sedman concluded that 'there may well be a *built in* or preformed mechanism in approximately 40 per cent of the population to exhibit depersonalization; that the factors which initiate such a response are not specifically those associated with clouding of consciousness; or where clouding of consciousness appears to be playing a part it may well be the presence of another common factor that is more relevant'. Thus, the relationship between depersonalization and brain pathology remains unclear; depersonalization is certainly not pathognomonic of organic diseases.

Depersonalization is sometimes associated with self-induced organic states. Thus, it occurs following the ingestion of alcohol or drugs especially psychotomimetics such as LSD (Sedman & Kenna, 1964), mescalin, marijuana (Szymanski, 1981), cannabis (Carney *et al.*, 1984), and with sensory deprivation. It is also described as a side-effect with prescribed psychotropic drugs, such as the tricyclic antidepressants, but because of the common association between depersonalization and depression, it is difficult always to attribute cause.

Depersonalization: neurotic or psychotic?

Sometimes there has been considerable confusion as to whether depersonalization can be distinguished from the disorders of self-image described in Chapter 11 as occurring in schizophrenia. In fact, passivity experiences have even been described as a variant of depersonalization. However, Meyer (1956), as cited by Sedman (1970), has distinguished schizophrenic ego disturbances from depersonalization on phenomenological grounds; that is, on the description by the patient of his own internal experience. It is, of course, well recognized that true depersonalization symptoms do occur in schizophrenic patients, especially in the early stages of the illness alongside definite schizophrenic psychopathology.

Depersonalization is commonly described in manic-depressive disorder; however, the symptoms only occur in the depressive phase and there are no references to depersonalization occurring in mania (Sedman, 1970). Anderson (1938) considered that *ecstasy states* occurring in manic-depressive disorders were the obverse of depersonalization and that, whilst the former occurred in mania, the latter occurred with depression. Sedman (1972) in an investigation of three matched groups, each of 18 subjects, with depersonalization, depressive and anxiety symptoms considered that the results stressed the importance of depressed mood in depersonalization, whilst anxiety seemed to carry no significant relationship.

Many other authors have stressed the close association between the symptoms of depersonalization and anxiety. For instance, Roth (1959, 1960) described the *phobic anxiety depersonalization syndrome* as a separate nosological entity, but saw it as a form of anxiety neurosis upon which the additional symptoms are superimposed in a particular group of individuals. He considers depersonalization to be more common with anxiety than with other affective disorders, for example, depression. The phobic symptoms are usually agoraphobic in nature. The patient, most often female, married and in the third decade of life, has a great fear of being conspicuous in an embarrassing way in public; for example, fainting or being taken suddenly ill on a bus or in a supermarket. Fear of leaving the house unaccompanied develops from this, so that the patient is frightened of being at a distance from familiar surroundings without some supporting figure to whom she can turn. She may be unable to go out of the house at all, even with her husband. She may feel panicky on her own at home, and so keeps her child off school.

Depersonalization symptoms are commonly described in association with agoraphobia, other phobic states and panic disorder. It may appear as an isolated symptom and Davison (1964) has described episodic depersonalization in which other aetiological factors are not prominent. In the International Classification of Diseases (World Health Organization, 1977), a distinct category of depersonalization syndrome is described (ICD 9, 300.6) with features:

> A neurotic disorder with an unpleasant state of disturbed perception in which external objects or parts of one's body are experienced as changed in their quality, unreal, remote or automatized. The patient is aware of the subjective nature of the change he experiences. Depersonalization may occur as a feature of several mental disorders including depression, obsessional neurosis, anxiety and schizophrenia; in that case the condition should not be classified here but in the corresponding major category.

However, symptoms of depersonalization are commonly found in association with many varied neurotic conditions and, in practice, the different neurotic syndromes are not mutually exclusive but overlap in their symptomatology (Sims, 1983).

Certain personality types are more regularly associated with complaint of depersonalization and may therefore be regarded as predisposing: anankastic or obsessional personality disorder has frequently been implicated. Such personalities are, 'characterized by feelings of personal insecurity, doubt and incompleteness leading to excessive conscientiousness, checking, stubborness and caution. There may be insistent and unwelcome thoughts or impulses which do not attain the severity of an obsessional neurosis. There is perfectionism and meticulous accuracy and a need to check repeatedly in an attempt to ensure this. Rigidity and excessive doubt may be conspicuous' (World Health Organization). Introversion, as measured on the Eysenck Personality Inventory, is also found to be associated with greater frequency of depersonalization symptoms (Reed & Sedman, 1964). When symptoms are active, the neuroticism score on this scale is also raised but returns to normal levels on recovery.

In psychoanalytic theory, depersonalization has taken on a rather different meaning, and with this different explanations for origin. Psychoanalysts have been less concerned with describing the phenomena than the underlying concept of the alienation of the ego. For example, in the work of the existentialist school as typified by Binswanger (1963) there is discussion of the *depersonalization of man*:

> This depersonalization has by now gone so far that the psychiatrist (even more than the psychoanalyst) can no longer simply say, 'I', 'you', or 'he' wants, wishes etc.–the only phrases that would correspond to the phenomenal *facts*. Theoretical constructs dispose him, rather, to speak instead of *my, your,* or *his* Ego wishing something. In this depersonalization we see at work that aspect of psychiatry's founding charter that is most at odds with every attempt to establish a *genuine* psychology. An explanation of this baleful influence need go no further than the clearly recognized task that psychiatry, since Griesinger, has set itself–namely, to create a psychology that, on the one hand, serves to bring a reified functional complex into relation with a material 'organ' but that, on the other hand, allows this organ itself to be divided into and understood in terms of its functions.

This clearly is quite a different sense of the word than the phenomenological, with which this chapter has been concerned.

The distressing experience of depersonalization with a feeling of unreality remains central to description of the disordered self. The disturbance which causes this may be organic or environmental, psychotic or existential. Concern about the experience of self and of the environment most commonly occur together.

References

Ackner B (1954) Depersonalization I. Aetiology and phenomenology II. Clinical syndromes. *Journal of Mental Science 100*, 838–72.

Anderson EW (1938) A clinical study of states of 'ecstasy' occurring in affective disorders. *Journal of Neurology and Psychiatry 1*, 1–20.

Binswanger L (1963) Being-in-the World. (transl. Needleman J, 1975). *Selected Papers of Ludwig Binswanger* Basic Books. London: Souvenir Press.

British Medical Journal (Leading Article) (1972) Depersonalization syndromes. *British Medical Journal 4*, 378.

Carney MWP, Bacelle L & Robinson B (1984) Psychosis after cannabis abuse. *British Medical Journal 288*, 1047.

Davison K (1964) Episodic depersonalization: observations on seven patients. *British Journal of Psychiatry 110*, 505–13.

Jackson JH (1884) Croonian Lectures on Evolution and Dissolution of the Nervous System. In Taylor J (ed.) *Selected Writings of John Hughlings Jackson*, Vol. II, 1958, pp. 3–120. London: Staples Press.

Kennedy RB (1976) Self-induced depersonalization syndrome. *American Journal of Psychiatry 133*, 1326–8.

Langfeldt G (1960) Diagnosis and prognosis of schizophrenia. *Proceedings of the Royal Society of Medicine 52*, 595–6.

Lewis C Day (1948) The Neurotic. In *Poems 1943-1947*, pp. 76–77. London: Cape.

Mapother E (1935) cited by Mayer-Gross (1935).

Mayer-Gross W (1935) On depersonalization. *British Journal of Medical Psychology 15*, 103–22.

Meyer JE (1956) Studien zur Depersonalisation. *Psychiatrie et Neurologie (Basel) 132*, 221–32.

Reed GF & Sedman G (1964) Personality and depersonalization under sensory deprivation conditions. *Perceptual & Motor Skills 18*, 659–60.

Roth M (1959) The phobic anxiety-depersonalization syndrome. *Proceedings of the Royal Society of Medicine 52*, 587–95.

Roth M (1960) The phobic anxiety-depersonalization syndrome and some general aetiological problems in psychiatry. *Journal of Neuropsychiatry 1*, 292–306.

Scharfetter C (1980) *General Psychopathology: An Introduction*. Cambridge: Cambridge University Press.

Schilder P (1935) *The Image and Appearance of the Human Body: Studies in the Constructive Energies of the Psyche*. London: Kegan Paul.

Sedman G (1970) Theories of depersonalization: A reappraisal. *British Journal of Psychiatry 117*, 1–14.

Sedman G (1972) An investigation of certain factors concerned in the aetiology of depersonalization. *Acta Psychiatrica Scandinavica 48*, 191–219.

Sedman G & Kenna JC (1964) The occurrence of depersonalization phenomena under LSD. *Psychiatrie et Neurologie (Basel) 147*, 129–37.

Sedman G & Kenna JC (1965) Depersonalization in temporal lobe epilepsy and the organic psychoses. *British Journal of Psychiatry 111*, 293–9.

Sims ACP (1983) *Neurosis in Society*. Basingstoke: Macmillan.

Szymanski HV (1981) Prolonged depersonalization after marijuana use. *American Journal of Psychiatry 138*, 231–3.

World Health Organization (1977) *International Statistical Classification of Diseases, Injuries and Causes of Death* 9th Revision. Geneva: World Health Organization.

13

Disorder of the Awareness of the Body

I know I have the body of a weak and feeble woman,
but I have the heart and stomach of a king
Queen Elizabeth I (1588)

To some, ill health is
a way to be important,
Others are stoics,
a few fanatics,
who won't feel happy until
they are cut open.
WH Auden (1972)

Many descriptions of mood, cognition, volition and other psychological functions are expressed in physical terms: 'a heavy heart', 'bone headed', 'guts and determination'; the list in everyday use is endless. There is no division between subjective experience of self and of body. A 10-year-old girl put this relationship: 'You feel better if you've done your homework; if you haven't you get a horrible pain in your stomach'.

Bodily complaint without organic cause

Classification of these disorders is difficult, partly because the symptoms are obscure in origin and partly because there are different theoretical bases for the words used. For example, *conversion hysteria* refers to the presumed unconscious *conversion* of an unacceptable affect into a physical symptom; *hypochondriasis* refers to a concern with symptoms and with illness that the outside observer regards as excessive–the same amount of concern or complaint but associated with pathology that the doctor regards as justifying it would not be deemed hypochondriacal; *dysmorphophobia* is a phenomenological term and refers to the subjective experience of dissatisfaction with bodily shape or form.

In the Diagnostic and Statistical Manual of Mental Disorders, Third Edition (DSM III) (American Psychiatric Association, 1980) the conditions discussed in this chapter are described under *Somatoform Disorders* and *Factitious Disorders*. Somatoform disorders include *Somatization disorder* (300.81), *Conversion disorder* (300.11; or Hysterical neurosis, conversion type), *Psychogenic pain disorder* (307.80), *Hypochondriasis* (300.70, or Hypochondriacal neurosis), and Atypical somatoform disorder (300.71). Placing conversion disorder in an entirely different diagnostic category from *Dissociative Disorders* (hysterical neuroses, dissociative type), which logically belong together, is an example of the arbitrary and inappropriate division of symptoms into bodily and psychological. The

171

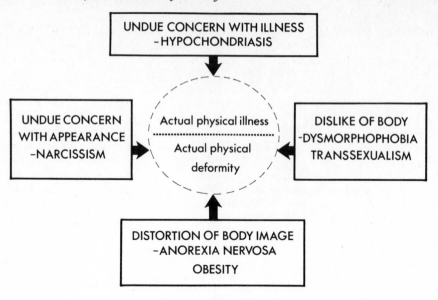

Fig. 13.1 Disorders of bodily complaint

gender identity disorders form a logical association with other disturbance of body image and identity such as dysmorphophobia; however, for the sake of convenience they are dealt with separately with other psychosexual disorders in Chapter 14.

HYPOCHONDRIASIS

Hypochondriasis describes that awareness in which the person takes undue account of the symptomatic component of his sensorium. There are many different modes of expression: minor pain and discomfort dominate his life and occupy his attention; he may have unreasonable fears about the likelihood of developing serious illness, and feels a need to take excessive precautions; he may misinterpret benign blemishes as having sinister pathological significance. Hypochondriacal symptoms are very common and usually transient. Only a minority come to medical attention and only a selected atypical proportion of these are seen by psychiatrists.

There is a distinction between illness fears, when there are no bodily symptoms, and fears and distress arising associated with bodily symptoms. This shows the overlap between illness phobia (unreasonable fear of developing illness) and hypochondriasis (preoccupation with symptoms). There is often difficulty in diagnosis when a person with demonstrable physical pathology complains excessively about his symptoms; his complaints appear to be out of proportion to the anticipated suffering and disability of the illness. The clinician may be in doubt as to whether there is further resistance to treatment and the necessary medical examination and investigation tends to reinforce the patient's symptoms. Somatic symptoms without organic pathology are extremely common, and may result from misunderstanding the nature and significance of physiological activity aggravated by emotion (Kellner, 1985). The mechanisms underlying hypochondriacal symptoms include misinterpretation of normal bodily sensations, conversion of unpleasant affect after depression into physical symptoms and the experience of autonomic symptoms directly caused by disorder of mood.

Explicit in the diagnosis of hypochondriasis is the condition of the patient himself. Implicit, however, is the doctor, who labels his patient *hypochondriacal* and deems him *sick*. In a society which is so conscious of physical health and the external physical appearance, the patient may have to shout hypochondriacally because the doctor will only listen organically. What the symptoms communicate to other people is an important component of all disorders of bodily awareness; concentrating on the subjective aspects of symptoms should not detract from their social implications. Hypochondriasis is not uncommonly an iatrogenic condition induced by the doctor's failure to listen to his patient's story and inability to give appropriate weight to psychosocial aspects contributing to symptoms.

What is hypochondriasis?

By derivation, the word *hypochondria* refers to the anatomical area below the rib cage (Figure 13.2), and hence dysfunction of the liver or spleen. Such words as *atrabilious* or *melancholia* refer to the black bile which was considered to be associated with hypochondriacal complaint and depressed mood. A better synonym is the word *valetudinarian*, derived from *valetudo*–the state of health. Kenyon (1965) has defined hypochondriasis as morbid preoccupation with the body or state of health.

Is hypochondriasis a separate condition–a symptom or a syndrome, a noun or an adjective? In the older psychiatric classification, and also surprisingly in

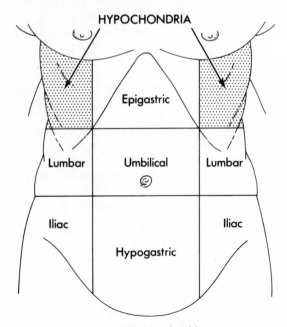

Fig. 13.2 The hypochondrium

DSM III, hypochondriasis is given a separate designation. However, in the International Statistical Classification of Diseases, 9th Revision (World Health Organization, 1977), and also in the more detailed rubric of DSM III, it is used adjectivally to describe one type of neurotic disorder. This conforms with Fischer-Homberger's dictum (1972) that hypochondriasis of the eighteenth century is equivalent to neurosis of the present century. Hypochondriasis is not an unitary condition but a disorder of content rather than of form. The content is the excessive concern with health, either physical or mental. The form of the condition may be very variable. *Hypochondriacal* is best retained as a description rather than as a discrete disease entity (Kenyon, 1976).

Barsky and Klerman (1983) have considered that the word hypochondriasis is used to describe four quite distinct concepts:

1 It describes a psychiatric syndrome characterized by physical symptoms disproportionate to demonstrable organic disease, fear of disease and the conviction that one is sick, preoccupation with one's body, and pursuit of medical care.
2 Hypochondriasis is seen psychodynamically as a derivative of aggressive or oral drives or as a defence against guilt or low self-esteem.
3 It results from a perceptual amplification and augmentation and a cognitive misinterpretation of normal bodily sensations.
4 It is socially learned illness behaviour to which the philosophy and practice of the medical profession lends support; these concepts are not alternatives but are all present to a different extent in the individual sufferer. Some individuals use a *somatic style* to describe perception of internal discomfort.

The diagnostic categories used in DSM III (American Psychiatric Association) are summarized in Table 13.1. In hypochondriasis 'the predominant disturbance is an unrealistic interpretation of physical signs or sensations as abnormal, leading to preoccupation with the fear or belief of having a serious disease'.

Bridges and Goldberg (1985) have assessed somatic presentation of psychiatric disorder in primary care in a series of 500 inceptions to illness amongst 2500 attenders. Their operational criteria for *somatization* were as follows:

i   *consulting behaviour*–seeking medical help for somatic manifestations and not presenting psychological symptoms;
ii *attribution*–patient considers somatic manifestations to be caused physically;
iii *psychiatric illness*–psychiatric diagnosis justified by psychiatrist;
iv *response to intervention*–research psychiatrist is of the opinion that treatment of the psychiatric disorder would benefit somatic symptoms.

These authors consider that somatization is a common mode of presentation of psychiatric illness and partly explains the failure of family doctors to detect psychiatric disorders in primary care.

When hypochondriacal symptoms were assessed in medical out-patients using a self-report questionnaire, structured interview and perusal of medical records, the DSM III criteria for hypochondriasis were found to be consistent (Barsky *et al.*, 1986). Disease conviction and fear, bodily preoccupation and somatic symptoms were intercorrelated, and also correlated with depressive symptoms.

Table 13.1 Somatoform disorders in DSM III

Syndrome	Diagnostic criteria
Somatization disorder	A Physical symptoms for several years beginning before age of 30 B Complaints of at least 14 symptoms for women and 12 for men out of a list of 37 symptoms
Conversion disorder	A Change in physical functioning suggests physical disorder B Psychological factors considered to be aetiological C Symptom not under voluntary control D Cannot be explained by known pathology E Not solely pain or sexual dysfunction F Not due to Somatization disorder or Schizophrenia
Psychogenic pain disorder	A Severe prolonged pain B Pain inconsistent anatomically or pathologically or excessive C Psychological factors considered to be aetiological D Not due to other mental disorder
Hypochondriasis	A Preoccupation with the fear or belief of having a serious illness B No physical evidence to support individual's unrealistic interpretation C Fear or belief of having disease persists despite reassurance D Not due to other mental disorders
Atypical somatoform disorder	Residual category

Trying to distinguish between organic and psychological elements is often a fruitless task. Psychological conflict may be mediated via physical illness, and a physical illness results in psychosocial sequelae. Both somatic and psychological symptoms occur, and it is perfectly possible for a patient to have an hypochondriacal reaction to a clearly defined organic illness. Stoeckel (1966) regarded the following as being the features of hypochondriasis: bodily complaint; attitudes and beliefs about the body; concerns about illness; and, the act of complaining to the doctor or complaining too often.

A patient who regards himself as having symptoms of illness communicates this to relatives and also to the doctor in a tacit request for both help and labelling (Parsons, 1951). In order to come to medical attention, the person has to carry out a particular set of actions; that is, undertake *illness behaviour* (Mechanic, 1962 & 1986). Illness behaviour is an important determinant of association between physical and mental illness; they may sometimes be more apparent than real (Benjamin *et al.*, 1984). Kennedy (1980) suggested that doctors force the *sick role* upon their patients, so that hypochondriasis becomes a necessary response.

There is overlap between hypochondriasis and dysmorphophobia and other body image disorders. Dissatisfaction with the body may be experienced as narcissism, an absorption with the appearance of the body; or hypochondriasis, an absorption with symptoms. There may be distortion of the body image without fear of illness as, for example, in anorexia nervosa or gross obesity. There is not necessarily any actual body image disturbance in hypochondriasis.

There are very marked cultural differences in the presentation of symptoms of disordered mood; somatization of emotional distress applies to both anxiety and depression (Rack, 1982). The predominance of description of somatic over mood symptoms in depressive illness has been reported from India, Pakistan,

Bangladesh, Hong Kong, the West Indies and various parts of Africa. The reasons for this include the expectations the patient has for what the doctor can do; the use of somatic symptoms as metaphor for distress; and the social unacceptability of psychological symptoms.

Psychopathology of the hypochondriacal patient

The *content* of hypochondriasis is the excessive concern with health, either physical or mental. Possible *forms* of the condition are listed in Table 13.2. These forms can include the following:

1   An *hallucinatory* voice may say to the patient: 'you have cancer, you are moribund'.

2   A *secondary delusion* associated with affective illness may occur in which the patient unreasonably believes he has cancer; he is quite unable to accept his doctor's reassurance. The belief is understandable in terms of the patient's overall depressed mood state. That such secondary delusions could be associated with affective psychoses was clearly described by Cotard (1882): '... she blamed herself and felt guilty. After some months she entertained hypochondriacal delusions, believing that she had no stomach and that her organs had been destroyed; she attributed these beliefs to the effects of an emetic which she had, in fact, been given...'

3   The *delusion* may be *primary* in nature. A patient believed that he had been innoculated under a general anaesthetic with a transmissible cancer because others believed him to be homosexual.

4   Hypochondriasis often manifests as an *overvalued idea*. Such a person is constantly worried and concerned about the risk of illness and the need to take precautions in ways that his friends find ridiculous; for instance, in the lengths that he will go to avoid a possible carcinogen. He considers it perfectly reasonable that he should take due care to maintain his health, but he agrees that his measures are excessive. He cannot stop himself, night or day, from thinking, worrying and trying to prevent illness. Such an overvalued idea is found reasonable, or at least not alien to the person's nature, but preoccupies the mind to an unreasonable extent; the whole energy and being becomes directed towards this single idea.

5   The hypochondriacal idea may take the form of an *obsessional rumination* in which the possibility of a particular illness or a form of words, as 'I have cancer', may occur. This is recognized as being both 'alien to my nature', but also 'coming from inside myself'. It is resisted, yet occurs repetitively.

6   Without its amounting to a delusion, patients may often have hypochondriacal symptoms of a non-specific nature in the course of a *depressive* illness. It may be possible to reassure them concerning any particular symptom, but this does not make them feel better in their mood, nor does it prevent the occurrence of further hypochondriacal symptoms in the form of depressive ruminations.

Table 13.2 Psychopathology of Hypochondriasis

1 Hallucination	5	Obsessional rumination
2 Secondary delusion	6	Depressive rumination
3 Primary delusion	7	Anxious preoccupation
4 Over-valued idea		

7 In the context of acute or chronic anxiety, the patient may be prone to multitudinous worries concerning illness and fears of illness. The normal sensorium is interpreted as symptoms; symptoms are interpreted as serious illness. Most hypochondriacal symptoms occur in relation to anxiety and depression; the other forms of disorder are much less frequent.

The commonest bodily symptoms implicated in hypochondriasis are: musculo-skeletal; gastro-intestinal, including indigestion, constipation and other preoccupations with malfunction; central nervous system, including headache (Kenyon, 1964). The most commonly affected parts of the body are: head and neck; abdomen; and chest. In 16% of patients, symptoms are predominantly unilateral, and of these, 73%, according to Kenyon, were left-sided. There was no significant physical abnormality found in 47% of those admitted to a psychiatric ward for hypochondriasis. Pain was prominent in 70% of patients. Hypochondriasis may be associated with smell, bodily appearance, sexual hypochondria, ear, nose and throat symptoms, and ophthalmological abnormalities (Karseras, 1976), such as *asthenopia*, which includes such complaints as ocular discomfort, aching eyes, soreness, pressure in or around the eyes, tiredness of the eyes, grittiness, chronic redness, feelings that the eyes are pushed out on stalks, tightness of the skin across the bridge of the nose, or pricking of the skin around the eyes. Photophobia is a common hypochondriacal complaint, as are 'floaters'–muscae volitantes–photopsia, and sometimes diplopia.

Hypochondriacal complaint may relate to psychological symptoms and the fear of mental illness. In this context, sleep is often involved, with subjective feelings of sleep not occurring at all; not occurring in sufficient amount; or not being of satisfactory quality. Fear of madness and inevitable psychiatric deterioration is commonly associated with acute anxiety disorders and also with depressive illness.

Diagnosis of hypochondriasis from other conditions

Hypochondriasis is an important presentation of depressive illness, and was quite clearly recognized by Schiller, for instance, when writing about the illness affecting his pupil Grammont on the 26 June 1780 (Dewhurst & Reeves, 1978):

> ...in my view the ailment is nothing but a case of true hypochondria, that unfortunate condition, wherein one is the lamentable victim of the intimate sympathy between the abdomen and the soul, an illness that afflicts deeply reflective and emotional spirits and the majority of great men of learning. The close connection between the body and the soul makes it extremely difficult to discover the origin of the complaint and to ascertain whether it originates from the body or the soul.
>
> ... Gradually, a state of physical disorder came to be associated with the derangement of his reason–I dare not offer an opinion on whether there was an underlying organic cause in the abdomen. Then came digestive disturbances, exhaustion and headaches, which, as the effects of a disturbed state of mind, in turn aggravated his mental condition still further.
>
> This led to the terrible state of melancholy into which he fell for some weeks. He despaired of his own strength, often telling me that he was not a human being since he could not think; that he could not see any reason for remaining alive as he had no purpose in life, and other things of a similar nature.

This presentation of depression as somatization often misleads the doctor in primary care into missing the underlying depressive illness. Because of the emphasis upon, and rewards accruing from, bodily symptoms in childhood and in many cultures, patients often selectively complain about physical symptoms and minimize the mood disorder and cognitive aspects of depression (Katon *et al.*, 1982). Somatization within depression is regarded as a coping mechanism that protects the individual from psychological pain. Culture, childhood experience and the stage of development of the individual's coping mechanisms all emphasize this process. This concentration by the individual upon the somatic symptoms of depression, with relative under-reporting of emotional and cognitive symptoms, has a profound effect upon interactions with health care systems because physicians are also somatizers. Diagnosis, investigation and treatment are likely to be influenced by this at great cost to the individual and the system. 'Somatization is a metaphor for personal distress'.

Hypochondriacal neurosis (ICD 9) is a common diagnosis. The International Statistical Classification of Diseases ascribes a category to hypochondriacal neurosis (300.7) but in fact hypochondriacal symptoms may occur in all neurotic disorders and neurosis cannot be tidily compartmentalized (Gelder, 1986).

In schizophrenia, hypochondriasis manifests with the bizarre symptomatology associated with that condition. The diagnosis is made on the presence of abnormal form.

Hypochondriasis may occur in the context of an organic psychosyndrome. Diagnosis is made by precise assessment of the mental state; looking for the appropriate features. Hypochondriasis and an organic state may of course coexist.

In children, hypochondriasis of the parents may be communicated to a child to produce hypochondriacal symptoms in him. This is an extremely common situation and it is often easy to see how hypochondriasis becomes a type of learned behaviour. Two much rarer conditions have been described: the *masquerade syndrome* (Waller & Eisenberg, 1980) occurs in children who have required long-term medical treatment for serious illness; as they improve physically, they manifest hypochondriacal school phobia associated with separation anxiety, and use their previous physical disability as a reason for not leaving home and returning to school. Meadow (1977) has described *Munchausen's syndrome by proxy*, where a parent produces factitious illness in the child–a complaint of haematuria in the child may be caused by the mother placing blood in his urine. This may on occasions be a form of hypochondriasis in the parent reflecting his/her over-concern for the child's health.

There is overlap between the terms *hysteria* and *hypochondriasis*. This is discussed further in the section on hysteria.

The term *somatization disorder* is used in DSM III to designate a condition with recurrent and multiple somatic complaints of several years' duration, for which medical attention has been sought but which are apparently not due to any physical disorder. The disorder begins before the age of 30 and has a chronic but fluctuating course. Complaints are often presented in a dramatic, vague or exaggerated way. Such individuals receive medical care from a number of physicians, sometimes simultaneously, and complaints are invariably made in many different organ systems. This is synonymous with the condition previously called Briquet's syndrome (De Souza & Othmer, 1984). In the terminology used in practice in the United Kingdom and categorized in the International Classification of Diseases, this disorder would be considered polysystematic, polysymptomatic, chronic, *hypochondriacal neurosis*.

especially at times of great stress such as during war, after disaster, in hospi..
emergency departments and with grave physical illness.

It is important to take into account the effect hysterical symptoms have upon
other aspects of a patient's behaviour and social relationships. Symptoms result
in his being regarded as *ill* or *disabled*, and this alters the way he or she is
perceived both by relatives and friends and by the medical and related
professions. There may be long-term physical consequences of hysteria, for
example, contractures; this is the ultimate mimicry hysteria shows of organic
conditions.

Classically, mood in hysteria is described as *belle indifference*. Such mood
occurred in a girl aged 20 with severe disability which had entailed her using
crutches for the past two years. She smiled with sublime resignation at her
unfortunate situation. However, some patients with conversion symptoms show
higher autonomic arousal than do anxious and phobic patients (Lader &
Sartorius, 1968). Hysterical patients often describe feeling extremely anxious at
the time of interview. They may also describe depression, and it is of course
important to decide whether depression is the primary diagnosis or not. They
may quite frequently manifest anger and hostility towards their relatives and
also those treating them; this may be overt or concealed.

In the history of hysteria, abnormal sexual behaviour has commonly
ccompanied other symptoms. This seems less frequent in contemporary
ccounts, perhaps because the general climate towards sexual expression has
ome more permissive and therefore sexually provocative behaviour evokes
comment.

ions from the term 'hysteria'

dering such an indefinite term as hysteria it is important to exclude
s that are psychopathologically separate. *Hysterical personality disorder*
1.5) is characterized by shallow, labile affect; dependence on others,
appreciation and attention; suggestibility and theatricality, with a
of sexual frigidity and over-responsiveness to stimuli. Although
occur in those with hysterical personality disorder, it may also be
on other personality types; and people with hysterical
not necessarily develop hysteria. This personality type is better
word *histrionic*.

nction is between hysteria and *deliberate disability* (Hawkins *et*
escribes mainly young, single women who feign illness and
edures which endanger life; sometimes they are involved in a
n. A patient, an ECG technician, presented with repeated
e hypoglaecemia following self-injection with insulin;
burns on accessible parts of the body that failed to heal.
necessary to demonstrate that the symptoms must have
ious, deliberate action of the patient.

SS

have been used to describe this condition. These
ess, *deliberate disability*, *Munchausen's syndrome*,
factitious disorders. It is important to make the

In dealing with hypochondriasis, one is often met with the nagging suspicion
that there may be concealed physical illness and, of course, this is usually the
fear of the patient. Hypochondriasis and severe physical illness may coexist, and
these two diagnoses should not be polarized in terms of either/or.

HYSTERIA

Hysteria is an old-fashioned word, the existence and meaning of which has been
argued over for centuries (Veith, 1965). More recently, Slater (1965) wished to
reject the diagnosis of hysteria, while retaining the word as an adjective to
describe certain types of symptoms and personality. Lewis (1975) summarized
this controversy: 'The majority of psychiatrists would be hard put to it if they
could no longer make a disgnosis of "hysteria" or "hysterical reaction"; and in
any case a tough old word like hysteria dies very hard. It tends to outlive its
obituarists.' Hysterical symptoms are extremely common, but the primary
diagnosis of hysteria is not.

What is hysteria?

The International Classification of Diseases 9th Revision (World Health
Organization, 1977) uses a traditional description of hysteria, whilst DSM III
(American Psychiatric Association, 1980) removes the term altogether by
fragmenting it into different parts. Merskey (1979) retained the term 'as a
medical issue, to treat patients who have it as subject to illness, and to accept
that it is a valid diagnosis embracing... symptoms....' British psychiatry has in
general implemented ICD 9 for diagnosis (Bewley, 1979).

The implications which may be drawn from the classification of hysteria in
ICD 9 are: (1) symptoms are psychogenic; (2) the causation is unconscious; (3)
symptoms carry some sort of advantage to the patient; (4) they occur by the
mediation of the processes of *conversion* or *dissociation*. Conversion and
dissociation are common mechanisms of hypochondriacal and pain symptoms,
although often overlooked. Hysteria is an example of the International
Classification being based upon psychodynamic formulation in that *conversion*
involves an unacceptable affect or perception of current life circumstances being
converted into physical symptoms. The symptoms do not carry aetiological
implications, but their descriptive use refers to symptoms suggesting
neurological disease such as amnesia, paralysis, difficulty in walking, and so on
(the so-called pseudoneurological or grand hysterical symptoms) (Guze, 1970).
The question that haunts psychiatrists and other physicians is, of course, how
can one be sure that the disturbance is psychogenic?

Conversion implies the behaviour of physical illness without evidence of
organic pathology; the patient is not aware of psychogenicity. *Dissociation*
implies 'a narrowing of the field of consciousness with selective amnesia. There
may be dramatic but essentially superficial changes of personality, at times
taking the form of a fugue (wandering state). Behaviour may mimic psychosis,
or rather the patient's idea of psychosis' (ICD 9). Dissociation can therefore be
seen as a form of conversion in which environmental stresses result in illness
behaviour in the psychological, rather than the physical, realm. Thus, the
symptoms of hysteria may be considered to be motor, sensory (including pain),
or psychological.

At ten-year follow-up of patients diagnosed with hysteria at a neurological hospital, many were found to have subsequently developed a serious physical or psychiatric illness; and for this reason the existence of hysteria as a diagnostic category was questioned (Slater & Glithero, 1965). At follow-up, 113 patients diagnosed as hysterical by psychiatrists revealed 60% to have shown evidence of affective disorder, and only 13% retained a consistent picture of hysteria (Reed, 1975). However, Merskey and Buhrich (1975) carried out a follow-up on patients diagnosed as having motor conversion symptoms at a neurological hospital and a control group of other patients from the same clinical setting. They found a higher rate for organic symptoms at follow-up in the control group. From follow-up studies of neurological or psychiatric patients, when the diagnosis of hysteria has been highly inclusive, other organic and psychiatric conditions have commonly manifested at follow-up; but there are still 15–20% who retained the diagnosis of hysteria. Hysteria exists but is much less common than previously thought.

Briquet's syndrome has developed from the concept of hysteria developed by the St Louis group (Perley & Guze, 1962; Guze, 1967); most of these patients had severe personality disorder and showed chronic hypochondriacal symptoms.

Clinical syndromes of hysteria

For the diagnosis of hysteria to be made, positive psychological features must be present, as well as organic features absent; it is important to emphasize the danger of diagnosing hysteria for chronic and obscure physical symptoms. Thus for *astasia–abasia* to be considered hysterical, the symptom should have a psychogenic aetiology; the patient is unaware of this, and the symptoms can be seen to be a way of dealing with stress. If symptoms are clearly consciously produced, deliberate disability, malingering or artefactual illness is present. One may have to distinguish between the symptoms of the original illness, for example head injury, and a secondary hysterical reaction (Sims, 1985a).

The *Ganser syndrome* is described in Chapter 4, and the confused issue of organic and hysterical symptoms. Hysterical *pseudodementia*, a most unsatisfactory term, is sometimes regarded as synonymous with Ganser syndrome and organicity requires investigating. However, pseudodementia is also used to describe the agitated symptoms that appear superficially similar to dementia occurring in old people with affective disorders.

Multiple personality, in which the patient assumes in series a number of different personalities, was described by Morton Prince (1905). His patients showed hysterical symptoms, but several of them also showed organic pathology. Sometimes these personalities claimed to know the other personalities in the same person and intensely disliked them, and sometimes they denied all knowledge of them. This dissociative symptom of hysteria is discussed with disorders of singleness in Chapter 11.

Epidemic, communicated or *mass* hysteria has been known and described from earliest times; for example, the physical symptoms of conversion type associated with the millenialist movements of the Middle Ages (Cohn, 1958); in a closed female community in a French seventeenth century convent (Huxley, 1952); and amongst Lancashire mill girls (St Clare, 1787). A rather similar epidemic

spread through a school in Blackburn 180 years later with symptoms of over-breathing, dizziness, fainting, headache, shivering, pins and needles, nausea, pain in the back or abdomen, hot feelings and general weakness (Moss & McEvedy, 1966). The spread of such epidemics has been described: they almost always occur in young females; they often start with a girl of high status in her peer group who is unhappy; they tend to occur in largest numbers in the younger children in a secondary school, that is, just after the age of puberty; they appear to affect most severely those who on subsequent testing are found to be the most unstable.

War neurosis, or shell shock, may be hysterical in nature when conversion symptoms occur in the absence of organic disorder. There are other transcultural forms of hysteria described, for example, *latah* (Yap, 1951). T̶ has a number of different names in slightly different forms in v̶ communities in South-east Asia, but characteristic is hypersugge̶ automatic obedience, coprolalia, and various echo phenomena. It̶ lower social class women exposed to sudden overwhelming stres̶ considered an acute catastrophic reaction: 'Such a reaction doe̶ occur in the western world except in special stress situation̶ disaster or drastic social change' (Kiev, 1972).

It would be unrewarding to list all the possible sym̶ hysterical origin: motor, sensory, pain, and alterations̶ the use of skilled examination and additional neuroph̶ example, in the investigation of hysterical blindne̶ demonstrate discrepancy between the severity̶ dysfunction, which may be minimal or absen̶ of hysterical symptoms is well demonstrat̶ visual field of an hysterical patient compl̶ context, is a contentious issue; it is un̶ complaint is of pain. Pain also comm̶ course, may indicate organic path̶ with hysteria include fugues,̶ personality. Acute, good pr̶

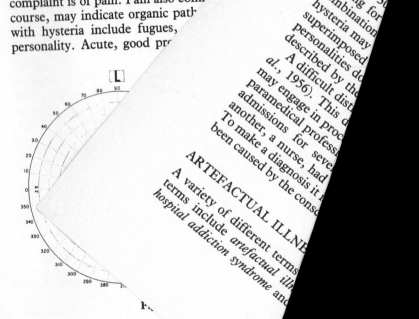

Table 13.3 'Factitious Disorders' in the Cumulated Index Medicus – 100 consecutive titles of articles

Terms used and their frequency			
Factitious (ial)	38	Fictitious	2
Pseudodementia	27	Pathomimia, pathomimicry	2
Ganser	4	Pseudostigmata	1
Feigned	4	Counterfeit	1
Munchausen	4	Simulated	1
Artefactual	4	Impostor	1
Surreptitious	3	Secretan's syndrome	1
Artificial	3	Psychogenic	1
Dermatitis artefacta	2	Masquerade	1

distinction between these and *malingering* which has obvious pejorative implications and should only be used when there is no possibility of doubt; for instance, even when the patient admits to feigning symptoms, there is often evidence of psychiatric illness (Hay, 1983). When the term *factitious disorders* was searched for in the Cumulated Index Medicus in the 1980s, one hundred consecutive titles of articles showed the different terminology of Table 13.3.

Factitious disorder is a term used in DSM III and implies that symptoms are not real, genuine or natural, but produced by the individual and under voluntary control. From external evidence and upon the subjective judgement of the observer, illness is considered to be simulated and the behaviour that results in the symptoms to be deliberate and purposeful. Where there is a goal that is obviously recognizable with a knowledge of environmental circumstances, then the diagnosis is *malingering* rather than factitious disorder; for instance, if symptoms are deliberately produced for compensation or to avoid military service. 'Malingering is the voluntary production and presentation of false or grossly exaggerated physical or psychological symptoms. The symptoms are produced in pursuit of a goal that is obviously recognizable with an understanding of the individual's circumstances rather than of his or her individual psychology' (American Psychiatric Association).

In factitious disorder, there is no apparent goal other than to assume the sick role, and it is therefore regarded as psychopathological rather than in any way as being adaptive. Factitious disorder may present with psychological symptoms

Table 13.4 Diagnostic criteria for factitious disorder (from DSM III)

Diagnostic criteria for Factitious Disorder with Psychological Symptoms
A. The production of psychological symptoms is apparently under the individual's voluntary control.
B. The symptoms produced are not explained by any other mental disorder (although they may be superimposed on one).
C. The individual's goal is apparently to assume the 'patient' role and is not otherwise understandable in light of the individual's environmental circumstances (as is the case in Malingering).
Diagnostic criteria for Chronic Factitious Disorder with Physical Symptoms
A. Plausible presentation of physical symptoms that are apparently under the individual's voluntary control to such a degree that there are multiple hospitalizations.
B. The individual's goal is apparently to assume the 'patient' role and is not otherwise understandable in light of the individual's environmental circumstances (as is the case in Malingering).

as in the Ganser syndrome or pseudodementia; or it may present with physical symptoms, as in complaints of acute abdominal pain without pain at all; be self-inflicted, as in the production of abscesses by injection into the skin, or haematuria by deliberate abrasion of the urethra; or an exaggeration of a pre-existing physical condition such as overdosage of insulin in a known diabetic. Chronic factitious disorder with physical symptoms is a synonym for the Munchausen syndrome; it is an important part of this condition that the patient seeks and achieves hospital treatment by deception. Diagnostic criteria for factitious disorder are shown in Table 13.4.

NARCISSISM

In classical mythology, Narcissus was punished for his disdain of Echo's admiration by being condemned to fall in love with his own image in the pool. An exaggerated concern with one's self-image, and especially with personal appearance, is called *narcissism*. The absorption with self and excessive self-love arise in the presence of feelings of insecurity about the self: there is some imminent threat to the body or to the integrity of oneself. The fixation of interest upon, and admiration of, himself impairs other interpersonal relationships. The term is mostly used in psychoanalysis and is often associated with sexual and gender abnormalities. It is, strictly, an abnormal attitude to the body rather than an abnormality of body image. The features of this state are described with literary insight in the *Picture of Dorian Gray* by Oscar Wilde (1948).

Narcissism is not essentially different from hypochondriasis in that the For example, the same qualities of attention to personal appearance that would result in a woman being considered well-dressed might be considered narcissistic in a man; perhaps current trends towards uniformity of the sexes are altering this. The term *narcissism* cannot be used in descriptive psychopathology unless the patient himself describes what he considers to be an excessive concern with his own appearance and a consequent inability to relate to other people. Using it indiscriminately about a patient makes it into a pejorative blunt instrument that does not add to one's knowledge of internal state.

Narcissism is not assentially different from hypochondriasis in that the former is fear of deterioration of bodily appearance, but the processes by which this may occur are seen in illness terms; whilst hypochondriasis is fear of illness itself. Our social standards for determining which blemishes in appearance are cosmetically acceptable are influenced by general pressures to conform in society and by availability of medical resources. Thus, in Britain now, any young person, irrespective of their financial state, will expect to have a relatively minor deformity of their nose corrected; whilst in the seventeenth century, Cardinal Richelieu, one of the wealthiest men in Europe, held his eminent public position whilst suffering offensive anal ulceration and suppurating sores that made his life miserable and eventually killed him (Bailly, 1939).

Narcissism is especially associated with ageing and the fear of growing old. De Beauvoir (1972) described the concern with facial appearance of growing old. This has a lot in common with the over-valued idea of dysmorphophobia; there may also be evidence of depression.

DISLIKE OF THE BODY

Distortion of body image and dislike of the body are subjectively different experiences. However, they often occur together. It is, for example, usual in anorexia nervosa and obesity to experience both features. It is important in elucidating symptoms to make a distinction.

Dysmorphophobia

There are many people dissatisfied with the way they look, and of course this does not of itself constitute a psychiatric symptom. However, unreasonable loathing or excessive preoccupation with a disliked feature may result in psychiatric referral. Such people may shown generalized disapproval or it may be concentrated upon one feature of their appearance. According to Andreasen and Bardach (1977), the primary symptom of dysmorphophobia is the patient's belief that he or she is unattractive.

Dysmorphophobia has been defined as the primary complaint of some external physical defect thought to be noticeable to other people, but, objectively, their appearance lying within normal limits (Hay, 1970). Patients presenting to a plastic surgeon for cosmetic rhinoplasty were examined psychiatrically. They were, as a group, more disfigured than a control group, and they showed some psychological disturbance, in that 40% showed personality disorder. There was, however, no relationship between the degree of deformity and amount of psychological disturbance. Hay and Heather (1973) commented that when surgery was carried out, those patients with minimal disfigurements did as well as those with more marked defects, both subjectively in description of their self-image and on psychological testing. They considered that the degree of deformity was not of major importance in coming to a decision with regard to operation.

Those complaining about their face, and especially their nose, do so in extreme and exaggerated terms despite the deformity often being quite minimal. The dissatisfaction with their appearance and the extent to which they feel others are aware of their disfigurement are quite out of proportion, as are the discomfort and disturbance in function: 'agonizing pain' and 'total inability to breathe'. Because of the extreme degree of reaction they show they may contemplate radical remedies, for example wishing to have their nose amputated or threatening to kill themselves. Dysmorphophobia is a relatively common disturbance of self and usually takes the form of an *over-valued idea*.

The complaint of dysmorphophobia is made by the subject in relation to others, but not usually based upon the opinion of others. So a patient complains of his nose, or the small size of her breasts and considers that others will regard them as ugly or unattractive. Often the appearance is well within normal limits with no deformity, but the patient is convinced that surgery will be beneficial. Patients often present in their late teens or early twenties. There is quite often underlying personality disorder of anankastic or affective type; there may be neurotic depression as a reaction to the complaint; and such patients not infrequently talk of, and attempt, suicide.

A female student, aged 20, was referred to the psychiatric clinic following an overdose. When asked her problem, she burst into tears and said, describing the small size of her breasts: 'Basically there is a big difference between me and other girls. I've always been self-conscious. I used to pad myself. Even my mother made fun of me. I've tried to convince myself I would change physically. I don't feel like a total woman. I have to buy clothes that look ridiculous on top. My present boyfriend I have been going out with for over a year always talks about other girls he has. He went to a dance and danced with another girl, I knew that it was because she was bigger-busted than me. I was always aware of my figure, that I am not attractive... I detest myself, I hate my body... I don't like my boyfriend touching me there, I can't wear nice clothes, I can't make the best of what I already have... even my little sister of 16 has more than I have ever had'.

This girl hated herself because of the small size of her breasts which she construed as an intolerable deformity, and she was contemplating suicide. Using the technique described by Kelly (1955) for obtaining elements and constructs concerning the way she regarded her body, a repertory grid representing her mental state is shown in Figure 13.4. For her, *breasts* are the *massgebend*, a polarized element quite different from the way she regards any other organ; they are associated with the constructs of *loathing*, *I endure* and *too small*.

It is of interest to note that surgery can result in restitution of normal body image. In a study of eleven young women with no other disease and breast size not grossly inappropriate for body size requesting reduction mammoplasty, Hollyman *et al.* (1986) found after surgery body image had returned to normal; self-confidence, feelings about femininity and sexual attractiveness were also enhanced.

Dysmorphophobia is sometimes described by schizophrenic patients. It may occur as the first symptom as the condition develops and the clinician should therefore look carefully for suggestive symptoms. It may also be present in the

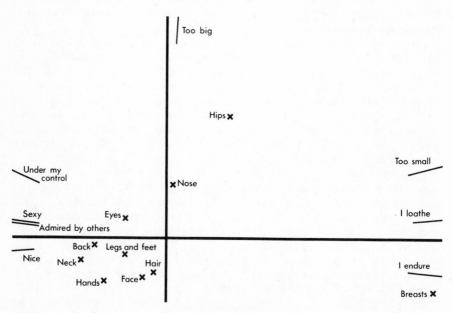

Fig. 13.4 A repertory grid representing the mental state of a girl who complained of the size of her breasts (Sims, 1985b)

established case and will then show characteristic schizophrenic symptomatology. A 19-year-old girl of West Indian extraction, previously diagnosed schizophrenic, said:

> The Spirit is a man, he feels warm and moves in me. I can't feel yet. I've got to pray for my new body. I'll have it in March. I will have to look beautiful, I don't feel beautiful at the moment, I don't look nice enough. I'll have a nice face, nice teeth, red eyebrows, red eyes, pupils red and smooth red lips. My skin will be light and I'll have long fair thick hair down to my knees. My voice will be different and I'll have a new tongue. I'll speak many languages. I'll sing too. My brain and my mind will be the same. I'll have long finger nails, a smaller waist, bigger breasts and my legs will be a bit shapelier. My figure will change from 33″ 24″ 35″ to 38″ 18″ 36″.

Transsexualism

This is discussed in more detail in Chapter 15. It is a disorder of content in which the person believes that true gender identity is at variance with biological and physical characteristics. Psychopathological form is usually that of an over-valued idea.

DISTURBANCE OF FEEDING AND BODY SIZE

Disturbance of feeding occurs with various conditions in which alteration of body image either causes eating disorder or results from it. Three conditions will be discussed: obesity; anorexia; and bulimia nervosa. Once again, it is the subjective aspects, the effect on self-image, that concerns us here and not the physical aspects.

Obesity

Obesity has many causes: physiological; genetic; cultural; and social; and one cannot therefore generalize about the mental state of obese people. It is important to distinguish those whose obesity began during childhood from those becoming obese later. The childhood group are likely to have hypercellular adipose tissue. They have much more difficulty in maintaining weight reduction and they are likely to become depressed while dieting.

In discussion of the body image phenomena of obesity, Kalucy (1976) considers that adolescence is the critical stage of development when primary disorders of shape and body experience appear. Obesity in adolescents in diet-conscious western societies results in self-loathing and self-denigration. The presence of any physical deformity at this stage of life is likely to provoke revulsion from the self-image; they feel especially physically loathsome with regard to the opposite sex. They may avoid mirrors and any other reminder of their shape. There is also present a distortion of body size in that they often over-estimate their size. This is interesting in comparison with anorexia nervosa patients who also often over-estimate their size and whose behaviour of dieting and food rejection may start when they are mildly obese at the time of puberty.

Anorexia nervosa

Anorexia nervosa is an illness which occurs mainly in young women; the proportion of male cases seen ranges from one in twenty to about one in ten in

different series (Dally & Gomez, 1979). There is a failure to eat, low body
weight and amenorrhoea. It is considered by Crisp (1975) that the disorder is
primarily a *weight phobia*, a fear of increasing body weight, and not only a
feeding disorder similar to those of childhood. Prominent is the fear of loss of
control–if one eats normally one will be unable to stop and therefore become fat.
As well as an abnormal self-image there are also abnormal attitudes towards
food, gender and sex. How does the patient with anorexia nervosa see herself? It
is in part a narcissistic disorder according to Bruch (1966), who has called it 'the
pursuit of thinness'. Anorexia nervosa is a condition which seems to be
becoming more common in the United Kingdom (Kendell *et al.*, 1973). It is
much rarer in India, and its prevalence may well be linked to social attitudes
towards thinness, dieting and slimming. In an affluent and well-nourished
society slimness is regarded as beautiful, and dieting may become a social norm
which acts as a persuasive pressure on an impressionable adolescent female,
whose body weight has increased a little more than average at puberty. If there
are other psychological difficulties and social conflicts, the slimming may get
out of control. In a country where there is much malnutrition, fatness is
considered healthy and the parents of a plump child are applauded as good
providers. Anorexia nervosa is relatively rare in Negroes. It has been
consistently found to be more common in people of higher social class since
Fenwick's description in 1880.

Patients with anorexia nervosa often deny their thinness and sometimes claim
to be too fat. Because of their extreme concern over their physical size and
weight, a technique was devised by Slade and Russell (1973) to investigate
bodily perception in anorexics. This involved comparing real size in subjects
(measured by an anthropometer) and perceived size, which was measured by the
observer moving horizontal lights to a distance that the subject estimated as the
width across four body regions: face, chest, waist and hips. When compared
with an age-matched normal control group, anorexic patients significantly
overestimated their own perceived width at all regions, with the face being
overestimated by more than 50%. Although actually thinner at chest, waist and
hips, anorexic patients saw themselves as fatter than normal women.

The body image disturbance could not be accounted for by a general
perceptual disorder as anorexics were fairly accurate at the measurement of
width of wooden blocks, and also extremely accurate at measuring physical
height. They tended to overestimate the width of other people, but not as much
as themselves. The body image distortion tended to lessen as patients put on
weight, especially if they did so slowly. It was shown that a greater degree of
body image disorder held a worse prognosis. Slade and Russell considered that
'patients with anorexia nervosa show a faulty appreciation of their own body
image in the sense that they perceive their bodies as possessing an exaggerated
girth'. It was found by Garfinkel *et al.* (1979) that some anorexic subjects tend to
overestimate body size and that this overestimate was stable over a year and not
affected by weight change.

Experimental work by Button *et al.* (1977) has called into doubt the finding
that anorexics overestimate their size while normal females are very accurate.
They consider that disturbance of body perception is variable among anorexics.
It is only present amongst some patients at certain stages during their illness.
Those who vomit were found to overestimate their size. Normal females are not
homogeneous with regard to body perception. It is considered that abnormal

sensitivity about body size with body perception disturbance occurs in states other than anorexia nervosa.

Strober *et al.* (1979) assessed perception of body size, subjective experience of body image distortions and differentiation of body concepts by asking adolescent anorexic patients and controls to draw the human figure soon after hospital admission and six months later. Both groups tended to overestimate size at both times, but 'experiences denoting estrangement from the body, insensitivity to body sensations, and weakness of body boundaries were more prevalent in anorexics, and persisted at high levels after frank symptoms of weight and eating disorder had subsided'. There was a greater degree of a more persistent body image distortion in those who vomited. These authors considered that 'defects in body image formation render the anorexic vulnerable to their manifest pathology, which is itself activated by maturational conflicts unique to adolescence'.

The underlying fear of loss of control, and the incessant need for vigilance concerning any calorie that enters the mouth, influences all other areas of the patient's life. Obsessional tidiness and cleanliness may be manifested, and control of other people at home. An anorexic patient controlled the behaviour of her parents and twin sister by threatening to starve herself yet further if they would not co-operate. She weighed not only her own food but that of all the other members of the family. Before her illness she and her sister both weighed about nine stone, but as her anorexia progressed she insisted on her twin eating her food, which the patient cooked. As a result the patient dropped in weight to just over five stone, whilst her sister reached thirteen stone.

Bulimia nervosa

This condition has only been described relatively recently (Russell, 1979). Although the patient is currently of normal or near-normal weight, there is usually a history of anorexia nervosa with weight loss (Fairburn & Cooper, 1984).

The characteristic eating disorder is of gross preoccupation with food, with episodic binge-eating or gorging. This is frequently countered with self-induced vomiting and other methods of weight reduction such as abuse of drugs, for example laxatives or amphetamine-like drugs, or voluntary starvation. Weight is thus maintained with a fragile stability–sometimes weight loss may reach anorexic proportions and sometimes there may be mild obesity (associated with feelings of guilt). The fear of putting on weight and the dominating preoccupation with food is an over-valued idea.

There are often changes of body image similar to anorexia nervosa–the patient regards herself as being excessively fat. This may be associated with the mood of depression (often feelings of guilt and unworthiness and a conviction of a need for punishment). Various abnormal behaviours may occur including alcohol abuse, shop-lifting (especially involving stealing food) and deliberate self-harm. A variety of serious physical complications may result from rigorous self-induced vomiting or purging.

Underlying factors are particularly centred on doubts concerning femininity (Lacey *et al.*, 1986). Poor relationships with parents, academic striving, parental marital conflict, and poor relationships with the patients' own peers also occur. These patients described major life events in the areas of sexual conflict, major changes in life circumstances and experience of loss.

Organic changes in body image

Disease of, and trauma to, the brain alter the body image in a variety of ways. This is either due to damage of the conceptualized object; for example, amputation with phantom limb; or blindness necessarily altering the way one sees oneself; or damage to the process of conceptualization itself, for example, section of the corpus callosum. Often, of course, there is scattered damage, as with arteriopathy or multiple sclerosis, and these two features cannot be separated.

The expression *body image* as used in neurology was defined by Critchley (1950) as the mental idea which an individual possesses as to his own body and its physical and aesthetic attributes. Visual sensation, tactile impulses and proprioceptive stimuli contribute to the formation of body image but are not essential–following amputation of a limb, a phantom limb retaining the integrity of the body image occurs in the vast majority of cases. The body image 'lives on the fringe of awareness and is by no means obtrusive in ordinary circumstances. It is however available and can be brought into consciousness as soon as the stream of attention voluntarily or involuntarily focuses upon it' (Critchley). Morbid changes in the body image may show enhancement, diminution (or ablation) or distortion.

PATHOLOGICAL ACCENTUATION OF BODY IMAGE (HYPERSCHEMAZIA)

Pain or discomfort causes the affected part of the body to loom large. After dropping a heavy weight on his great toe a man felt his body to be 'an insubstantial shell around a huge throbbing toe'. Such a description of the painful organ seeming larger in size is frequent following surgery and traumatic injury.

Critchley gives several examples of neurological lesions causing enhancement of an organ:

1 with partial paralysis of a limb, the affected segment gives the impression of being too heavy and too big; for example, with Brown-Séquard paralysis (unilateral lesion of the spinal cord) the side with the pyramidal signs is hyperschematic whilst the other side with loss of pain and temperature sensation is perceived as normal in body scheme;
2 unilaterally, following thrombosis of the posterior inferior cerebellar artery;
3 in multiple sclerosis, again unilaterally.

Hyperschemazia may also occur with peripheral vascular disease where the affected limb feels larger and heavier. It may also occur in acute toxic states. Non-organic cases occur with hypochondriasis, depersonalization states and with hysteria, for example, hysterical pseudocyesis.

DIMINISHED OR ABSENT BODY IMAGE (HYPOSCHEMAZIA; ASCHEMAZIA)

This may occur when afferent and efferent innervation is lost, for example with transection of the spinal cord the patient may feel sawn off at the waist.

Hyposchemazia may accompany the sensory deprivation of weightlessness, for instance, under water. With vertigo the patient may feel excessively light, as if floating in the air.

Parietal lobe lesions may result in complicated states of diminution of the body image. Critchley cites a patient with embolism of the right middle cerebral artery:

> 'It felt as if I was missing one side of my body (the left), but it also felt as if the dummy side was lined with a piece of iron so heavy that I could not move it... I even fancied my head to be narrow, but the left side from the centre felt heavy, as if filled with bricks.' At one time he thought that his paralyzed leg belonged to the man in the next bed. His body felt to him half as wide as it should have done. Lying on the left side gave him the sensation that he was 'lying on a void'... that he was at the extreme edge of the bed and would presently fall off. In the early days he also felt that he had no penis at all. On this account he was clumsy with the urinal and the bed was frequently soiled. His sensation of owning a penis returned quite suddenly one morning in association with an erection, and it afterwards felt quite normal.

In *hemisomatognosia* (hemidepersonalization), the patient feels as though the limbs on one side are missing; this may occur as part of an epileptic aura. *Anosognosia* describes the lack of awareness of disease which may, for instance, occur with neglect of a hemiplegic limb.

Again, non-organic conditions such as depersonalization may also show diminution of body image. An anxious and depersonalized patient described: 'I don't feel at all the same person. Sometimes my head feels so numb when I walk to the shops. I feel I've left half my body behind'. This was clearly an *as if* experience.

DISTORTION OF THE BODY IMAGE (PARASCHEMAZIA)

This may occur with enhancement or diminution of the body image. It is described with hallucinogenic drugs such as mescalin, marijuana and LSD. Parts of the body may feel distorted, twisted, separated from the rest of the body or merged with the external environment. With hashish:

> the sensations produced were those of exquisite lightness and airiness... I expected to be lifted up and carried away by the first breeze... the walls of my frame were burst outward and tumbled into ruin, and without thinking what form I wore... I felt that I existed throughout a vast extent of space. The blood pulsed from my head, sped through uncounted leagues before it reached my extremities; the air drawn into my lungs expanded into seas of limpid ether, and the arch of my skull was broader than the vault of heaven... I was a mass of transparent jelly, and a confectioner poured me into a twisted mould (Taylor, 1856).

Distortion of body image may occur with epileptic aura and also rarely with migraine. Autoscopy is a related reduplicative phenomenon and may occur in similar circumstances.

Phantom limb

This occurs in the majority of amputees. As well as occurring with the loss of a limb, this type of distortion of body image is relatively common after surgical removal of an eye, the rectum or the larynx. If an amputee experiences a generalized peripheral neuritis involving sensation, paraesthesiae will also occur in the phantom limb. The amputee is aware of the phantom limb in space and also experiences pain in the space conceived as being occupied by the limb.

With time the limb appears to change in size. The image shrinks, but unevenly; distal joints shrink more slowly than proximal. The limb feels fixed: if an arm, flexed at the elbow; if a leg, spastic with all joints extended–this causes the patient difficulty, for instance, in walking upstairs. The limb may feel twisted and painful.

Orbach and Tallent (1965) described the body concepts of patients five to ten years after the construction of a colostomy. These patients had a conviction that they had been seriously damaged:

> They believed that their bodily intactness and integrity had been violated. In common with such beliefs many patients on a fantasy level perceived the operation as a physical or sexual assault. Patients who fantasized the surgery as a sexual assault were supported in this belief by the colostomy stoma, a new opening in the front of the body. Most men regarded this opening as evidence of having been feminized, while women often interpreted it as the addition of a second vagina. The bleeding from the stoma reinforced the fantasy of a second vagina because it was interpreted as comparable to menstruation.

In one fifth of patients, preoccupation about the bodily processes concerned with food intake and elimination

> was embodied in a replacement concept which attempted to establish equality between intake and evacuation by eating approximately as much as had recently been evacuated. A majority of the remaining patients communicated a sense of confusion about the machinery and functioning of their bodies.
>
> When colostomy patients were initially studied and reports published the constriction of activity and of the life space was emphasized. It is now apparent that the constriction is paralleled by a body concept of being damaged and fragile as a consequence of the injury.

Phantom limb pain may be psychologically determined (Parkes, 1976). Forty-six amputees were studied four to eight weeks and thirteen months after amputation, but a third to a half showed moderate disturbance tending to persist a year later.

Body image is not necessarily associated with abnormal sensation or perception. The hypochondriac may believe he has cancer although he has no physical symptoms. The transsexualist experiences his body normally, but he hates it and especially his penis. The narcissist is inordinately concerned with his body; nevertheless he is quite accurate in his objective quantitative perception of self, that is he knows how long his nose is or how far he can throw a cricket ball. Where sensation is abnormal or even deficient altogether in some modality, for example with blindness or deafness, body image is undoubtedly altered, but this alteration does not in any way imply mental illness; the alteration of body image is appropriate to the disability.

Culture bound disorders of body image

Various culturally determined hysterical conditions have been described by Langness (1967). These conditions have in common a sudden, dramatic onset related in time to a psychosocial upset. Manifestation of these conditions are: grossly unusual behaviour; volatile mood; transient occurrence of alteration of speech; depersonalization with altered body awareness; and symptoms somewhat similar to delusions and hallucinations. The course of these conditions is usually limited to one to three weeks, but may recur with further episodes. They appear to be more likely in those predisposed with hysterical personalities. The precise symptoms are often localized to that particular culture and demonstrate how neurotic symptoms in their content comply with the expectations of the society in which they occur. For instance Adair, writing from Bath in 1786, described how fashion influenced the great and opulent in the choice of their diseases and considered that Queen Anne's nervousness resulted in the transfer of similar symptoms 'to all who had the least pretensions to rank with persons of fashion'.

Some of the culturally localized disorders of awareness of the body are summarized in Table 13.5 (from Kiev). The variability of such syndromes is immense but the preoccupation with bodily organs and functions is common to many of them. The bizarre nature of symptoms, for example *koro*, in which there is fear of the penis shrinking into the abdomen, is often explained by a faulty knowledge of human anatomy and physiology and may seem naive to doctors practising in Europe. However, it is not generally known how ignorant British patients are concerning the organization and functions of the organs they cannot see. Hospital out-patients were compared with doctors by Boyle (1970) in their understanding of commonly used medical terms. As might be expected the doctors were consistent in their use of terms, but patients had enormous variation in their understanding of such terms as 'piles', 'least starchy food', 'palpitation', 'jaundice', 'flatulence'. When asked to detail the surface anatomy of internal organs, for example, bladder, kidneys, thyroid gland, the patients showed great variation, and were generally quite inaccurate. There are also bizarre anomalies of body image and function occurring in practice in the United Kingdom. A mill girl from Lancashire complained of migrainous headaches and ascribed these to insufficiently heavy periods. This explanation was found to be culturally acceptable to her peers.

Table 13.5 Culture bound disorders of body image (after Kiev)

Disorder	Diagnostic equivalent	Site	Key symptoms
Koro	Anxiety state	S.E. Asia	Belief that the penis will retract into the abdomen and cause death
Frigophobia	Obsessive–compulsive neurosis	East Asia	Morbid fear of the cold, preoccupation with loss of vitality, compulsive wearing of layers of clothes
Latah	Hysteria	Malaysia	Hypersuggestibility, automatic obedience, coprolalia, echolalia, echopraxia, echomimia, altered consciousness, disorganization, depression and anxiety
Evil eye	Phobic neurosis	Mexico N. Africa	Strong glances are harmful, precautions taken to avoid or counteract evil eye
Voodoo	Phobic neurosis	Haiti	Violation of taboo may result in death
Windigo	Depressive reaction	Canadian Indians	Fear of engaging in cannibalism and of becoming a sorcerer; depression of mood
Amok	Dissociative state	Malaysia	Neurasthenia; depersonalization, rage; automatism, violent acts

References

Adair JM (1786) *Medical Cautions for the Consideration of Invalids, Those Especially who Resort to Bath.* Bath: Dodsley & Dilly.

American Psychiatric Association (1980) *Diagnostic and Statistical Manual of Mental Disorders*, 3rd Edn. Washington: American Psychiatric Association.

Andreasen NC & Bardach J (1977) Dysmorphophobia: Symptom or disease? *American Journal of Psychiatry 134*, 673–5.

Asher R (1951) Munchausen's syndrome. *Lancet i*, 339–41.

Auden WH (1969) The art of healing: In memoriam David Protech, M.D. In *Epistle to a Godson*. London: Faber & Faber. *Collected Poems 1976*, p.626. London: Faber & Faber.

Bailly A (1939) *The Cardinal Dictator* (transl. Miles H, 1939). London: Jonathan Cape.

Barsky AJ & Klerman GL (1983) Overview: Hypochondriasis, bodily complaints and somatic styles. *American Journal of Psychiatry 140*, 273–83.

Barsky AJ, Wyshak G & Klerman GL (1986) Hypochondriasis: an evaluation of the DSM III criteria in medical out-patients. *Archives of General Psychiatry 43*, 493–500.

Benjamin S, Barnes D, Falconer G & Hoare E (1984) The effect of illness behaviour on the apparent relationship between physical and mental disorders. *Journal of Psychosomatic Research 28*, 387–95.

Bewley T (1979) Implementation of the 9th International Classification of Diseases. *Bulletin of the Royal College of Psychiatrists 188*.

Boyle CM (1970) 'Difference between patients' and doctors' interpretation of some common medical terms'. *British Medical Journal 2*, 286–89.

Bridges KW & Goldberg DP (1985) Somatic presentation of DSM III psychiatric disorders in primary care. *Journal of Psychosomatic Research 29*, 563–9.

Bruch H (1965) Anorexia nervosa and its differential diagnosis. *Journal of Nervous & Mental Diseases 141*, 555–566.

Button EJ, Fransella F & Slade PD (1977) A reappraisal of body perception disturbance in anorexia nervosa. *Psychological Medicine 7*, 235–43.

Carney MWP (1980) Artefactual illness to attract medical attention. *British Journal of Psychiatry 136*, 542–47.

Cohn N (1958) *The Pursuit of the Millenium.* London: Secker & Warburg.

Cotard M (1882) Nihilistic delusions. In Hirsch SR & Shepherd M (eds) *Themes and Variations in European Psychiatry*, 1974. Bristol: John Wright.

Crisp AH (1975) Anorexia nervosa. In Silverstone T & Barraclough B (eds). *Contemporary Psychiatry*. Ashford: Headley Brothers.

Critchley M (1950) The body image in neurology. *Lancet i*, 335–41.

Dally P & Gomez J (1979) *Anorexia Nervosa.* London: Heinemann.

De Beauvoir S (1970) *Old Age* (transl. O'Brian P, 1972). London: André Deutsch & Weidenfeld and Nicolson.

De Souza C & Othmer E (1948) Somatization disorder and Briquet's syndrome: An assessment of their diagnostic concordance. *Archives of General Psychiatry 41*, 334–6.

Dewhurst K & Reeves N (1978) *Friedrich Schiller: Medicine, Psychology and Literature.* Oxford: Sandford Publications.

Enoch MD & Trethowan WH (1979) *Uncommon Psychiatric Syndromes*, 2nd Edn. Bristol: John Wright.

Fairburn CG & Cooper PJ (1984) The clinical features of bulimia nervosa. *British Journal of Psychiatry 144*, 238–46.

Fenwick S (1880) *On Atrophy of the Stomach and on the Nervous Affections of the Digestive Organs.* London: Churchill.

Fischer-Homberger E (1972) Hypochondria of the eighteenth century–neurosis of the present century. *Bulletin of the History of Medicine 46*, 391–401.

Ganser SJM (1898) A peculiar hysterical state *Archiv fur Psychiatrie und Nerven Krankheiten 30*, 633–40 Transl. Schorer, CE (1965) *British Journal of Criminology 5*, 120–26.

Garfinkel PE, Moldofsky H & Garner D (1979) The stability of perceptual disturbances in anorexia nervosa. *Psychological Medicine 9*, 703–8.

Gelder MG (1986) Neurosis: another tough old word. *British Medical Journal 292*, 972–3.

Guze SB (1967) The diagnosis of hysteria: what are we trying to do? *American Journal of Psychiatry 124*, 491–98.

Guze SB (1970) The role of follow-up studies: their contribution to diagnostic classification as applied to hysteria. *Semin. Psychiat. 2*, 392–402.

Hawkings JR, Jones KS, Sim M & Tibbetts RW (1956) Deliberate disability. *British Medical Journal i*, 361–7.

Hay GG (1970) Dysmorphophobia. *British Journal of Psychiatry 116*, 399–406.

Hay GG (1983) Feigned psychosis: A review of the simulation of mental illness. *British Journal of Psychiatry 143*, 8–10.

Hay GG & Heather BB (1973) Changes in psychometric test results following cosmetic nasal operations. *British Journal of Psychology 122*, 89–90.

Hollyman JA, Lacey JH, Whitfield PJ & Wilson JSP (1986) Surgery for the psyche: a longitudinal study of women undergoing reduction mammoplasty. *British Journal of Plastic Surgery 39*, 222–4.

Huxley A (1952) *The Devils of Loudon*. Harmondsworth: Penguin.

Jaspers K (1959) *General Psychopathology* (transl. Hoenig J & Hamilton MW, 1963). Manchester: Manchester University Press.

Kalucy RS (1976) Obesity: an attempt to find a common ground among some of the biological, psychological and sociological phenomena of the obesity/overeating syndromes. In Hill OW (ed.) *Modern Trends in Psychosomatic Medicine 3*. London: Butterworths.

Karseras AG (1976) Psychiatric aspects of opthalmology. In Howells JG (ed.) *Modern Perspectives in the Psychiatric Aspects of Surgery*. London: Macmillan.

Katon W, Kleinman A & Rosen G (1982) Depression and somatization: a review. *American Journal of Medicine 72*, 127–35 & 241–7.

Kellner R (1985) Functional somatic symptoms and hypochondriasis. *Archives of General Psychiatry 42*, 821–33.

Kelly GA (1955) *The Psychology of Personal Constructs*. New York: Norton.

Kendell RE (1972) A new look at hysteria. *Medicine 30*, 1780–83.

Kendell RE, Hall DJ, Hailey A & Babigian HM (1973) The epidemiology of anorexia nervosa. *Psychological Medicine 3*, 200–203.

Kennedy I (1980) Unmasking medicine. *The Listener* 600–604, 641–44, 677–79, 713–15, 745–48, 777–79.

Kenyon FE (1964) Hypochondriasis: a clinical study. *British Journal of Psychiatry 110*, 478–88.

Kenyon FE (1965) Hypochondriasis: a survey of some historical, clinical and social aspects. *British Journal of Medical Psychology 38*, 117–33

Kenyon FE (1976) Hypochondriacal states. *British Journal of Psychiatry 129*, 1–14.

Kiev A (1972) *Transcultural Psychiatry*. Harmondsworth: Penguin.

Lacey JH, Coker S & Birtchnell SA (1986) Bulimia: factors associated with its etiology and maintenance. *International Journal of Eating Disorders 5*, 475–87.

Lader M & Sartorius N (1968) Anxiety in patients with hysterical conversion symptoms. *Journal of Neurology, Neurosurgery and Psychiatry 31*, 490–95.

Langness LL (1967) Hysterical psychosis: the cross-cultural evidence. *American Journal of Psychiatry 124*, 143–152.

Lewis AJ (1975) The survival of hysteria. *Psychological Medicine 5*, 9–12.

Meadow SR (1977) Munchausen syndrome by proxy. *Lancet 2*, 343–45.

Mechanic D (1962) *Students Under Stress: A Study in the Social Psychology of Adaption*. New York: Free Press.

Mechanic D (1986) The concept of illness behaviour: culture, situation and personal predisposition. *Psychological Medicine 16*, 1–7

Merskey H (1979) *The Analysis of Hysteria*. London: Baillière Tindall.

Merskey H & Buhrich NA (1975) Hysteria & organic brain disease. *British Journal of Medical Psychology 48*, 359–66.

Moss PD & McEvedy CP (1966) An epidemic of over-breathing among schoolgirls. *British Medical Journal 2*, 1295–1300.

Orbach CE & Tallent N (1965) Modification of perceived body and of body concept. *Archives of General Psychiatry 12*, 126–35.

Parkes CM (1976) The psychological reaction to loss of a limb: the first year after amputation. In Howells JG (ed.) *Modern Perspectives in the Psychiatric Aspects of Surgery*. London: Macmillan.

Parsons T (1951) Illness and the role of the physician: a sociological perspective. *American Journal of Orthopsychiatry 21*, 452–60.

Perley MJ & Guze SB (1962) Hysteria—the stability and usefulness of clinical criteria. A quantitative study based on a follow-up period of 6 to 8 years in 39 patients. *New England Journal of Medicine 266*, 421–26.

Pilowsky I (1967) Dimensions of hypochondriasis. *British Journal of Psychiatry 113*, 89–94.

Prince M (1905) *The Dissociation of a Personality*. New York: Longman.

Rack P (1982) *Race, Culture and Mental Disorder*. London: Tavistock.

Reed JL (1975) The diagnosis of 'hysteria'. *Psychological Medicine 5*, 13–17.

Russell GFM (1979) Bulimia nervosa: an ominous form of anorexia nervosa. *Psychological Medicine 9*, 429–48.

Sims ACP (1985a) Head injury, neurosis and accident proneness. In Trimble MR (ed.) *Advances in Psychosomatic Medicine: Neuropsychiatry*. Basel: Karger.

Sims ACP (1985b) Neurotic illness: conserving a threatened concept. *British Journal of Clinical Pharmacology 19*, 95–155.

Slade PD & Russell GFM (1973) Awareness of body dimensions in anorexia nervosa: cross-sectional and longitudinal studies. *Psychological Medicine 3*, 188–99.

Slater E (1965) Diagnosis of hysteria. *British Medical Journal 1*, 1395–99.

Slater E & Glithero E (1965) A follow-up of patients diagnosed as suffering from hysteria. *Journal of Psychosomatic Research 9*, 9–13.

St Clare W (1787) Country News in *The Gentleman's Magazine 57*, 1, 268. Cited by Hunter R & Macalpine I (1963) *Three Hundred Years of Psychiatry*. London: Oxford University Press.

Stoeckel JD (1966) Hypochondriasis. *International Journal of Psychiatry 2*, 330–31.

Strober M, Goldenberg I, Green J & Saxon J (1979) Body image disturbance in anorexia nervosa during the acute and recuperative phase. *Psychological Medicine 9*, 695–701.

Taylor B (1856) *Putnams' Monthly Magazine 8*, 233.

Veith I (1965) *Hysteria: The History of a Disease*. Chicago: University of Chicago Press.

Waller D & Eisenberg L (1980) School refusal in childhood—a psychiatric-paediatric perspective. In Hersov L & Berg I (eds) *Out of School*. Chichester: John Wiley.

Wilde OFFW (1948) *The Picture of Dorian Gray*. London: Unicorn Press.

World Health Organization (1977) *International Statistical Classification of Diseases. Injuries, and Causes of Death*, 9th Revision. Geneva: World Health Organization.

Yap PM (1951) Mental illness peculiar to certain cultures. *Journal of Mental Science 97*, 313–27.

14

Disorders of Gender and Sexuality

Transsexualism is something different in kind. It is not a sexual mode or preference. It is not an act of sex at all. It is a passionate, lifelong, ineradicable conviction, and no true transsexual has ever been disabused of it...

I myself see the conundrum in another perspective, for I believe it to have some higher origin or meaning. I equate it with the idea of soul, or self, and I think of it not just as a sexual enigma, but as a quest for unity. For me every aspect of my life is relevant to that quest–not only the sexual impulses, but all the sights, sounds and smells of memory, the influences of buildings, landscapes, comradeships, the power of love and of sorrow, the satisfactions of the senses as of the body. In my mind it is a subject far wider than sex; I recognise no pruriency to it, and I see it above all as a dilemma neither of the body nor of the brain, but of the spirit.

Morris (1974)

This chapter only attempts to outline the range of disorders of gender and sex. More detailed information, both on symptoms and treatment, are found in textbooks on this topic (Gagnon & Simon, 1967; Bancroft, 1974; Rosen, 1979; Feldman & MacCulloch, 1980; Bancroft, 1983). The social, cultural and relationship aspects are not dealt with fully in this chapter. Marital dysfunction and disorders of pregnancy and the puerperium are discussed here for convenience: there are often associations in the mind of the sufferers between their present state of conflict and their role as woman, spouse, sexual partner and mother.

Gender describes the lifelong state or category of an animal as regards masculinity and femininity. *Sex* describes its physical manifestation with an implication of its participation in the appropriate copulatory activity for that gender: male or female. The difference of meaning between the two words *gender* and *sex* has become blurred with usage. The sex of a child is, of course, normally assigned at birth. Mistaken or uncertain assignment at this stage will have serious psychological implications at a later stage. Gender identity is normally established by about the age of 18 months: the child knows that he is a boy and that this is different from being a girl; he begins to learn what are masculine interests and behaviours and to apply them to himself. This begins to occur from the beginning of the establishment of language. This development does not occur in a vacuum: it is strongly reinforced by the parents and by society in general. If there had been faulty assignment at birth, this establishment of gender identity upon the ascribed sex overrides the biological sex.

This *core gender identity* is the private view of *own* gender, which the subject retains, and is established very early in life. It is biologically influenced and also strongly socially reinforced. It remains throughout life. The tendency is, once having settled on gender, for subsequent development to encourage that gender identity to become more pronounced.

Gender role is the working out of this gender identity in a social milieu–the public aspect of gender. So the little boy plays the role of the man, the father, in his games of pretence and later plays the role in adult life. Gender role is developed on the basis of gender identity but is not fixed or immutable like gender identity. Qualities such as aggressiveness, gentleness, effeminacy may be seen as having gender role connotations, but gender role is on a continuum: a male person with masculine gender identity may play a female gender role either consistently or occasionally. Sexual behaviour, which lies dormant until puberty, is clearly related to gender identity and role, but is not wholly dependent upon them for its orientation. The pattern of sexual behaviour that becomes established is dictated by the fantasy life, especially masturbation fantasies, of that person based on his previous memories; by the time of life and his physical constitution; and by the availability of sexual outlets, as well as by gender. Cultural norms and patterns establish the framework which limits the possibility for sexual expression.

Gender identity disorders

There is in these conditions a lack of congruence between biological sex and gender identity. Gender identity is usually clearly established as male or female in early childhood but, occasionally, there is a feeling of discomfort and inappropriateness about his or her biological sex, with a persistent wish to be of the opposite sex and repudiation of his own anatomy. Such children involve themselves in stereotypical behaviour of the other sex and prefer to cross-dress. The vast majority of such children eventually develop normally in gender identity and sexual behaviour; a few become predominantly homosexual; and very few indeed are eventually, as adults, established in transsexualism.

Psychotic disturbances of gender identity and role are common. In fact, with schizophrenia, the disturbance of self-image is global and virtually always affects feelings about sex and gender. Schizophrenic patients often describe delusions and hallucinations with sexual content. They quite often believe that they may be changing sex; that they are homosexual; or they believe that other people believe them to be homosexual. A schizophrenic man aged 32 believed he was changing into a woman because, 'I went back for the clock... everybody seemed to move inside my body the next day... I started to wind the clock and thought to myself, "What time did Tom say that he was going to call for me?" He was the last one I thought of going into the bedroom with. I couldn't get him out of my mind. I like the chap but I couldn't care less about him. My sister said, "Don't forget to bring in the clock". I don't know what the clock has got to do with it'. Depressive delusions may also be associated with gender, and these have the usual nihilistic or guilt-ridden content.

TRANSSEXUALISM

In this condition there is a disturbance of body image with a disorder of core gender identity; a discrepancy between anatomical sex and the gender the person ascribes to himself. Wearing clothing of the opposite sex (transvestism) occurs as a means of personal gratification without genital excitement in transsexualism. It is much commoner in biological males than females, but occurs in both sexes. The sufferer from this anomaly feels he should have been of the other gender, 'a female spirit trapped in a male body', and is quite unconvinced by scientific tests that show him to be indisputably male. The strength of this bizarre conviction is described in *Conundrum* by Jan Morris with literary éclat: 'I was three or perhaps four years old when I realised that I had been born into the wrong body, and should really be a girl... through each year my every instinct seemed to become more feminine, my entombment within the male physique more terrible to me'.

Another transsexual described himself:

> I know that I am biologically a man but it is all a horrible freak of nature. Really I am a woman and by some accident I have got a male body. I think as a woman and have female feelings and interests, and am only comfortable when wearing women's clothes and in a feminine job. So, genuinely, I am a woman... I am not against homosexuals although I am not one myself. When I have sex with a man, you must remember that I am really a woman.

The transsexual may even succeed in persuading his partner about the 'mistake' of his body. His belief is an *over-valued idea*, often taken to an extreme degree. He may change his name to a feminine one by deed poll, change the description of sex on his employment card and seek surgery to achieve 'restitution to my rightful appearance'.

Transsexualists describe their feelings about their body as having been present from early childhood: the feeling of comfort and 'rightness' they experienced when wearing their sister's dress; how they 'fell naturally' into female pursuits and interests. The difference of self-image from the biological sex is usually, in their own account, clearly established before puberty. In the development of the condition a mutually dependent relationship with the mother and an absent or abnormal father has often been described. Background family dynamics, of dependence upon a dominant mother and a weak or absent father, are by no means universal for transsexuals and, of course, may precede entirely normal sexual development.

Many transsexuals experience disturbance in their life situation from personality disorder, but transsexualism is also compatible with a stable way of life. A biological female aged 45 had lived for over 20 years as the masculine proprietor of a hardware shop in a small country town. He lived with his sister and brother-in-law and their family and did all the carpentry, plumbing, and painting jobs about the house. The family accepted his gender as 'a male person'. His presenting complaint to his doctor was that if he needed to go to a Public Convenience at a football match, he could not use the male toilet, and he was in danger with the law in the female one. Although he showed no other psychological abnormality at extensive psychiatric interview, at a fifteen-year follow-up he had killed himself.

Transsexuals usually describe difficulties in adjustment at school and they tend to have jobs below their intellectual level. If married, the male transsexual tends to be envious of his wife's femininity, pregnancy and motherhood. The transsexual is repelled by his external genitalia and he repudiates his biological sex. Their intense preoccupation with feminine pursuits is often a caricature of womanhood; a pretentious consciousness of femininity unusual in women. They tend, if biologically male, to have a stereotyped male attitude to what it is to be female–a transsexual with muscular, male physique expatiated on the delights of having silky underwear next to the skin and how 'it is so feminine'; another considered an idyllic existence was to sit at home in the evening knitting woollen baby clothes.

Sexual deviation

Most of the descriptive accounts in this area are concerned with the nature of the behaviour rather than the subjective experience of the person who carried out that behaviour. The phenomenologist is concerned with such questions as–why did this person carry out this sexual behaviour; and why now? Interest lies in the current subjective state of the individual and in understanding the background from which it emerged. Most of the answers to the questions will only be revealed on detailed phenomenological enquiry; unfortunately such enquiry is often omitted in favour of behavioural analysis and symptomatic treatment. Figure 14.1 represents graphically a notion of Scott's concerning the relationship between deviant sexuality and society.

The definition of sexual perversion (deviation) ascribed to Scott (1964) and quoted by Wakeling (1979) is as follows:

> The elements of a comprehensive definition of sexual perversion should include sexual activity or fantasy directed towards orgasm other than genital intercourse with a willing partner of the opposite sex and of similar maturity, persistently recurrent, not merely a substitute for preferred behaviour made difficult by the immediate environment and contrary to the generally accepted norm of sexual behaviour in the community.

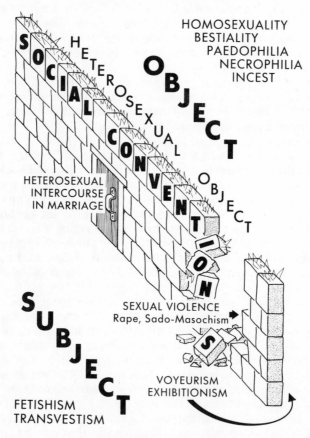

Fig. 14.1 Deviant sexual activity

The types of sexual deviation listed below are categorized according to the predominant behaviour, but there is overlap between different types of behaviour, and within each type there is much variation in pattern, attitude and socio-cultural aspects. Phenomenological description of self-experience associated with these behaviours varies from the aggressively political stance of some homosexuals that theirs is normal behaviour, to the extreme of guilt and self-loathing sometimes culminating in suicide, which may occur with any deviation. Fantasies of domination and destruction are more serious predictors of violent sexual acts than sexual arousal alone; the feature of these behaviours is that violent fantasy is required for sexual excitement.

Masturbation

This is mentioned to demonstrate how what is regarded within the social context as deviant will change in response to alterations of attitude in society. Masturbation in the nineteenth century was not only regarded as sexual deviation, but a substantial cause of serious physical and mental illness, and was recognized in its own right to be a dangerous disease entity (Englehardt, 1981). This should make us wary of too readily labelling what we regard as unacceptable as deviant, mentally ill or pathological. Much of the psychopathology, especially anxiety and depression, of those caught in the act of masturbation one hundred years ago could be ascribed to the social sanctions and dire consequences attributed to it in the public, and medical, mind rather than to the act itself.

HOMOSEXUALITY

There has been debate as to whether homosexuality should be regarded as deviation and classified as mental illness, and some have considered it as an alternative form of normality. The International Classification of Diseases (World Health Organization, 1977) includes it; while DSM III (American Psychiatric Association, 1980) omits it. However, the latter includes within its classification *ego-dystonic homosexuality* where the individual explicitly states that the sustained pattern of homosexual arousal is unwanted and a source of distress, and there is a desire to acquire heterosexual arousal.

Homosexuality is the preference for sexual behaviour with a member of one's own rather than the opposite sex, either in fact or in fantasy, or in both. There is not necessarily disturbance of gender identity, but such effeminate male homosexuals have conflicts concerning masculinity and femininity (Rosen, 1979). There is often dissonance of gender in that the gender identity is usually clearly male, but the role is construed by the person himself as female.

The factors contributing to male homosexuality have been summarized by Bancroft (1975) as 'push' and 'pull' factors. The 'push' factors involve anxiety about the heterosexual role. This may be based on learned reluctance of involement in hetero-sexual contact, incestuous feelings towards the mother, lack of confidence in sexual potency, fear of failure in heterosexual relationships or impaired gender identity with fear of rejection of his masculinity by women. The 'pull' factors include sexual drive, the feeling of need for a one-to-one emotional relationship, self-esteem engendered by the partner's attraction, eroticization of a person who is otherwise a threatening object, and material gain. Bancroft stresses that an important determinant of whether a person continues with homosexual behaviour is his ability to tolerate the idea of himself as homosexual; the challenge to his self-esteem may outweigh the positive reinforcement he experiences.

In female homosexuality, there is a definite preference for erotic attraction to another female, commonly implying some physical expression (Kenyon, 1975). Disturbance in gender identity is not usually conspicuous, but gender role is often quite markedly masculine. *Lesbians* more often described disturbance in their early life than heterosexual women, with a poor relationship with a mother who was more likely to have died prematurely or had mental illness. They also described more often poor relationships with the father, disturbed parental marriage, and an unhappy childhood. Family attitudes towards sex were less accepting; they had rarely received sex instruction from their mother and a quarter reported a family history of homosexuality. Lesbians were more likely to have experienced a traumatic heterosexual approach during childhood. More of the lesbian group felt that they were not fully feminine, and their lifestyle and choice of occupation had been more likely to result in proximity and access to other women.

Certainly since the Kinsey Reports, in which many thousands of Americans were questioned about their sexual behaviour (Kinsey *et al.*, 1948 & 1953) it has been realized that there are gradations from exclusive homosexuality to exclusive heterosexuality, as shown in Table 14.1, and there may be a discrepancy between fantasy and practice in the relative proportions. Also, homosexuality and heterosexuality are not fixed and immutable: there is the

Table 14.1 The Kinsey scale

0	Exclusively heterosexual
1	Predominantly heterosexual, only incidentally homosexual
2	Predominantly heterosexual, but more than incidentally homosexual
3	Equally heterosexual and homosexual
4	Predominantly homosexual, but more than incidentally heterosexual
5	Predominantly homosexual, but incidentally heterosexual
6	Exclusively homosexual

possibility of change in both directions, and this is influenced by environmental/social and internal/psychological factors. A person who has not previously manifested homosexual experience may do so for the first time, even in late middle-age, in response to some life crisis, especially if the problem is associated with confidence in himself as a mature and competent adult or with marital difficulties. A person who has shown homosexual practice for decades may change to heterosexual identity, initially, and practice subsequently–for example, in association with religious conversion (Pattison & Pattison, 1980). The cognitive change precedes behavioural change, which precedes orientation or preference. Because of this possibility of change it is better to use the word *homosexual* as an adjective rather than a noun; a person is not *an* homosexual, although he or she may regard themselves as having homosexual orientation.

The vast majority of those whose sexual practice is homosexual will not consult a psychiatrist and make no longstanding complaint of psychiatric symptoms. Those who do make complaint specifically related to their homosexuality (ego-dystonic) are most likely to do so on one or both of two grounds: (1) feelings of guilt that they are unable to expunge; this relates to their background social, cultural and religious beliefs about the nature of relationships; and (2) breakdown of relationships. For a variety of reasons, homosexual relationships are brittle, jealousies intense and severe feelings of loss and abandonment occur frequently when such relationships are severed.

A recent example of dysphoric mood associated directly with homosexuality is the fear of Acquired Immune Deficiency Syndrome (AIDS). The syndrome of fear of AIDS may be very similar, in its psychological symptoms, to the disease itself in the early stages, as anxiety and depression may be prominent in either (Miller *et al.*, 1985). In AIDS the sufferer feels lethargic, loses appetite and weight, and sweats excessively. There is an increasing concern among homosexual men concerning the development of AIDS and there are some who show a pseudo-AIDS syndrome, of psychogenic cause, which can result in considerable disability.

Writing in 1986, the spectre of an AIDS epidemic among homosexual men in the next few years has all the ingredients for epidemic anxiety—a discrete, vulnerable subculture who communicate both the infection and the mass neurosis:

> The male gay community is gripped with fear of AIDS. There is a widespread folk-myth that... AIDS has been sent as retribution... The anonymous, and semi-anonymous, nature of much male gay sex—and the extent of recreational sex—means that many gay men simply do not know whether or not they have had sex with someone who is now suffering from AIDS—or with someone who has had sex with someone who is now suffering from AIDS—or with... and so it goes on (Macourt, 1985).

OTHER FORMS OF SEXUAL DEVIATION

These are termed paraphilias in the Diagnostic and Statistical Manual of Mental Disorders (American Psychiatric Association). Like homosexuality, these forms of behaviour are statistically abnormal, and as attitudes to sexual behaviour are emotionally charged in society, deviation from the norm, abnormal behaviour, is regarded in a pejorative way: there is a marked social stigma. Subjective experience of deviance in sexual behaviour is determined by the social context. This has been categorized by Gagnon and Simon (1967) into three types:

1 *Normal* deviance, including such behaviour as masturbation, pre-marital intercourse, and oral sex which have been in the past and are still, in some communities, regarded as deviant.
2 *Subcultural* deviance, including homosexuality and transsexualism, where although the larger society rejects this behaviour as deviant, an accepting subculture can be found.
3 *Individual* deviance where no such subculture exists, for instance with exhibitionism or incest. Within this classification individual deviance is seen to carry a much higher risk of ostracism, alienation and consequent psychiatric symptoms.

Psychological symptoms are common for many different forms of behaviour, and are especially related to: feelings about oneself—frequently guilt, shame and disgust; and, problems with relationships—concentration upon these behaviours as the predominant sexual activity will adversely affect a long-term sexual and loving relationship.

Bestiality (zoophilia)

This describes any type of sexual intercourse with animals; it is a criminal offence. It is most likely to be indulged in by those of limited intellectual capacity and restricted social outlet for whom access to animals is easy; for example, a shy, mentally handicapped, adolescent boy living on a farm.

Paedophilia

Paedophilia is defined as 'an exaggerated affection for children' (Critchley, 1978), and 'the expressed desire for immature sexual gratification with a pre-pubertal child' (Mohr *et al.*, 1964). An adult engages in sexual activity with a child of the same or opposite sex. *Paederasty* is anal intercourse practised by adults with boys. The adult in such activity is guilty of a criminal offence and physical contact of a sexual kind is regarded as an assault, even though the majority of such actions are not violent in nature. Where the child is an older girl (over 12), the offender is often a young male, relatively indiscriminate about sexual partners, but neither consistently deviant nor psychiatrically ill. For younger children below the age of puberty, the adult is likely to be substantially older than the child, more consistently interested in sexual activity with children, and more likely to show psychiatric illness such as schizophrenia, hypomania, alcoholism, dementia or mental handicap (Bancroft).

Paedophilia is associated with extreme social disapproval and, despite recent attempts by those involved to establish a subculture, such people feel themselves to be utterly rejected. Severe depressive reaction is associated with shame and self-loathing; suicide is not uncommon. In prison such individuals require protection from serious physical assaults by their fellow inmates.

Transvestism

This is the persistent wearing of clothes of the opposite sex. Usually the cross-dresser is a heterosexual man who carries out the behaviour for the purpose of sexual excitement. However, the term encompasses all types of cross-dressing from occasional, solitary wearing of female clothes or more persistent wearing of, for example, one female undergarment, to the regular wearing by a male of entirely female clothing.

Transvestism is carried out for the following reasons or in these contexts:

1   In entertainment or theatre, as female impersonators.
2   To provoke heterosexual erotic excitement as part of fetishistic, masturbatory or coital ritual (a man was impotent in intercourse with his wife unless he was wearing high-heeled feminine shoes).
3   Within homosexual relationships cross-dressing has a symbolic significance. The aim is not to simulate the opposite sex, but rather to carry out a burlesque, pointing fun at the image of the opposite sex (Brierley, 1979). There is also the political posture of establishing the right of the homosexual not to conform to the social conventions of his or her own sex.
4   Exhibitionistic cross-dressing occurs in which a man dressed partly in female clothes exposes himself to a female person. The intention, again, is not to pass as a female but to frighten the victim and express a hostile sexual message in the context of relationship difficulties with women.

5 Cross-dressing has been used as a device; for example, to escape from prison, to serve in a one-sex profession, or to gain entry to a harem!
6 Gratification of social role without sexual excitement is the form transvestism takes in transsexualism.

In all these situations, except perhaps (5), it is vastly more common for biological males to wear female clothes, than vice versa. However, this could be challenged with the undoubtedly true contention that it is much easier for females to wear male (or nearly masculine) garments without social disapproval. Such well-known behaviour as the cross-dressing of Joan of Arc is quite exceptional; most forms of sexual deviation are predominantly male.

Exhibitionism

The main sexual pleasure and gratification is derived from exposure of the genitals to a person of the opposite sex (Snaith, 1983a). This is the commonest of sexual offences; from the victim's point of view the behaviour is a nuisance but not dangerous. Whilst exhibitionism is predominantly male, the offence of *indecent exposure* is confined to men; this is perhaps more of a cultural context, rather than a difference of individual experience between the sexes. The victim of indecent exposure is female, adult or child, and there is often an intention to surprise, shock or even insult, the observer. The exhibitionist exposes his genitals and may masturbate whilst doing so; he may return regularly to the same spot where passers by will see him, and repeat his behaviour persistently, despite numerous court appearances and punishments. The compulsive nature of the behaviour is strongly marked in that there is an overriding compulsion to act in some way, even though the individual himself recognizes the act as senseless. It is quite exceptional for such people to proceed to any other type of sexual deviation. Such individuals are often passive, inadequate men with problems in relationships and low self-esteem; they may show personality disorder of asthenic or inadequate type.

Fetishism

Etymologically this means 'the worship of inanimate objects' (Christie-Brown, 1983), but implies repeated sexual preoccupation and excitement with non-living objects; these come to take central importance in achieving orgasm. Fetishes may be articles of clothing, perhaps shoes of the opposite sex; substances and textures, for example, rubber or shiny black plastic; or even parts of the body, such as hair or nails. To be regarded as deviant, fetishism must be essential for orgasm, and causing problems, for instance in the relationship between partners; it may occur within the context of sexual intercourse or masturbation. Fetishism is almost exclusively male.

The sexual behaviour may involve masturbation using the fetish alone, or the fetish may be incorporated within sexual activities involving another person.

Voyeurism

In order to achieve sexual excitement, as the preferred or exclusive method, such a person repetitively looks at unsuspecting people who are naked, getting undressed or engaged in sexual activity ('Peeping Tom'). No other sexual contact with the observed individual is attempted; masturbation may take place during viewing or afterwards whilst recalling the memory. The voyeur often has fantasies of humiliating or embarrassing the victims with the knowledge that they have been observed.

Sado-masochism

Sexual arousal is in response to the infliction of pain, psychological humiliation or ritualized dominance or submission. Sadism is the infliction of pain or suffering upon another for sexual excitement, and masochism the passive experience of being made to suffer to achieve sexual stimulation. The latter often involves submission in various forms of *bondage*, being tied up and constrained, often associated with *flagellation*. Sado-masochistic fantasies, of a mild kind, occur during intercourse or masturbation in both sexes, often within marriage, but more violent fantasies and practices are predominantly or exclusively male in nature. Sado-masochism is quite common among those who are exclusively homosexual; among those who are heterosexual, it frequently results in marital breakdown.

The polymorphously perverse

The various sexual preferences, above, are not necessarily exclusive to any one individual. Thus a person who shows one form of deviation is more likely to find sexual arousal in another–sadism, masochism, transvestism, fetishism. Such a person, showing many different abnormalities is described as *polymorphously perverse*.

Necrophilia

Necrophilia, which is extremely rare, involves achieving sexual excitement through contact with a dead body; it may occur in association with homicide.

SEXUAL VIOLENCE–RAPE

Rape is sexual intercourse by a male with a female, not his wife, who at the time does not consent. For the act to be regarded legally as rape, it must involve vaginal penetration by the penis, and the man must be aged over 14.

Buggery refers to anal intercourse and is more commonly homosexual; buggery with violence is endemic in some prison populations, where it is more an expression of physical domination than sexual gratification.

Heterosexual assault, rape, usually involves physical violence, sometimes extreme. Violence is usually a more important part of the motivation than sexual excitement. Holmstrom and Burgess (1980) considered that sexual assault had four principal meanings: (1) power and control over the victim, (2) expression of anger or hatred, (3) in group rape, camaraderie experienced by rapists, and (4) sexual experience, which was never the dominant theme. On the other hand, the violence of sexual assault is itself found to be sexually stimulating. Rapists in prison were found to develop erection during audio description of rape scenes, while non-rapist prisoners did not (Abel *et al.*, 1978).

In terms of mental symptoms associated with sexual behaviour, the victim of rape should, of course, also be considered. Although the characteristics of rape victims are not dissimilar to other victims of violence, in the victim's subjective experience this form of violence has different implications. The way it is regarded by the public and dealt with by the police and others often produces feelings of guilt and shame that exacerbate what is already an appalling experience. Rape and its consequences are a significant factor for victims in producing long-term psychiatric morbidity and psychosocial disability.

INCEST

Under the Sexual Offences Act, 1956, it is an offence for a man to have sexual intercourse with a woman whom he knows to be his granddaughter, daughter, sister (or half-sister), or mother; and it is an offence for a woman over the age of 16 years to permit a man of similar affinity to have intercourse with her by her consent (Bluglass, 1979). Incest probably occurs in all social class groups, the mean intelligence of offenders is probably higher than that of other sexual offenders and mental illness is unusual; although a substantial minority of offenders show such abnormalities of personality as being violent and irascible, maladjusted at work, alcoholic and having a previous criminal record. There is also a relatively normal group of otherwise well-adjusted individuals.

Brother–sister and mother–son relationships are rare; father-daughter incest is the most common type, both in fact and to come to court. Bluglass considered the following to be predisposing factors:

1　A man returning home after many years of separation to find an ageing wife and a young daughter, who now seems almost a stranger and also a temptation.
2　The loss of a wife by divorce, separation, or death, leaving a bereaved father alone with an adolescent daughter who becomes a substitute wife providing love, solace and sexual comfort.
3　Gross overcrowding, physical proximity, and alcoholism leading to sexual intimacy.
4　A lack of social contact outside the family as a result of poverty and geographical remoteness.
5　Anxiety associated with a lack of sexual potency.
6　Marital disharmony and rejection or a decrease in marital sexual activity.
7　Psychopathic characteristics of poor impulse control, aggressiveness, and lack of guilt feelings, with or without any of the above.

The father may have severe feelings of guilt and depression whilst the relationship is still continuing and after discovery and sentencing. Such depression will require treatment and there is considerable risk of suicide. The daughter may also show subsequent psychiatric disability: four out of twenty-six daughters subsequently showed frank psychiatric symptoms; eleven developed character disorder; and five frigidity or aversion to sexual relations with their husbands (Lukianowicz, 1972).

Psychosexual dysfunction

Symptoms associated with 'normal' heterosexual intercourse are extremely frequent; the more the interviewer allows the patient to express him- or herself freely, the more likely they are to be described. Symptoms may be associated with the functions of the genital organs during intercourse (sexual dysfunction), with the subjective feelings during intercourse (sexual difficulties), and with the sexual relationship; of course, these areas overlap.

SEXUAL DYSFUNCTION

For men, this includes erectile and ejaculatory difficulties; for women, various inhibitions of sexual excitement and orgasm, and also genital pain and discomfort occur.

Male sexual dysfunction

Lack of, or inhibited, sexual excitement during intended sexual activity is manifested by partial or complete failure to achieve or maintain an erection throughout sexual intercourse (*erectile dysfunction*–previously *impotence*). There may also be *delay* or *absence of* ejaculation following an adequate phase of sexual excitement. *Premature ejaculation* may take place before the man wishes it, and clearly out of his control (Cooper, 1970). When any of these symptoms or more than one occurs persistently, this would be regarded as dysfunction. This may be responsible for causing further symptoms such as anxiety and loss of self-esteem, or result from psychological symptoms such as anxiety or fatigue. It can be seen how sexual dysfunction and neurotic illness become a mutually reinforcing vicious circle.

Female sexual dysfunction

In women *inhibited sexual excitement* (previously *frigidity*) is shown by partial or complete failure to achieve or maintain the lubrication and swelling of the genitalia during the sexual act. There may also be persistent delay or absence of orgasm following normal sexual excitement and activity. Coitus may also be associated with persistent genital pain (*dyspareunia*) or involuntary spasm of the vaginal musculature (*vaginismus*). As in the male, this may both cause further psychological symptoms and result from them.

SEXUAL DIFFICULTIES AND THE SEXUAL RELATIONSHIP

Doctors tend to classify symptoms into the above categories of dysfunction. However, patients regard as more serious in promoting sexual dissatisfaction such difficulties as inability to relax, lack of interest in sex, distaste or revulsion: 'too little foreplay', 'too little attention after intercourse' (Frank *et al.*, 1978). These symptoms are extremely common: the subjective experience during intercourse; the interaction with the partner and other aspects, such as fantasy, is as important as the more mechanical elements involved.

   The sexual relationship with the partner is, of course, crucial. One cannot consider, categorize or treat the sexual symptoms of one partner without taking into account the characteristics, attitudes and expectations of the other. If one partner is either experiencing symptoms or dissatisfaction in the sexual relationship, the other partner may also be dissatisfied.

Marital dysfunction

This subject is discussed here briefly because such symptoms are undoubtedly presented to the psychiatrist frequently; however, fuller description and details of practical management are outside our scope. Dominian (1980) has reviewed this topic.

Marital problems have repercussions outside as well as inside the sexual sphere, and for others as well as the partners themselves. Thus, disturbance of relationships within the family, and especially within the marriage, is seen as a more potent factor in promoting later emotional and neurotic difficulties for children than separation of the child from a parent alone (Rutter, 1972). Marital discord, separation and divorce is often due to the disparity between giving and receiving affection, an imbalance between care-giving and the need for attachment. When one partner in a marriage suffers from mental illness there is a much increased likelihood for the other partner also to be affected (Hagnell & Kreitman, 1974). Diagnosis, then, is usually neurosis or personality disorder for the wives, and frequently alcoholism in the husbands.

Vulnerability for marital disorder occurs especially within the earliest years of marriage, with nearly half of all divorces in the first nine years. The highest rate for separation is within the first year of marriage and, for divorce, in the third year. Marked changes in the role of women in society and of attitudes towards marriage have contributed to the increase in breakdown. The change of attitudes towards marriage has been described by Dominian as a change from *institution* to *relationship*. There have been changes in the law facilitating divorce in several countries; and there has also been an increase in prosperity and longevity (with consequent increase of very long marriages), and a decrease in the number of children per family.

In a person with diminished self-esteem, expectations from relationships are blighted by past failure and, through feeling incompetent, such a person fails to build a relationship. A chronic need to be appreciated by other people may be manifested as excessive dependence, or attempting to deal with conflict by extreme self-sufficiency, preventing any sort of closeness developing which may damage the relationship. Alternatively, there may be problems in the ability to trust the partner, which may show itself in a studied callousness, demonstrating no apparent need for the other partner. Learning how to form emotional bonds occurs early in childhood and longstanding disturbance of the ability to make relationships may be due to a defect at this stage.

Marriage problems are very common amongst psychiatric patients: for example, as agoraphobic symptoms remit in treatment, marital problems which originally were denied become more obvious. Such a wife may describe her husband as 'golden' because of his resigned tolerance towards her neuroticism, but, despite a relationship in which arguing does not take place, there are frustrations and resentments in the marriage, and the wife feels unable to express her feelings, or 'be herself'. There is a tendency for neurotic people to marry each other, and also for inappropriate behaviour arising from one partner's neuroticism to be the stress, provoking neurotic symptoms in the other. Sometimes the choice of partner is an inappropriate way of trying to make up for longlasting deficiencies in the individual. Such misguided union may well end in breakdown.

Marital problems are rarely presented to the doctor straightforwardly. Other symptoms are described first, and only in discussion do the difficulties within the marriage loom large. Any of the whole gamut of neurotic, psychosomatic, or drug and alcohol-dependent symptoms may be associated with marital dysfunction. Insomnia is particularly frequent, as are also depression and anxiety, and somatic complaints such as abdominal pains, headache, frequency of micturition, dyspareunia and backache. While the wife is likely to present with psychosomatic symptoms, the husband often denies his marriage problems, escaping into the solace of alcohol excess. More than half of alcoholic men, by the time they receive treatment, are already separated or divorced. Problems in the marriage are both a result of the excess drinking and also a cause of it.

Attempted suicide is extremely common following marital difficulties. In a study of self-poisoning, 68% of married men and 60% of married women described marital disharmony as the major precipitating factor (Kessel, 1965). Thirty per cent of the marriages of the men and 26% of the women had broken down; and in 17% the break-up had been within a month of the suicide attempt. In a study of parasuicide from Oxford (Bancroft *et al.*, 1977) a decade later, an even higher proportion of married men and women complained of marital problems. Half of the married men described an extra-marital affair in the previous twelve months; very frequently a quarrel had preceded the suicide attempt by a few days, and was considered to have provoked the act. Completed suicide is also related to marital difficulties; an established and continuing marriage relationship offers some protection against suicide.

Problems of personality are a potent source of difficulty in marriage, either in provoking disharmony or becoming manifest because of marriage problems. This may be true of any of the recognized personality types (Chapter 20), for instance paranoid, dysthymic, schizoid, or obsessional.

Environmental factors such as financial difficulties, discordant work patterns or interests, relationships with the in-laws and so on, may precipitate marital problems. One spouse may have a neurotic need to look after a sick person, and marries the other because of his handicap. His recovery may frustrate her need for this dependence. Conflict over diverse educational and intellectual interests may occur; or disagreement arises because one partner has a completely different approach to child-rearing from the spouse.

Disorders of pregnancy and the puerperium

It remains an enigma why epidemiological studies should regularly show for most mental illnesses a considerable excess of females over males. Biological, social and psychological explanations have been given. There are some disorders specifically associated with female sex, gender and role. Thus, psychological symptoms may be associated with the menarche, with menstruation and amenorrhoea, with pregnancy and the puerperium and with the menopause. Some of these have been mentioned in Chapter 5. These disorders are only discussed briefly here and the reader is referred to a review by Snaith (1983b).

DISORDERS OF PREGNANCY

Pregnancy is the most dramatic and rapid change in bodily form that occurs in adult life, and there is realistically a gross change in body image accompanying it. The subsequent change of role of the woman becoming a mother further accentuates the changing self-image through pregnancy. It is not surprising, therefore, that there are often disturbances such as anxiety, depression, hypochondriasis or hysterical conversion in this process. It is more surprising that these disturbances may affect the husband as well as the wife herself. The abnormality of self-awareness when a husband experiences obstetric symptoms during his wife's pregnancy or parturition is called the *Couvade syndrome* (Enoch & Trethowan, 1979).

The Couvade syndrome takes its name from a ritual that has been observed in different cultures over many centuries in which the father of the child to be born mimics the behaviour of his wife through labour. At the onset of her labour, he is put to bed, simulates labour pains and remains 'convalescent' for some days after 'delivery'. Gross forms of the Couvade syndrome are very rare, but minor symptoms in the husband directly associated with his wife's pregnancy are quite common. It has been described in other members of the family.

Couvade symptoms in the husband occur from the third month of pregnancy onwards. They are most frequent in the third and ninth month. Symptoms complained of are very variable and include loss of appetite, toothache, nausea and vomiting (often morning sickness), indigestion, vague abdominal pains, constipation and diarrhoea. The chronological relationship with the wife's pregnancy is more important for making the diagnosis than the nature of the symptoms. Anxiety, tension, insomnia, and instability are common complaints and there is preoccupation with his wife's condition. The symptom can be seen as a *conversion* of the husband's anxiety over his wife's health into somatic symptoms. It is not delusional: the husband with Couvade syndrome does not believe himself to be pregnant!

Pseudocyesis is the occurrence of a false pregnancy. It can occur both in women and men, although understandably much more commonly in women. Hysterical pseudocysesis occurs quite dramatically, with swelling of the abdomen to simulate a full term pregnancy. This disappears under general anaesthetic, but the muscular spasm producing depression of the diaphragm and lumbar lordosis returns as the patient regains consciousness. Delusions of pregnancy in men have been described in schizophrenia, depressive psychosis, senile dementia, cerebral syphilis, and following encephalitis. The delusion remains at the level of a fixed belief without somatic concomitants. Similar delusions of pregnancy occur in psychotic women, who may be post-menopausal or virginal, or both.

Less exotic but more common symptoms associated with pregnancy are the presence of anxiety and depression. This is not uncommon during pregnancy. It may be endogenous or reactive and, if the latter, is due to pregnancy itself or its associations. Psychotic disturbance may occur during pregnancy but is more common in the puerperium.

PUERPERAL DISORDERS

The three usual presentations are 'maternity blues', puerperal psychosis or chronic depressive disorder (Gelder *et al.*, 1983). The term *puerperal*, referring to the life epoch, is to be preferred to post-partum or post-natal, which latter should logically refer to the baby.

Between one-half and two-thirds of women experience a brief episode of lability of mood, tearfulness and irritability, often starting on the third or fourth day after normal delivery. The condition is more common in primigravida, and in those who previously suffered premenstrual tension or depressive symptoms before delivery.

Puerperal psychosis is not a distinct disease entity; affective, schizophrenic or organic psychoses occur, but now with good obstetrics and nutrition, and asepsis, 80% of cases are affective. Affective features may occur with schizophrenic psychoses and altered consciousness and disorientation, with either affective or schizophrenic psychoses, to a greater extent than with non-puerperal disorders. Puerperal psychoses often have a very acute onset and are florid in their symptoms; mania is relatively common amongst puerperal affective psychoses.

In a few patients, depressive symptomatology of lesser severity may persist for months, or sometimes even for years, after childbirth. This is associated with the changes in lifestyle, looking after a baby, changes in relationships with husband and others and alteration of self-image. It is more frequent in those who have previously experienced affective disorder.

References

Abel GG, Barlow DH, Blanchard EB & Guild D (1978) The components of rapists' sexual arousal. In Neale JM, Davison GC & Price KP (eds) *Contemporary Readings in Psychopathology*, 2nd Edn, pp. 217–233. New York: John Wiley.

American Psychiatric Association (1980) *Diagnostic and Statistical Manual of Mental Disorders*, 3rd Edn. Washington: American Psychiatric Association.

Bancroft J (1974) *Deviant Sexual Behaviour*. Oxford: Clarendon Press.

Bancroft JHH (1975) Homosexuality in the male. In Silverstone T & Barraclough B (eds) *Contemporary Psychiatry*. Ashford: Headley Brothers.

Bancroft J (1983) *Human Sexuality and its Problems*. Edinburgh: Churchill Livingstone.

Bancroft J, Skrimshire A, Casson J, Harvard-Watts O & Reynolds F (1977) People who deliberately poison or injure themselves: their problems and their contacts with helping agencies. *Psychological Medicine* 7, 289–304.

Bluglass RS (1979) Incest. *British Journal of Hospital Medicine* 22, 152–57.

Brierley H (1979) *Transvestism: A Handbook with Case Studies for Psychologists, Psychiatrists and Counsellors*. Oxford: Pergamon Press.

Christie-Brown JRW (1983) Paraphilias: Sadomasochism, fetishism, transvestism and transsexuality. *British Journal of Psychiatry 143*, 227–31.

Cooper AJ (1970) Guide to treatment and short-term prognosis of male potency disorders in hospital and general practice. *British Medical Journal i*, 157–59.

Critchley M (1978) *Butterworths Medical Dictionary*, 2nd Edn. London: Butterworths.

Dominian J (1980) *Marital Pathology: An Introduction for Doctors, Counsellors and Clergy*. London: Darton Longmann & Todd & the British Medical Association.

Engelhardt HT (1981) The disease of masturbation: Values and the concept of disease. In Caplan AL, Engelhardt HT & McCartney JJ (eds) *Concepts of Health and Disease*, pp. 267–280. Reading, Massachusetts: Addison-Wesley.

Enoch MD & Trethowan WH (1979) *Uncommon Psychiatric Syndromes*. Bristol: John Wright.

Feldman P & MacCulloch M (1980) *Human Sexual Behaviour*. Chichester: John Wiley.

Frank E, Anderson C & Rubinstein D (1978) Frequency of sexual dysfunction in 'normal' couples. *New England Journal of Medicine* 299, 111–5.

Gagnon JH & Simon W (1967) *Sexual Deviance*. New York: Harper & Row.

Gelder M, Gath D & Mayou R (1983) *Oxford Textbook of Psychiatry*. Oxford: Oxford University Press.

Hagnell O & Kreitman N (1974) Mental illness in married pairs in a total population. *British Journal of Psychiatry 125*, 293–302.

Holmstrom LL & Burgess AW (1980) Sexual behaviour of assailants during reported rapes. *Archives of Sexual Behaviour 9*, 427–46.

Kenyon FE (1975) Homosexuality in the female. In Silverstone T & Barraclough B (eds) *Contemporary Psychiatry*, pp. 185–200. Ashford: Headley Brothers.

Kessel WIN (1965) Self poisoning. *British Medical Journal 2*, 1265–70 & 1336–40.

Kinsey AC, Pomeroy WB & Martin CE (1948) *Sexual Behaviour in the Human Male*. Philadelphia: Saunders.

Kinsey AC, Pomeroy WB, Martin CE & Gebhard PH (1953) *Sexual Behaviour in the Human Female*. Philadelphia: Saunders.

Lukianowicz N (1972) Incest: Part I: Paternal incest; Part II: Other types of incest. *British Journal of Psychiatry 120*, 301–14.

Macourt MPA (1985) AIDS, Gay Liberation and Pastoral Care: a problem concerning the fusion of pastoral care with an emerging ideology in a time of conflict. *Pastoral Studies Conference, University of Birmingham*.

Miller D, Green J, Farmer R & Carroll G (1985) A 'Pseudo-AIDS' syndrome following from fear of AIDS. *British Journal of Psychiatry 146*, 550–1.

Mohr JW, Turner RE & Jerry MB (1964) *Paedophilia and Exhibitionism*. London: Oxford University Press.

Morris J (1974) *Conundrum*. London: Faber & Faber.

Pattison EM & Pattison ML (1980) 'Ex-gays': Religious mediated change in homosexuals. *American Journal of Psychiatry 137*, 1553–62.

Rosen I (1979) *Sexual Deviation*, 2nd Edn. Oxford: Oxford University Press.

Rutter M (1972) *Maternal Deprivation Reassessed*. Harmondsworth: Penguin.

Scott PD (1964) Definition, Classification, Prognosis and Treatment. In Rosen I (ed.) *The Pathology and Treatment of Sexual Deviation*. London: Oxford University Press.

Snaith RP (1983a) Exhibitionism: A clinical conundrum *British Journal of Psychiatry 143*, 231–5.

Snaith RP (1983b) Pregnancy-related psychiatric disorder *British Journal of Hospital Medicine 29*, 450–6.

Wakeling A (1979) A General Psychiatric Approach to Sexual Deviation. In Rosen I (ed.) *Sexual Deviation*, 2nd Edn, pp. 1–28. Oxford: Oxford University Press.

World Health Organization (1977) *International Statistical Classification of Diseases, Injuries and Causes of Death*, 9th Revision. Geneva: World Health Organization.

──15──

The Psychopathology of Pain

Pain is a subjective experience which occurs only in consciousness
Bond (1976)

Since Aristotle, pain has been classified not as a perception but as a mood state and so excluded from the five senses. It is conceptually a most difficult topic, hard to describe and to categorize: the only aspect that is clear is that it represents a state of subjective suffering of the patient. But what does he mean by 'my pain': where is it and what is it? Certainly the *meaning* of the pain is more than the pain itself, and often it is the reason for the sensation being interpreted as suffering. A patient with soreness of the throat believed herself to have a cancer of the throat; her mother had died of that condition. The relation between symptoms and their meaning is not straightforward. Another patient believed herself to be suffering from venereal disease without having been exposed to the risk. But she had previously been successfully treated for Hodgkins disease. She had no fears concerning her existing, and potentially lethal, illness but only admitted consciously to fearing the impossible.

Among psychiatric patients the complaint of pain may be associated with diagnostic uncertainty (Anstee & Fleminger, 1977). Ten per cent of patients discharged from a psychiatric unit in a general hospital had an 'uncertain' diagnosis at the time of discharge: nearly one-fifth of these were complaining of pain. At long-term follow-up, nearly half of those complaining of pain remained undiagnosed; of those in which a diagnosis could by then be made, neuroses and depressive psychoses were commonest, with *atypical facial pain* and physical illness (abdominal neoplasm and coronary disease) less frequent. When pain, without known cause, is the major symptom it is very difficult to apply the usual psychiatric diagnoses.

Phenomenological aspects of the experience of pain are not well charted, although in general medicine this is, above all others, the area where phenomenology could be most helpful. The psychiatrist is often confronted with the problem of whether the pain is physical or mental, organic or functional, medical or psychiatric; and, of course, the answer is, often, both. We may then be requested to assess how much of the pain is psychogenic, although this is virtually impossible because, following Aristotle, pain is a state of mind, even when there is such an obvious cause as a haematoma under the fingernail.

Organic or psychogenic

The transmission of pain results in a subjective, conscious experience. For an account of the anatomical basis for pain and also the physiological and

214

biochemical mechanisms the reader is referred to Bond (1984). There is a threshold for pain: light pressure is perceived as touch, heavy pressure as pain. An explanation for this has been suggested in the *gate theory* of Melzack and Wall (1965), who considered that painful stimulation through the thin myelinated and unmyelinated fibres results in positive feedback in the substantia gelatinosa; this is transmitted in the lateral spinothalamic tract. However, this gate is under the influence of the higher centres which can override the local input, as demonstrated by the effect of *attention*: sometimes pain is not *felt* when attention is directed away from the affected site. Current biochemical theories are also important in accounting for the mediation of pain.

More recent theories involve the study of pre-synaptic and post-synaptic mechanisms in the central nervous system (Nathan, 1980). Electrical stimulation in various sites in the brain stem, including the medulla oblongata, periaqueductal grey matter and the hypothalamus around the third ventricle, may produce analgesia. Endogenous opiate substances (endorphins) have been discovered to inhibit nerve fibres reporting noxious events. This was initially discovered following electrical stimulation in the periaqueductal grey matter of the brain stem in rats but has subsequently been demonstrated in humans (Bond, 1976).

The temptation to regard pain simply as any other sensation creates certain dilemmas. For example, what is the subjective experience of the person who complains of severe pain with no organic pathology detectable, or the person with mild pathology who complains of excruciating pain? How does one assess the person with apparently painful injury who claims he did not notice any pain at the time?

Purely organic, physiological terms, and also psychological, emotional words have been used. Beecher (1959) believed that pain could be defined, and listed many distinguished physiologists and psychiatrists to support his case. However, Merskey (1976) considers that pain is a psychological experience, private to the individual, but tending to be described in terms of damage to the body, and so defined pain as 'an unpleasant experience which we primarily associate with tissue damage or describe in terms of such damage, or both'.

Clearly, irrespective of the physical stimulus, psychological factors are enormously important in the appreciation of pain. Doctors have frequently, through neglecting subjective evaluation, missed the important distinction between the experience of pain and the physical causes of pain (Noordenbos, 1959). The patient assumes that his pain indicates the presence of physical illness, but pain of various types is a very common symptom in many psychiatric conditions without there being physical pathology.

The experience of psychogenic pain has been associated with particular personality types (Engel, 1959). The most important traits of personality associated with pain are those of anxiousness; depressiveness and the cyclothymic personality at the depressive pole; hysterical, hypochondriacal and obsessional traits (Bond, 1976). Subjects with such personality traits to abnormal extent are especially likely to respond to life stresses with pain. Complaints of pain are common in neurosis generally, especially with chronic anxiety or hysterical traits (Merskey, 1965).

Pain commonly occurs in those patients, usually female, who complain of multiple physical symptoms in many different bodily systems but without evidence of physical disease. Such a conglomeration of symptoms, starting before the age of 30 and often continuing for decades, was described by Perley and Guze (1962). They called this condition *hysteria*, and later the label *Briquet's syndrome* was used (Woodruff *et al.*, 1971; Cloninger *et al.*, 1975); more recently, the term *somatoform disorder* has been applied (DSM III, American Psychiatric Association, 1980), but in English usage it would conform more with chronic *hypochondriacal neurosis* (World Health Organization, 1977: ICD 9, 300.7). Psychogenic pain disorder is defined in DSM III, as: 'a clinical picture in which the predominant feature is the complaint of pain, in the absence of adequate findings and in association with evidence of the etiological role of psychological factors. The disturbance is not due to any other mental disorder'.

It is important to be very careful in attempting to distinguish pain of physical origin from that which is largely psychogenic; generalizations can be dangerous. However, Trethowan (1977) considers that there are certain important differences between pain of psychiatric and organic origin. These are as follows:

1   Pain associated with psychiatric illness tends to be more diffuse and less well-localized than pain due to a physical lesion. It spreads with a non-anatomical distribution.
2   Pain is complained of as a constant feature. It may become even more severe at times but it persists unremittingly. Physical pains usually have more definite provocative agents and are relieved by various measures.
3   Psychogenic pain is clearly seen to be associated with an underlying disturbance of mood which appears to be primary both in terms of time and causation.
4   It seems to be much more difficult accurately to describe the quality of psychogenic pain. The patient is in no doubt that he is suffering, that the pain is very unpleasant and that he feels he cannot bear it. But in contrast to painful damage to a defined organ where pain may be described as burning (skin), shooting (nerve) or gripping (heart muscle), the patient with non-organic pain can find no adequate words for description.
5   A further addition to this list is the finding of progression of the severity and extent of the pain over time–unusual for a purely physically mediated pain (Tyrer, 1986).

Pain and heightened sensation

Generalized increase in sensory input may be experienced as pain. This is exemplified by hyperacousia: the patient complains of noises being uncomfortably loud. There is no objective improvement in his capacity to hear, but the threshold at which sound is perceived as unpleasantly loud is lowered. Noises, even a normal speaking voice, are described as painful to listen to.

With lysergic acid diethylamide (LSD) intense pain may be experienced in the limbs which seem to the sufferer to be twisted or contorted. Similarly, in the early stages of thiamine deficiency there may be increased sensitivity to pain. In these situations there is an alteration to perception of sensations so that they are experienced as pain.

During consciousness the person receives countless sensations from all over his body, such as itching, distension, pressure, borborygmi, mild aching, thumping, warmth, and so on. These form the *sensorium* of the body image; they make possible the location of self in space. Most of these sensations, for most of the time, escape attention. However, occasionally the person concentrates and may take action to eliminate the sensation–scratch his ear or cross his legs. Attention to such sensations, especially if linked to an unpleasant emotion, may occasion the experience of pain. Noticing the sensation results in fear and the distress of this emotion is perceived as pain.

This would appear to be the explanation for the *vital feelings* of depression, described in Chapter 16. Vital feelings are the localization of depression in a bodily organ, complained of, perhaps as pain, in the head or chest or elsewhere. On further questioning, symptoms are described as being unpleasant, painful pressure or even a feeling of misery and depression in that organ: morbid interpretations of ordinary bodily sensations. The sensation is unpleasant but normal and would be ignored in health. With disorder of affect the sensation may be morbidly interpreted as due to cancer, tuberculosis or venereal disease. There are, of course, also actual physical changes in depression; for example, slowing of peristalsis and decreased gastro-intestinal secretions, and these may also provoke unpleasant sensations such as spasm and constipation.

Diminished pain sensation and pain craving

In certain situations there is a decrease in the perception of pain. Thus, in acute drunkenness, there is diminished appreciation due to the central depressant action of alcohol, and opiates similarly are analgesic through their action on the central appreciation of pain.

Attention is also an important factor in the perception of pain. Excitement or aggression, as in footballers or soldiers, may render the subject oblivious of serious injury. When a wound has advantages to the patient, for example enabling a soldier to leave the battlefield, it causes less pain than when the injury is seen as wholly disadvantageous. Various psychological techniques can reduce the experience of pain including hypnosis, various stratagems in childbirth, placebo medication and, possibly, acupuncture. In hysterical dissociation there may be localized anaesthesia and analgesia for the affected limb; for example, the patient may describe no perception of pin-prick sensation.

A blunting and perverting of pain perception is described in severe subnormality, resulting occasionally in gross self-damage. The patient may bang his head so that there is chronic haematoma formation, bite himself, or otherwise harm himself repeatedly causing permanent damage. Meanwhile he appears to experience no pain or even discomfort. Self-damage of a gross nature also occurs sometimes in schizophrenia–for example, self-castration in a patient of ours. Self-application of constricting bands has been described in schizophrenic and organically disordered patients (Dawson-Butterworth *et al.*, 1969). These are most often applied to the left arm; despite extensive tissue damage, the patient does not complain of pain.

Self-inflicted harm occurs also in those of disturbed personality without intellectual deficiency. Prominent amongst these are the *wrist slashers*. These patients are usually female (Graff & Mallin, 1967), and typically 'an attractive, intelligent, unmarried young woman, who is either promiscuous or overtly afraid of sex, easily addicted, and unable to relate to others... she slashes her wrists indiscriminately and repeatedly at the slightest provocation, but she does not commit suicide. She feels relief with the commission of her act'. The behaviour is seen as a way of relieving internal tension that has become intolerable.

A different explanation for the damage is proposed by Gardner and Gardner (1975). They consider that female non-psychotic 'delicate self-cutters' are markedly obsessional in personality. There is a compulsive and ritualized element in repeated self-cutting which the patient has come to accept as a satisfactory way of relieving tension.

Pain without organic cause

There is a high prevalence of pain in almost all medical settings; it is a common complaint in medical, surgical, gynaecological and psychiatric practice. Recalcitrant cases may be referred to a pain clinic, and prominent amongst such referrals are those in whom no organic basis can be found to account for the complaint of pain (Tyrer, 1985). Pain in the back and in the head and face particularly are often found not to be associated with organic lesions. From 3-50% of patients have measurable psychiatric disturbance.

There is a variety of possible mechanisms to explain the presence of pain without physical disease: autonomic nervous activity may be interpreted and elaborated through fear of possible consequences; normal sensations may be experienced as painful in situations of stress, or in fear; relatively minor pain and discomfort of benign cause may be misinterpreted as being more ominous than it really is.

Classification of non-organic pain is complex. As well as occurring without other DSM III diagnosis in psychogenic pain disorder, pain also may be conspicuous with hypochondriasis, with somatoform disorder and, especially, with major depressive disorder. In Tyrer's series, two-thirds of those patients without organic cause and with measurable psychiatric disturbance were diagnosed as suffering from major depressive disorder. The remainder had personality disorders, anxiety state, hysteria and drug dependence; paraphrenia and organic brain syndrome also occurred, but rarely.

Pain without adequate organic explanation is one of the most difficult problems psychiatrists are called upon to treat. In a study of patients with pain referred to psychiatrists in a general hospital, the head and neck was the most common site, followed by the back, abdomen, arm or leg, rectum or genitalia, and chest (Pilling *et al.*, 1967). Of these medical and surgical patients, in 32% pain was the presenting complaint and it was considered that these patients 'spoke to their physicians in terms of pain or other organic symptoms rather than anxiety, depression and the like'.

It is, of course, wholly understandable that someone suffering pain should be miserable and that chronic pain or the anticipation of recurrent pain should provoke depression of mood. This is often so much taken for granted that no steps are taken to alleviate the depressed mood if the cause of the pain is obvious. However, if the perception of pain is considered to have two separate contributions–the sensory perception and the investing affect–efforts to relieve the latter, if successful, will produce a global diminution of pain. Pain can be a cause of depression, and in this situation treatment for the depression is appropriate.

There is an association between abdominal pain in childhood and the subsequent demonstration of hypochondriacal symptoms in adult life (Apley, 1975). He found such children typically to be 'highly strung, fussy and excitable', to have an increase of such symptoms as fearfulness, nocturnal enuresis, sleep disturbance and appetite difficulties, and to come from 'painful families'.

PAIN AND LOSS

The model for this topic is the *phantom limb* pain so often experienced in amputees. Pain is experienced within a limb that is not there; that is, spatially, pain is located outside the patient. However, this is not an hallucination. The person knows full well that he has lost his leg and the *feeling* of pain is inside himself. The body image takes a very long time to adjust to a change such as an amputation and it may never fully adjust. The sensory cause of the pain is probably located in the stump but its cortical perception is still represented for the intact limb, and so pain may be experienced as a painful weight on the absent foot, or the leg being twisted.

Parkes (1976) has pointed out the importance of viewing amputation in its psychological context, both for understanding the symptoms and making a prognosis.

PSYCHOGENIC FACIAL PAIN

It has been known for a long time that many patients with chronic pain at a variety of sites, do not have abnormal physical signs and do not manifest serious organic illness. Atypical facial pain is an especially frequent and intractable example, manifesting no organic signs but causing great suffering; the patient is referred from surgeon to dentist to pain clinic physician to psychiatrist, often without benefit. Such pain has often been associated with depression. Lascelles (1966) described a series of ninety-three patients suffering from prolonged facial pain, of whom the majority suffered from *atypical depression* with intense fatigue, tension and sleep disorder superimposed upon 'obsessive' personality; fifty-three of these patients responded well to antidepressant therapy.

More recently Blumer and Heilbronn (1982) have seen chronic, intractable pain without organic cause as being a variant of depressive illness. Garvey *et al.* (1983) investigated the association between headache and depression in 116 patients suffering from major depressive disorder. These patients experienced during a non-depressed period a similar rate for headache to non-depressive control subjects, but they had a markedly increased rate during depressive episodes. Feinmann *et al.* (1984) investigated the efficacy of an antidepressant, dothiepin, in the treatment of psychogenic facial pain. Seventy-one per cent of patients were free of symptoms at nine weeks, compared with 47% in a placebo group; at a twelve-month follow-up, 81% of patients were pain free. Good prognostic indicators for successful treatment included pain following an adverse life event, minimal previous surgical intervention, and freedom from pain after nine weeks' treatment. Such studies would suggest an association between facial pain without physical signs and depressive illness.

Pain and suffering

Pain is an appropriate study for the phenomenologist in that the external signs may be irrelevant and the subjective experience all important. The chief problem in assessing pain is the extraordinary difficulty a patient has in describing the quality of his pain: the greater the psychogenic component of the pain, the more difficult it is to find the right words to describe it. Sometimes, it seems that pain may be needed as a neurotic solution to a neurotic conflict: for the equilibrium to remain it is necessary for the pain to be retained. It has been considered by Trethowan that such a patient 'is not suffering from pain at all. What she is suffering from is suffering'.

There are differences between the person suffering from organically determined pain and the chronic sufferer with multiple symptoms whose pain is considered psychogenic. The latter truly suffers but does not show the physical correlates of severe pain. It seems that the state of suffering in which this person exists finds expression, dons respectability, and can only be communicated when it is transformed peripherally into a specific pain. Pain may occur with little suffering, as in the injection of local anaesthetic that, after the small prick, brings relief from a worse pain. Suffering may also occur without pain; but it may also be described as pain, and this may be the nature of many neurotic complaints of pain. This transposition of affect is wholly understandable when one considers the semantics of suffering. Suffering of all non-physical kinds–indignation, humiliation, disappointment–finds expression in pain terms: 'taking pains, feeling crushed, bruised self-esteem, rubbing salt in the wound, getting one's fingers burnt, searing remarks'. It is not just that pain is a metaphor for suffering, but in many situations suffering can only be experienced and explained by the sufferer in *pain* terms.

So the use of pain words can be construed metaphorically and the neurotic may follow this to its logical conclusion and concretize the unbearable and humiliating suffering of his daily existence into complaints of localized physical pain. The experience of pain is a physical sensation that takes on an affective component for its expression and interpretation. This affective component– suffering–may occur without the physical, and sometimes still be experienced by the person himself as pain. This is, of course, a closely related phenomenon to the dissociation described for hysteria.

References

American Psychiatric Association (1980) *Diagnostic and Statistical Manual of Mental Disorders*, 3rd Edn. Washington: American Psychiatric Association.

Anstee BH & Fleminger JJ (1977) Diagnosis 'uncertain': a follow-up study. *British Journal of Psychiatry 131*, 592–8.

Apley J (1975) *The Child with Abdominal Pains*, 2nd Edn. Oxford: Blackwell Scientific.

Beecher HK (1959) *Measurement of Subjective Responses, Quantitative Effects of Drugs*. New York: Oxford University Press.

Blumer D & Heilbronn M (1982) Chronic pain as a variant of depressive disease: the pain-prone disorder. *Journal of Nervous & Mental Diseases 170*, 381–406.

Bond MR (1976) Psychological and psychiatric aspects of pain. In Howells JG (ed.) *Modern Perspectives in the Psychiatric Aspects of Surgery*, pp. 109–139. London: Macmillan.

Bond MR (1984) *Pain: Its Nature, Analysis and Treatment*, 2nd Edn. Edinburgh: Churchill Livingstone.

Cloninger CR, Reich T & Guze SB (1975) The multi-factorial model of disease transmission III Familial relationships between sociopathy and hysteria (Briquet's syndrome). *British Journal of Psychiatry 127*, 23–32.

Dawson-Butterworth K, Wallen GDP & Gittleson NL (1969) Self-applied constricting bands. *British Journal of Psychiatry 115*, 1255–59.

Engel GL (1959) 'Psychogenic' pain and the pain prone patient. *American Journal of Medicine 26*, 899.

Feinmann C, Harris M & Cawley R (1984) Psychogenic facial pain: presentation and treatment. *British Medical Journal 288*, 436–8.

Gardner AR & Gardner AJ (1975) Self-mutilation, obsessionality and narcissism. *British Journal of Psychiatry 127*, 127–32.

Garvey MJ, Schaffer CB & Tuason VB (1983) Relationship of headaches to depression. *British Journal of Psychiatry 143*, 544–7.

Graff H & Mallin R (1967) The syndrome of the wrist-cutter. *American Journal of Psychiatry 124*, 36–42.

Lascelles RG (1966) Atypical facial pain and depression. *British Journal of Psychiatry 112*, 651–9.

Melzack R & Wall PD (1965) Pain mechanisms: a new theory. *Science 150*, 971.

Merskey H (1965) The characteristics of persistent pain in psychological illness. *Journal of Psychosomatic Research 9*, 291.

Merskey H (1976) The status of pain. In Hill O (ed.) *Modern Trends in Psychosomatic Medicine 3*, pp. 166–186. London: Butterworths.

Nathan P (1980) Recent advances in understanding pain *British Journal of Psychiatry 136*, 509–12.

Noordenbos W (1959) *Pain: Problems Pertaining to the Transmission of Nerve Impulses which Give Rise to Pain*. London: Elsevier.

Parkes CM (1976) The psychological reaction to loss of a limb: The first year after amputation. In Howells JG (ed.) *Modern Perspectives in the Psychiatric Aspects of Surgery*, pp. 515–533. London: Macmillan.

Perley MJ & Guze SB (1962) Hysteria–the stability and usefulness of clinical criteria. A quantitive study based on a follow-up period of 6-8 years in 39 patients *New England Journal of Medicine 266*, 421–26.

Pilling LF, Bannick TL & Swenson WM (1967) Psychological characteristics of patients having pain as a presenting symptom. *Canadian Medical Association Journal 97*, 387.

Tyrer S (1985) The role of the psychiatrist in the pain clinic. *Bulletin of the Royal College of Psychiatrists 9*, 135–6.

Tyrer SP (1986) Learned pain behaviour. *British Medical Journal 292*, 1–2

Trethowan WH (1977) *Pain as a Psychiatric Symptom*. Unpublished.

Woodruff RA, Clayton PS & Guze SB (1971) 'Hysteria': Studies of diagnosis, outcome and prevalence. *Journal of the American Medical Association 215*, 425–28.

World Health Organization (1977) *International Classification of Diseases*, 9th Revision. Geneva: World Health Organization.

— 16

Affect and Emotional Disorders

> I wish to inform you that I have received the cake. Many thanks, but I am not worthy. You
> sent it on the anniversary of my child's death, for I am not worthy of my birthday; I must
> weep myself to death; I cannot live and I cannot die, because I have failed so much, I shall
> bring my husband and children to hell. We are all lost; we won't see each other any more; I
> shall go to the convict prison and my two girls as well, if they do not make away with
> themselves because they were born in my body.
>
> A patient of Emil Kraepelin (1905)

Assessing and observing changes in mood is essential in psychiatry, but at the same time very difficult. In a study of patients with physical symptoms of depression the condition was most commonly associated with diagnostic doubt (Anstee & Fleminger, 1977), and in another study depressed affect was a major cause of somatic problems (Brenner, 1979). However, the terms used are not standardized, nor mutually exclusive. Different languages, unlike the names given to physical objects, have an entirely different range of descriptions of mood so that one is left wondering whether it is just the terms which differ in different cultures or perhaps even the experience of emotion itself. So *Angst* cannot be translated into English with a single equivalent word; neither can *depression* be precisely translated into German. The word *feeling* describes an active experience of somatic sensation, touch, as well as the passive subjective experience of emotion. Feelings are also personal convictions, predictive forecasts and social sensibilities. All these nuances of meaning are somewhat different from the use with regard to mood.

Traditionally, *feeling* has been used to describe a positive or negative reaction to an experience; it is marked but transitory. *Affect* is used to describe differentiated specific feelings directed towards objects. *Mood* is a more prolonged prevailing state or disposition. In practice, these terms are used more or less interchangeably. Similarly, *emotion* is often used with regard to the physiological and psychosomatic concomitants of mood, but this use is not specific.

Mood describes the state of the self in relation to its environment. There is an enormous range of variation of what could reasonably be called *normal* mood. Pathological mood, that is mood from which the patient suffers or mood which causes disturbance or suffering to others, also varies very greatly, and the extent to which it is acceptable to others in its expression is different in different social contexts. The clinician has to ask two questions concerning the mood of his patient: is the person suffering? is the expression of mood inappropriate in this social setting? Psychopathology of mood is confined to those situations where there is an affirmative answer to at least one of the questions, and treatment is directed towards improving the mood.

Like other human characteristics mood arises in the context of a diathesis. Whereas the physical constitution forms the tendency for developing, for example, a prolapsed intervertebral disc, personality is closely associated with the type, quality and direction of mood. So, a person of cyclothymic personality is more prone to morbid states of elation and excessive activity or taciturn dejection and retardation.

In the phenomenological assessment of mood, Jaspers (1959) has concentrated on three main aspects: the involvement of self; the contrast of opposites; and the nature of the object of feeling. Feelings are a feature of *self*, but by a process of empathy they may be ascribed to other objects of awareness. So, I experience my own feeling of sadness; I can also make a judgement that another person is sad because he looks sad, and even that a picture is sad because of its content and the affect that it evokes in me. A diagrammatic representation of some of the subjective experiences of mood is shown in Figure 16.1.

Affect is experienced in *contrasts*. This customary human characteristic of polarizing mood into opposites is made use of in the applications of Personal Construct Theory (Kelly, 1955), and in the use of Visual Analogue Scales (Aitken, 1969) in rating change of mood (Fig. 16.2). Feelings may have a

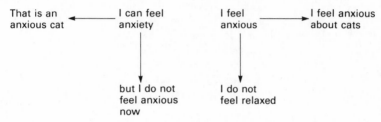

Figure 16.1 Subjective evaluation of mood

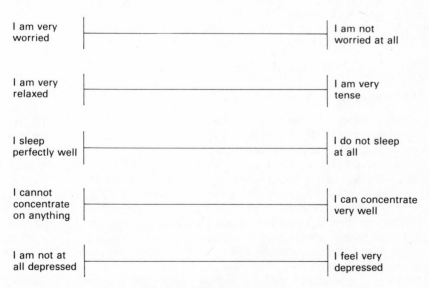

Figure 16.2 Visual analogue scale

definite object, for instance, a fear of cats; exposure to cats or to the idea of cats then evokes the emotion of anxiety. Feelings may also be without object, for example, free-floating anxiety in which the sufferer is in no doubt about the reality of his somatic and psychological symptoms of anxiety but can ascribe it to no definite cause, precipitant or object.

COMMUNICATION OF MOOD

'No man is an Island, entire of it self' (John Donne, 1571-1631), and in no area of life is this more true than that of feelings. Our feelings are very much affected by those around us. They are observable and understandable to other people and this is not accidental, they are actually signalled as a non-verbal message. The affect itself is not directed towards another person, but the expression of the affect is conveyed both deliberately and unintentionally to others.

Research on facial expression indicates seven main groups of emotion as being discriminated by the observer (Argyle, 1975). These are happiness, surprise, fear, sadness, anger, disgust/contempt, and interest. Emotions are communicated non-verbally by different parts of the body; for example, by the face (especially the eyes), gesture, posture, tone of voice and general appearance, especially the choice of clothes. In assessing the emotional state of others, those who are better at communicating emotion non-verbally are also better at reading it. The communicator assesses the other's affective response but he also in part evokes it. A person who is cheerful on meeting someone else will greet him cheerfully and induce a feeling of cheerfulness, even if transitory, which he then reads as the other person being cheerful. This has important implications in the way that mood is assessed. It would seem that emotion is evaluated empathically. Without having to go through this elaborate argument in words, the observer says to himself 'if I felt how I estimate the feelings of that person from his appearance, I would feel very unhappy; he is unhappy'. This is, of course, the empathic method as described earlier, and it takes place spontaneously and without deliberate training. Assessment of others' mood does not need to become verbal to be acted on. It takes place rapidly and is followed by the appropriate behavioural response from the observer.

THE CATEGORIZATION OF EMOTION

Jaspers has categorized feelings in the following ways:

1 According to the *object* of the emotion. This would include such diverse feelings as fear of snakes, patriotism, servile submission. The range of possible contents of emotion is, of course, limitless.

2 Feelings can be categorized according to their *source*. These may be localized feeling sensations: affect experienced in individual regions or areas of the body. There can be vital feelings affecting the whole body in which an emotion is described subjectively as being physical but affecting the whole organism in a complete way. Psychological feelings are the emotions we commonly describe as sadness, joy, and so on. Finally, Jaspers describes spiritual feelings, an expression which falls uncomfortably on the uncomprehending ears of our defective secular culture.

3 It would be possible to evaluate emotion according to its *biological purpose*. This would provoke a discussion of the theory of instinct.

4 *Feeling* state is a description of all the different feelings occurring at any one time and describes the affective state of the individual at that time; for example, a state of arousal, feeling of anergia.

5 Emotion has been categorized traditionally according to *duration and intensity*. Thus, feeling is an individual emotional reaction. *Affect* is a complex but momentary emotional perturbation. *Mood* is a more prolonged emotional state which influences all aspects of the mental state.

6 There is an important distinction within the ambiguous word *feeling* which means both emotions and sensations. Emotion refers to a state of the self, whilst sensation refers to elements of perception.

Pathological changes in mood

CHANGES IN MOOD

Most often in psychiatric practice, subjective description of *change* in the experience of emotion is for the worse–a state of dysphoria, meaning the condition of 'being ill at ease'; more rarely the patient may describe the onset of ecstacy or euphoria. The subjective experience of change of mood can be quantified and represented graphically as in Figure 16.3, which shows a part of

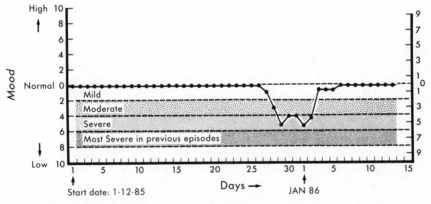

Figure 16.3 Mood chart kept by a depressed patient who had had acute bronchitis

a mood chart a previously depressed patient had recorded; he had noticed an association between an acute attack of bronchitis and exacerbation of depressive symptoms.

Bodily feelings associated with mood

Mood and somatic symptoms has been discussed in Chapter 13. Changes in bodily feeling are important in a number of conditions. Physical illness frequently precipitates a loss of the accustomed sense of well-being. This is subjectively experienced as a generalized lowering of vitality and may be associated with other abnormalities, for instance, hypochondriasis or dissociation.

Feelings of capacity

There may be a loss of the normal feeling of self-sufficiency and the appropriate sense of self-esteem. Competence in any field of life is linked with a reasonably accurate knowledge of self-capacity–the ability to know one's own limits and not attempt the impossible. Loss of the accustomed feeling of capacity to achieve what is known to be within a person's capacity may occur with psychotic depression; it may also be a neurotic development. The resultant feelings of helplessness and hopelessness have been described by Schmale (1958) and others in the 'giving-up given-up complex'.

Increased feelings of capacity may be experienced in mania. A young, unemployed lorry driver was an in-patient undergoing investigation on a medical ward. He developed a manic episode and conducted a ward round late one night. Going to a bed of a particularly timid and sick patient he announced: 'I am a Professor of Medicine from the British Medical Association. With the treatment you are getting from Dr X you are going to die, but don't worry, I'll make sure you're alright'.

Absence of blunting and flattening of feeling

Apathy is the absence of feeling; there may be *blunting* or *flattening* of affective response. The patient himself is often not aware of his deficiency but when pointed out to him, may agree that there is a lack of any sort of emotional reaction. Apathy is often associated with anergia and lack of volition. The schizophrenic patient so afflicted has no desire or internal drive to work or find a job. He may be so apathetic that he does not dress or even feed himself properly. He will respond to continual persuasion or cajoling, but otherwise remains inert and passive.

The terms 'blunting' and 'flattening' are not identical, although both may occur in schizophrenia. *Blunting* implies a lack of emotional sensitivity, such as was displayed by the schizophrenic girl who, with obvious relish for the sensational effect, took her visitors up to the bedroom to show them her mother who had been dead for forty-eight hours. *Flattening* is a limitation of the usual range of emotion and is often associated with anergia amongst schizophrenics. The individual does not express very much affect in any direction, although that which is expressed is appropriate in direction.

Feeling of a loss of feeling

This is subtly but significantly different from apathy. It is experienced by the patient as a loss, a deficiency and is all-pervasive–anger, love, pleasure and so on. The patient resents or does not understand it, suffers very greatly and often feels guilty about the feeling. It is a subjective experience of loss of feelings that were formerly present, rather than an objectively observed absence. A depressed young woman said 'I have no feelings for my children. That is wicked. They are beautiful children'. A person with religious belief may experience this loss of feeling with a religious content: they no longer believe in God. On more detailed eliciting of their subjective experience, they are likely to describe a loss of the feeling of assurance associated with their faith, rather than any actual change in the content of their beliefs. This affect occurs particularly in depressive psychosis, but also occasionally in personality disorders and schizophrenia. Milder forms are experienced as *depersonalization*. The patient complains that his feelings are numbed, diminished, made remote from himself, to which is ascribed the unmelodious word, de-affectualization.

In *anhedonia* there is a total inability to enjoy anything in life or even get the accustomed satisfaction from everyday events or objects. This would seem to be a fundamental symptom of depressive illness. A highly intelligent and perceptive man suffering from psychotic depression said: 'I have a sort of uncanny feeling. I know what I am reading is amusing but I am not at all amused by it'. Anhedonia is also described as a symptom in schizophrenia, in which it is especially likely to be social—absence of the ability to feel pleasure in relationships (Cutting, 1985).

Often the very way the patient describes the loss of the ability to feel feelings demonstrates that feelings are still there. A girl described how she no longer felt anything for her boyfriend: 'It is nothing to do with him, it is me'. She did not feel she could love anyone and she was in a quandary because she thought it impossible to proceed with the affair, but could not break it up 'because it would hurt him very much and I would hate to do that'.

Feeling of impending disaster

This experience of dread or apprehension is, of course, a common and normal emotion and would be quite appropriate, for example, for the idle student awaiting his examination results. However, a nameless dread without reasonable cause is seen with various morbid mental disorders. A graphic and terrifying example was written by the poet William Cowper (1822, posthumously) during an acute episode of psychotic depression:

> Hatred and vengeance,–my eternal portion,
> Scarce can endure delay of execution,–
> Wait with impatient readiness to seize my
> Soul in a moment.

Ecstasy

Ecstasy and euphoria are normal phenomena; psychiatrists are only concerned with them when they occur inappropriately or to an abnormal degree. Heightened states of happiness such as euphoria and ecstasy sometimes occur in people with mental illness or abnormality of personality. Understandably, most psychiatrists writing about the mood state of ecstasy have described its occurrence in psychotic patients, but with the pattern towards increased numbers of psychiatric out-patient referrals, neurotic patients giving a previous description of less bizarre ecstatic symptoms are being seen. The patient may describe a calm exalted euphoria amounting to ecstasy, although this tranquil mood state is relatively uncommon and usually short-lived. In schizophrenia, ecstatic mood may be associated with exalted delusions, for example, the chronic patient who sat placidly enraptured on a long-stay ward, knowing herself to be the Queen of Heaven and waiting for a messenger to inform her that she was to take over the rule of the world. Ecstatic states, usually with a histrionic flavour, may occur in hysterical dissociation and may be associated with religious stigmata (Simpson, 1984). Bizarre, mass hysterical phenomena, often with religious associations, are usually of this type; for example, the Devils of Loudun as described by Aldous Huxley (1952). The social, institutional and group psychological prerequisites for the development of epidemic hysteria (Sirois, 1982) are usually present in these situations and mismanagement is usually responsible for the development from isolated hysteria to an epidemic. Ecstasy, solemn elation or excessive exuberant expansiveness, may also be seen in epilepsy and in other organic states, for example, in general paresis.

Characteristic of ecstasy is that it is self-referent; for example, the flowers of spring 'open for *me*'. There is an alteration of the boundaries of self so that the person may feel 'at one with the universe', or he may 'empty myself of all will' so that 'I am nothing but feelings'. The change in ego boundaries does not usually have the aspect of interference with self that accompanies passivity experiences. In ecstasy, the abrogation of self is experienced as being voluntary.

Euphoria is a state of excessive unreasonable cheerfulness; it may communicate itself like the cheerfulness of mania, or it may seem inappropriate and bizarre. It is commonly seen in organic states, especially associated with frontal lobe impairment.

Feelings attached to the perception of objects

Objects may evoke an emotional response in a normal person, for instance: comfortable familiarity towards an armchair in which one rests after an energetic walk; apprehensive dislike towards a dentist's chair. This normal affective response may be exaggerated pathologically. Excessive feelings of fear amounting to terror may remain associated with objects, or, alternatively, profound and inappropriate happiness. The objects to which affect is attached may not only be physical inanimate objects but also thoughts, and patterns of thoughts, and people. The occurrence of certain ideas may regularly be associated with specific pathological emotion, perhaps resulting in phobia. Any object of perception may be invested with idiosyncratic affect.

Feelings directed towards people

These may be disturbed in a number of different ways. Affect may be absent or deadened, increased and excessive or distorted. It may also be ambivalent–both loving and hating, rejecting and over-protecting synchronously. A girl described in Chapter 14, suffering from anorexia nervosa, would take great care to cook enormous meals for her twin sister, to whom she was very close: the sister became grossly obese at 14 stone, whilst the patient reached 5 stone. In answer to remonstrations about feeding her sister, she said: 'I look horrible, so she should look horrible as well'.

Free-floating emotion

This is commonly described in psychiatric disturbance and in his original description of anxiety neurosis, Freud (1895) considered that the condition was characterized by free-floating anxiety. A powerful affect seems to have no goal and is associated with no object. The patient describes himself as feeling generally anxious, not anxious about anything in particular but just anxious. This free-floating anxiety has somatic and psychological concomitants. It may seem to be localized physically in certain areas of the body. Other free-floating affects occur such as restlessness, tension, gloom, despondency, euphoria, and so on.

Experience and expression of emotion

These are separate stages but closely linked. The expression of mood may be abnormal in a number of ways. Mood may be censored or denied so that it never gains expression. It may be altered, and this is the theoretical explanation of conversion in hysteria, that is, an affect becomes unbearably intense and is therefore *converted* by a presumed unconscious mechanism into physical symptoms. The expression of mood may be impulsive and explosive, with inadequate control and a lack of empathic feeling.

Hypochondriasis is very commonly associated with disorders of mood, for example, anxiety or depression. There is background perception of sensations from many different parts of the body skin surfaces, joints and viscera. A process of introspection and concentration of consciousness on individual organs or regions, coupled with the memory for past experience of the subject, or others known to him, causes him to experience these as morbid. When individual perceptions of the self become linked with unpleasant affect they become one of the bases of the multifaceted term *hypochondriacal preoccupation*.

A speculative hypothesis that clinicians have found helpful is the term *alexithymia* which was coined by Sifneos (1972) to describe a specific disturbance in psychic functioning, characterized by difficulties in the capacity to verbalize affect and elaborate fantasies. This was originally introduced to describe psychosomatic disorders occurring in individuals with difficulty expressing their emotions. The link with absence or diminution of fantasy is a consistent finding (Nemiah & Sifneos, 1970). The communicative style shows markedly reduced or absent symbolic thinking so that inner attitudes, feelings, wishes and drives are not revealed; few dreams and a paucity of fantasies are reported (Taylor, 1984). Thinking is literal, utilitarian and concerned with the minutiae of external events. These individuals have great difficulty in recognizing and describing their own feelings and in discriminating between emotional states and bodily sensations. They show a stiff robot-like existence 'almost as if they are following an instruction book'; there may be stiffness of posture and lack of facial expression. They show an impaired capacity for empathy in their interpersonal relationships. Alexithymic characteristics have been found, especially amongst patients with psychosomatic disorders, somatoform disorders, psychogenic pain disorders, substance abuse disorders, post-traumatic stress disorder, masked depression, character neuroses and sexual perversions.

Somatization in patients with mental disorder can be defined as the selective perception and focus on the somatic manifestations of the disorder with denial or minimization of the affective and cognitive changes (Katon *et al.*, 1982). As a method of expression of emotion it is also reported in transcultural studies, especially in the Indian subcontinent; according to Rack (1982) this is associated with a relative paucity of words to denote mood in the vocabulary. Murphy and coworkers (1964) studied basic depressive symptomatology in 30 countries and showed how culture changes illness and the way dysphoria is expressed. Bavington (1981), studying depression in a predominantly Pathan culture in Pakistan, found somatization to be expressed in 45% of cases; hypochondriasis was present in 55%, hysterical features in 60%, feelings of guilt in 50%, paranoid ideas in 38%, suicidal thoughts in 75%, diurnal variation in 18%, retardation in 50%, and irritability in 80% of depressed patients. Bavington explains these somatic ideas by the presence of vital feelings rather than poverty of language.

VITAL FEELINGS

Vital feelings was a term used by Wernicke (1906) to describe certain somatic symptoms occurring in the affective psychoses. The word *vital* comes from the concept of the *vital self* which describes the close relationship of the body to awareness of self; the way we experience our bodies and the impression we consider our physical presence makes on others. So, vital feelings are those that make us aware of our vital self. These are the feelings of mood which appear to emanate from the body itself; localized and somatized affect. For example, depressed patients commonly complain of headache. On more informed enquiry, the patient may say 'it's not exactly a pain, but more an unbearable feeling of pressure like a tight band around the head'; 'a feeling of misery, like a black cloud pressing on my head'. The head is the commonest site for vital feelings, but they may also occur in the abdomen: 'I have a dull feeling in my bowels, they are slowing down and blocking'; in the chest: 'it feels like a weight bearing down on my chest, stopping me breathing'; in the eyes: 'everything looks black, dark and drab; my eyes are heavy, I cannot see properly'; in the legs: 'my legs are terribly heavy; I cannot walk I feel so exhausted'. They may occur in other regions of the body, for instance, the bladder, the feet, the hair and so on. The features which appear to be constant are the association of the localized body sensation with the prevailing depressed mood, the sensation of weight, tension, heaviness, even depression, in the particular organ, and a consequent loss of function: 'I cannot think properly... my bowels are blocked'.

Schneider (1920) considered vital feelings to be of paramount diagnostic significance in depressive illness, equivalent to the first-rank symptoms in schizophrenia, the core of cyclothymic depression and autonomic in origin. He considered these feelings to be common in depression. It would seem that Dupré (1913), writing about what he called *coenestopathic states*, was describing the same symptom: 'Coenestopathic states are, indeed, so common as to figure among the most frequent features of the psychoses'. He described *coenesthesia* as the 'deep but more or less indefinite awareness that we have of our own bodies and the general tone of functional activity'. Coenestopathic states are 'the distressing feelings which emanate from one or other of the coenesthesic areas... a change in the normal quality of physical feeling in certain parts of the body'. They are localized but there is no local pathogenic lesion. Dupré claimed that coenestopathic states were autonomous, not associated with other psychiatric disorders; but, in describing the affects with which they are associated, he appears to describe affective disorders. The mood of depression may be described as a global loss of vitality in which all functions are affected and all performances depressed.

A change in vital feelings does not only occur in depression. The bizarre feelings that the schizophrenic has about his body is a change in the way he expresses himself, often further elaborated by delusions. It should be noted that the term *vital* is used rather differently in *vital anxiety states*. These states have been described (Lopez Ibor, 1966) in which the anxiety is thought to be endogenous developing relatively acutely in people of stable personality.

The depressive content of what phenomenologists would consider to be vital feelings varies very greatly; for example: 'I have turned to stone... I have a feeling of depression in my chest... it is a pain, a knot, a weight... I have a cloud on my head, a feeling of nothingness...'. Burns (1971) commented with regard to respiratory vital feelings: 'A striking feature of the breathlessness described by the patients with depression was its fairly sudden onset and cessation, corresponding exactly with the onset and resolution of the depressive illness'.

Trethowan (1977, 1979) has considered that lowering of vitality is fundamental to the experience of depressive illness. He has described this as 'a lowering of vitality which is all-pervasive and leads to a marked loss of ability of the subject to function as he did before he became ill in terms of both mind and body'.

RELIGIOUS FEELINGS

Psychiatrists have not increased the credibility of their specialty in the first three-quarters of the twentieth century by posing as the universal experts on the experience of life and how it should be led. Expert knowledge of the abnormal does not preclude ignorance of the normal and the psychiatrist can never generalize from the sample of people selectively referred to him to the whole of mankind. This discrepancy can become very obvious in the area of *ecstatic* and *religious experience*. The psychiatrist sees a most unrepresentative group of those having some form of religious experience, which latter according to Greeley may amount to over 40% of the adult population of the USA, more males than females, more stable than unstable, more happy than unhappy.

The anthropology of ecstasy (Lewis, 1971) can be traced through Christian and other cultures and only makes contact with recognizable mental illness at a few points. William James (1925), in *The Variety of Religious Experience*, demonstrated the vast extent of the phenomenology of religion, and showed how unwise it would be to equate the surprising with the pathological. Once again, the phenomenological dichotomy of *form* and *content* is important. For a person whose predominant thinking in health is religious, the content of their mental illness, if they become psychiatrically disordered, may well be religious also; but it is the *form* of the condition by which the doctor will decide whether they are ill or not and, if so, what is the precise nature of their illness. Thus, although a religious person with manic–depressive illness in manic phase will describe bizarre religious flights of ideas, pressure of talk and ecstatic mood, there is no such thing *ipso facto* as 'religious mania'.

Accounts vary as to the extent of psychopathology amongst converts to religious groups and sects; it is probably associated with the nature of the group. Thus Ungerleider and Wellisch (1979) found no evidence of severe mental illness in one study; while Galanter (1982) described evidence of emotional problems amongst adherents to Divine Light, the Unification Church, Baba and Subud.

The indicators for establishing a religious experience as psychiatrically morbid are:

1　The phenomenology of the experience conforms with psychiatric illness.
2　There are other recognizable symptoms of mental disturbance.
3　The life style, behaviour and direction of personal goals of the person subsequent to the event are consistent with the natural history of mental disorder, rather than with an enriching life experience.
4　The personality of the person is disordered in a way with which such behaviour would be consistent.

With the following signs, the experience is more likely to be intrinsic to the person's belief and less likely to denote psychiatric illness:

1　The person shows some degree of reticence to discuss the experience, especially with those he believes to be unsympathetic.
2　It is described unemotionally with matter-of-fact conviction and appears 'authentic'.
3　The person understands, allows for and even sympathizes with the incredulity of others.
4　He usually considers that the experience implies some demands upon himself.
5　The religious experience conforms with the subject's recognizable religious traditions.

In his clinical practice, the psychiatrist is likely to come across patients describing religious experience; in some he will feel this is symptomatic of mental illness, but in others it is clearly intrinsic to the values of the patient, and independent of illness, even though illness be present.

Manic–depressive mood

Certainly since the writings of Kraepelin, the apparently opposite mood states of mania and depression have been recognized as occurring in the same illness–frequently at different times and stages of the illness in the same patient; more rarely at the same time in the same patient. Although depression occurs more frequently than mania in bipolar illnesses, the first attack of mania may occur even after the age of 60 (Shulman & Post, 1980).

Although they are described separately, it is important to realize that these mood states may occur together. Mania and depression are not opposite mood states; they are both pathological, and the opposite would be freedom from morbid emotion. Agitation and overactivity may occur with depression, irritability and a feeling of frustration with mania. It is usual for a person to go through a depressive phase before becoming manic, and again on the return from mania before reaching a state of normal mood. A patient, now depressed, having previously been manic, described this: 'The first fine careless rapture has disappeared. I feel more tired and moody'.

DEPRESSION OF MOOD

Core experience: psychological and physical

Depression of mood is very common, and depression of such persistence and intensity as to be regarded as illness frequently occurs. There is considerable discussion as to what is the central core of depression. Of course, arguments advocating biochemical, psychodynamic, or conditioning factors as initiating causes are not mutually exclusive. It affects virtually all physical and psychological functions; for example, using a tachistoscopic method, Powell and Hemsley (1984) were able to show that depression influenced perception. The word *depression* is a misnomer, as depressive illness may occur without the patient making a complaint of depression as a symptom (*depressio sine depressione*); for this reason *melancholia* may be preferred. However, this term is used in the Diagnostic and Statistical Manual 3rd Edition (American Psychiatric Association, 1980) to describe one aspect of *major depressive disorder*. The subjective symptoms are very variable. The mood varies from indifference and apathy to profound dejection, despondency and despair. *Anhedonia*, the complete inability to experience pleasure, is a constant feature; it is experienced as joylessness and revealed in facial expression, speech, behaviour and life style.

A slowing down of the ability to initiate thought or action is noted by the observer as *retardation*. A patient, describing this after recovery, said: 'it feels as if treacle has been poured into my head through your ears'. Psychic retardation is experienced subjectively as an inability to fulfil normal obligations, as loss of coping. The proneness to self-blame often results in the patient describing himself as lazy and good for nothing. There is a catastrophic lowering of self-esteem as a cognitive component. Beck (1967, 1979) considered that there is a pre-depressive constellation of attitudes or assumptions developed from previous experiences. The patient has a negative view of himself; he interprets his ongoing experiences in a negative way and he has a negative view of the future.

Brown and Harris (1978), in a study of depressed women in inner areas of London, considered that provoking agents such as adverse life events potentiated already existing *vulnerability factors* to promote depression. These latter included lack of a close confidante; loss of mother before the age of 11; three or more children under the age of 14 at home; and no employment outside the home. Ingham *et al.* (1986) studied in Edinburgh the relationships between self-esteem, vulnerability and psychiatric disorder in the community. It is complex, but certain life circumstances influence feelings of self-esteem independent of illness. Anxiety as well as depression has effects on self-esteem.

Agitation and purposeless restlessness add to the discomfort and to inability to achieve anything. This anxiety and preoccupation with gloomy thoughts impairs concentration. Diurnality of mood is often prominent with the patient feeling at his worst, and perhaps most suicidal, when he wakes early in the morning or, alternatively, somewhat later in the morning. The degree of depression and misery may sometimes successfully be concealed; this is the presentation of *depressio sine depressione* (smiling depression) in a patient who appears not to be depressed in the consulting room but may, much to his doctor's dismay, kill himself.

Concentration, application and decision making become difficult, painful and sometimes impossible. The person describes difficulty or impossibility in fantasy and recollection of emotion. This is described as loss of memory and loss of feeling. Often this loss of mental function makes the patient believe he is 'going mad' or 'losing his mind', a sort of mental hypochondriasis. The retardation of physical function readily leads to a generalized or localized somatic hypochondriasis. A very depressed middle-aged woman described her bodily feelings: 'I have a feeling like having an injection at the dentist's. My face feels numb, but at the same time painful all over'.

Anxiety is a common concomitant with depression and may completely obscure the latter. In agitated depression, agitation and restlessness is extreme and the patient carries a serious suicide risk. Histrionic behaviour may also obscure the underlying depressive illness. A patient who was actually profoundly depressed kept picking her skin and pulling her hair, saying, 'look, I can't feel anything when I do this to myself'.

The affect of depression may be localized somatically in vital feelings (see above). It may take the form of profound misery or dejection. There is usually a feeling of loss of capacity, helplessness and a feeling that the patient cannot cope. Absence of feelings is often described, or it may be described as an inexplicable loss of feelings 'that ought to be there'.

Feelings of guilt and unworthiness are prominent in depressive illness of endogenous type. This has long been known; for example, Plutarch in the first century AD described a person: 'He looks on himself as a man whom the gods hate and pursue with their anger... "Leave me," says the wretched man, "me the impious, the accursed, hated of the gods, to suffer my punishment"' (Zilboorg & Henry, 1941). The patient may blame himself for having allowed himself to get into this state of mind. He is full of self-reproach and recrimination for all sorts of peccadilloes from the distant past. For all that goes wrong around him he takes personal blame; this may be of delusional intensity. As well as delusions of guilt and unworthiness, hypochondriacal and nihilistic delusions are relatively common in depression, especially when it occurs in the elderly.

Delusions occur in psychotic depression. It is important to make the distinction between a belief about the state of the world coloured by current mood–'I feel that I must have done something to my brain as I can't think properly', from an actual delusional belief–'I can't think at all, it is impossible, my brain is dead'. The former is a metaphorical statement, the latter a belief held with conviction. In practice, there is often a grey area between frank depressive delusions and emotionally laden views of the world.

Suicidal thoughts

'I feel as though I want to destroy myself. There is no point in going on'. Suicidal ideas, ruminations and impulses are common. A detailed study of suicide from a literary point of view has been written by Alvarez (1971). He is concerned with the background and the reasons for suicide and attempted suicide in many well-known writers, especially poets. He writes about suicide as 'letting go': 'I have to admit that I am a failed suicide... Seneca, the final authority on the subject, pointed out disdainfully that the exits are everywhere:

each precipice and river, each branch of each tree, every vein in your body will set you free... Yet despite all that, I never quite made it'.

Plans for suicide may not be executed only because of the degree of *retardation*–occasionally electroconvulsive therapy may lessen retardation after three or four treatments and thereby increase the risk of suicide, because improvement from depression of mood and lowered self-esteem due to guilt feelings has not yet occurred. Death is often welcomed with a sense of relief. A psychotically depressed patient, when offered admission to hospital, accepted with resignation: 'I will come in and there you will kill me. It is what I deserve'. It is frequently described afterwards by the relatives of suicides that in the days or hours preceding their death they were happier and more tranquil than they had been for a long time.

Homicide of those close to the patient followed by suicide is a real danger with depressive illness. A profoundly depressed man felt that life was not worth living, that he had failed completely and the world was intolerable. The only person he cared for was his five-year-old son and he did not want to condemn him to what he anticipated would be a lifetime of misery. He put his son on the handlebars of his bicycle and rode over the quay into the harbour intending to kill them both. The boy was drowned but the father was rescued and resuscitated. Subsequently, he responded to treatment for his endogenous depression.

Depersonalization

Depersonalization, which is common in depression, may be manifest as loss of feelings or the ability to feel. This is a milder form of what may progress in severe illness to nihilistic delusions: 'my body has been changed to water', or 'I am dead; I have no feelings and no will'. Depersonalization is described in Chapter 12. When it occurs in healthy people it is noticed but associated with little emotion, but when it is complained of as a symptom, it is described as being extremely unpleasant. The patient usually finds it very difficult to describe the experience but is quite adamant that it is one of the most unpleasant experiences he has ever had.

'That internal restlessness'

'That Internal Restlessness and Disorder in Man, which has been the Complaint of All Ages' was part of the title of James Vere's book (1778) in which restlessness of mood is associated with instinctual conflict in a way that anticipates Freud's theory of anxiety–the resultant conflict from the opposing forces of the superego and id. Mood is a variable expression of the self; it may be a transient feeling reactive to a certain situation or it may be a more longlasting, sustained, inexplicable mood that is regarded as endogenous.

Internal restlessness also describes the emotions of neurotic disorder–anxiety, irritability and the situational fears of phobic state. These, with obsessional disorders, are discussed in Chapter 17.

DEPRESSION AND LOSS

Any social situation of transition is associated with some disturbance of emotion (Parkes, 1971). Depression is the affect associated with experience of loss. It is not the intention here to enter into theoretical aspects but to discuss the subjective experience. Parkes (1976) has demonstrated how loss of a person, loss of a limb and even loss of a home are stressful in similar ways, and that there is a mental process going on in which the person is 'making real inside the self events which have already occurred in reality outside'. This process is associated with marked psychic pain and unhappiness. An example of depression associated with the threat of loss of a loved object was a taxi driver who owned his own car which was the only thing he valued in life. During an episode of profound depression, he polished the taxi to perfection, took it into the garage, connected a pipe to the exhaust of the car, started the engine and killed himself.

Grief

The immediate experience of loss is shock and numbness. The suddenly bereaved person may say that he cannot believe that it has happened to him. He just feels numb and empty. He may describe depersonalization feelings. There is a tendency to deny that the loss has happened. A woman was referred to a surgeon for a lump in the breast. At operation the mass was found to be malignant and the breast was amputated. For several days after the operation she was unable to accept that the painful area under the dressing signified the loss of her breast rather than a minor excision.

Following initial shock and denial come the pangs of grief. This is an acute feeling of loss with prominent anxiety as well as grieving–*anxious searching*. The implications of the experience of loss begin to be realized and this may cause the person feelings of anxiety amounting to panic: 'However am I going to cope without him?' The somatic symptoms of anxiety may be present as well as the psychological.

Three distinct patterns of *morbid grief* have been observed (Lieberman, 1978):

1   phobic avoidance of persons, places or things related to the deceased, combined with extreme guilt and anger about the deceased and his death;
2   a total lack of grieving with anger directed towards others and over-idealization of the deceased;
3   physical illness and recurrent nightmares of the deceased.

These patterns have relevance for treatment using the behavioural method of *forced mourning*.

When the experience of loss has been accepted as a reality, *depression*, the affect appertaining to loss, occurs. The person feels very low and hopeless, perhaps with the lowering of vitality and apathy of depression. He becomes resigned to his situation but sees no way out: 'There is simply no future for me now'. Not surprisingly this state is often associated with suicidal ideas and impulses, and there is an increased mortality from suicide and other causes in the six months subsequent to bereavement (Parkes *et al.*, 1969).

As the state of grieving is resolved the person gradually overcomes this despairing hopelessness. There is an attitude of mind which results in reorganization and redirection. He gradually makes decisions and carries out activities that demonstrate his emotional and intellectual acceptance of the loss and intention to continue his life as well as possible, although still remembering the loss. This stage of *resolution* may be postponed for many years, as with Queen Victoria's grieving for Prince Albert.

Parkes (1976) discriminates between the subjective experience of *external loss* and *internal change*. The external loss is shown by pining for the lost object. Separation anxiety occurs both in bereaved people and in amputees, and is associated with anxious searching: a bereaved person was walking up and down the street wondering if she would see her husband whom she knew to be dead. In these circumstances misperception of strangers as being the lost relative may happen. A man whose father had died some long time before thought he heard his father's voice in another room, and then realized it was his son. People return to places associated with the lost person or keep articles which belonged to them sacrosanct. The *pseudohallucinations of bereavement* described by Rees (1971) would seem to be a feature of this anxious searching. These are usually experienced as pleasant and reassuring but may occasionally be a horrific memory of the person when ill and suffering. In a small proportion of amputees, phantom limb pain is incapacitating. Parkes considered that this was at least in part psychologically determined and an equivalent of separation anxiety. He demonstrated similar affective experiences in those compulsorily rehoused from the slums of Boston.

Internal change with a sense of mutilation is common to people with different types of loss. Amputees feel themselves to be badly damaged both in their function and in their self-image. Because a man has lost his leg, he will be unable to carry out his previous activities as before and may feel himself to be less of a man. Similarly, the woman with an amputated arm may prefer a cosmetic but useless prosthesis rather than a more functional hook. She may feel the affront to her self-image of a mutilated arm more than the loss of function. Parkes and Napier (1975) stress the social associations of loss in their discussion of prevention and alleviation of the problems resulting from amputation. Widows also describe a feeling of loss within themselves due to their bereavement; there is, of course, often a real loss of status. Those rehoused often described an internal change on moving: 'something of me went'.

Helplessness and hopelessness

Engel (1967) has studied the life setting in which illness develops, observing that the onset of illness often coincides with a time when the patient was assailed with real or threatened loss or separation, and was experiencing great difficulty with coping. Patients have described this affect as 'discouragement', 'despair', 'giving up' or 'depression' (Schmale, 1958, 1965). These authors considered that the effect contributes to the emergence of somatic disease when the necessary predisposing factors are present. The different facets of this emotional set have been described as the *giving-up given-up complex* and five subjective characteristics have been delineated (Engel, 1968). These are:

1 The affect of helplessness and hopelessness. The patient describes himself as being at the end of his tether, unable to cope and not knowing which way to turn. He talks about giving up and of being incapable of any action to resolve his dilemma.

2 There is a loss of self-esteem. He feels himself no longer to be competent or in control. He may feel himself to be damaged, maimed or mutilated.

3 There is loss of gratification in his relationships and roles in life. He may express dissatisfaction with his marriage or his job, and he feels a failure in achieving his ambitions.

4   There is a disruption of the normal sense of continuity between past, present and future. The future seems bleak and hopeless.
5   There is a painful remembering of times when his self-esteem and sense of well-being were lowered. This reactivation of memory especially concerns past failures, embarrassments and griefs. Feelings of giving-up may be directed towards an idea (a cherished ambition) or an object, as well as towards a person or even himself.

These affects of helplessness and hopelessness have been described as a psychological disturbance preceding becoming ill (Schmale & Iker).

Low self-esteem is an important facet of the vulnerability theory in the social origins of depression. Thus, it is not just feelings of loss but feelings of hopelessness that also results in depressive mood: the self is construed as worthless and the world meaningless, and the social situation is such that no amelioration is possible. This is frequently the soil in which the neurotic depression grows.

MANIA

Mania is a word with a long history. Hare (1981) considers that the early descriptions of intellectual deterioration with excitement were made because of the association with organic deterioration from poor general health during the nineteenth century. As the physical health of the population improved, it was possible to describe separate conditions with different natural histories. However, mania still forms a much higher proportion of affective psychoses occuring puerperally than of affective disorders occuring at other stages of life (Dean & Kendall, 1981).

Mania refers to elation, acceleration of thinking and over-activity. It has become conventional to refer to all but the most severe cases as suffering from *hypomania*. This is unfortunate as one does not refer to hypodepression, and the person using the term *hypomania* often gives the impression that wrong diagnosis is permissible to a greater extent than if the term *mania* had been used. A young manic in-patient described his internal state: 'I feel hypersuffused with experience... I am developing a close secretarial relationship with Camilla Brown (another young patient)... I feel like a rocket with the blue paper lit, standing in a bottle and just ready to take off'.

In pure form it is characterized by excessive cheerfulness, rapid train and association of thought, and over-activity. The speed of thinking and the ready ability to form associations results in rapid and apparently sparkling conversation (see Chapter 8). Puns and clang associations abound; for example, in a case quoted by Bingham (1841):

> A fine bold lady, well dressed and well known to the officers of a certain house, 'a regular madwoman', as they called her, was brought thither by her friends. She was no sooner announced than every missile and instrument of attack was carefully removed out of her way. She opened the conference by a familiar address to the physician under whose care she had been before and was going to remain, by saying to him, 'Well, Doctor M(orrison), but I beg pardon, I forgot whom I was speaking to–it is Sir A(lexander). Well, Sir A–, since I had the pleasure of seeing you last, I have been benighted, and you have been knighted...

An excellent ward sister, Sister Boddy, with whom I once had the privilege to work was greeted by a young manic patient: 'Sister Boddy, Sister Anatomy!'

Manic thinking

Exceptional *distractibility* is shown in the way external events, such as a noise in the street outside, are immediately incorporated into conversation. The rapid association of thought is called *flight of ideas* (see Chapter 8) and the incessant need to talk and express these ideas *pressure of talk*. Behavioural changes result from this elevation of mood and acceleration of thinking and activity. Restless activity associated with grandiose schemes is often seen: a patient buried mattresses in his garden because he felt it would improve the quality of his vegetables by making compost. Manic patients often go on spending sprees well beyond their means, or get involved in sexual affairs in a manner unlike their normal character. A manic patient said, 'my thinking feels hot'. Their overactivity and superabundance of energy involves other people, who find themselves having to cope with the elaborate projects that the manic patient sets in operation. An example of this is the case of folie à deux described by Ropschitz (1957) in Chapter 19.

Usually, the manic looks at his world with complete, unshakeable and unjustified optimism. However, he is intolerant of authority, when relatives and doctors try to curtail his restless overactivity, showing itself in *manic irritability*, when he feels all his brilliant ideas are frustrated by the lack of vision of everyone else. He has no insight into his illness but feels better, more alert, more healthy then ever before. He believes his thinking to be greatly improved and feels other people are dull and slow in comparison.

Kraepelin considered that there were three fundamental components to the symptomatology of manic–depressive psychosis: level of mood; psychic activity; and motor activity. Characteristically, in mania, these functions are elevated, whilst in endogenous depression they are depressed. In agitated depression, the mood is depressed whilst activity is increased and the patient moves restlessly and purposelessly about, wringing his or her hands. Thinking may be increased showing what Mapother and Lewis (1937) have called 'a ceaseless roundabout of painful thought'. These changes are represented diagrammatically in Figure 16.4. In affective disorders, restlessness and

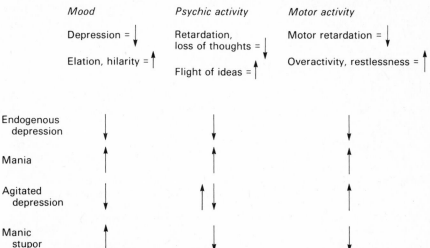

Figure 16.4 Kraepelin's triad: the components of manic-depressive psychosis

retardation of body or mind may occur in the same patient, and sometimes rather surprisingly at the same time. It was an observation of great significance of Kraepelin to demonstrate how these apparent polar opposites of madness should in fact be part of the same condition. *Mixed affective states* are those in which features of mania and depression are seen during the same episode of illness. Thus the features of Kraepelin's triad can be mixed in any combination in the affective disorders.

A THIRD FUNCTIONAL PSYCHOSIS?

Not uncommonly, the mental state of a patient is clearly psychotic, but not obviously revealing either manic–depressive psychosis or schizophrenia. Quite often, such conditions show features of both major psychoses; more rarely the presentation is quite different. A variety of different terms have been used to describe a third functional psychosis (Table 16.1). Reference is only made here to some of the syndromes described. For more information the reader is recommended to consult a textbook of psychiatry, for instance Gelder *et al.* (1983). The term *schizo-affective psychosis* introduced by Kasanin in 1933, is used in several quite different ways: delusions, hallucinations and thought disorder are described. The International Statistical Classification of Diseases (World Health Organization, 1977) places them diagnostically within schizophrenia. However, Procci (1976), in his thorough survey of the literature, emphasizes the scant resemblance of a well-defined minority to nuclear schizophrenia, and sees them as more related to affective psychoses. He focuses on the group of young, acute onset patients with good premorbid history, presence of external precipitants, affective features and heredity coupled with positive criteria for Bleulerian schizophrenia; this dilemma demonstrates the over-inclusiveness of Bleuler's description of schizophrenia (1911).

Table 16.1 The third functional psychosis

State	Author	Description
Schizophreniform states	Langfeldt (1939)	Schizophrenics who recover, acute onset, psychogenic precipitants, depressive symptoms and family history, confusion during acute episode, extroversion of personality, pyknic body build
Schizo-affective psychosis	Kasanin (1933)	Good premorbid function, mixed schizophrenic and affective features, recovery after a few months
Dementia praecox	Kraepelin (1919)	Obsolete term
Dementia praecox with cyclical course	Dunton (1910)	Obsolete term
Catatonic syndrome	Kiley (1913)	Acute onset of catatonic symptoms, no premorbid personality changes, good prognosis
Benign stupor	Hoch (1921)	Aged 15–25, acute onset of catatonic symptoms, inactivity, intellectual interference, affectless, negation
Recovered schizophrenics	Kant (1940)	Acute onset, clouding of consciousness, extroversion, pyknic build, affective features and family history, young, often prior diagnosis of affective psychosis

Not infrequently, as has been demonstrated by Carlson and Goodwin (1973), in the acute phase of a bipolar affective psychosis a patient will show symptoms suggestive of schizophrenia, such as thought disorder, bizarre behaviour, ideas of reference, delusions and hallucinations. It has been described how a proportion of people who have had schizophrenic features in one episode develop manic features of an affective psychosis in a subsequent episode (Lipkin et al., 1970). Some patients with remitting schizophrenic illnesses subsequently present with clear-cut affective disorders (Sheldrick et al., 1977). There are also some who are initially diagnosed manic–depressive and subsequently reclassified schizophrenic (Hoch & Rachlin, 1941).

Kuriansky, Deming and Gurland (1974) have demonstrated that there was a shift in diagnosis in the USA from 1932 to 1956 towards schizophrenia. Baldessarini (1970) showed a shift towards diagnosis of affective psychoses from 1960 to 1968, and he linked this with the introduction of lithium for the treatment of mania and schizo-affective psychosis.

Slater and Roth (1969) regard the controversy over schizo-affective psychosis as largely unnecessary. They consider that careful diagnosis of schizophrenia and manic–depressive psychosis will include most cases. The term *schizo-affective psychosis* has been used loosely to imply any of the following four situations:

1 A patient has previously had an attack of schizophrenia with first-rank symptoms and now has a quite definite episode of affective psychosis.
2 A patient who had a previous manic–depressive illness, now has a definite schizophrenic illness.
3 A patient appeared to be suffering from schizophrenia and manic–depressive psychosis simultaneously, and both illnesses can be clearly delineated.
4 The psychosis seems to be somewhere between schizophrenia and manic–depressive psychosis and the doctor is not sure which diagnosis is correct. It is recommended that diagnosis should be made only after careful elucidation of the phenomenological symptoms.

Helmchen and Hippius (1967) found that half a sample of 120 admissions for schizophrenia also manifested depressive symptoms at the time of admission to hospital, and this finding has been subsequently confirmed. The possible explanations for this association of schizophrenic and depressive symptoms has been discussed by Hirsch (1986); he considers that depressive symptoms are an integral part of the schizophrenic syndrome (Knights & Hirsch, 1981).

References

Aitken RCB (1969) Measurement of feelings using visual analogue scales. *Proceedings of the Royal Society of Medicine 62*, 989–93.

Alvarez A (1971) *The Savage God: A Study of Suicide*. London: Weidenfeld & Nicolson.

American Psychiatric Association (1980) *Diagnostic and Statistical Manual of Mental Disorders*, 3rd Edn. Washington: American Psychiatric Association.

Anstee BH & Fleminger JJ (1977) Diagnosis 'uncertain': a follow-up study. *British Journal of Psychiatry 131*, 592–8.

Argyle M (1975) *Bodily Communication*. London: Methuen.

Baldessarini RJ (1970) Frequency of diagnosis of schizophrenia versus affective disorders 1944 to 1968. *American Journal of Psychiatry 127*, 759–63.

Bavington J (1981) *Depression in Pakistan.* Leeds: Transcultural Psychiatry Society (UK) Workshop.

Beck AT (1967) *Depression: Clinical, Experimental & Theoretical Aspects.* New York: Hoeber.

Beck AT, Rush AJ, Shaw BF & Emery G (1979) *Cognitive Therapy of Depression.* New York: The Guilford Press.

Bingham N (1841) *Religious Delusions.* London: Hatchard.

Bleuler E (1911) *Dementia Praecox: or the Group of Schizophrenias.* New York: International University Press.

Brenner B (1979) Depressed affect as a cause of associated somatic problems. *Psychological Medicine* 9, 737–46.

Brown GW & Harris T (1978) Social Origins of Depression: A study of psychiatric disorder in women. London: Tavistock.

Burns BH (1971) Breathlessness in depression. *British Journal of Psychiatry 119*, 39–45.

Carlson GA & Goodwin FK (1973) The stages of mania. *Archives of General Psychiatry 28*, 221–28.

Cowper W (1822) Written during a period of insanity. In Bruce J (ed.) *The Poetical Works of William Cowper*, Vol. III, pp. 340–341. London: Bell & Daldy.

Cutting J (1985) *The Psychology of Schizophrenia.* Edinburgh: Churchill Livingstone.

Cutting JC, Clare AW & Mann AH (1978) Cycloid psychosis: an investigation of the diagnostic concept. *Psychological Medicine 8*, 637–48.

Dean C & Kendell RE (1981) The symptomatology of puerperal illness. *British Journal of Psychiatry 139*, 128–33.

Dupré E (1913) Les Cénestopathies, Mouvement Médical 3–22 (transl. Rohde M, 1974) In Hirsch SR & Shepherd M (eds) *Themes & Variations in European Psychiatry* Bristol: John Wright.

Engel GL (1967) A psychological setting of somatic disease: The giving-up–given-up complex. *Proceedings of the Royal Society of Medicine 60*, 553–55.

Engel GL (1968) A life setting conducive to illness: The giving-up–given-up complex. *Annals of International Medicine 69*, 293–300.

Freud S (1895) On the grounds for detaching a particular syndrome from neurasthenia under the description 'anxiety neurosis'. *Standard Edition of the Complete Psychological Works of Sigmund Freud Vol. III*, pp.90–115. London: The Hogarth Press.

Galanter M (1982) Charismatic religious sects and psychiatry: an overview. *American Journal of Psychiatry 139*, 1539–48.

Gelder M, Gath D & Mayou R (1983) *Oxford Textbook of Psychiatry.* Oxford: Oxford University Press.

Hamilton M (1976) The role of rating scales in psychiatry. *Psychological Medicine 6*, 347–49.

Hare E (1981) The two manias: A study of the evolution of the modern concept of mania. *British Journal of Psychiatry 138*, 89–99.

Helmchen H & Hippius H (1967) Depressive syndrome im verlauf neuronleptischer therapie. *Nervenarzt 38*, 445.

Huxley A (1952) *The Devils of Loudun.* London: Chatto & Windus.

Hirsch S (1986) Depression 'revealed' in schizophrenia. In Kerr A & Snaith P (eds) *Contemporary Issues in Schizophrenia*, pp. 459–462. London: Gaskell.

Hoch P & Rachlin HL (1941) An evaluation of manic–depressive psychosis in light of follow-up studies. *American Journal of Psychiatry 97*, 831–43.

Ingham JG, Kreitman NB, Miller PMcC, Sashidharan SP & Surtees PG (1986) Self-esteem, vulnerability and psychiatric disorder in the community. *British Journal of Psychiatry 148*, 375–85.

James W (1902) *The Varieties of Religious Experience: A Study in Human Nature.* New York: Longmans, Green & Co.

Jaspers K (1959) *General Psychopathology* (transl. Hoenig J & Hamilton MW (1963). Manchester: Manchester University Press.

Kasanin J (1933) The acute schizoaffective psychoses. *American Journal of Psychiatry 13*, 97–126.

Katon W, Kleinman A & Rosen G (1982) Depression and somatization: a review. Part 1. *American Journal of Medicine 72*, 127–35.

Kelly GA (1955) *The Psychology of Personal Constructs.* New York: Norton.

Knights A & Hirsch SR (1981) 'Revealed' depression and drug treatment for schizophrenia. *Archives of General Psychiatry 38*, 806–11.

Kraepelin E (1905) *Lectures on Clinical Psychiatry*, 3rd Edn. (transl. Johnston T, 1917). New York: W Wood.

Kuriansky JB, Deming WE & Gurland BJ (1974) On trends in the diagnosis of schizophrenia. *American Journal of Psychiatry 131*, 402–05.

Lewis IM (1971) *Ecstatic Religion: An Anthropological Study of Spirit Possession and Shamanism.* Harmondsworth: Penguin.

Lieberman S (1978) Nineteen cases of morbid grief. *British Journal of Psychiatry 132*, 159–63.

Lipkin KM, Dyrud J & Meyer G (1970) The many faces of mania: Therapeutic trial of lithium carbonate. *Archives of General Psychiatry 22*, 262–67.

Lopez Ibor JJ (1966) *Neuroses as Mood Disorders.* Madrid: Editorial Gredos.

Mapother E & Lewis AJ (1937) In *PRICE'S Textbook of Medicine*, 5th Edn. London: Oxford University Press.

Murphy HBM, Wittkower ED & Chance NA (1964) A cross-cultural inquiry into the symptomatology of depression. *Transcultural Psychiatry Review.*

Nemiah JC & Sifneos PE (1970) Affect and fantasy in patients with psychosomatic disorders. In Hill OW (ed.) *Modern Trends in Psychosomatic Medicine–2*, pp. 26–34. London: Butterworth.

Parkes CM (1971) Psycho-social transitions: a field for study. *Social Science & Medicine 5*, 101–15.

Parkes CM (1976) The psychological reaction to loss of a limb: The first year after amputation. In Howells JG (ed.) *Modern Perception in the Psychiatric Aspects of Surgery*, pp. 515–533. London: MacMillan.

Parkes CM, Benjamin B & Fitzgerald RG (1969) Broken heart: A statistical study of increased mortality among widows. *British Medical Journal 1*, 740–43.

Parkes CM & Napier MM (1975) Psychiatric sequelae of amputation. In Silverstone T & Barraclough B (eds) *Contemporary Psychiatry*, pp. 440–446. Ashford: Headley Brothers.

Powell M & Hemsley DR (1984) Depression: A breakdown of perceptual defence? *British Journal of Psychiatry 145*, 358–62.

Procci WR (1976) Schizo-affective psychosis: Fact or fiction? A survey of the literature. *Archives of General Psychiatry 33*, 1167–78.

Rack P (1982) *Race, Culture and Mental Disorder.* London: Tavistock.

Rees WD (1971) The hallucinations of widowhood. *British Medical Journal 4*, 37–41.

Ropschitz DH (1957) Folie à deux: a case of folie imposée à trois. *Journal of Mental Science 103*, 589–96.

Schmale AH (1958) Relationships of separation and depression to disease: A report on a hospitalized medical population. *Psychosomatic Medicine 20*, 259–77.

Schmale AH & Iker HP (1966) The affect of hopelessness and the development of cancer. I. Identification of uterine cervical cancer in women with atypical cytology. *Psychosomatic Medicine 28*, 714–21.

Schneider K (1920) The stratification of emotional life and the structure of the depressive states. *Z ges. Neuol Psychiat. 59*, 281.

Sheldrick C, Jablensky A, Sartorius N & Shepherd M (1977) Schizophrenia succeeded by affective illness: catamnestic study and statistical enquiry. *Psychological Medicine 7*, 619–24.

Shulman K & Post F (1980) Bipolar affective disorder in old age. *British Journal of Psychiatry 136*, 26–32.

Sifneos PE (1972) *Short-Term Psychotherapy and Emotional Crisis.* Cambridge, Massachusetts: Harvard University Press.

Simpson CJ (1984) The stigmata: pathology or miracle? *British Medical Journal 289*, 1746–8.

Sirois F (1982) Epidemic hysteria. In Roy A (ed.) *Hysteria*, pp. 101–116. Chichester: John Wiley.

Slater E & Roth M (1969) *Clinical Psychiatry*, 3rd Edn. London: Baillière Tindall & Cassell.

Taylor G (1984) Alexithymia: Concept, measurement and implications for treatment. *American Journal of Psychiatry 141*, 725–32.

Trethowan WH (1977) *The Psychopathology of Depression.* Unpublished.

Trethowan WH (1979) Affective Disorders. In Trethowan WH (ed.) *Psychiatry*, Chapter 10. London: Baillière Tindall.

Ungerleider JT & Wellisch DK (1979) Coercive persuasion (brainwashing), religious cults, and deprogramming. *American Journal of Psychiatry 136*, 279–82.

Vere J (1778) *A Physical and Moral Enquiry into the Causes of That Internal Restlessness and Disorder in Man, Which Has Been the Complaint of All Ages.* London: White & Sewell.

Wernicke C (1906) *Fundamentals of Psychiatry.* Leipzig: Thieme.

World Health Organization (1977) *International Statistical Classification of Diseases, Injuries and Causes of Death*, 9th Revision. Geneva: World Health Organization.

Zilboorg G & Henry GW (1941) *A History of Medical Psychology.* New York: Norton.

—17

Anxiety, Irritability, Phobia and Obsession

Montanus speaks of one that durst not walk alone from home for fear that he should swoon or die. A second fears every man he meets will rob him, quarrel with him or kill him. A third dares not venture to walk alone, for fear he should meet the devil, a thief, be sick; fears all old women as witches; and every black dog or cat he sees he suspecteth to be a devil; every person comes near him is malificiated; every creature, all intend to hurt him, seek his ruine; another dares not go over a bridge, come near a pool, rock, steep hill, lye in a chamber where cross beams are for fear he be tempted to hang, drown or precipitate himself. If he be in a silent auditory, as at a sermon, he is afraid he shall speak aloud, at unawares, something undecent, unfit to be said. If he be locked in a close room, he is afraid of being stifled for want of air, and still carries bisket, aquavitae, or some strong waters about him for fear of deliquiums, or being sick; or if he be in a throng, middle of a church, multitude, where he may not well get out, though he sit at ease he is certase affected. He will freely promise, undertake any business beforehand; but when it comes to be performed he dares not adventure, but fears an infinite number of dangers, disasters, etc... They are afraid of some loss, danger, that they shall surely lose their lives, goods, and all they have; but why they know not.

Robert Burton (1621)

These four abnormal phenomena are common amongst neurotic disorders. What makes them abnormal is their severity, their prolonged duration, their occurrence in reaction to what could be considered an inadequate situational stress, and the deleterious effect they have upon social functioning. Each of them has a normal, even necessary, aspect: it is appropriate to be anxious at the beginning of a speech in public; it is normal for a parent to express irritability when an 8-year-old son breaks a window–it is a necessary learning experience for him; fear is necessary for coping when an individual suddenly discovers him or herself to be surrounded by poisonous snakes; meticulous checking and checking again is an important part of learning to be a competent airline pilot.

These four symptoms may all occur together, especially in response to increased situational stress. They may also occur in pairs. Anxiety and irritability are phenomenologically related; in irritability, aggressiveness is added to the subjective experience of tension. Anxiety and phobia are related in that phobia is anxiety occurring in a specific situation. Phobia and obsession are related in that those experiencing either of them suffer a loss of freedom of action and, in both, a self-examining attitude is maintained (Scharfetter, 1980). These four states are all more likely to occur with anankastic and dysthymic personality disorders, and with other neurotic disorders. They often occur in depressive illness and may be associated with depersonalization or hypochondriasis.

Patients may have insight and present themselves as suffering from–'phobia', 'obsession', 'anxiety state'. However, the lay use of each of these terms is significantly different from psychiatric use and it will be more usual for the clinician to diagnose the state from a description of the mood or thought process.

Mood in neurotic disorders is an exaggeration or distortion of the normal mood that might occur in similar circumstances. Mood is the state of drive, energy or tension from which action takes place. It is characteristic of the mood in neurosis that it is ineffective in producing action to deal appropriately or effectively with the problems that provoked it. It is therefore pathological as a response to the factors that caused it and in the effects which it facilitates.

Anxiety

Anxiety is a universal emotion that it would at times be maladaptive not to experience; it is a necessary part of the response of the organism to stress. Lader and Marks (1971) have discussed the features of anxiety in terms of the emotion being normal or pathological. In rather concrete terms: a man, who discovers that he is sharing a field with a bull, feels acutely anxious and runs at top speed for the gate; if, six weeks later, when back in the city, he has a panic attack and has to lie down because someone mentions a part of the city called 'The Bullring', his response is clearly maladaptive and his anxiety pathological.

Anxiety may also be polarized between *state* and *trait*. Anxiety state is the quality of being anxious now, at this particular time, probably as a reaction to provoking circumstances. Anxiety trait is the tendency over a long time, perhaps throughout life, to meet all the vicissitudes of life with an habitual excessive degree of anxiety; it is often associated with dysthymic personality disorder (Chapter 20). Anxiety as a description of the experience of normal emotion is not different in quality, only quantitatively, from anxiety state (Hamilton, 1959). Characteristic of the mood of anxiety are feelings of *constriction*. The word is etymologically associated with the idea of narrowness, stricture, 'straits'; and in early usage was located in the praecordium and prominently associated with angina (Sims, 1985). The patient with anxiety state may feel restless, uncertain, vulnerable, trapped, breathless, choked. As well as feeling frightened and worried, hypochondriacal ideas and feelings of guilt are often prominent. Symptoms of anxiety occur pathologically in *anxiety states* without obvious external cause. The anxiety is not attached to any specific provoking object and so it is termed *free-floating anxiety*.

There is also a contrast between the experience of anxiety as a subjective emotion and the objective occurrence of physiological somatic changes normally associated with that affect; some of the commoner symptoms are shown in Table 17.1 (Tyrer, 1982). Tyrer considers irritability to be a symptom *of* anxiety state but Snaith and Taylor (1985) showed that irritability is an independent mood state which may be associated *with* anxiety–or any other mood disorder. Although it is usual to find the psychological and physical aspects associated and related in intensity, this may not necessarily be so. The patient may complain of feeling extremely anxious but show minimal somatic expression; in hysteria, marked physical changes have been described when the patient does not complain at all of feeling anxious. These three dichotomous aspects of anxiety are represented in Figure 17.1.

Table 17.1 Symptoms of anxiety (Tyrer, 1982)

Somatic and Autonomic	Psychic (psychological)
Palpitations	Feelings of dread and threat
Difficulty in breathing	Irritability
Dry mouth	Panic
Nausea	Anxious anticipation
Frequency of micturition	Inner (psychic) terror
Dizziness	Worrying over trivia
Muscular tension	Difficulty in concentrating
Sweating	Initial insomnia
Abdominal churning	Inability to relax
Tremor	
Cold skin	

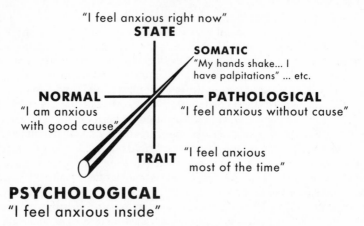

Fig. 17.1 Three-dimensional model of anxiety symptoms

Patients with anxiety disorder describe characteristic ideational components, concentrating on themes of personal danger and especially physical harm (Hibbert, 1984). The 'most important' thought of patients included: 'I may panic in front of others'; 'I may die of a heart attack while asleep'; and, 'I am going to have a heart attack'. Fear of physical, psychological or social disaster occurred during panic attacks. Stressful life experiences in the preceding twelve months, and some physiological disturbance other than anxiety immediately before the symptoms, were commonly described.

Other psychological functions are affected by acute anxiety. The capacity for reflection is decreased, and the field of conscious awareness narrowed; this obviously has survival value for instant physical action but is a disadvantage when planning, reviewing and taking many different factors into consideration is important. The variations of activity with anxiety are seen, for instance, after the experience of disaster: some victims will be numb and inert; others tense, restless and constructively overactive; and others still panic-stricken and incapable of sustained activity.

In the Present State Examination (Wing *et al.*, 1974), *general anxiety* is contrasted with *situational anxiety*; that is, the tendency to become anxious in certain defined situations. This latter is discussed later with phobic states. Under *general anxiety* is included free-floating autonomic anxiety, panic attacks and the observation during interview that the patient appears to be anxious, tense, worried or apprehensive. Free-floating anxiety comprises such autonomic components as blushing, 'butterflies in the stomach', choking, difficulty in getting the breath, dizziness, dry mouth, giddiness, palpitations, sweating and trembling, dilated pupils, raised blood pressure; parasympathetic aspects include nausea, vomiting, frequency of micturition and diarrhoea.

Panic attacks occur as discrete episodes of somatic or autonomic anxiety associated with marked psychic anxiety as an extreme sense of fear. The attack ends either with a complete interruption to the patient's current stream of behaviour so that he lies on the floor, rushes into the open air, runs back into the house, or 'collapses'; or he terminates his current behaviour voluntarily so that the attack remits more gradually. In either case, there is something about his mode of activities which was precipitating or perpetuating the attack. The patient makes this association for himself and he goes to elaborate lengths to avoid provoking a panic attack. This may be the antecedent condition for development of a phobic state. The duration of the attack varies from less than a minute to several hours, but is normally about ten to twenty minutes. Frequency of occurrence may be up to many times per day.

Panic disorder has been established as a separate diagnostic category in DSM III (American Psychiatric Association, 1980). For this to be present, at least three panic attacks should have been experienced during a three-week period without marked physical exertion or a life-threatening situation. At least four of the following symptoms should be present for diagnosis: dyspnoea; palpitations; chest pain or discomfort; choking or smothering sensations; dizziness; feelings of unreality; paraesthesiae; hot and cold flushes; sweating; faintness trembling; or fear of dying or going mad.

The psychic quality of feeling anxious or tense is more difficult to measure than the physiological correlates. Words are idiosyncratic in their meaning, and so there is a tendency to judge the veracity of the patient's statement that he is 'terribly anxious' according to the severity of the autonomic symptoms occurring concurrently. However, it is possible by using serial rating scales to compare the patient's subjective experience at different times. Self-description of anxiety includes worry, brooding, sleeplessness through preoccupation with contents of the thoughts, and so on.

Phobic states

Phobias, or unreasonable fears, have been described for many centuries. For example, Benjamin Rush (1798) defines phobia as 'a fear of an imaginary evil, or an undue fear of a real one,' and then produces a list of eighteen phobias, partly humorously intended; this is reproduced in Table 17.2. *Agoraphobia* was originally described by Westphal (1871); this condition, literally fear of the market-place, causes very severe disability. Animal phobias have been contrasted by Marks (1970): 'If ever we are tempted to think that all phobic states are a unity which reflects the same disorder and aetiology, we can quickly dispel this illusion simply by looking at the startling contrast between animal phobias and agoraphobias. These two conditions differ radically in onset, course, symptomatology, response to treatment and psychological measures'. Solyom *et al.* (1986) divided the symptomatology of 199 patients into three

Table 17.2 Species of Phobia according to Rush (1798)

1.	The Cat Phobia	10.	The Faction Phobia
2.	The Rat Phobia	11.	The Want Phobia
3.	The Insect Phobia	12.	The Doctor Phobia
4.	The Odour Phobia	13.	The Blood Phobia
5.	The Dirt Phobia	14.	The Thunder Phobia
6.	The Rum Phobia	15.	The Home Phobia
7.	The Water Phobia	16.	The Church Phobia
8.	The Solo Phobia	17.	The Ghost Phobia
9.	The Power Phobia	18.	The Death Phobia

categories: agoraphobia (80 patients), social phobia (47 patients) and simple phobia (72 patients). Agoraphobia included 'fear of leaving home, of being alone at home or on the street, in crowds, of travelling by car, bus or train'. Social phobia involved 'fear of performing–speaking, writing, eating, urinating in public or in the presence of others'. Simple phobia described a single but life-disrupting fear, such as of animals, heights, disease, aeroplanes, insects and so on.

A more comprehensive subdivision of phobic states is contained in Table 17.3 from Marks (1969). Since agoraphobia literally means fear of the market-place, this is often appropriate nowadays, as often the most phobic situation for such people is in the supermarket. Agoraphobia is, in fact, a heterogeneous collection of disorders and not an entity (Snaith, 1981). It includes both those who have a fear of being under public scrutiny and therefore who avoid public places; and also those with illness fears in either a public place where they become noticeable or an exposed place where they will not receive help.

Table 17.3 Subdivisions of phobic neurosis (after Marks, 1969)

Phobias of External Stimuli	*Phobias of Internal Stimuli*
Agoraphobia	Illness phobias
Social phobias	Obsessive phobias
Animal phobias	
Miscellaneous specific phobias	

Illness phobia is different from hypochondriacal preoccupation in that, with the former, avoidance occurs. Thus the criteria for phobia, according to Marks (1969), are:

1 Fear is out of proportion to the demands of the situation;
2 It cannot be explained or reasoned away;
3 It is not under voluntary control;
4 The fear leads to an *avoidance* of the feared situation.

A 28-year-old married woman said: 'My fear problems are worst... I am afraid of catching cancer. I am afraid of catching it from the hospital (Radiotherapy hospital one mile away)... I bought a scarf from a shop and the assistant frightened me... the look of her, she hardly had any hair and looked very old... I thought I had caught it from her and so I had to wash the house. I cleaned the whole house and it made me poorly. I had to move house because of the hospital and I cannot go back to that shop ever again'.

Phobias are unreasonable and inappropriate fears. Subjectively, they take the form of *situational anxiety*; anxiety is associated with specific circumstances or objects, and may result in *avoidance*. Situational autonomic anxiety, unlike free-floating anxiety, arises only with specific causes. Such fear-provoking situations include being in a crowded place (agoraphobia), or a confined space (claustrophobia), or perhaps on one's own, or looking down from a high place; phobias may follow a stimulus which is idiosyncratic to this particular person. Provoking causes are frequently animals or parts of animals; for example cat, mouse, spider, snake, feathers, bird. This specific type of anxiety may then generalize so that the person starts by being phobic for cats, but becomes so frightened that she might meet a cat, that all the time she spends out of home she lives in a state of dread; eventually this bears only a tenuous relationship with the original cause.

There is also some relationships between phobias, especially agoraphobia and depression (Schapira *et al.*, 1970). Persistent fear and foreboding, often of a situational nature, may occur with other depressive symptoms. Phobic states do on occasions respond to antidepressent therapy.

Roth (1959) has described the phobic–anxiety–depersonalization syndrome as a separate nosological entity, but sees it as a form of anxiety neurosis upon which the additional symptoms are superimposed in some individuals; phobic symptoms are usually social and agoraphobic. This is seen most often in younger married women. Typically, such a patient shows agoraphobia so that she cannot travel on a bus or go shopping in a supermarket for fear of being conspicuous in public–either fainting or being taken suddenly ill in one of these places. She is likely to describe panic attacks on some of the occasions when she has attempted these things in the past. She develops a relationship of complete dependency on her husband whom she may describe as 'a golden husband'. His work and other interests outside the home are severely curtailed. Fear of leaving the house unaccompanied may result in the husband staying off work to cope with household duties. The children are often involved in her symptoms also: they may be constrained to stay home from school so that she does not have to be on her own. She is chronically anxious and may experience depersonalization, either as episodes which come and go unaccountably or as a continuously unpleasant state.

Phobias are overpowering and compelling in their nature, dominating the whole of life. Like obsessions they are repetitive, resisted unsuccessfully, regarded by the subject as senseless and irrational but at the same time as coming from inside of him- or herself. Some authors therefore describe them as *obsessional fears*. Often compulsive behaviour, such as hand-washing, arises out of a phobia; for instance, fear of dirt and contamination. Prominent in the subject's description of his phobia is that he is controlled by it; that the fear is something from inside himself (in no way controlled from outside).

Irritability

Irritability of the patient may be observed by others, or experienced subjectively directed towards others (outward) or towards the self (inward). Irritability, outwardly expressed, is considered to be a disorder of mood in its own right and independent of anxiety, depression or other mood state (Snaith & Taylor, 1985): 'Marked irritability does not attract a caring response from the health care professions'. Outwardly expressed irritability is particularly commonly associated with puerperal mood disorder; whilst inwardly directed irritability was described in those with obsessional neurosis. In the Irritability, Depression and Anxiety (IDA) Scale, two subscales were developed for irritability (Snaith *et al.*, 1978): Outwardly Directed Irritability and Inwardly Directed Irritability. Snaith and Taylor (1985) have defined irritability for use in the context of psychopathology: 'Irritability is a feeling state characterized by reduced control over temper–which usually results in irascible verbal or behavioural outbursts, although the mood may be present without observed manifestation. It may be experienced as brief episodes, in particular circumstances, or it may be prolonged and generalized. The experience of irritability is always unpleasant for the individual and overt manifestation lacks the cathartic effect of justified outbursts of anger'.

The severity of irritability probably has an inverse correlation with age; it occurs in both men and women. It is useful to make a distinction between the subjective mood of irritability and the observation of violent behaviour, although these may overlap. Severe irritability may cause considerable distress to patients, relatives and health care professionals; there may be no other psychiatric symptomatology present. The factors that predispose to irritability are not clearly known.

Obsessions and compulsions

The patient may be troubled by thoughts that he knows to be his own but which he finds repetitive and strange; he finds he is unable to prevent their repetition. These obsessional thoughts have, according to Lewis (1936), three essential features: a feeling of subjective compulsion, a resistance to it and the preservation of insight. These features distinguish obsession from voluntary repetitive acts and social ceremonies. The word *obsession* is usually reserved for the thought, and compulsion for the act. The sufferer knows that it is his own thought (or act), that it arises from within himself, and that it is subject to his own will whether he continues to think (or perform) it; he can decide not to think it on this particular occasion (but it does and will recur). He is tormented by the fear of what may happen if he disturbs the routine. There is no disturbance of consciousness or of the awareness of the possession of his own thought. The person usually functions satisfactorily in other areas of his life uncontaminated by the obsessional thought, but as the obsessions become more severe there is increasing social incapacity, and misery that can grossly disrupt his whole lifestyle.

A midwife, aged 32, kept thinking after she had finished her spell of duty at hospital that she might have pushed an airway down the throat of a baby that she had delivered. She telephoned the ward repeatedly to check that the infant was well. She frequently made sure that her dog's collar was secure when she was out walking in case he escaped and was killed by traffic. When a little boy and his mother visited her home, she gave him a glass of 'pop'. However, she had to drink what she had just poured out for him herself, although she disliked it, to make sure it really was pop and not something harmful. The accumulation of more and more symptoms eventually prevented her from working or carrying out any reasonable social life. She knew that these were her own notions, that they were stupid, but she could not stop herself thinking and performing them.

The compulsive behaviour often provokes further anxiety in the patient; the need both to perform the action and to preserve social acceptability. Although wide areas of life are often implicated in compulsive rituals, it is often striking how the obsessional omits other areas from his obsessionality. The patient who excoriates his hands by excessive washing and devotes a substantial portion of each day to the pursuit of cleanliness may drive to work in a dirty and ill-serviced car and work in an untidy office! The dilemma of obsessional symptoms remains that they are both reckoned as part of the patient's own behaviour, and resisted unsuccessfully: that is, they are under voluntary control but not altogether experienced as voluntary. The patient has an awareness that this particular act or thought is voluntary and can be resisted, with difficulty, but the overall pattern of thinking or behaving is experienced subjectively as inevitable–it is ultimately futile to struggle. The action sometimes 'appears to be against the will of the patient, and often seems to have the quality of disgust or repulsion; this urge to do something yet to be repelled by it, is said to be a singular characteristic of the obsessional state' (Beech, 1974).

Obsession may occur as thoughts, images, impulses, ruminations or fears; compulsions as acts, rituals, behaviours. Schneider's definition (1959) emphasizes that there is no loss of contact with reality: 'An obsession occurs when someone cannot get rid of a content of consciousness, although when it occurs he realizes that it is senseless or at least that it is dominating and persisting without cause'. Thus, hallucinations, delusions and mood disturbances cannot be obsessional in form. The craving of an alcoholic for his beverage or the abnormal drive of sexual deviation are not compulsive in a strict sense. They do not contravene the person's will, although he may dislike himself intensely for having such wishes.

Obsessional ideas may be simple or complicated. A tune or a few notes may become repetitive and be resisted, or a sequence of words, 'The British Socialist Party', be reiterated irritatingly inside his head. The obsessions or compulsions may be more complex, and ritualistic; for example, a patient who tried to shut the car door after getting out, found this very difficult because he was afraid that the act of shutting would produce unpleasant, obscene, repetitive thoughts. For this reason he had to go to elaborate lengths to put the car in a certain place, check all the doors before getting out, check them all again after getting out and turn the key whilst looking in a particular direction.

The images may be vivid but are always known by the patient to be his own thoughts. Ruminations are often pseudophilosophical, irritatingly unnecessary, repetitive and achieve no conclusion. A priest has an inner impulse to utter swear words in church, or a mother an impulse to harm her child–both quite frequent complaints of obsessional patients. Reassurance that he will not harm himself or others or act on the impulses, can be given to the obsessional, provided it is truly obsessional in form, that he is not concurrently depressed, and that there is not coexisting asocial personality disorder.

Obsessions occur in the context of obsessive–compulsive neurosis, as the major symptom of the condition. However, they also occasionally occur in other circumstances. The depressed patient with an obsessional personality may show obsessions and compulsions which clear when his illness is treated. Obsessional states are more common where obsessional personality is present but this personality type is not a prerequisite. Obsessional symptoms may occur in schizophrenia when they usually have a bizarre character. Apparent obsessional symptoms may arise *de novo* in an older person associated with an organic psychosyndrome. However, the element of resistance characteristic of obsessionality is usually not present. It seems that the person carries out repetitive behaviour in order to cope with the uncertainties of his life caused by his failing memory and performance. Similar repetitiveness and stickiness of thinking occurs with epilepsy, following head injury and with other organic states; but again this is not truly obsessional in nature.

Obsessionality and anankastic personality

The discussion above has been concerned with obsessive–compulsive neurosis. The following description is more concerned with *trait* obsessionality, the features of the person with obsessional or *anankastic personality*. The general features of this personality type are discussed in Chapter 21. However, because there is so much confusion between obsessive–compulsive symptoms and obsessionality as a way of life, it is appropriate to digress and give some attention to the latter at this point.

In their thinking, anankasts tolerate ambiguity less readily than normals. They like to have decisions made, but will delay making a decision until they have reached a greater degree of certainty than is required by other people. As they grow older they become increasingly rigid in their thinking. They constrict their thinking to deal more comfortably with daily events, and this requires them to make sweeping generalizations of a narrow and prejudiced sort. Reed (1969) has considered the thinking of the obsessional to be *under-inclusive*; that is, in a test for over-inclusiveness he will put too few members into a category. This is a further example of the anankast's indecision and doubt in performing new tasks and craving for certainty. He has to be completely sure of getting it right.

Janet regarded as the central experience of patients suffering from obsessional neurosis *sentiment d'incomplétude, incompleteness* (Cooper & Kelleher, 1973). This was demonstrated as a personality trait present in a proportion of normal subjects when a principal components analysis was carried out on the Leyton Obsessional Inventory, completed by 302 supposedly normal men and women. The three distinct components of this personality trait demonstrated were: *clean and tidy, incompleteness* and *checking*.

Another attempt to explain anankastic thinking has used personal construct theory and the use of the repertory grid. Makhlouf Norris (1968) found what she described as *monolithic* and *segmented systems* to be characteristic of obsessional thinking. In monolithic systems, there are clusters of related constructs which are not related to other groups of constructs. These systems do not allow conceptualization of the person's environment and the people in it to form a single whole with all the ambiguities and qualifications this would require: 'Independent judgements with opposing implications cannot be made. Therefore the tendency is to make judgements which mean the same thing'. The limitation of these systems is that they cannot be modified by changing circumstances, and so the obsessional has an extreme reluctance to make decisions because of the inadequacy of his conceptualization in making predictions: 'In uncertainty he creates islands of certainty in which he can control events, he tries to create a condition in which his objective probabilities are invariably 1.00–an obsessional idea or compulsive act. It is a symbolic miniature act with a dual function; that of bridging the gap between self and ideal self, and also confirming the inferiority of the self'. Makhlouf Norris proposes total correlation between the obsessional's own observed and expected behaviour, because it is rigidly self-controlled.

Because he lacks links between different construct systems, the anankast is intolerant of any uncertainty. Fransella (1974) has summarized this: 'Threat is seen as the awareness of imminent comprehensive change in one's core structures. It would indeed be threatening for the person with only a very limited part of his system functioning as an integrated whole, to be confronted with the prospect of letting even a limited part of it go momentarily out of his control–he must hang on at all costs. Thus, he over-defines, under-includes, he misreads the evidence, he does everything to help him hang on to the meaning when he perceives threat to this system... Invalidation is a threat to the whole system'. The rigidity of his constructs and his obsessionality are confined to the way he sees himself and the relation of self to not-self. In other areas, his constructs are very loose and obsessionality is not present.

Two other features of the anankastic personality connected with intolerance of uncertainty and feelings of incompleteness are *insecurity* and *sensitivity*. Even when every possible check and precaution has been introduced the anankast still fells insecure about his activities. Fundamentally, this is associated with the way he sees himself in relation to others: he is uncertain about the way they regard him and extremely sensitive concerning the slightest suggestion of criticism.

It is very important to make the distinction between the form of obsessions or compulsions and anankastic thinking. Often they overlap; a person with anankastic personality may have discrete episodes of obsessive–compulsive neurosis. However, in terms of understanding the patient's symptoms, in diagnosis, in prognosis and for treatment these two phenomena should be considered separately.

References

American Psychiatric Association (1980) *Diagnostic and Statistical Manual of Mental Disorders*, 3rd Edn. Washington: American Psychiatric Association.

Beech HR (1974) *Obsessional States*. London: Methuen.

Burton R (1621) *The Anatomy of Melancholy, What It Is. With All the Kinds, Causes, Symptomes, Prognostickes, and Severall Cures of it by Democritus Junior*. Oxford: Cripps.

Cooper J & Kelleher M (1973) The Leyton Obsessional Inventory: a principal components analysis on normal subjects. *Psychological Medicine 3*, 204–8.

Fransella F (1974) *Thinking and the obsessional*. In Beech HR (ed.) *Obsessional States*, pp. 175–196. London: Methuen.

Hamilton M (1959) The assessment of anxiety states by rating. *British Journal of Medical Psychology 32*, 50–55.

Hibbert GA (1984) Ideational components of anxiety: their origin and content. *British Journal of Psychiatry 144*, 613–24.

Lader MH & Marks IM (1971) *Clinical Anxiety*. London: Heinemann.

Lewis AJ (1936) Problems of obsessional illness. *Proceedings of Royal Society of Medicine 29*, 325–36.

Makhlouf Norris F (1968) Concepts of the Self and Others in Obsessional Neurosis Studied by an Adaptation of the Role Construct Repertory Grid. University of London, PhD Thesis.

Marks IM (1969) *Fears and Phobias*. London: Heinemann.

Marks IM (1970) The classification of phobic disorders. *British Journal of Psychiatry 116*, 377–86.

Reed GF (1969) 'Under-inclusion': A characteristic of obsessional personality disorder I & II. *British Journal of Psychiatry 115*, 781–90.

Roth M (1959) The phobic anxiety–depersonalization syndrome. *Proceedings of the Royal Society of Medicine 52*, 587–95.

Rush B (1798) On the different species of phobia. *The Weekly Magazine of Original Essays, Fugitive Pieces, and Interesting Intelligence, Philadelphia*. In Hunter R & McAlpine I (1963) *Three Hundred Years of Psychiatry 1535–1860*, pp. 669–70. London: Oxford University Press.

Schapira K, Kerr TA & Roth M (1970) Phobias and affective illness. *British Journal of Psychiatry 117*, 25–32.

Scharfetter C (1980) *General Psychopathology: An Introduction*. Cambridge: Cambridge University Press.

Schneider K (1959) *Clinical Psychopathology*, 5th Edn. (transl. Hamilton MW). New York & London: Grune & Stratton.

Sims ACP (1985) Anxiety in historical perspective. *British Journal of Clinical Practice, Supplement 38, 39*, 4–9.

Snaith P (1981) *Clinical Neurosis*. Oxford: Oxford University Press.

Snaith RP, Constantopoulos AA, Jardine MY & McGuffin P (1978) A clinical scale for the self assessment of irritability, anxiety and depression. *British Journal of Psychiatry 132*, 164–71.

Snaith RP & Taylor CM (1985) Irritability: definition, assessment and associated factors. *British Journal of Psychiatry 147*, 127–36.

Solyom L, Ledwige B & Solyom C (1986) Delineating social phobia. *British Journal of Psychiatry*.

Tyrer P (1982) Anxiety. *British Journal of Hospital Medicine 27*, 109–16.

Westphal C (1871) Die Agoraphobie: eine neuropathische Erscheinung. *Archiv. fur Psychiatrie und Nerven Krankheiten 3*, 138–61.

Wing JK, Cooper JE & Sartorius N (1974) *The Measurement and Classification of Psychiatric Symptoms*. Cambridge: Cambridge University Press.

18

Urge, Drive & Will: Disturbance of Volition

There is a vice that most I do abhor,
And most desire should meet the flow of justice,
For which I would not plead, but that I must;
For which I must not plead, but that I am
At war 'twixt will and will not.
William Shakespeare, *Measure for Measure*, II.ii.29.

This is an area of psychiatry that is even less well-charted than others. There is no comprehensive model that satisfactorily encompasses the various terms used. Therefore, until we have a more general theory and set of definitions, it is best to rely mostly on the subjective descriptions given by patients and upon the unequivocal observations made of them.

Definitions proposed by Scharfetter (1980) are as follows:

1 *Need* (a phenomenological concept): a striving towards a particular object, state or action, that is experienced as a desire.
2 *Drive* (a) as a construct: an inclination to satisfy certain primary, that is, innate needs; (b) as activity: the individual's basic mode of expression.
3 *Instinct* (a construct): an innate pattern of behaviour which leads to drive-satisfaction.
4 *Motivation* (a) as a phenomenological concept: a more or less clearly experienced mood or affect which is governed by needs and which moves us to actions which satisfy these needs; (b) as a construct: a hypothetical activating factor.
5 *Will* (a phenomenological concept): a goal-directed striving or intention based on cognitively planned motivation.

Scharfetter then describes those primary needs, which are innate and not learned as *hunger*, *thirst*, *breathing*, *urination* and *defecation*, *sleep* and *self-preservation*. Other needs are not essential for survival; their demands can be postponed and they are more affected by acquired patterns of behaviour; such as sexual drive, social or community drive, drive to care for one's young, drive to movement and play and exploratory drive (curiosity). Secondary needs are acquired and vary with the individual, for example smoking.

Human beings are so complex that, although primary needs require rapid satisfaction, they only account for a small proportion of the individual's psychic experience and action. Whilst I write this I allow myself to become aware of the primary need for breathing–but I shall not be giving it a thought ten minutes from now. The acquired primary needs and secondary needs have more influence upon the individual mental state.

Motivation, as a phenomenological concept, is readily understood by the layman but is ultimately tautologous: 'I do it because I am motivated'; 'I am motivated to do it'. However, it is a concept that in psychiatry we cannot do without. Similarly *will* is a necessary concept, but we have great difficulty in comprehending it, partly because the will itself is not unitary but often in conflict with itself, as has been clearly recognized for two millenia in this Biblical quotation. 'So I find it to be a law that when I want to do right, evil lies close at hand. For I delight in the law of God, in my inmost self, but I see in my members another law at war with the law of my mind and making me captive to the law of sin which dwells in my members'. This conflict, which causes consternation to the mentally healthy, may paralyse the activity of neurotic patients.

Activity is discussed in a subsequent chapter. Abnormalities of need and motivation ultimately express themselves as disturbance of volition and these will now be described.

Disturbance of volition

In terms of the self-description of the subject, any of the following phenomenological abnormalities resulting in observed disturbance of volition may occur: there could be a disturbance of the *need*, for example, an absence of hunger; abnormality of *motivation* may occur with, for example, no experience of the necessary affect to move the individual towards finding food, despite his having the physical pangs of hunger; there may be a disturbance of *will*, for example, in an individual who feels hungry and wishes to have food but either cannot move himself out of his present state of apathy sufficiently to seek to obtain it, or alternatively, deliberately denies his feeling of need for food and abstains. Of course, very frequently these elements are mixed.

ORGANIC CAUSES

Biological drives such as appetite, sleep and thirst are located anatomically in and around the mid-brain. Localized disease in this area of either a structural or biochemical nature is therefore likely to result in disturbance of drive and, hence, volition. Hormonal, metabolic and neurophysiological mechanisms affect volition. Thus, the need for food, expressed in hunger and resulting in seeking food, is affected by the state of fullness of the gastro-intestinal tract; by the secretion of insulin from the pancreas; by sensory innervation of the gut wall; as well as by regulation in the appetite centre. Physical illnesses have both a specific and a generalized effect upon volition.

Excessive appetite (bulimia) may occur with conditions such as tumour affecting the hypothalamus, and result in gross obesity; obesity may be associated with hypoventilation and excessive sleeping (hypersomnia) in the Pickwickian syndrome (Burwell *et al.*, 1956); periodic somnolence and intense hunger with voracious overeating occur in the Kleine–Levin syndrome (Critchley, 1962). Excessive thirst and fluid intake (polydipsia) occurs with disease of the posterior pituitary or the kidney (nephrogenic diabetes insipidus, for example, with lithium treatment). Loss of appetite (anorexia) may occur with localized disease of the mid-brain, resulting in severe cachexia; however, it is very much more common as a feature of any severe debilitating physical illness.

SCHIZOPHRENIC DISTURBANCE OF VOLITION

In schizophrenia, the disturbance of volition is much more at the level of *motivation* or *will* than of *need*. There may be abnormality of appetite with polyphagia and consequent obesity, as occurs in some chronic schizophrenic patients; however, this is not usual. Deluded schizophrenics who believe that their food is being poisoned may refrain from eating as a consequence; that is, of course, a deliberate act of will. The more conspicuous disturbance, however, is *loss of volition* that results in withdrawal from normal social interaction, for instance lack of motivation to obtain and continue in employment, or diminished sexual drive resulting in decreased fecundity, especially in male schizophrenics.

This symptom was described by Bleuler (1911) as *disturbance of initiative*, according to Lehmann (1967). It is also recognized amongst the so-called negative symptoms of what Crow (1980) has designated Type II schizophrenia. The *negative traits*–emotional apathy, slowness of thought and movement, underactivity, lack of drive, poverty of speech and social withdrawal–are a major barrier to effective rehabilitation in chronic schizophrenic patients (Wing, 1978). Although positive symptoms, such as delusions, hallucinations and thought disorder, are more conspicuous, especially in the earlier stages of a schizophrenic illness, the prognosis is probably affected to a greater extent by the loss of volition.

Schizophrenic patients regularly describe wanting to 'get married, set up home and have a family' or 'get a good job and earn a living'; they may describe detailed and elaborate plans to do this, but actually initiating the practical steps to carry out these objectives does not materialize. A young man suffering from schizophrenia would come regularly to the out-patient clinic to describe how he was intending to become a market gardener. He would go to great lengths discussing the economic aspects of the project, and he had a particular enthusiasm for compost-making for which he had invented his own new apparatus–on paper. In practice, he lived in a one-bedroom flat in an old house surrounded by an overgrown and totally derelict garden. Over several years acquaintance he never cut one sod or cultivated a single plant.

AFFECTIVE DISTURBANCE OF VOLITION

Abnormalities of volition in affective illnesses are associated with abnormality of activity; retardation being prominent in depression, and overactivity in mania. In depression, motivation is impaired rather than will. A severely depressed managing director continued to worry about his plans for his company, but he found himself unable to make himself do anything about it. Loss of motivation occurs alongside loss of other affect. *Anhedonia* (see Chapter 16) or loss of ability to experience enjoyment is a prominent symptom in depressive illness (Snaith, 1986) and also occurs in schizophrenia. Depressed patients normally describe loss of interest in their previous hobbies and enjoyments in life. This anhedonia results in loss of motivation to carry out these activities. Such patients also describe lack of appetite and loss of all interest in food; this may result in marked loss of weight.

In mania there is commonly increased activity, a subjective feeling of greater energy, effectiveness and self-confidence; such a person may initiate all sorts of new projects. Manic patients are prone to drink too much alcohol, but they do not usually overeat, perhaps because they are readily distracted and tend to interrupt their meals with other new enterprises. Such people describe it as being very easy to make decisions, and their flight of ideas results in starting many tasks which they do not carry through to completion.

An elderly man lived with his wife in a late-nineteenth century semi-detached house in an industrial town. The first intimation of his manic illness was a desperate cry for help from his wife to their family doctor that he was destroying the house. At interview at home, one could see his many uncompleted building projects in the house. He said that he had thought it improper that every time his wife went to the toilet she should have to go through the back yard, where she could be seen by the neighbours. He had therefore knocked a hole in the wall between the kitchen and toilet to give internal access. Before he could get round to tidying the brickwork and putting in a new door, he had realized that the electric wiring was very old and so he had removed all the cables from the ground floor of the house. He was thinking of renewing the wiring, but then decided that his wife would like a brand new bathroom. It was at this point that his wife realized that he was ill and consulted their doctor.

DISTURBANCE WITH NEUROSIS AND PERSONALITY DISORDER

Neuroses and personality disorders overlap to a considerable extent: 60% of a population previously treated for neurotic disorder were found to show abnormality of personality at follow-up, while only 25% of an apparently normal group showed abnormality to the same extent (Sims & Gooding, 1975). Neurotic reaction is more prone to occur in those whose abnormal personality predisposes them. Personality disorder is present when the abnormality of personality is of such degree as to cause the patient himself or other people to suffer (Schneider, 1958).

In neurotic disturbance there is no loss of *need*; in fact, the needs are felt more keenly. Motivation and will are present but, because of neurotic attitudes and patterns of thinking, they fail to achieve the desired goals. This is closely associated with *attribution*–the neurotic believes that the circumstances of his life are not attributable to his own action (for more detail in this area see Antaki and Brewin, 1981); and to beliefs about *locus of control*–the neurotic considering himself to be subject to an external locus of control (Rotter, 1966). According to Schneider, the treatment of neurosis begins with the ability of the patient to accept responsibility for his actions.

Chronic low self-esteem and anxious over-involvement with self, results in a paralysis of willing. There is not a loss of will or of motivation but a conflict of direction of motivation; or, as in the quotation at the beginning of this chapter, 'I am at war 'twixt will and will not'. The patient has low self-esteem and devalues himself; he assumes he will not be able to cope with the demands made upon him and feels incapable of effective action. He considers himself to be a victim of circumstances, 'the tyranny of inevitability', in that he cannot materially alter his environment. He does not know what he can hope to achieve and therefore attempts either nothing or the unattainable.

Hysterical dissociation, with automatism affecting volition, is phenomenologically quite different from passivity of volition–a delusion of control occuring as a schizophrenic symptom. In both, the experience of activity is that it is not under personal control. In *made volitional acts* or passivity, the action is carried out in conditions where there is awareness of self (Jaspers, 1962); the person shows normal consciousness at the time and has full memory for the action afterwards. However, in hysterical states there is dissociation from the self or ego–the patient is not aware of the act and of the self at the same time. During the hysterical dissociation, there is diminished experience of self at the time of the automatic act; and in retrospect there is limited recollection for the time during which automatism occurred.

References

Antaki C & Brewin C (1981) *Attributions and Psychological Change*. London: Academic Press.

Bleuler E (1911) *Dementia Praecox or the Group of Schizophrenias* (transl. Zinkin J, 1950). New York: International Universities Press.

Burwell CS, Robin ED, Whaley RD & Bickelmann AG (1956) Extreme obesity associated with alveolar hypoventilation–a Pickwickian syndrome. *American Journal of Medicine 21*, 811–18.

Critchley M (1962) Periodic hypersomnia and megaphagia in adolescent males. *Brain 85*, 627–56.

Crow TJ (1980) Molecular pathology of schizophrenia; more than one disease process? *British Medical Journal 280*, 66–8.

Jaspers K (1959) *General Psychopathology*, 7th Edn. (transl. Hoenig J & Hamilton MW, 1963). Manchester: Manchester University Press.

Lehmann HE (1967) Schizophrenia. In Freedman AM & Kaplan HI (eds) *Comprehensive Textbook of Psychiatry*. Baltimore: Williams & Wilkins.

Rotter JB (1966) Generalized expectancies for internal versus external control of reinforcements. *Psychological Monographs 80(1)*, 1–28.

Scharfetter C (1980) *General Psychopathology: An Introduction*. Cambridge: Cambridge University Press.

Schneider K (1950) *Psychopathic Personalities*, (transl. Hamilton MW, 1958). London: Cassell.

Sims ACP & Gooding KM (1975) The psychiatric outcome of 'normal' people at follow-up. *Journal of Psychiatric Research 12*, 167–75.

Snaith RP (1986) *The Concepts of Depression*. Unpublished.

Wing JK (1978) *Reasoning about Madness*. Oxford: Oxford University Press.

19

Impulsive & Aggressive Acts

Dying
Is an art, like everything else.
I do it exceptionally well.

I do it so it feels like hell.
I do it so it feels real
I guess you could say I've a call.
                    Sylvia Plath (1962)

This poem by Sylvia Plath (1932–1963), who committed suicide by coal-gas poisoning within four months of writing it, highlights the dilemma of impulsive and aggressive acts: although the actual behaviour appears impulsive, it occurs against a background that made that final impulse more likely. What was it about the person or the circumstances that resulted in the impulsive act happening *then*? Impulsive behaviour is not usually wholly impulsive, and this raises the next question of *responsibility*–as both a legal and a philosophical issue.

Impulsive acts are 'executed forcefully with no deliberation or reflection, under the influence of a compelling pressure that restricts the subject's freedom of will. Since reflective control or consideration is lacking, the consequences of such acts are not thought out or taken into consideration' (Scharfetter, 1980). It will be seen that this is not an all-or-nothing phenomenon. Voluntary inhibitions will be present to a varying extent, from completely preventing the act, modifying or delaying it, to not existing at all, when the act takes place unrestrained.

Aggression is defined as 'a verbal or physical attack on other living creatures or things' (Scharfetter, 1980), and *aggressiveness* as a readiness to be aggressive. In general ethological terms, this is required by animals for survival, and by man to cope with individual conflicts and problems in his society. However, in a more restricted psychopathological sense, aggression involves deliberate or reckless damage and destruction, and is accompanied by negative emotions such as anger, fear, despair, spite or rage.

The two concepts of aggression which Scharfetter contrasts are an *innate drive* and an *acquired response*. The former theory is followed both by ethologists, such as Lorenz (1966), and in classical psychoanalysis in the writings of Freud and Adler (1929); if aggression is an innate drive, it must find some form of expression. Learning theory would suppose that aggression is an acquired reaction in response to external stimuli, especially the expression of others' aggressive behaviour, and it is reinforced by the success it achieves.

RESPONSIBILITY

The legal term *diminished responsibility* only has relevance for homicide trials in England and Wales in the Homicide Act 1957, which states: 'where a person kills or is party to a killing of another, he shall not be convicted of murder if he was suffering from such abnormality of mind (whether arising from a condition of arrested or retarded development of mind or any inherent causes or induced by disease or injury) as substantially impaired his mental responsibility for his acts and omissions in doing or being party to the killing'. However, the concept of individual responsibility has much greater significance for forensic psychiatry than homicide alone, and for all types of management and treatment of mental illness it is relevant.

'To be judged mentally ill is judged, to a greater or lesser extent, not responsible' (Kennedy, 1981). Distinction is often made between *psychosis* and *neurosis*. The concept of psychosis, because of defect of insight and reality judgement, implies a different understanding of personal responsibility from neurosis, where morbid subjective experiences are not confused with external reality. Whether a person is decreed responsible, in both a layperson's and a legal sense, depends ultimately upon whether he is considered to be ill; but, as Kennedy has pointed out, *illness* itself is a judgemental term that depends upon the perspective of the observer. Clearly, there are important legal, philosophical and theological issues involved, but they are not the concern of a work on psychopathology. More detailed consideration of this complex subject from both the psychiatric and forensic standpoint is found in Whitlock (1963).

If one concentrates on the phenomenological aspects, both the psychotic and the neurotic patient have a conscious feeling of being responsible for most of their actions, as does a normal, healthy person. So, when a man, be he healthy, psychotic or neurotic, reflects on the action of scratching his head, he knows with absolute certainty that he was completely and solely responsible for that action; it was *his* action. Most of the time, for most activities, a person is so certain of what is self that he does not give a moment's consideration to whether he is responsible for such activities or not: it is an assumption of life. However, it is worthwhile looking at the following six situations from a phenomenological point of view:

1 A person feels responsible for his action, but the action is based upon delusional, psychotic thinking. A chronic schizophrenic patient used to walk eight miles and prostrate himself in front of a village maypole; on occasions he had taken his clothes off and been charged with indecent exposure. He believed himself to be in communication with the sun and that the sun needed him to carry out this action. He was in no doubt that this was his action and that he was wholly responsible. However, an outside observer would not consider him to be guilty of the consequences of his action because the action directly resulted from his delusional state.

2 A person may feel responsible for an action and not actually be responsible. This is most dramatically demonstrated by those who confess to having perpetrated horrific murders. Sometimes, such a person will be found to be suffering from schizophrenia and has, because of the publicity concerning the murder, incorporated its details in his delusional system, but this is not always so. Occasionally, a person with grossly anankastic personality may be consumed with self-doubt as to whether he might have committed the murder or not, 'perhaps in my sleep... maybe I have lost my memory', and so on.

3 A person feels responsible for his activity, and is responsible. Even the most grossly disturbed psychotic patient feels, and is responsible for, most of the actions of everyday life—getting up and dressing; eating breakfast; walking along

the corridor; and so on. EW Anderson used to say that 'mental illness is no excuse for bad manners'. Neither the staff nor the patient himself should automatically assume that, when a chronic schizophrenic attacks a fellow patient, he is not responsible because of his psychotic condition. Mentally ill people may, on occasions, be selfishly aggressive and meanly antisocial in the same way, and for the same reasons, as a healthy person. After a fracas on the ward, when the doctor remonstrated with a patient, encouraging him not to assault the other patient again, the patient said 'I probably will, I don't like him'. This man was in no doubt about his responsibility for his own action.

4   A person does not feel responsible, for psychotic reasons, for his action. The most frequent cause for this is passivity experience. A schizophrenic in-patient poured his bowl of porridge over another patient's food. He claimed that he had been made to do this by someone else against his will. Like (1) above, the outside observer would not hold him responsible for the consequences of his action, but regard them as a direct result of the psychotic illness.

5   A person denies responsibility for his action, but is responsible. This is conceptually the most difficult situation. For instance, a young man with asocial personality disorder while cohabiting injures a woman's 2-year-old daughter from a previous marriage. The man claims, through his Counsel, that he is not responsible because of his own extremely deprived upbringing and his personality disorder. However, it is his own volitional act and, even if an outside observer could predict his action, it would still remain his action, his responsibility, and ultimately voluntary (MacKay, 1973). Of course, extenuating circumstances should be taken into account during court proceedings, but the phenomenological aspect of responsibility should not be denied. Arising from studies of attribution is the finding that normal people will grossly deceive themselves to excuse their socially unacceptable behaviour, and that this can occur by surreptitious progression from relatively minor antisocial acts to gross physical harm directed at other people (Milgram, 1965).

6   A person may not feel responsible for his action and is not–a true accident. Thus, the engine driver who runs over a suicide laying himself across the track need not, and should not, hold himself responsible for the latter's death.

Automatism occuring in the context of epilepsy is important, both clinically and legally. An accused person must have acted voluntarily to be guilty of the act; in this context, automatism is defined in law as the state of a person who, although capable of action, is not conscious of what he is doing. *Insane automatism* implies disease of the mind, especially psychomotor epilepsy, and is equivalent to a plea of insanity. It is important to demonstrate that epilepsy and automatic behaviour were present before the homicidal act. *Non-insane automatism* occurs where the dysfunction of the mind is transitory, such as following alcohol, drugs or anaesthesia; or associated with sleep disorder such as sleepwalking.

Psychopathology of impulsive and aggressive behaviour

There is nothing that is likely to result in referral to psychiatric services more quickly than the public exhibition of inexplicable impulsive and aggressive acts. Also, there is nothing more likely to be labelled as madness by the lay public. In practice, such public behaviour is commonly associated with mental illness. In a study of mentally disturbed people coming to the attention of the police, there was a tendency for such people to create their disturbance near the city centre rather than at the periphery. Of the situations resulting in the involvement of the police, assault and damage were frequent, but it was the bizarreness of the behaviour that marked the person as being mentally ill; for example, a man who proffered a windscreen wiper as fare for travelling on a bus, or a woman who presented herself mute at a hostel. On subsequent admission to hospital diagnosis was predominantly of psychotic illness (57%), schizophrenia accounting for 40% (Sims & Symonds, 1975).

Excessive aggression, and especially unprovoked inappropriate or mis-directed aggression, is much more often presented for psychiatric evaluation than a pathological lack of aggressive behaviour. However, the latter may also be a manifestation of illness. Excessive aggression may be considered both in terms of the underlying psychiatric illness, and according to the specific nature of the behaviour.

PSYCHIATRIC ILLNESS AND AGGRESSIVE BEHAVIOUR

Aggressive behaviour may be shown with almost any psychiatric condition. It is, of course, not necessarily associated with the illness, but may be an expression of the individual's underlying personality and constitution, and of the specific frustrations in his current social context. The McNaughton rules as applied to homicide was an attempt by the judiciary, albeit not a very successful one, to apportion how much blame should be ascribed to the illness, in terms of delusions consequent upon it, and how much to the moral turpitude of the individual (West & Walk, 1977). This distinction between mental illness and criminality as cause of homicidal behaviour was based, therefore, on phenomenology; upon the patient's own subjective assessment of the meaning of his behaviour. The abnormal mental phenomena occurring and accounting for violence will depend for its form upon the nature of the psychiatric illness.

Personality disorder

Impulsive and aggressive behaviour is particularly characteristic of what ICD 9 describes as *explosive personality disorder*-'instability of mood with liability to intemperate outbursts of anger, hate, violence or affection. Aggression may be expressed in words or in physical violence. The outbursts cannot be readily controlled by the affected persons, who are not otherwise prone to antisocial behaviour' (World Health Organization, 1977). Fortunately, this personality abnormality does not occur very frequently in clinical practice. A person whose usual mood may be equable shows what is regarded as a grossly excessive expression of emotion in response to relatively minor stimuli; the emotion may be of anger, fear, misery, anxiety or rage, and often results in violent behaviour. So the violence here results from the phenomena of sudden, excessive and uncontrollable outbursts of emotion.

Such people are likely to be very destructive in interpersonal relationships. During the intervals between explosive outbursts they are likely to be able to form relationships, but their unpredictable swings of mood are disruptive and they tend to be manipulative and dominating, using their explosiveness to control those around them.

Impulsive and aggressive acts may also be associated with the *asocial* or *psychopathic personality*. Such people are heedless of the consequences of their actions; they especially do not empathize with the emotions experienced by others consequent upon their own destructive behaviour. A sociopathic curate experienced sorrow when he was discovered by his vicar scrounging sums of money from elderly female parishioners; but he had no feeling of remorse or understanding for how the vicar felt in having misplaced his confidence in him. Henderson (1939) described creative, inadequate and aggressive psychopathy. Those with asocial personality will show different kinds of impulsive behaviour depending upon which of these three qualities predominate.

With hysterical or histrionic personality disorder, impulsive acts occur, although these are not usually aggressive.

Alcohol is a complicating factor which renders a person with any type of personality disorder more liable to impulsive or aggressive action through the pharmacological action of central disinhibition of higher centres.

Neurosis, depression and mania

Aggressiveness is not particularly a characteristic of neurotic illness, although impulsive and inappropriate behaviour may occur. Irritability is a regular feature and may on occasion find expression in impulsive aggression; for example, non-accidental injury of a child by its neurotic, socially deprived and frustrated parent (Smith *et al.*, 1973). In both neurosis and depressive illness, impulsive action may result from disturbance in attitudes and emotion.

Mass disasters frequently provoke neurotic reaction. However, in the *impact phase* of acute catastrophe, such as an earthquake, fire, bombing or other major disaster, the victims are usually dazed, stunned or bewildered; it is in the subsequent *recoil phase* that emotional release occurs and a small proportion of victims exhibit 'psychopathic liberation' such as looting, rape and heavy drinking (Kinston & Rosser, 1974). Reactions to stressful situations, either natural or man-made, for example, imprisonment or the experience of being trapped underground in a mining disaster, may take the form of impulsive aggression.

There is a very great risk of suicide with depressive illness. This may be consistent, experienced over a considerable time, and resisted because of feelings of duty towards family or glimmerings of hope for a successful outcome to treatment; or it may be a sudden impulse to 'end it all' superimposed upon consistently lowered mood. In this latter instance, close relatives sometimes describe an amelioration of mood in the few hours or days before successfully completed suicide, as if having finally made the decision brings some relief. Retardation and apathy, which are frequently present in depressive illness, may render suicide less likely. However, the earlier stages of effective treatment, for instance with electroconvulsive therapy, may result in initial lessening of retardation without concurrent improvement in mood, and so the risk of suicide may be temporarily increased. Other self-destructive behaviour may occur with depression, and homicide followed by attempted suicide also occurs more frequently. A case is described in Chapter 16 of a depressed man who intended to drown his greatly loved young son and himself but only succeeded in the former. With depressive illness motor retardation may render any concerted activity less likely. However, if retardation does completely inhibit action, the mood of hopelessness accounts for suicidal behaviour.

In mania, the mood disturbance may result in aggressive behaviour. There may be frenzied violence of an ineffective kind or the patient may be consistently more irritable, resulting in aggression on relatively slight provocation. Not only aggressive but other impulsive behaviour of florid kind may occur in mania; one manic patient, a doctor, 'cured' a pilot with a phobia for flying by suggestion and then immediately persuaded him to hire an aeroplane to fly himself and two other in-patients from their hospital in the North of England so that they could all visit their unsuspecting psychiatrist who was on holiday in Italy (Ropschitz, 1957).

Schizophrenia

Apparently meaningless, aggressive or self-destructive acts may take place as a result of the abnormal mental state. However, it can usually be shown that these actions take place in direct response to abnormal phenomena such as auditory hallucinations, delusions or passivity experiences. A man cycling along a canal towpath was assaulted by another man walking in the opposite direction and carrying a long length of rubber tubing. The police apprehended the assailant and after questioning requested a psychiatric opinion. The man, who proved to be schizophrenic said: 'As I walked along I had a pain in my stomach. Then I heard a voice which said, "If you hit him the pain will go". So I hit him with the rubber pipe'. The aggressive act was a direct response to an auditory hallucination and, in fact, it is this psychopathological form which most frequently accounts for violence in schizophrenia. The homicidal attack on 20 January 1843 by Daniel McNaughton upon Edward Drummond, the Prime Minister's Private Secretary was a direct response to his persecutory delusion. McNaughton believed: 'The Tories in my native city have compelled me to do this. They follow and persecute me wherever I go, and have entirely destroyed my peace of mind... in fact, they wish to murder me. It can be proved by evidence' (West and Walk, 1977).

It has been postulated that the very rare phenomenon of *clinical vampirism*, drinking the blood of a victim, is usually associated with a schizophrenic disorder (Prins, 1984). This condition, which overlaps to some extent with necrophilia, needs to be seen in its symbolic and anthropological context.

Investigating the contribution made to acts of extreme violence by schizophrenic psychopathology, Taylor (1985) concluded that in 82% of those who were schizophrenic and had committed a violent act, the offence was attributable to the illness. Two hundred and three male prisoners who had committed a violent offence and were remanded for psychiatric examination were interviewed, 121 of these were psychotic with active symptoms in all but nine cases. Twenty per cent of actively ill men were directly driven to offend by their psychotic symptoms, and a further 20% probably so. Passivity delusions were especially frequent in precipitating violent acts in this series.

Undirected, frenzied violent behaviour may occur with acute catatonic schizophrenia. However, this is now extremely rare. Other impulsive actions, which are not at all aggressive in nature, may occur in schizophrenic patients in response to hallucinations, delusions or associated with loss of volition or blunting of social behaviour. This could include hoarding, or unhygienic and antisocial behaviour. This is more common in those who are institutionalized and show chronic defect states.

Impulsive and aggressive acts are not uncommon in schizophrenia. They may occur in response to auditory hallucinations–voices that command or invite the patient to carry out certain actions. Alternatively, the violence may be directed against what the patient believes to be the source of the voices in order to get rid of them. Delusions of persecution may result in action to eradicate the presumed perpetrator. With passivity experiences or delusions of control, violence may be directed at an external influence that is believed to be controlling the person in some way.

Organic states

Inexplicable impulsive acts of aggression, episodes of irritable mood, bad temper of sudden onset and without adequate provocation, petty behaviour of unexpected spitefulness and malevolence, may occur with various organic psychosyndromes, often as an early sign of illness, in people who previously did not show such traits of character. These symptoms may herald a dementing process with increasing irritability and loss of control; such behaviour is characteristic of post-encephalitic Parkinsonism, following head injury, or in epileptic automatism during convulsive discharge. A recent deterioration in behaviour with the occurrence of such inexplicable aggression should always raise the suspicion of a developing organic lesion, and detailed examination neurologically and of the mental state should be carried out.

Aggressive outbursts may occur, often associated with alteration of consciousness and hallucinosis, in acute, toxic confusional states. Irritability and aggression is commonly seen with hypoglycaemia after excess dosage of insulin in diabetes, and with hypoxia in incipient respiratory failure. It may occur with other metabolic illness. Of particular importance are the acute organic psychosyndromes due to intoxication with alcohol or other drugs. The relationship between alcohol abuse and crime is complex: 'the variations on the alcohol–crime connection are legion' (Edwards, 1982); repeated episodes of acute alcohol intoxication combined with uncontrollable violence are a particular problem.

MODES OF BEHAVIOUR

Psychiatric associations have been sought for different types of impulsive or aggressive behaviour. There is a temptation for the layperson to make the illogical leap 'because that act was so appalling and so incomprehensible to me, the person who committed it must have been mad'. Thus, some have thought that all murderers must be mentally ill. Careful investigation of the psychopathology will correct this misunderstanding. Violent sexual behaviour has already been discussed in Chapter 14; in most instances of rape, taking pleasure in violence is more prominent in the psychopathology than sexual gratification. The following terms are only considered very briefly; more detailed description will be found in a textbook of forensic psychiatry (Bluglass & Bowden, 1987).

Fire-setting (arson)

Although fire-setting is considered here (and also in DSM III) with impulse control disorders, this behaviour may be pre-planned, deliberate and apparently convey a non-verbal message. Thus Geller (1984) described 'arson by consumers of public sector mental health services who want to communicate a wish and/or a need for a change in location of those services. Fires may be set to return to a state hospital, to preclude placement from the hospital to a "less restrictive" setting, or to express dissatisfaction with one's current locus of services'. Of fourteen such patients, eight were diagnosed as psychotic (six schizophrenic) and three as showing mental retardation. In another series of seventeen cases, seven showed mental retardation, eight had neurotic reactions and two were classified under personality disorder (Zeegers, 1984).

Scott (1977), in reviewing *malicious fire-raising*, considered that incendiarists could be divided into those with clear-cut motives and those whose motives are either blurred or absent. An example of the former is the person who works for profit by insuring a building and then arranging for it to be burnt down. Fire has also been used to conceal murder and is of course regularly used in vengeance or retribution, or by political extremists. Motiveless arson may occur among those with overt psychiatric disorder or organic brain disease; for example, half-accidentally in a demented person or in response to hallucinatory voices in schizophrenia. It may also occur without overt psychiatric illness following adverse circumstances but out of proportion to them; for example, a student failing his examination sets light to the college library. There is also a group of people, the 'fire-bugs' (Lewis & Yarnell, 1951), with psychopathic personality, who repeatedly set fires to satisfy such inner desires as wishing to help firemen, to be a hero or to enjoy destruction; some of these may gain sexual satisfaction only through this act and masturbate while watching their conflagration—fire fetishists. Fire-setting is quite commonly associated with a degree of mental subnormality. Fire-setting is usually a male activity (6:1, males:females), and most common between the age of 16 and 25.

Acute binge drinking

The history of western Europe and the lands populated by its emigrants is steeped in alcohol: the ceremonies of all life epochs and rites of passage are solemnized with alcohol; and contracts and relationships are symbolically sealed by drinking together. Alcohol is used for important events in the family, and the greatest effects of its abuse are also upon the family; a person with an alcohol problem usually affects the lives of others (Orford & Harwin, 1982). In medical practice, alcohol abuse is also important; the most conservative estimate is that at least 15% of patients admitted to general hospitals (in New Zealand) have an alcohol-related illness or disability, and in a further 10–20% this is a significant contributing factor to admission; in about 50% of fatal traffic accidents alcohol is involved (Bieder *et al.*, 1982).

Acute binge drinking, with a pattern of repeated loss of control is one of the many patterns of the *alcohol dependence* syndrome (Royal College of Psychiatrists, 1979). The elements of this syndrome are: (1) subjective awareness of compulsion to drink; (2) narrowing of the drinking repertoire (drinking in order to relieve or avoid withdrawal symptoms, and therefore a similar amount each day); (3) primacy of drinking over other activities, (4) altered tolerance to alcohol (initially increased tolerance but eventually decreased in the late stages of alcohol dependence); (5) repeated withdrawal symptoms (from shakiness, tremor, sweating, nausea, agitation and tenseness to convulsions and delirium tremens); (6) relief or avoidance of withdrawal symptoms by further drinking; (7) reinstatement after abstinence.

Glue-sniffing

Impulsive and self-destructive behaviour follows fashions and is in part determined by learning and by availability. This is exemplified by the phenomenology of intoxication with toluene-based adhesives and butane (Evans & Raistrick, 1986). In 1982, 3-5% of 15-year-olds in the United Kingdom had misused volatile substances at some time. Solvent intoxication is similar to alcohol in that initial stimulation of central nervous function is followed by depression. Both toluene and butane abusers described elevation of mood and hallucinations; nearly one-quarter of subjects experienced the dangerous delusion of being able to fly or swim. Amongst the group of toluene abusers, thoughts were more likely to be slowed, time appeared to pass more quickly and tactile hallucinations were more commonly reported than in the butane group. The toluene subjects were more likely to sniff only in a group setting and were more definite in their sanction against taking other drugs.

Shoplifting

Stealing from shops is a major economic problem, estimated to cost the honest shopper about 2% of the cost of what he or she buys (Segal, 1977). Unlike much other crime, shoplifting is predominantly a female activity (83%), with 50% of offenders being aged under 18 years, and about 4.5% of shoppers stealing at each shop, irrespective of city or country studied (Fisher, 1984). In one study, one in ten shoplifters were found to be recidivists and these frequently had also had convictions for prostitution and drug-related offences. More recently, the female predominance of shoplifting has been questioned; with high unemployment, young males are now more frequently involved.

In different series, about 2% of shoplifters were referred for psychiatric assessment by the courts, but when all women accused were assessed nearly 20% were found to have identifiable psychiatric disorder. Summing different studies, diagnostically 33% of psychiatrically disturbed shoplifters were suffering from neuroses, psychosomatic disorders or compulsive behaviour; 17% from personality disorders; 15% from psychotic disorders; 11% from mental handicap; 5% from organic disorders, such as dementia; and 3% from alcohol and/or drug abuse. Gibbens *et al.* (1971) have particularly commented on the association between depression and shoplifting. Significant recent or current physical illness was also an important factor.

The word *kleptomania* is now discounted. However, Fisher has classified stealing from shops into five categories in some of which adverse psychological and social factors make a contribution: (1) 'professional' shoplifters; (2) shoplifters with a severe functional or organic psychiatric disorder at the time of the offence; (3) reactive shoplifters (transient reaction to emotional stress); (4) young shoplifters (may reflect underlying social, emotional or family problems); (5) shoplifting as an abnormal learned behaviour.

Violence and homicide

Psychiatrists are usually requested to report when offenders plead guilty or are found guilty of charges of homicide; a term which covers murder, manslaughter and infanticide (Bluglass, 1979). There is therefore considerable knowledge of the mental state some time after homicide, but it is often difficult to extrapolate to the perpetrator's subjective state at the time he committed the act. Murder is classified as *normal* or *abnormal*, depending upon the legal outcome; and at least one-third of murders are classified as abnormal. Most frequently, the psychiatric diagnosis is depression, and suicide or a suicide attempt often follows the killing. Occasionally, an unpredictable murderous attack takes place in the context of a schizophrenic illness: a patient of Bluglass, because he believed that a piece of cotton in his car indicated that his girlfriend had been having sexual relations with his father, strangled her and drove the body to a police station. More rarely, homicide may be associated with mental subnormality, epilepsy or cerebral tumour.

Homicide may frequently follow the ingestion of alcohol (in Scotland 58% of males and 30% of females). Other drugs are less common, but marijuana, LSD, amphetamines and barbiturates have been implicated. Hypnotic trance has been incriminated on rare occasions.

Asocial personality disorder may be found to be present in a convicted murderer and is sometimes cited in a plea of diminished responsibility. The individual claiming amnesia for the time of the act is difficult to evaluate. This is rarely associated with organic or psychotic factors; more often with low intelligence, hysteria, alcohol intoxication, sexual excitement or rage. Malingering, hysterical amnesia and other psychogenic explanations for amnesia are virtually impossible to distinguish and may be a matter of degree (Gibbens & Hall-Williams, 1977).

Deliberate self-harm

This is not the place to review the vast literature on overdosage and deliberate self-harm. However, it is appropriate to make some mention of motivation for such actions. Kessel (1965) introduced the term *self-poisoning* as a behavioural description of people who take an overdose of drugs. Over the twenty years from 1960 to 1980 admission to hospital for this behaviour became about six times more frequent in the United Kingdom. The term *deliberate self-harm* has been used by Morgan *et al.* (1975) 'as a non-fatal act, whether physical injury, drug overdosage or poisoning, carried out in the knowledge that it was potentially harmful and, in the case of drug overdosage, that the amount taken was excessive'.

The reasons people gave for taking overdoses were studied by Bancroft *et al.* (1976) on interviewing 128 subjects in Oxford immediately after recovering from their overdose. Forty-four per cent of subjects expressed a 'wish to die'; it was considered that in some cases this was used as a socially acceptable motive and did not always express suicidal intent. Thirty-three per cent were 'seeking help', 42% 'escaping from the situation', 52% 'obtaining relief from a terrible state of mind', and 19% 'trying to influence someone'. The mood state of these patients at the time of the attempt was, in order of frequency: 'lonely', 'failed', 'worried', 'angry' and 'sorry'; in 92% at least one of these affects was described.

Trying to investigate the self-experience at the time of suicide can, of course, only be conjectural. Barraclough *et al.* (1974) have found evidence of mental illness in 93%, and depressive illness in 70% of completed suicides. The symptoms of these depressives appeared to have been similar in type but more severe than an unselected sample of depressed patients. There is a difference in mental state between those using violent methods such as jumping, drowning, hanging and shooting oneself, and those using less violent methods such as coal-gas poisoning in past decades, and self-poisoning nowadays. Self-mutilation using physical acts, for example wrist-slashing, probably demonstrates a different psychopathology from self-poisoning (Morgan, 1979).

Soranus, in the first century AD, recognized the danger of mentally ill people destroying themselves by jumping from a height, and he recommended looking after them on the ground floor (Zilboorg & Henry, 1941). In a study of such behaviour, called *autokabalesis*, occurring in a psychiatric hospital population, nearly 75% were suffering from schizophrenia and related conditions (Sims & O'Brien, 1979). Self-poisoning represented 95% of episodes of self-harm (Morgan *et al.*), and when psychiatric diagnosis was carried out for these, it was usually associated with neurotic or depressive illness.

Diminished aggression

Decreased aggressiveness may accompany reduced drive; it is seen in organic, psychotic and psychogenic disturbance. It is frequently associated with apathy in acute organic disorders, such as encephalitis, or in progressive dementia, although irritability and fractiousness may also occur. Generalized debilitating physical illness is normally accompanied by listlessness and apathy.

In schizophrenia, aggression is usually markedly reduced with lack of volition and failure to initiate any directive activity; however, unprovoked violence sometimes occurs. In depressive psychosis also, reduced aggression is much the most common presentation; however, homicide, quite often associated with suicide, is certainly described amongst severely depressed individuals with depressive delusions.

A consistently low level of aggressiveness may occur as a personality characteristic; for example, with *asthenic* disorder of personality. It may be seen as part of a neurotic reaction or during adverse life situations: for instance, with the grief of bereavement or the unhappiness of feeling lonely. A certain degree of aggression is necessary for many of the social activities of normal life and its absence impairs functioning. Pathological lack of aggression is closely associated with disorder of volition (Chapter 18).

References

Adler A (1929) *Problems of Neuroses*. London: Kegan Paul, Trench, Trubner.
Bancroft JHJ, Skrimshire AM & Simkin S (1976) The reasons people give for taking overdoses. *British Journal of Psychiatry 128*, 538–48.
Barraclough GM, Bunch J, Nelson B & Sainsbury P (1974) A hundred cases of suicide: clinical aspects. *British Journal of Psychiatry 125*, 355–73.
Bieder L, O'Hagan J, Whiteside E & Paton A (1982) *Handbook on Alcoholism for Health Professionals*. London: Heinemann.

Bluglass R (1979) The psychiatric assessment of homicide. *British Journal of Hospital Medicine 22*, 366–77.

Bluglass R & Bowden P (1987) *Principles and Practice of Forensic Psychiatry*. Edinburgh: Churchill Livingstone.

Edwards G (1982) *The Treatment of Drinking Problems: A Guide for the Helping Professions*. London: Grant McIntyre.

Evans AC & Raistrick D (1986) Phenomenology of intoxication with toluene based adhesives and butane gas. Unpublished.

Fisher C (1984) Psychiatric aspects of shoplifting. *British Journal of Hospital Medicine 31*, 209–12.

Geller J (1984) Arson: An unforseen sequela of deinstitutionalization. *American Journal of Psychiatry 141*, 504–8.

Gibbens TCM & Hall-Williams JE (1977) In Whitty CWM & Zangwill OL (eds) *Amnesia*. London: Butterworth.

Gibbens TCN, Palmer C & Prince J (1971) Mental health aspects of shoplifting. *British Medical Journal 3*, 612–5.

Henderson DK (1939) *Psychopathic States*. New York: Norton.

Kessel WIN (1965) Self poisoning. *British Medical Journal 2*, 1265–1270, 1336–1340.

Kennedy I (1981) *The Unmasking of Medicine*. London: George Allen & Unwin.

Kinston W & Rosser R (1974) Disaster: Effects on mental state and physical state. *Journal of Psychosomatic Research 18*, 437–56.

Lewis NDC & Yarnell H (1951) *Pathological Firesetting*. Nervous and Mental Disease Monographs No. 82. New York.

Lorenz K (1963) *On Aggression* (transl. Latzke M, 1966) London: Methuen.

Mackay DM (1973) The logical indeterminateness of human choices. *British J. Phil. Sci. 24*, 405–8.

Milgram S (1965) Some conditions of obedience and disobedience to authority. *Human Relations 18*, 57–75.

Morgan HG (1979) *Death Wishes? The Understanding and Management of Deliberate Self-Harm*. Chichester: Wiley.

Morgan HG, Burns-Cox CJ, Pocock H & Pottle S (1975) Deliberate self-harm: Clinical and socio-economic characteristics of 368 patients. *British Journal of Psychiatry 127*, 564–74.

Orford J & Harwin J (1982) *Alcohol and the Family*. London: Croom Helm.

Plath S (1962) Lady Lazarus. In Ted Hughes (ed.), 1981 *Sylvia Plath: Collected Poems*. London: Faber & Faber.

Prins H (1984) Vampirism–legendary or clinical phenomenon. *Medicine Science and the Law 24*, 283–93.

Ropschitz DH (1957) Folie à deux: a case of folie imposée à quatre and à trois. *Journal of Mental Science 103*, 589–96.

Royal College of Psychiatrists (1979) *Alcohol and Alcoholism*. London: Tavistock.

Scharfetter C (1980) *General Psychopathology: An Introduction*. Cambridge: Cambridge University Press.

Scott D (1977) Malicious fire-raising. *Practitioner 218*, 812–7.

Segal M (1977) Psychiatry and the shoplifter. *Practitioner 218*, 823–7.

Sims ACP & O'Brien K (1979) Autokabalesis: an account of mentally ill people who jump from buildings. *Medicine Science and the Law 19*, 195–8.

Sims ACP & Symonds RL (1975) Psychiatric referrals from the police. *British Journal of Psychiatry 127*, 171–8.

Smith SM, Hanson R & Noble S (1973) Parents of battered babies; a controlled study. *British Medical Journal iv*, 388–91.

Taylor PJ (1985) Motives for offending among violent and psychotic men. *British Journal of Psychiatry 147*, 491–8.

West DJ & Walk A (1977) *Daniel McNaughton: His Trial and the Aftermath*. Ashford: Headley Brothers.

Whitlock FA (1963) *Criminal Responsibility and Mental Illness*. London: Butterworth.

World Health Organization (1977) *International Statistical Classification of Diseases, Injury and Causes of Death*, 9th Revision. Geneva: World Health Organization.

Zeegers M (1984) Criminal fire-setting: a review and some case studies. *Medicine & Law 3*, 171–6.

Zilboorg G & Henry GW (1941) *A History of Medical Psychology*. New York: Norton.

20

Disturbance of Movement and Behaviour

By ceaseless action, all that is subsists.
Constant rotation of the universal wheel
That nature rides upon, maintains her health,
Her beauty, her fertility. She dreads
An instant's pause, and lives but while she moves.
Its own revolvency upholds the world.
William Cowper *The Task* (1784)

Behavioural and movement disturbances may have crucial diagnostic significance, especially when there is difficulty with verbal explanation. However, as
the emphasis of this book is on subjective description of abnormality, these
disorders are only discussed briefly. The distinction between movement and
behaviour is wholly arbitrary, as will be shown, especially when schizophrenia is
considered.

Disturbance of movement

Movement may be increased or speeded up, reduced or slowed down, or it may
show various qualitative abnormalities. Some of these disorders of movement
are involuntary and are appropriately regarded as neurological; some are
voluntary but carried out unconsciously; and some are deliberate actions (of the
will). The words used mostly describe the objective characteristics of the action
to the outside observer, not the subjective experience of the actor.

These disorders of movement are now considered briefly, starting with
abnormalities of increased movement–*agitation* and decreased movement–
retardation. The movement disorders of some psychiatric conditions are then
described. On occasions there is, of course, movement disorder with other
psychiatric illnesses and not infrequently there will be psychiatric sequelae with
primary movement disorders other than Parkinsonism.

AGITATION

Agitation implies mental disturbance causing physical restlessness and increased
arousal; it is phenomenologically a description of a subjective mood state
associated with and resulting in physical expression. The patient may describe
his affect as 'feeling agitated', and both he and the external observer see motor
restlessness as being logically connected with this. It is demonstrated in many
different mental states–pathologically it may occur with affective psychoses,

schizophrenia, organic psychosyndromes such as senile dementia, or with neuroses and personality disorders, especially anxiety neurosis. Agitation is quite often a symptom with physical illness, for example, hyperthyroidism or hypoparathyroidism. It is an important component of severe depressive illness. Although retardation is more commonly seen with endogenous depression, agitation may occur, either without retardation, in alternating phase with retardation, or concurrently with retardation in a *mixed affective state*. *Agitated depression* is described as a variant of manic–depressive psychosis, depressed type (ICD 9, 296.1 World Health Organization, 1977) and with severe depression of mood may accompany so-called *involutional melancholia*. Practical clinical importance of this mood state ensues from the fact that, whereas suicidal impulses may be prevented from expression by retardation, agitation with restlessness may render such behaviour more likely. An early response to treatment following electroconvulsive treatment may result in the patient becoming less retarded and therefore at greater suicidal risk.

Hyperactivity describes the mental state in which there is increased motor activity, possibly with aggressiveness, over-talkativeness or unco-ordinated physical activity. The term is descriptive of behaviour rather than of subjective psychic state. Restless hyperactivity or *hyperkinesis* may occur with a variety of different physical assaults upon the brain but is especially prominent as a sequel to head injury in children, in whom it may be associated with impulsive disobedience and explosive outbursts of anger and irritability (Black *et al.*, 1969); it is also associated with childhood epilepsy when there is brain damage.

RETARDATION

Retardation has two quite different meanings in psychiatry. *Motor retardation*, the sense in which it is used here, implies slowness of the initiation, execution and completion of physical activity; it is frequently associated with retardation of thought, for example, in severe depressive illness. The patient subjectively describes himself as having difficulty with thinking, 'my thoughts are slowed up', and also with initiating and carrying out spontaneous activity. *Mental retardation* is a synonym for mental handicap or mental subnormality; it is an unfortunate term as, although there is intellectual deficit, there may be no physical slowness; in fact, there may be overactivity, especially if there is brain damage.

Retardation is so prominent a symptom of the severe endogenous type of depression that it was in the past used to name the condition, *retarded depression*. There is restricted movement, a posture of dejection and decrease of muscular tone. Gesticulation is reduced, as is the emotional component of facial expression.

Retardation with slowness of motor activity is also seen with other causes of mental slowness as in various organic psychosyndromes and with physical illnesses. The extreme of retardation–no voluntary movement at all–is known as *akinesis* and occurs with muteness in *stupor*.

DISORDER OF MOVEMENT IN SCHIZOPHRENIA

For the sake of convenience, three types of abnormality may be recognized in schizophrenia: isolated abnormalities of movement and posture which are now discussed; more complex patterns of disordered behaviour described later in the chapter; and the presumed effects upon movement of the neuroleptic drugs which are often used in large dosage and for a long time in schizophrenia. Some of the odd motor disorders that occur are described first, and then the disturbances of chronic schizophrenia are listed.

Motor disorders

Catatonia means a state of increased tone in muscles at rest, abolished by voluntary activities, and thereby distinguished from extra-pyramidal rigidity. The category *catatonic schizophrenia* was introduced by Kraepelin and is characterized by the presence of the motor disorders described below. It is very difficult to classify the precise nature of the odd and abnormal posture in schizophrenia. *Waxy flexibility* (flexibilitas cerea) and *psychological pillow* occur but are both rare conditions. In waxy flexibility when the limbs of the patient are put into any posture by the interviewer, they will be retained in that position for a sustained period (a minute or more). Psychological pillow, where the patient's head is maintained a few inches above the bed, may continue for hours. In *stereotypy*, a bizarre uncomfortable posture also may be retained for some hours.

There are two types of abnormal movement in schizophrenia: *idiosyncratic voluntary movements* or *mannerisms*, and *spontaneous involuntary movements*. Mannerisms are shown in odd, stilted, voluntary movements and patterns of behaviour. The patient may claim to be unaware of these acts or explain them in terms of his delusions.

It is sometimes difficult to distinguish mannerisms from the stereotypic movements or posture–movements which are not goal-directed but are carried out in an unvarying way in any individual patient. It is important to attempt to distinguish either of these types of movements from the abnormal movements of *Parkinsonian syndromes*, which occur quite frequently in schizophrenics treated with phenothiazine and butyrophenone drugs (see below). *Grimacing* is a common feature in schizophrenia; *Schnauzkrampf* (literally snout spasm) is a characteristic facial expression in which the nose and lips are drawn together in a pout.

Abnormality of the *execution* of *movement* may result from schizophrenic experiences. At times he resists stimuli, for example the interviewer's request to raise his arm, and shows *negativism*. At other times he demonstrates excessive compliance amounting to *automatic obedience*: not only does he raise one arm but he raises the other arm and then stands up with both arms raised in dramatic response to the request. This alternation of co-operation and opposition produces the diffident unpredictable behaviour of *ambitendency*.

Obstruction is the equivalent in the flow of action to thought blocking in the flow of speech. Whilst carrying out a motor act, the patient stops still in his tracks. After a pause he continues with the act or he may proceed to do something else. Usually, he cannot account for his obstruction but may do so in terms of passivity, 'my action was stopped'.

Abnormal movements manifested in the interaction with the interviewer may reveal excessive co-operation or opposition. *Mitgehen, echopraxia, automatic obedience* and *advertence* are symptoms of excessive co-operation. In mitgehen (literally, German, *to go with*) the interviewer can move the patient's limbs or body by directing him with fingertip pressure 'as if one was moving an anglepoise lamp' according to Hamilton (1984). When the patient imitates the interviewer's every action the symptom is called *echopraxia*; this occurs despite the doctor asking him not to. Automatic obedience denotes a condition in which the patient carries out every command in a literal, concrete 'zombie-like' fashion. To demonstrate these symptoms of excessive co-operation, the patient should be asked to resist the interviewer. Mitgehen and echopraxia still occur. This inability to accede to instructions to resist occurs with *forced grasping*. The interviewer presents his hand to be shaken but at the same time asks the patient not to shake it; every time the patient does shake hands the interviewer has great difficulty in getting his hand away again. In *advertence*, the patient turns towards the examiner when he addresses him; again it has a bizarre, exaggerated and inflexible quality.

Opposition occurs as a negative response to all the approaches of the examiner. The patient resists the examiner when the latter attempts to move his limbs. When addressed the patient turns away: *aversion*. Negativism is not just a refusal of the patient to do what he is asked; it is an active process of resisting all attempts to make contact with him. Opposition may sometimes manifest itself in muteness.

The abnormal movements of schizophrenia are strongly suggestive of neurological abnormality. This is supported by the deficits that have been demonstrated in chronic schizophrenics in the transfer of information between the two hemispheres when manual tasks involving touch are carried out without other sensory cues (Carr, 1980).

Disorder in chronic schizophrenia

Motor disorder in the mentally ill may be ascribed to the abnormal mental state, to treatment or to independent undiagnosed neurological disease (Rogers, 1985). Rogers studied motor disorders in 100 extremely chronic psychiatric in-patients, fifty-nine women and forty-one men, with a mean length of current admission of 42.8 years. Ninety-two of these patients had had a diagnosis of schizophrenia at some time and all of them showed some current motor disorder.

Motor disorders were listed under the ten categories of Table 20.1. These abnormalities were: difficulty with the initiation, efficient execution of, or persistence with, *purposive motor activity* resulting in restriction of the motor

Table 20.1 Percentage of patients with current motor disorder ($n = 100$) (Rogers, 1985)

Motor disorder	% of whole group
Purposive movement	97
Speech production	95
Posture	86
Tone	85
Facial movements or postures	74
Head, trunk or limb movements	67
Activity	64
Stride or gait	48
Eye movements	48
Blinking	38

repertoire available; *speech production* with twenty-two patients normally mute, twenty-five never initiating spontaneous conversation, fifty-three showing 'outbursts' of shouting, singing or talking and fifty-one inarticulate or barely audible at interview; *posture* and *tone* with a tendency to flexion associated with varying degrees of rigidity and typically affecting the head or neck; *abnormal movement* or *postures* of *oro-facial muscles* with rapid or slow contractions of different muscle groups; abnormal movements of the *head, trunk* or *limbs* which might be brief, jerky, and semi-purposive in quality; *abnormal activity* might occur in outbursts or continuously with behaviour, such as hitting out at others, stamping, touching or following other people; *stride* or *gait* might show shuffling, slowness, not swinging the arms, or turning with head and neck 'in one piece'; conjugate deviation of the *eyes*, often up and laterally with deviation of the head in the same direction; *blinking* markedly increased or decreased in rate, sometimes in 'bursts'.

Ninety-eight of these hundred patients had had motor disorder recorded prior to 1955 before any treatment with neuroleptic drugs. There was considerable variability between the type of motor disorder recorded before 1955 and observed currently. Disorder of eye movements, tone, gait and blinking were recorded less commonly. Movement disorder in this group of patients was compared between those currently receiving neuroleptic drugs, those not treated for one month, one year, or five years, and those never having received medication: with the possible exception of facial movements, which were more frequent in those having received treatment in the last year, there was no difference in the frequency of abnormal movements.

MOTOR DISORDER IN PARKINSONISM

The disturbance of basal ganglia resulting in Parkinsonian symptoms has two main causes of relevance to psychiatry: Parkinson's disease and symptoms secondary to the exhibition of psychotropic drugs. Some of the motor symptoms are similar in these two conditions, but the overall clinical picture differs.

Parkinson's disease

In Parkinson's disease, as well as motor symptoms, there are frequent sensory, autonomic and psychiatric abnormalities. Parkinson's original description in 1817 implied an absence of perceptual (as opposed to sensory) abnormality, and does not comment on 'psychiatric status', which would then have been an unknown concept.

Primary or secondary sensory abnormalities may occur and there may be autonomic under- or over-activity. However, the most conspicuous symptoms are in motor function: slowing of emotional and voluntary movement (Walton, 1985), muscular rigidity, akinesia, tremor and disorders of gait, speech and posture. There is not necessarily any mental change; however, depression is very common (Mindham, 1970), intellectual deterioration may occur, and personality disorder is sometimes associated. Psychotic episodes have also been described. A very excellent description of the symptoms and subjective experience of Parkinsonism is given by Sacks (1973).

Extrapyramidal side-effects of neuroleptic drugs

The extrapyramidal movement disorders produced by antipsychotic drugs are described in detail by Marsden *et al.* (1986). These include drug-induced Parkinsonism with the classical Parkinsonian triad of rigidity, tremor and akinesia, and also such symptoms as abnormalities of gait, speech, and posture, excessive salivation, difficulty with swallowing, the characteristic *facies* and greasy skin. *Akinesia* varies from being mild in degree (dyskinesia) with immobile, blank, expressionless face; limited movements with loss of such associated motor activity as the arms swinging when walking; and lack of spontaneity to more severe and generalized absence of movement; this may start soon after beginning neuroleptic medication. Cog-wheel rigidity and 'pill-rolling' of the fingers, tremor of the hands or peri-orbital tremor may occur, but are less common than akinesia.

Akathisia, motor restlessness, occurs frequently. There is a subjective experience of motor unease with a feeling of being unable to sit still, a need to get up and move about, to stretch the legs, tap the feet, rock the body. Akathisia may occur at the same time as the akinesia of drug-induced Parkinsonian and presents the contrasting state of a subjective urge to move and physical impairment of movement. Akathisia is a difficult symptom to evaluate: to distinguish it from other causes of inner restlessness, restlessness of the legs should be found to be especially prominent.

Acute dystonic reactions include a variety of intermittent or sustained muscular spasms and abnormal postures. There may be protrusion of the tongue, grimacing, oculogyric crises, blepharospasm, torticollis, opisthotonus, and other hyperkinetic exaggerated actions of face, head, trunk or limbs.

The association of so-called *tardive dyskinesia*, in which repetitive, purposeless movements of the facial muscles, mouth and tongue occur (sometimes with choreoathetotic limb movement and respiratory grunting) with the exhibition of psychotropic drugs is disputed. There is no doubt that facio-bucco-linguo-masticatory dyskinesia occurs in many chronic, especially elderly, psychotic patients on neuroleptic medication, but is it causally connected with drugs? The word *tardive* is used as the syndrome was considered to be a late consequence of drug treatment; however, there are cases described who have never received neuroleptic drugs and the precise relationship remains to be elucidated–it may be simply a late stage of the illness. In practice, the extrapyramidal symptoms secondary to medication are difficult to evaluate and measure in terms of severity, problematic in accounting for aetiologically, but important in the satisfactory management of the patient. At a three-year follow-up of psychiatric patients receiving antipsychotic medication, oro-facial dyskinesia increased from 39% to 47% of the sample with a few developing the disorder anew and a few remitting (Barnes *et al.*, 1983). There was an association between dyskinesia and age over 50, and the presence of akathisia, but none with the use of antipsychotic drugs; in fact those on high dosage were unlikely to have the condition. These dyskinesic symptoms also occur in Huntington's chorea and in senile chorea.

HUNTINGTON'S CHOREA

This is a hereditary condition, inherited as a Mendelian dominant, which manifests usually in early middle life and is characterized by choreiform movements and dementia. Jerky, rapid, involuntary movements start in the face and upper limbs. Dysarthria and disorder of gait also occur before the intellectual impairment. The progressive dementia with inertia and apathy may be accompanied by irritability and occasional outbursts of excited behaviour. Occasionally, the dementia occurs as the first sign of the illness.

Various psychological abnormalities have been described in the prodromal stage before manifestation of chorea and dementia. These may be anxiety, reactive depression and the features of peronality disorder, especially antisocial behaviour. It is not known if this is truly an early symptom of the illness or part of the psychosocial reaction to this appalling and doom-laden condition.

Other dementing illnesses

Non-specific deterioration of motor behaviour occurs with other dementing illnesses, especially increasing clumsiness and incoordination and eventually inertia and akinesia. In senile dementia, which is much commoner in females than males, the course is usually steadily and smoothly progressive. Death generally occurs within five years of the onset of the condition, often within six months of admission to hospital, from intercurrent infection or progressive inanition. In arteriosclerotic dementia, males and females are approximately equally affected; the course is fluctuating and stepwise in progression, and usually slower in achieving its eventually fatal outcome than senile dementia.

TICS AND GILLES DE LA TOURETTE'S SYNDROME

Tics are usually rapid, repetitive, co-ordinated and stereotyped movements, most of which can be mimicked and are usually reproduced faithfully by the individual (Macleod, 1981). In Gilles de la Tourette's syndrome, multiple tics are accompanied by forced vocalizations which often take the form of obscene words or phrases–*coprolalia* (Lishman, 1978). The condition starts in childhood under the age of 16; there are multiple motor tics and unprovoked loud utterances which may amount to shouted words which are obscene.

The condition is more common in boys than girls and usually starts between the ages of 5 and 8 with simple tics. The vocalizations usually begin as unrecognizable sounds but may progress to 'four-letter' swear words. Both tics and utterances are likely to occur with emotional stress. The subject often tries desperately hard not to vocalize the word and this may be accompanied by considerable anxiety. Aetiology of the condition is not known.

Disturbance of behaviour

There is no clear demarcation between disturbance of movement and of behaviour, and the distinction made here is arbitrary. Thus with Parkinsonism, and to a greater extent catatonic schizophrenia, an individual abnormal movement may be elaborated into an abnormal pattern of behaviour.

BEHAVIOURAL DISORDERS OF SCHIZOPHRENIA

Disorder of movement is characteristic of *catatonia* in which the patient may become immobilized in one attitude due to increased muscle tone at rest; it is usually seen in schizophrenia but has been described with frontal lobe tumour and some other organic conditions. There are abnormalities of posture and of movement, frequently shown in the actions made in relation to another person–the interviewer. Thus *waxy flexibility* describes the situation where a posture of the limbs is maintained indefinitely after being manipulated into that attitude by the observer. Behaviour, the composite of actions, may also be abnormal, and this is characteristic of *catatonic schizophrenia*, with more than just one isolated abnormality of posture. It has often been commented that the incidence of catatonic schizophrenia has markedly declined. However, Mahendra (1981) has queried the existence of catatonic schizophrenia as a condition with classical Kraepelinian schizophrenic features *and* catatonia in the same patient. He believes many of the latter patients to have suffered from neurological disease, perhaps post-encephalitic, from epidemic and endemic viral infections. If this were so, the presumed association between schizophrenia and catatonia was fortuitous.

One could make a vast catalogue of the bizarre, and sometimes unpleasant, behaviour demonstrated by chronic schizophrenic patients, but this could never be exhaustive. Certain types of behaviour patterns are described here with examples. Schizophrenic *stupor* occurs, although rarely. The patient is mute and akinetic, although from the alertness of the eyes and the occasional excursion into abrupt activity or speech he is clearly conscious. It can be distinguished from depressive or manic stupor by the obvious abnormalities of mood in the stupor of the affective psychoses. A schizophrenic patient sat mute and motionless with her arms held in stereotyped, twisted posture for hours at a time. This symptom is almost never seen nowadays with adequate treatment of schizophrenic symptoms.

Negativism, as described above under motor disorders, may influence the behaviour of the patient substantially. A schizophrenic patient was interviewed in prison. He was brought to the door of the doctor's room. When the doctor invited him to enter, he took two steps backwards. To get him to enter, the doctor had to ask him to go away. When the doctor put his hand out to shake hands, the patient put his hand behind his back, and reversed behind the desk. He would not sit down until he was politely asked to remain standing.

Excitement occurs in catatonia; sometimes a patient is mute and motionless for a time and then unpredictably becomes overactive and aimlessly destructive. A chronic schizophrenic patient, normally calm, would suddenly and unaccountably rush headlong across the ward and charge head-first into the wall. On occasion this behaviour was directed at a window and he had cut himself severely in the past.

Impulsive behaviour may not always be manifested as excitement; it may be carried out in contradistinction to the patient's habitual behaviour. A normally respectable and tranquil elderly female patient would suddenly make sexual assaults on unsuspecting male visitors to the hospital.

Hoarding is a common feature in chronic schizophrenics and is not confined to those in institutions. A patient used to put in a small tin insects and pieces of rubbish found around the hospital, such as cigarette ends and small pieces of string. She did not appear to use her assortment but was constantly collecting more items.

There may be *mannerisms* and idiosyncracies of behaviour as well as of single movements. One totally mute male chronic patient used to retire to the top of a remote staircase above a ward where he ingeniously and delicately cut keys that would open any door in the hospital. He would exchange these for cigarettes with other patients, despite remaining silent.

Multitudinous other forms of abnormal behaviour are manifested in schizophrenia. Flagrant stealing occurs, sometimes with a manneristic flavour, such as the patient who 'stole' bed-springs, much to the discomfort of the occupants. Unprovoked aggression and 'nastiness' are seen. Patients may exhibit childish naughtiness or grotesque dirtiness; self-immolation and suicide occur. This may take place in obedience to auditory hallucinations or as part of a delusion. One patient regularly heard a voice that instructed him to jump out of the window; he was prevented on many occasions but finally took the reinforced window frames with him in leaping to his death.

It has been queried whether impairment of performance in schizophrenia could be associated with a lesion of the corpus callosum. Theoretically, this could result in dysfunction of interhemispheric transfer of information. When chronic schizophrenic patients were compared with 'matched' controls for a task in intermanual transfer, that is using their right and left hands for tasks that require touch alone and therefore information to be conveyed from one hemisphere controlling each hand to the other, schizophrenic patients showed a gross deficit in intermanual transfer (Carr, 1980). However, the overall difference between schizophrenics and controls was so great as to overshadow the differences within the schizophrenic group.

BEHAVIOURAL SIGNS OF EMOTIONAL DISTURBANCE

Psychiatrists have learnt that they must listen to their patients; they are less skilled in observing them and coming to useful, testable hypotheses. Internal medicine has, traditionally, made great diagnostic use of physical signs and psychiatry also would do well to use behavioural signs as indicators, not proof, of possible disturbance. Trethowan (1977) has noted, in addition to the evidence for catatonia and Parkinsonism, the following behaviour, as opposed to neurological signs, which may be of value diagnostically in psychiatry.

1   *The handshake* may be limp and lifeless as in the asthenic adolescent or sufferer from simple schizophrenia, or vice-like in mania; the hand of the schizophrenic patient with negativism may be withdrawn when the interviewer offers his, or the manic or personality disordered patient may insist on shaking hands contrary to the doctor's intention.

2   *Other forms of hand behaviour* which may be significant include bitten or picked nails, clenched hands with blanched knuckles and restless fidgeting with the fingers; all these may indicate acute or chronic anxiety. Heavily cigarette-stained fingers obviously reflect the large number of cigarettes smoked and the extent to which each cigarette is consumed; it may also show a degree of tension. Tremor may reveal alcoholism with alcohol withdrawal. In 'Trethowan's wedding ring sign' a woman during history-taking unconsciously reveals her marital difficulties by constantly sliding her wedding ring on and off her finger.

3   *The feet* may be used for restless pacing in agitated depression. Akathisia, as described above, with an inability to keep the feet still may indicate excessive medication with phenothiazine drugs.

4   *Depressive facies and posture* sometimes lead to diagnosis before the patient

speaks. The patient may be slumped in the chair with a fixed expression of unmitigated grief on his face and a prominent 'crow's foot' between the eyebrows. Trethowan (1977) has commented on the greatly reduced blink rate with severely retarded depressives.

5 *Clothing* in mania may be distinctive and suggestive; both of the diagnosis and the hypereroticism that often accompanies it. Hair, make-up and dress may be unequivocal demonstrations of manic mood: 'Thus Stella, normally a fairly modest girl, appeared one day in my consulting room wearing an all black outfit consisting of net stockings, a mini-skirt which extended barely to vulva level, and a top with so deep a cleavage as almost to expose her umbilicus. As if this were not enough she had stuffed her red, white and blue jubilee panties into the top of her open handbag, for all to see' (Trethowan, 1977).

This list is far from exhaustive. The point is that clinicians should use their eyes and their previous clinical experience to form hypotheses in observation which they can subsequently test in the history or examination of mental state.

BEHAVIOUR OF HYSTERIA

In the International Classification of Diseases (World Health Organization), disturbances in hysteria are described: 'There may be dramatic but essentially superficial changes of personality sometimes taking the form of a fugue (wandering state). Behaviour may mimic psychosis, or, rather, the patient's idea of psychosis'. Conversion symptoms include such motor disturbances as hysterical paralyses, astasia–abasia and other disorders of gait and tremor, and also sensory disturbances.

The word *conversion* implies the conversion of an unpleasant and unacceptable emotion into a physical symptom. This is, of course, a theoretical interpretation of the dynamics of aetiology of the symptom. A characteristic example of conversion would be a girl, aged 20, who had spent a lot of time during her childhood in hospital. Four years previously she had been unable to walk and was pushed into the neurological ward in a wheelchair. No organic pathology was found. She was then transferred to a psychiatric ward and without further specific treatment her function gradually returned to normal. Two years later she complained of backache and after six months importuning, she persuaded an orthopaedic surgeon to operate on an intervertebral disc. Following the operation she walked with a stick, dragging one leg and saying the backache was unchanged. On physical examination, there was no voluntary movement of flexion or extension at the knee or ankle on the right side. However, there was no wasting or fasciculation of muscles. Tone was normal; knee and ankle jerks were brisk and equal, and both plantar responses were flexor. There was stocking anaesthesia of the right leg. She smiled as she described the way her disability limited her lifestyle and how limited was the effectiveness of the medical profession. When offered admission to hospital with the prognosis of complete relief of symptoms, she refused saying that she could not afford the time off work.

ANOREXIC BEHAVIOUR

The name of this condition is a misnomer; although some patients may claim to have no appetite, others admit to a voracious appetite which, with almost superhuman effort, they successfully control. The behavioural abnormality is a feeding disturbance or eating disorder; carbohydrate deprivation with carbohydrate starvation is characteristic.

The patient may resist the encouragement of her parents and the hospital staff to eat, often using deception such as hiding food in her clothes, holding it in her mouth and depositing it in a WC, or throwing it out of the window. She may make herself vomit or take purgatives to remove food. Anorexia may alternate with episodes of bulimia, when she eats excessively. This overeating is often bizarre in nature; for example, a 16-year-old girl persuaded her parents to lock the pantry door to prevent her stealing food and each parent had then to keep a key on their person. One evening, when they were both out, she broke the pantry window, climbed in and consumed everything she could. On the day she came to hospital, she got up at 5.30 a.m. and ate 1lb of raw sausages and a whole loaf of bread. Patients often feel very guilty about eating, and obtain a feeling of satisfaction from starving themselves and reducing their weight to cachexia.

Ritualistic behaviour may be shown in the preparation and eating of food. Very frequently, cooking or dietetics is their hobby with an array of exotic cooking books on the kitchen shelf. They are very interested in what other people eat–a married anorexic cooked her husband into obesity, 'like a Michelin man', she admitted, whilst she starved herself. Another patient recounted that if she were reading a novel and came to a description of food or eating, she would go back and read that passage several times with gloating excitement before continuing the book.

Abnormalities in sexuality, gender role and attitudes towards maternity of anorexic patients have been described (Bruch, 1973). Worries about oral impregnation, fatness resulting in childbirth and so on, appear to be much rarer in the better informed adolescents of today. However, there is often an expressed wish not to become an adult, a mother or a woman. An anorexic patient occupied the same room as a young woman admitted to hospital with her baby son. The anorexic girl intensely disliked and refused to look at the baby boy. She resented the attention that he received which was therefore no longer directed at her, previously having been the youngest person on the ward. She disliked him because he was male and would become a man. She hated the reminder that she was becoming a woman and would be capable of having a baby. It is quite common for the patient to be pleased that she is emenorrhoeic, and to try and limit weight gain so that periods do not recur. She may take the returning attention of boys, as she begins to put on weight and become attractive, as a signal that she needs to lose weight again. Sometimes her denial of food is seen as a self-imposed penalty for sexual thoughts or misdemeanours which occurred when she was at normal weight.

References

Barnes TRE, Kidger T & Gore SM (1983) Tardive dyskinesia: a 3 year follow-up study. *Psychological Medicine 13*, 71–81.

Black P, Jeffries JJ, Blumer D, Wellner A & Walker AE (1969) The post-traumatic syndrome in children. In Walker AE, Caveness WF & Critchley M (eds) *The Late Effects of Head Injury*. Springfield, Illinois: Thomas.

Bruch H (1973) *Eating Disorders: Obesity, Anorexia Nervosa and the Person Within*. London: Routledge & Kegan Paul.

Carr SA (1980) Interhemispheric transfer of stereognostic information in chronic schizophrenia. *British Journal of Psychiatry 136*, 53–8.

Hamilton M (1984) *Fish's Schizophrenia*, 3rd Edn. Bristol: Wright.

Lishman WA (1978) *Organic Psychiatry*. Oxford: Blackwell scientific.

Macleod J (1981) *Davidson's Principles & Practice of Medicine*, 13th Edn. Edinburgh: Churchill Livingstone.

Mahendra B (1981) Where have all the catatonics gone? *Psychological Medicine 11*, 669–71.

Marsden CD, Mindham RHS & MacKay AVP (1986) Extrapyramidal movement disorders produced by antipsychotic drugs. In Bradley PB and Hirsch SR, *The Psychopharmacology and Treatment of Schizophrenia*. Oxford: Oxford University Press.

Mindham RHS (1970) Psychiatric symptoms in Parkinsonism. *Journal of Neurology, Neurosurgery & Psychiatry 33*, 188–191.

Rogers D (1985) The motor disorders of severe psychiatric illness: a conflict of paradigms. *British Journal of Psychiatry 147*, 221–32.

Sacks OW (1973) *Awakenings*. London: Duckworth.

Trethowan WH (1977) Psychiatry's physical signs. *World Medicine November 16*, 19–21.

Walton J (1985) *Brain's Diseases of the Nervous System*, 9th Edn. Oxford: Oxford University Press.

World Health Organization (1977) *International Classification of Diseases*, 9th Revision. Geneva: World Health Organization.

21

The Expression of Disordered Personality

'But the impressions and actions of human beings are not solely the result of their present circumstances, but the joint result of those circumstances and of the characters of the individuals: and the agencies which determine human character are so numerous, (nothing which has happened to the person throughout life being without its portion of influence), that in the aggregate they are never in any two cases exactly similar. Hence, even if our science of human nature were theoretically perfect, that is, if we could calculate any character as we can calculate the orbit of any planet, *from given data*; still, as the data are never all given, nor ever precisely alike in different cases, we could neither make positive predictions, nor lay down universal propositions'.

John Stuart Mill (1811)

Mill states succinctly the difficulty of forming a structure of personality theory that is useful in clinical practice in *predicting* behaviour.

The term *personality disorder* is an abstraction built upon several tenuous theories; it is an untidy concept but it carries clinical usefulness. The way in which the term has been developed and its relationship with *neurosis* is dealt with elsewhere (Sims, 1983). The intention here is only to discuss the effects different types of personality have upon actions and behaviour. The clinician builds upon a profile for personality disorder starting with his meaning of the term *personality* which Schneider (1959) has defined as 'the unique quality of the individual, his feelings and personal goals'. This leads to a characteristic pattern of behaviour which allows us, to some extent, to predict his future actions and which makes this individual different. The clinical designation of personality is purely descriptive and carries no theoretical implications, otherwise there is a logical flaw in describing personality type in terms of consistent behaviour and at the same time claiming the *type* accounts for definite patterns of behaviour.

These characteristics of behaviour, including the capacity for relationships with other people, are brought together to describe *traits* or *personality types*; obviously to be clinically relevant these traits must have implications for the functioning of the individual. The distinction between *trait*, the predisposition associated with personality, and *state*, the current mental condition, is very important. These classifications of personality disorder based upon such lists of traits were categorized by Schneider (1923), and more recently in the International Statistical Classification of Diseases (World Health Organization, 1977) and in DSM III (American Psychiatric Association, 1980). Certain characteristics have clinical significance, such as the degree to which the person is aware of the feelings, and sensitive to the judgements, of other people. A person who carries this trait to excess is considered to have *obsessional (anankastic) personality*; too little is found in *asocial personality* (psychopathy). Abnormal personality is found when a personality trait considered to be clinically important is present to either too small or too great an extent to conform statistically with the mass of mankind.

Although Schneider's typology has been largely superceded by ICD 9 in general clinical use, it does show considerable reliability (Standage, 1979). When psychiatrists rated according to Schneider's criteria, considerable reliability was found for *asthenic, explosive, depressive* and *affectionless* types; *insecure* and *attention-seeking* types were overused; low reliability was found for the *fanatic, labile* and *hyperthymic* types.

Abnormality of personality has been described. What is *personality disorder*? Here Schneider's definition will suffice. Personality disorder is present when that abnormality of personality causes either the patient himself or other people to suffer:

1   A highly conscientious and meticulous Post Office sorter is promoted to Foreman Sorter after many years' reliable service. The appropriate response might be to be pleased at the increased pay and go and spend the first week's increment before receiving it. However, this man is fearful about the promotion. He worries that he may not be able to cope with the job, that he may not be able to persuade the men in his charge to sort letters to his own high standards, that he won't be able to mix socially with his superiors and equals, that he will make a fool of himself and that other people will laugh at him. He becomes miserable, anxious and retarded, and has to stop work. Because of his abnormal, obsessional (anankastic) personality he responds to the stress of promotion by becoming acutely distressed and developing neurotic depression.

2   A bland and plausible confidence trickster extracts without compunction the means of subsistence from an elderly widow. His psychopathic blunting of appreciation for the way others will experience his behaviour and their consequent feelings results in his causing suffering to others.

Personality abnormality is a part of the individual's constitution. Whether or not it manifests as personality disorder depends to a considerable extent on social circumstances. A highly abnormal personality which in one situation may be considered criminal psychopathy and be seen in a convicted prisoner, in another situation will be the driving force in a highly successful and relatively creative political revolutionary. Personality in an individual cannot be divorced from its social and cultural setting.

Having ascertained whether personality disorder is present, its type should be categorized using an accepted system. However, a caution is needed here. It is often extremely difficult to fit people into arbitrary categories of personality and the whole topic of classification is still highly unsatisfactory. It may be much better to use a few descriptive sentences for the personality, and probably best is to combine description with categorization. Three systems can be recommended: ICD 9 and DSM III referred to above, and the typological classification of personality disorder introduced by Tyrer and Alexander (1979); Table 21.1 is a composite of these classifications. They all start from the same point: the definition of personality; the evaluation of abnormality; and the observation of certain influential and regularly occurring traits. Tyrer and Alexander's five discrete categories of abnormal personality followed from a cluster analysis of personality data and is therefore a simplification of ICD 9, which itself was based originally upon Schneider. The DSM III has certain

Table 21.1 Comparison of personality types: ICD 9, DSM III & Tyrer

Tyrer & Alexander 1979	ICD 9 (World Health Organization, 1977)	DSM III (American Psychiatric Association, 1980)
	301.0 Paranoid	Paranoid
Dysthymic	301.1 Affective	
Schizoid	301.2 Schizoid	Schizoid
		Schizotypal
Sociopathic	301.3 Explosive	
Anankastic	301.4 Anankastic	Compulsive
	301.5 Hysterical	Histrionic
Passive dependent	301.6 Asthenic	Dependent
	301.7 Asocial	Antisocial
		Narcissistic
		Avoidant
	301.8 'Other'	Borderline
		Passive–aggressive
		Atypical, mixed or other

concepts added which have proved important in American psychiatry, although they are not necessarily found helpful elsewhere.

Paranoid personality disorder

The essential feature of this type of personality disorder is self-reference, the proper psychiatric sense of the word *paranoid*: such people misinterpret the words and actions of others as having special significance for, and being directed against, themselves. Theoretically, self-referent ideas could imply that others are always noticing them in an admiring and benevolent way; in practice, such people presenting in psychiatry have ideas of persecution. They mistrust other people, they are very sensitive and suspicious believing that others are against them and that what they say about them is derogatory. There are active and passive types of paranoid personality disorder; both types feel that others are 'getting at them' but their response differs.

The active paranoid personality manifests suspiciousness and is hostile and untrusting. Such a person is quarrelsome, litigious, quick to take offence, intensely suspicious and sometimes violent; he will go to enormous lengths to defend his rights or to address real or imagined injustices. He is extremely vigilant and takes precautions against any perceived threat. This is the sort of person who will march fearlessly across a field of young corn because he sees there is a public right of way on his map and the farmer has no right to violate this. They repudiate blame and may be regarded by others as devious, scheming and secretive. Such a person is intensely jealous of what he regards as his own belongings, which may be people as well as objects, and he spends a lot of time planning to 'get his own back'. He may be self-important and fanatical. Morbid jealousy may be shown and such a person may be involved in acts of violence because of imagined injustice. Such a personality may find creative expression in social and political life but is likely to be very destructive within the family.

A person with passive paranoid personality faces the world from a position of submission and humiliation. He assumes that whatever happens to him will be damaging. Like the active type he is suspicious, sensitive, self-referent and misconstrues circumstances and other people. He believes that other people will dislike him and that they will ultimately let him down. However, he accepts 'the slings and arrows of outrageous fortune' passively, bowing to the inevitable; he is vulnerable and frequently feels humiliated and unable to initiate any assertive activity.

A prominent characteristic of the paranoid personality is the presence of an over-valued idea (Chapter 7). This, alternatively described as a fixed idea (idée fixe), is a belief which might seem reasonable both to the patient and to other people. However, it comes to dominate completely the person's thinking and life, and instead of testing its validity he tends to consider that every circumstance of life substantiates it; it becomes the basis for action which is sometimes aggressive or self-destructive. It is quite distinct phenomenologically from both *delusion* and *obsessional idea*.

Affective (dysthymic) personality disorder

This abnormality of personality describes the situation where there is persistent life-long abnormality of mood, not amounting to illness, as opposed to those reactive or endogenous disturbances of affect which are of shorter duration and are regarded as illness. The three most frequent types of affective personality disorder show excessive lability of mood, persistent depressive stance towards life, or continuing anxious trait. Other abnormalities of personality may occur, such as persistent hypomania, but these rarely present to the psychiatrist.

Those with *cyclothymic personality* show marked fluctuations of mood; for instance, for a day, or a week, they may be optimistic, energetic, creative and garrulous; then, for a period they may become gloomy, morose, taciturn and unable to turn themselves to any useful activity. These cycles may be linked to other biological rhythms such as the menstrual cycle; they may, however, appear out of the blue, apparently unprovoked. A premorbid cyclothymic personality is thought to predispose to manic–depressive psychosis. Certainly Jamison (1986), in a study of manic–depressive illness and creativity found that amongst poets especially there was an excess of cyclothymic personality, of depressive illness and of suicide.

The *depressive* type of affective personality disorder, which is probably the commonest, is manifested by all-pervasive and permanent gloom and apprehensiveness. It leads to the diagnostic quandary: 'Is this depressive state or depressive trait?' Such people are usually gentle and sensitive, they take themselves and their activities seriously; they are often safety-conscious and hypochondriacal. A person with this personality structure coined aphorisms which revealed his mental set such as: 'There is no situation in life so bad as to be incapable of further deterioration', or 'Every silver lining has its cloud'.

It is important to distinguish anxiety *trait* from anxiety *state*. In the former there is often free-floating anxiety which is exacerbated by any overt predisposing cause. Such people often find the public side of life, for example at work, very much more stressful than the private side, within the family.

Schizoid personality disorder

This personality disorder is characterized by a lack of need for and defect in the capacity to form social relationships; such people show withdrawal from social involvement, emotional coolness and detachment, and indifference to the praise, criticism and feelings of other people.

These individuals are 'loners' with a disinclination to mix, and they appear somewhat aloof. They lack tender feelings and are not interested in the company of others. They are not depressed in mood, nor are they shy or sensitive towards other people, but they are solitary and prefer not to be involved in social occupations. Their interests and hobbies usually tend to increase their isolation from other people as they are more interested in things, objects and machines.

Close relatives may complain of subjects' emotional detachment, their inability to inspire strong feelings in others, their oddness and eccentricity, and their callous indifference to others' suffering. In a follow-up of former schizoid subjects, they were found to use psychological constructs less than a control group, and this pointed to the schizoid individual's lack of empathy (Chick *et al.*, 1979).

SCHIZOTYPAL PERSONALITY DISORDER

DSM III (American Psychiatric Association, 1980) introduces schizotypal disorder as a subtype. Such people do not have the characteristics of schizophrenia but show at least four of the following:

1   Magical thinking, for example, superstitiousness, clairvoyance, 'others can feel my feelings', bizarre fantasies or preoccupations in children.
2   Ideas of reference.
3   Social isolation.
4   Recurrent delusions, sensing the presence of a force or person not actually present.
5   Odd speech without loosening of associations or incoherence, for example, speech that is digressive, vague, over-elaborate, circumstantial or metaphorical.
6   Inadequate rapport in face-to-face interaction due to constricted or inappropriate affect.
7   Suspiciousness or paranoid ideation.
8   Undue social anxiety or hypersensitivity to real or imagined criticism.

This personality type has been thought to be associated with or predictive of schizophrenia. However, the list given above would not be considered to form one distinctive personality type in British or European psychiatry, and some of the phenomenological descriptions are questionable; for instance, the 'sensing of a force... not there' being described as a 'delusion'. Impaired 'smooth pursuit eye movements' was hypothesized as a biological marker for schizophrenia (Siever *et al.*, 1984). When 284 male students were screened for eye tracking and were independently evaluated for personality type, low accuracy trackers were significantly more likely to have schizotypal personality disorder according to DSM III criteria. However, as this type of personality is so indiscriminate, it is difficult to know whether this finding has any validity.

Explosive personality disorder

This personality disorder is not often encountered. The essential feature is liability to intemperate outbursts of mood; most frequently violent anger but occasionally inconsolable grief, extreme anxiety or uproarious hilarity. It is usually aggressiveness that brings them to the attention of the psychiatrist; with very slight provocation they may have become irritable and on occasions violent. They are treated with extreme circumspection by other people and their ill humour therefore becomes reinforced as it enables them to get their own way. They may exploit other people's fears of them to achieve their objectives, for example, the arbitrarily violent husband whose wife is completely dominated by him, through fear. Such personalities are disruptive and unpopular.

Those with this personality structure behave normally for most of the time and only occasionally explode in impulsive irritability, which is more common in younger people and may appear in either sex (Snaith & Taylor, 1985). In the system of classification advocated by Tyrer and Alexander, this personality type is not retained as distinct, but combined with paranoid and asocial personality to form a category of *sociopathic personality disorder*.

Anankastic personality disorder

Anankastic personality traits in moderate amount are valuable in society and for the success of the individual. However, when these traits are developed to an abnormal extent and interfere with the person's functioning, personality disorder is present and is characterized by perfectionism, rigidity, sensitivity, indecisiveness, a lack of capacity to express strongly felt emotion, and excessive conscientiousness. The pervading sense of insecurity is associated with extreme self-doubt and feelings of sensitivity concerning how other people view him.

Perfectionism and excessive attention to detail interferes with the overall grasp of subjects or situations. There is gross preoccupation with rules, efficiency, trivial details, procedures and protocol. One patient was making lists of the lists she had previously set herself. She could not throw away a list until everything on it had been completed, and as some of the items on the lists were things that she wished to remind herself to do regularly, she was accumulating such an ever-increasing number of lists as to be unmanageable. Efficiency and perfection are aimed at, but the excessively detailed manner in which the attempt to achieve them is made undermines the possibility of success. Often extreme orderliness in one area of life results in chaos in another; for example, the medical practitioner who kept the top of his desk in immaculate tidiness, but tipped all his case notes and other papers into the back of his car.

Rigidity in patterns of behaviour is characteristic. He values accuracy and thoroughness highly and respects other obsessional people for these qualities. He tends to keep fixed times and live to a regular programme altered only with the greatest misgivings. These constraints are extended to other people in that he insists that they submit to his way of doing things. There is often a lack of awareness of the feelings in others evoked by his behaviour. This anankastic control of other people is typified by Mrs Ogmore-Pritchard in Dylan Thomas' *Under Milk Wood* (1954), who imposes upon her husband the dictum: 'I must put my pyjamas in the drawer marked pyjamas... I must take my cold bath which is good for me'.

The anankast is extremely sensitive to the criticism, real or suspected, of other people; the slightest censure is 'taken very much to heart'. This awareness of other people's opinion makes him a conformist, not prepared to step out of line, always wishing 'to keep up with the Jones's'. He is rigid, formal, and self-controlled, not only in his public business but also at home and with his more intimate relationships.

Insecurity about his abilities and his relationships makes the anankast indecisive. He doubts his own capacity and only too easily finds himself agreeing in secret with those who criticize him. He vacillates and has great difficulty in making choices, constantly looking at situations from different points of view, 'weighing up the pros and cons'. He often finds himself in a position of ambivalence and may over-compensate for this indecisiveness by making arbitrary decisions which then become immutable upon insufficient evidence; or he may compensate for his legalistic rigidity by flaunting the law ostentatiously. Even in this his basic obsessionality and perfectionism is still manifest. The anankast finds the initiation or completion of any activity very difficult, but hard work is highly prized, and he is therefore prepared to carry on the middle part of the job indefinitely.

The obsessional's need for formality, and his feelings of sensitivity about how other people view him results in restricted ability to express tender emotion. He is unduly conventional, serious and formal. Stinginess is shown both with money and with the expression of feelings. Such a person actually experiences very strong affect but is quite unable to express this appropriately to other people.

The different facets of the anankastic personality disorder are of course interlocked. As traits of personality they are seen very frequently, not least among members of the medical profession. However, developed as a personality disorder, this way of life may be incapacitating, especially the indecisiveness and inability to express strong emotion. Depression, obsessive–compulsive neurosis and hypochondriasis are more commonly seen in such people.

Hysterical personality disorder

The word *histrionic*, used in DSM III and derived from playing on the stage, is a better term for this disorder, characterized by theatrical behaviour, craving for attention and excitement, excessive reaction to minor events and outbursts of mood, especially temper tantrums. In summarizing the description of twenty-two different authors, De Alarcon (1973) found the greatest agreement for hysterical personality disorder in the following features: histrionic behaviour, egocentricity, emotional lability, excitability, dependency, suggestibility, and seductiveness.

Characteristic of the disturbance in hysterical personality is the nature of their relationships, with limited ability to experience profound affect and communicate such feelings. There is a shallowness and lability of emotion and this is seen by others as lacking in genuineness, even though they are superficially charming–'the life and soul of the party'. They form excellent and rapid acquaintanceships with new people, but they have great difficulty sustaining a close long-term, mutually rewarding, exclusive relationship.

Mood is fluctuating and inconsistent, and they display towards other people a craving for attention, affection and appreciation. They are seen as egocentric, self-indulgent and inconsiderate of others. There is often extreme but superficial involvement with many different people in a short space of time, and such a person is seen as being manipulative, vain and demanding; the manipulativeness is often ineffectual and self-destructive. They are often superficially found very attractive, and achieve their short-term goals whilst being unable to sustain long-term relationships; for instance, marriage frequently ends in divorce. They may be dependent and helpless, constantly seeking reassurance and the approval of others. Gestures of deliberate self-harm, hysterical conversion symptoms, and abuse of alcohol and other drugs are common. Reactive depression is also frequently encountered, especially when a breakdown of relationships occurs. In a hospital study of those with hysterical personality disorder, Thompson (1980) found 83% of subjects to be female; there was a clear association with neurotic depression, overdosage, self-multilation, abuse of alcohol, and a history of criminality and sometimes violence. Tyrer and Alexander do not regard this as a distinct personality disorder, but combine it with asthenic personality disorder in a category of *passive dependence*.

Asthenic personality disorder

The asthenic personality is characterized by feelings of inadequacy of self and dependence upon other people. There is gross lack of self-confidence, initiative and drive. Such a person is unable to react to the changing demands of life and allows other people to assume responsibility for major areas of life. He may function reasonably well and appear inconspicuous when carried along through life by a dominant close relationship. However, when external stress occurs he lacks confidence and is unable to cope and craves long-term support and encouragement from relatives, his family doctor, social worker, minister, employer or surrounding social organizations. He may, for example, flourish in the Services but be unable to adjust to civilian life.

Such people tend to go through life with one dominant dependent relationship: for a man this may be initially his mother and subsequently his wife who takes over his mother's role. Crises resulting in psychiatric referral may occur when marriage breaks down, he loses his job, or after detection in crime or following physical illness. It is usually only after such situations that a person with this type of personality disorder comes to the attention of the caring professions. Dependence amounts to passive compliance with the aims and demands of the more dominant partner. There is a lack of vigour in maintaining aims and goals and in attempting to achieve these. They may describe themselves as depressed, but it is more a feeling of inertia and an inability to cope with their problems than the symptoms of affective disorder.

Asocial personality disorder

The essential, phenomenological abnormality of asocial (antisocial or psycho-pathic) personality disorder is primarily one of empathy. There is a defect in the capacity to understand other people's feelings, especially to comprehend how other people feel about the consequences of the person's own actions. This type includes those people considered to suffer from psychopathic personality within the meaning of the Mental Health Act 1983 (Bluglass, 1983). A normal person is prevented most of the time, by shame or by his capacity for empathy, from carrying out unpleasant actions towards other people. He does not want to be disliked and feels very keenly how it would be passively to be the recipient of such behaviour. It is this inability to feel for himself the discomfort that others experience as a result of his antisocial activities that appears to be absent in the psychopath. Despite such comprehensive descriptions as that of Cleckly (1941), in *The Mask of Sanity* and others, there are still considerable doubts as to whether this personality type forms a distinct category or not, and if it does, whether it should be considered within psychiatry or outside. This is succinctly expressed by Wootton (1959): psychopaths are 'extremely selfish persons and no one knows what makes them so'.

The concept of *moral derangement* was introduced by Benjamin Rush (1812), and of *moral insanity* by Prichard (1835), who considered this to occur among criminals who showed loss of feeling, of control, and of ethical sense; equivalent to mental disease but at a different level. It is important to stress that not all psychopaths are criminal, nor are all criminals psychopathic. Henderson (1939) described *creative, inadequate* and *aggressive psychopathy*, citing Lawrence of Arabia as an example of a creative psychopath. Asocial personality disorder, with conspicuous lack of conscience and in human sympathy, is found more often in males than in females; it is in many respects the opposite of anankastic personality.

This personality disorder should not be diagnosed unless the subject is aged over 18. However, in childhood or adolescence many of the following may have been demonstrated by the person subsequently diagnosed as asocial: truancy; expulsion or suspension from school for misbehaviour; delinquency; running away from home; persistent lying; repeated casual sexual intercourse; repeated drunkenness; substance abuse; theft; vandalism; school performance below expectation; repeated violation of rules at home and school; and fighting. Of course such behaviour may occur in normal children, especially with social deprivation, but it is their persistence and the presence of so many of these evidences of disturbed behaviour that may predict subsequent psychopathy.

Such a person may be meaninglessly cruel, callous and aggressive; be often cold emotionally, rejecting social norms, and showing irresponsibility in his relationships. He is often unable to maintain consistency at work with frequent unemployment, changes of occupation, absenteeism and poor relationships. Similarly, there are unsatisfactory relationships with sexual partners with a history of several separations or divorces, promiscuity, desertion and repeated marital arguments. Poor parenting results in conspicuous physical and psychological problems among his children, and the individual's aggressiveness may result in child abuse with non-accidental injury. As he ages, he is less likely to be in conflict with the law and less likely to be violent, but his affectionless inability to see the consequences of his actions, and the way other people suffer because of them, remains destructive within the family and in other institutions.

There is a failure to accept society's norms as regards social behaviour, drugs and alcohol, and personal property. A lengthy criminal record is frequently seen, as he fails to learn from his experiences (Craft, 1966). Such a person may feel miserable and depressed, even suicidal, when discovered in an unacceptable act, but this does not amount to the normal sense of feeling guilt. There is a failure to identify with the victim.

The definition of psychopathy proposed by Whiteley (1975) is as follows: the psychopath is an individual (1) who persistently behaves in a way which is not in accord with the accepted social norms of the culture or times in which he lives; (2) who appears to be unaware that his behaviour is seriously at fault; and, (3) whose abnormality cannot be readily explained as resulting from the 'madness' we commonly recognize, nor from 'badness' alone.

Failure to plan ahead and failure to honour obligations, for example, matrimonial or financial commitments, are repeated. There is a disregard for truth and also for safety, both for the individual himself and of others.

'Other' personality disorders

In DSM III certain other personality disorders are described. These mostly have a historical literature associated with them. However, it has not been thought necessary to include them as separate categories within British and European psychiatry. They are described below, in brief, for completeness.

NARCISSISTIC PERSONALITY DISORDER

This is categorized by a grandiose sense of self-importance or uniqueness; preoccupation with fantasies of unlimited success, power, brilliance, beauty or ideal love; an exhibitionistic need for constant attention and admiration; indifference, anger, or humiliation in response to criticism or indifference from others; and characteristic disturbances in interpersonal relationships, such as feelings of entitlement to special favours, taking advantage of other people, relationships with others that alternate between the extremes of over-idealization and devaluation, and lack of empathy.

AVOIDANT PERSONALITY DISORDER

This personality disorder is characterized by excessive sensitivity to rejection, humiliation or shame. There is unwillingness to enter into a relationship unless the person receives strong guarantees of uncritical acceptance. There is social withdrawal, despite a need for affection and acceptance, and the person has very low self-esteem, devaluing his own achievements, and is very aware of his personal shortcomings. Such people are exquisitely sensitive to the way they believe others will react to them.

BORDERLINE PERSONALITY DISORDER

This is a controversial concept; it appears to have characteristics of several of the categories described above. It has been used variously to describe a group of apparently neurotic patients who became psychotic while undergoing psychoanalysis, an enduring, unstable and vulnerable personality structure and a group of patients who 'almost' had schizophrenia (Leading Article, 1986). It is considered that at least five of the following should be present for the diagnosis to be made:

1   impulsivity or unpredictability in areas that are potentially self-damaging;
2   a pattern of unstable and intense interpersonal relationships;
3   inappropriate intense anger or lack of control;
4   identity disturbance in areas such as self-image, gender identity or long term goals;
5   marked lability of mood;
6   intolerance of being alone;
7   physically self-damaging acts such as self-poisoning, self-mutilation or recurrent accidents;
8   chronic feelings of emptiness or boredom.

PASSIVE–AGGRESSIVE PERSONALITY DISORDER

There is resistance to demands for adequate performance in both occupational and social functioning. This may be expressed through procrastination, dawdling, stubbornness, intentional inefficiency, or apparently deliberate forgetfulness. There is a pattern of occupational ineffectiveness resulting in a failure of job promotion or other benefits to the subject. It appears that more effective behaviour is well within the capacity of the individual.

These various 'other' personality disorders can be fitted into the list occurring in ICD 9 above. It is therefore recommended that their use diagnostically be avoided if at all possible. Borderline personality is found to be a particularly unsatisfactory term both logically and in clinical practice. It is difficult to see how a 'state' can logically be located on a 'line', either side of an indeterminate frontier perhaps, but not in one dimension. In clinical practice, making such a diagnosis often results in precluding accurate observation and being unprepared to retain an open mind.

References

American Psychiatric Association (1980) *Diagnostic and Statistical Manual of Mental Disorders*, 3rd Edn. Washington: American Psychiatric Association.

Bluglass RS (1983) *A Guide to the Mental Health Act, 1983*. Edinburgh: Churchill Livingstone.

Chick J, Waterhouse L, Wolff S (1979) Psychological construing in schizoid children grown up. *British Journal of Psychiatry 135*, 425–30.

Cleckley HM (1941) *The Mask of Sanity*. London: Kingston.

Craft M (1966) *Psychopathic Disorders*. Oxford: Pergamon Press.

De Alarcon RD (1973) Hysteria and hysterical personality disorder. *Psychiatric Quarterly 47*, 258–75.

Henderson DK (1939) *Psychopathic States*. New York: Norton.

Jamison KR (1986) Manic–depressive illness and accomplishment: creativity, leadership, and social class. In Goodwin FK & Jamison KR (eds) *Manic–Depressive Illness*. Oxford: Oxford University Press.

Leading Article (1986) Management of Borderline Personality Disorders. *Lancet 2*, 846–7.

Mill JS (1811) *A System of Logic Volume II*, 3rd Edn. London: John W Parker.

Prichard JC (1835) *A Treatise on Insanity and Other Disorders Affecting the Mind*. London: Sherwood, Gilbert & Piper.

Rush B (1812) *Medical Inquiries and Observations upon the Diseases of the Mind*. Philadelphia: Kimber & Richardson.

Schneider K (1950) *Psychopathic Personalities*, 9th Edn. (transl. Hamilton MW, 1958). London: Cassel.

Schneider K (1958) *Clinical Psychopathology*, 5th Edn. (transl. Hamilton MW, 1959). New York & London: Grune & Stratton.

Siever LJ, Coursey RD, Alterman IS, Buchsbaum MS & Murphy DL (1984) Impaired smooth pursuit eye movement: Vulnerability marker for schizotypal personality disorder in a normal volunteer population. *American Journal of Psychiatry 141*, 1560–6.

Sims ACP (1983) *Neurosis in Society*. Basingstoke: Macmillan.

Snaith RP & Taylor CM (1985) Irritability: Definition, assessment and associated factors. *British Journal of Psychiatry 147*, 127–36.

Standage KF (1979) The use of Schneider's typology for the diagnosis of personality disorder–An examination of reliability. *British Journal of Psychiatry 135*, 238–42.

Thomas D (1954) *Under Milk Wood*. London: Dent.

Thompson DJ (1980) A Comprehensive Study of Hysterical Personality Disorder. Unpublished Dissertation for degree of MSc. Faculty of Medicine, University of Manchester.

Tyrer P & Alexander J (1979) Classification of personality disorder. *British Journal of Psychiatry 135*, 163–7.

Whiteley JS (1975) The psychopath and his treatment. In Silverstone T & Barraclough B (eds) *Contemporary Psychiatry*. Ashford: Headley Brothers.

World Health Organization (1977) *International Statistical Classification of Diseases, Injuries and Causes of Death*, 9th Revision. Geneva: World Health Organization.

Wootton BF (1959) *Social Science and Social Pathology*. London: Allen & Unwin.

—22

Eliciting the Symptoms of Mental Illness

Well, let me see.... I read certain books and write certain others. I read thick ones and write thin ones.

Solzhenitsyn

Eliciting the symptoms involves observing the whole repertoire of behaviour and listening to an extensive description of the internal state and then reducing this to a few summarizing phrases. It is a difficult task, requiring persistence, a knowledge of the possible conditions of complaint, an ability to communicate, and a sensitivity to the needs and feelings of a person who is bewildered and distressed. This cannot be learned from a book, but a structure for case-taking which suggests likely areas for exploration is invaluable. There are many comprehensive schemes and they can often be traced to earlier textbooks with only slight modification. A summary of the scheme on which this chapter is based is shown in Table 22.1. A practical guide to history-taking and evaluation of the mental state, diagnosis, formulation and management is found in *Handbook for Trainee Psychiatrists* (Rix, 1987).

There is significant conflict of interest between the patient and the interviewer. The patient describes untoward experiences that he dislikes and make him feel upset. He wants to be rid of these experiences. One patient may, for example, say that he is depressed and miserable, or another may complain that his thoughts are being sucked out of his head by the Martians. In both instances the patient wishes the symptom to be removed and he feels that describing it to the doctor in the way that it is affecting him is the first stage in achieving this. The doctor needs to learn a lot of things from the patient which the latter would consider irrelevant. He needs to have a precise description of the symptoms and of the patient's state of mind. He needs to know about the patient's development and course through life; about his adjustment to his environment in general and to his symptoms in particular. To return to our examples, the doctor needs to know not only that the patient feels depressed: he must enquire about the precise nature of the 'depression', what the word implies to the patient, how the affect disturbs the routine of his life and what other symptoms are associated.

The person suffering at the hands of the Martians will be only too ready to talk about Martians. However, they are irrelevant to the interviewer, who is interested in exactly what the experience of 'thoughts being extracted' entails: what is the patient's evidence that this happens; what other abnormal mental phenomena are experienced? The reader can perhaps understand the patient's irritation if he can imagine that, after he had paid his gas bill, a final demand notice with an intimation that his gas supply was to be cut off came through the

Table 22.1 Outline for Psychiatric Examination

Patient's name	Age	Occupation	Marital status
Address			Source of referral

1 Reason for referral
2 Present illness: symptoms and their chronology
3 Previous medical history:
   i   physical
   ii psychiatric
4 Family history: father, mother, siblings, other relations, atmosphere at home
5 Personal history
   i   pregnancy
   ii   infancy
   iii   childhood and adolescence
   iv   education at school
   v   further education
   vi   occupation (and military service)
   vii   sexual history: puberty, menstrual
   viii marital history
   ix   children
6 Social data:
   i   life situation: currently working, housing situation, financial problems, relationships
   ii   crime, delinquency
   iii alcohol, drugs, tobacco
   iv social and religious affiliations
7 Premorbid personality
8 Mental state:
   i   appearance and behaviour
   ii   talk and thought
   iii   mood: subjective, objective, rapport
   iv   thoughts and beliefs: phobias, obsessions, compulsions, suicidal thoughts, delusions, misinterpretations
   v   experience and perception
   a   of the environment (hallucinations, illusions, derealization)
   b   of the body (hypochondriasis, somatic hallucinations)
   c   of the self (depersonalization, thought passivity)
   vi   cognitive state: orientation, attention, concentration and memory
   vii   insight
9 Formulation:
   i   description of person and problems
   ii   diagnosis and differential diagnosis
   iii   evidence for diagnosis
   iv   aetiological factors
   v   prognosis
   vi   management

letter box: on explaining to the authorities that his bill was already paid, they did not apologize nor say that they would correct their computer, but they started interrogating the harassed consumer as to why he should be so upset about it, and what was his evidence that he had been especially picked on by the authorities. Understandably, there is a real conflict of interest between the patient's wish for relief of symptoms and the doctor's need to start by making a diagnosis. A compromise is necessary.

The patient will quite quickly tire of the effort required to answer phenomenological questions; several short interviews are preferable to a marathon session: 'Never ask today what you can ask tomorrow'. The method should encourage the examiner to bracket out all preconceptions, and the patient to reflect upon his experiences under guidance from the examiner, who should not be digging for phenomena like a dog at a rabbit hole. It is important for the examiner to distinguish quite clearly between observations and inferences.

DIAGNOSIS AND LABELLING

Why make a diagnosis? There is clearly no very great value in attaching a label to a patient's complaint if exactly the same course of treatment would have been carried out whatever the label. It is of the essence of the work of a professional that his first task is carefully to collect information so that he knows exactly what problem confronts him within his professional competence, and therefore what action would be appropriate; this is what diagnosis implies.

In psychiatry, a multifactorial approach to understanding the causes of disability is the rule rather than the exception. This means that a narrow diagnosis, in purely organic or purely behavioural terms, is inadequate. The diagnosis needs to be made in the context of a formulation; this is discussed later in this chapter.

The psychiatric history

This account is chiefly interested in the way *taking the history* sheds light on the *mental state*. The nature and type of *referral* receives comment here; for example, from a general practitioner as an urgent problem, from a solicitor for court report, and so on. After recording the reason for referral the history will usually begin with the patient's *verbatim* description of his *present symptoms*, with the duration of each symptom and an account of the development of the illness. Using the patient's own words is valuable in giving insight into his state of mind and how he himself views his symptoms. It is helpful after receiving a catalogue of complaints to ask 'Which is the very worst of all these symptoms?' This reveals how the patient conceptualizes his problem and also suggests a satisfactory target for treatment.

A chronological account of the present illness reveals how the patient regards the development of his symptoms as well as giving information on the actual history. In the history one wants to know about the sequence of symptoms and the effects these symptoms had on the patient's lifestyle, about changes in behaviour, and alterations in physical function. It is appropriate at this point to note psychiatric symptoms of which the patient has been aware in the past, but for which he has never consulted a doctor nor received treatment. They may have relevance in the total picture of how the illness developed.

The patient feels it to be innately reasonable to describe chronologically and meticulously his previous *illnesses*, operations and accidents. He also will appreciate the logic of giving details of hospital and general practice treatment for mental illness and will usually give accurate information with regard to dates, duration, nature of treatment, in what hospital, and whether as an in-patient or out-patient. Treatment received from the family doctor is recalled less well: the dates are less reliable and often the patient does not know what was the nature of treatment nor what it was for.

The *family history* is concerned with genetic and environmental, pathoplastic features. History of mental illness, suicide, nature of treatment and so on is relevant for the first-degree relatives (those sharing 50% of the genetic material with the patient: parents, siblings, children) and more distant relatives. It is important to know about the quality of relationships, emotional bonding and interpersonal conflicts, both for the family in which the patient was a child and for the family in which the patient may be a parent. Relationships between individual members of the family are described and also the general emotional atmosphere, social and financial problems. The occupations of different family members gives information about the social context; record of health may be relevant, and also description of their personalities. Of course, the family is seen through the patient's eyes; this means that it is not a factual description but rather an account of the emotional impact the patient feels his family has made upon him. If the history from the patient is supplemented by an account from another *informant*, this bias of the patient's will itself give information which may be useful in subsequent treatment.

The *personal history* traces the stages of the patient's development, health and forming of relationships from conception, birth and infancy through childhood, school experiences, adolescence and further education to occupational, marital and sexual history. The factual details of these stages need to be recorded and also the way they have influenced the personality and attitudes of the patient, how he feels about them, how he has related to other people (teachers, work-mates), and how all these details are connected with the psychiatric condition. The emphasis throughout eliciting the history is on how the patient's account becomes meaningful; how he sees himself in relation to the world; and how his development and circumstances have been influential in provoking, exacerbating or ameliorating his present illness. The history is also used for collecting evidence on which a reasonable diagnosis, or differential diagnosis, can be made.

Premorbid, previous or usual personality

It shows considerable temerity on the part of the psychiatrist to presume to evaluate the previous personality confronted only with the patient in the present. It implies consistency of the personality as a backdrop upon which the vicissitudes of illness and other circumstances can make transitory patterns, but the underlying features remain constant. In clinical interview, the doctor assesses the patient's personality using three areas of information: first, he asks the patient to describe in detail his relationships with other people, interests and activities; secondly, the examiner studies the way in which the patient reacts to him in the interview situation; thirdly, he tries to help the patient to describe and demonstrate what he is like as a person, how he feels inside himself in different situations.

Personality assessment is not the exclusive preserve of psychiatrists or psychologists, but an important learned skill of many professionals who deal with people; for example school teachers, lawyers, even bank managers, although their terminology is different. Personality is that part of a person, excepting his physical characteristics, that makes him individual, that is, different from other people. Personality is revealed by a person's characteristic behaviour; if one can predict how he will react, what his behaviour will be in particular circumstances, then the basis of that prediction is the evaluation of his personality. Subjectively, personality is shown in the totality of a person's aims and goals, formed of everything which he values and to which he aspires. Personality is not a *thing* but an abstraction; one way of looking at human beings.

Categorization into normal and abnormal personality requires a further level of abstraction. *Normal*, an ordinary word in everyday use, needs to be used more rigorously in this context (see Chapter 1). It is best to confine 'normal' in medicine to its use in a statistical sense. It is *normal* if common to the majority; *abnormal*, if present only in the minority. A normal personality conforms therefore in its characteristics and the extent to which they are developed with the majority of mankind. Abnormal personality has some characteristics developed or underdeveloped to such an extent as to be quantitatively different from the mass of people.

This quantitative difference between normal and abnormal has to learned as a clinical skill. The aspirant to such expertise needs for a time to subject all the people who come within his horizon to a careful scrutiny of personality. What are the main constituents of this person's personality? Are they present or deficient to an abnormal extent? Such an assessment of patients, relatives and friends will gradually train the observer to become more acute in the evaluation of personality. Assessment of personality has not become useful clinically until it is effective in predicting behaviour, at least to some extent. So the first two important stages in the evaluation of personality are to ascertain the predominant traits; to establish personality type, and to decide whether these are present to an abnormal extent or not.

In the clinical interview there are various areas of dialogue with the patient that are likely to lead to useful information for depicting the detail and colouring of his personality–the *personality type*. Painting the picture and defining the type are both necessary clinical exercises. Social relations are investigated. How does he relate to his family? Is he detached or over-dependent? What sort of friendships does he form, with what sort of people and are they close-knit or superficial, with an exclusive few or an unlimited crowd? How do his interests and leisure activities involve him with others–social or solitary; structured or informal? How does he relate to bosses, workmates and employees at work? Is he a leader or a follower, an organizer, an isolant, pliant or truculent, co-operative, sympathetic, clubbable? His sexual preferences in social relationships should be noted.

The nature of his *interests* and activities are informative. What does he like doing in his spare time? If he is interested in sport, it is useful to know if he can feel partisan and involved and also whether he is a participant or observer. Enquiry is made of his preference and interests in films and literature: how he observes, criticizes and enjoys the material. To what social organizations does he belong? What are his religious beliefs and practice?

An account of his predominant *moods* is enquired for, and whether these are fluctuating or stable, responsive to precipitants or endogenous. Character traits imply a detailed adjectival list, for example, irritable, reserved, fussy and so on. It will, of course, be important to corroborate his description with an account from another person. Enquiry is made about his attitudes and values; his views about himself and his body; how he regards others close to him; his more general social values in religion, morality, politics, economics; how he feels events occur and can be made to occur. Drive and energy and the way these are expressed in ambition, lethargy, effectiveness and persistence is an important aspect of personality.

Study of his *fantasy* life is made: the frequency and duration of day-dreams and their content; whether these are goal-directed and realistic or dissociated from any expectation of fulfilment. Dreams and other supposed signs of unconscious psychic activity are useful, especially when the subject attempts to interpret them. We may comment on his habits of ingestion, inhalation and excretion; whether they are regular and to what extent he depends on this regularity. As the patient unfolds the facets of his personality so the overall emphases that he puts in areas of description become illuminating in understanding him as a whole person.

DIFFERENTIATION OF PERSONALITY DISORDER

Allocating the patient to a personality type without taking into account the infinite variability of individuals is quite inadequate. However, certain characteristics tend to occur together and are of clinical significance. Allocation to a particular category of personality disorder is made on the relative predominance of these different character traits. Having decided that a certain definite trait or traits are present in this individual to an abnormal extent, does the abnormality of personality cause the person himself or other people to suffer–that is, is personality disorder present?

If personality disorder is considered to be present, it is recommended that one of the classification systems described in Chapter 21 be used (World Health Organization, 1977; American Psychiatric Association, 1980; Tyrer & Alexander, 1979). None of these classifications is perfect, but conforming to an established scheme will facilitate communication. With greater consistency and the use of clearly laid down operational definitions it is hoped that research in this area will advance and this would have considerable clinical application.

More than one abnormal type of personality may be present in any individual; they are not mutually exclusive. In formulating the psychiatric history and evaluation of mental state, comment on premorbid personality should always be made, even if it is only to state that due to the ravages of the mental illness it is impossible to assess premorbid state. The predominant traits should be described, preferably with verbatim comments of the patient to illustrate them. The interviewer should decide whether these traits are there to a statistically abnormal extent and, if so, whether this amounts to personality disorder. The type of disorder should be differentiated.

The mental state examination

Every question that the doctor asks in taking the history or conducting an examination of the mental state should be carefully chosen to reveal useful information. It should be possible for the interviewer to interrogate himself, 'Why did I ask that question?', and know what precise area was being explored. There is no value in enquiring about the name of the patient's grandmother's dog if the answer does not have relevance to the clinical condition of the patient.

Unnecessary information is deplored for bothering the patient, needlessly wasting time and blunting the sharp edge of diagnostic enquiry. Knowing everything about the patient is neither necessary nor possible. Practical advice on conducting the psychiatric examination is found in Leff and Isaacs (1978).

As the interviewer asks each question he should be thinking what the possible answers to that question could be from a *reasonable* person in *this* context. For example, on asking an in-patient if he finds the ward routine helpful, a wide variety of answers would be reasonable and could be anticipated. They would reflect the patient's precipitating problems and underlying personality. A bizarre reply to the question or a response that does not answer the question, for instance 'occupational therapists are very powerful people', or 'the hospital is teaching me to discipline myself' are not themselves evidence of illness but are clues in the search for understanding of the patient's condition. In normal conversations one is trained, or trains oneself, to avoid asking embarrassing questions and so, when someone makes an odd remark, the tendency is to fill in the meaning of the response to make it sensible and avoid asking further questions in this area. This is exactly the opposite to phenomenological investigation, where the interviewer is looking for ways into the patient's private way of thinking. When the patient says something unreasonable, odd or unexpected, the interviewer must note it and, without embarrassing or disturbing the patient's equanimity, clarify the inner experience partly revealed. This will entail the use of the empathic method described in Chapter 1.

One of the difficulties for the aspiring phenomenologist is to know when to pursue what the patient reveals in more detail; where to make the incision for the psychopathological operation. There are two situations when this is particularly appropriate. The first is in the circumstances above when the patient 'puts a foot wrong' and makes a jarring or unexpected remark in the interview. The second is in looking for the appropriate psychopathological symptoms to make or confirm the diagnosis. Thus, in schizophrenia, passivity experiences or auditory hallucinations may not be volunteered but only made plain in detailed and careful direct questioning; or, in depression, vital feelings are only distinguishable from non-specific somatic symptoms when the diagnosis is being considered and that such symptoms as vital feelings occur is known by the interviewer.

Words limit as well as liberate. The clinical interviewer needs to be very careful not to restrain his patient's answers by imposing the shackles of psychiatric technical jargon. The question, 'Do you hear voices?', is a good example of this. The patient may truthfully answer 'No', and yet be suffering from almost continuous auditory hallucinations. This particular perceptual experience is most often described by patients and their doctors as 'voices'. However, phonemes may be thought of by the patient in quite other terms. He may make no distinction at all between the auditory perceptions, (1) 'voices' he hears for which an outside observer realizes there is an appropriate stimulus; and (2) auditory hallucinations. He may be largely oblivious of the form of the communication as (1) auditory and (2) hallucinatory because he is totally absorbed with its *content* (an order telling him to go to Strasbourg and preach).

Such a patient admitted to 'receiving messages' and on further questioning agreed that these messages were audible, emanating in various voices from sources outside his head but with no identifiable external source of sound. He said that sometimes these different people sending messages conversed with each other about him, jeering at his feeble thinking and telling each other his thoughts as he thought them. He never described these experiences as 'hearing voices'. Similarly, passivity experiences can be described by the patient using many different words and expressions. They are not confined to 'control' or 'influence', which two words are often used for non-passivity experiences; for example, the 'control' a manipulative wife enjoys of her placatory husband, or the 'influence' exerted over a young politician by his domineering father.

The psychiatrist's dilemma is forever to have his intentions misunderstood by his patients. He wishes to dissect out the *form* of the patient's illness in order to make a diagnosis and embark on a reasonable course of treatment. The patient is only interested in the *content* of his illness and is impatient with what appears to him to be the doctor's irritating preoccupation with irrelevant detail. The patient cannot always distinguish his normal or healthy thoughts or behaviours from those that are abnormal or pathological. He does not know which of his experiences are different, odd and therefore diagnostically important to the doctor. He cannot separate the abnormal processes from the suffering due to his mental state. His complaint may be that old acquaintances now refuse to acknowledge him in the street. He is not aware that this belief is not delusional but true, and the reason they avoid him is because of the deterioration in personal appearance and intellectual grasp due to early dementia. He would have the doctor be interested in the way he is abused and the resultant misery, but the doctor needs to amass the evidence for dementia and then set about finding a cause for this.

Almost every *technical term* in general medicine has diagnostic implications. This is also true in psychiatry. A symptom may not be pathognomonic of a certain condition, but nevertheless predominantly found with that illness. If the doctor uses the term *perseveration* in describing his patient's mental state to a colleague, he is by inference suggesting a diagnosis of an organic psychiatric state. If this is not the diagnosis, he has some hard explaining to do to justify the use of the word. Is it really perseveration or just the repetitious use of expressions found in a person who is retarded and shows poverty of expression? To avoid misunderstanding, it is best to use longer descriptions until the interviewer is sure that the symptom is truly present.

Observation of the *appearance* and *behaviour* of the patient is an invaluable supplement to his self-description. The observations of others, and at times other than the interview, need to be taken into account. As the interview proceeds, the interviewer more definitely pursues his real intention of finding out the meaning behind the words the patient uses. What is the patient feeling and experiencing? His own account may be a blind to prevent other people or even himself seeing how bad he really feels. The *empathic method* is invaluable in working out what he is implying. So also is acute, insightful and trained observation. *Observation* may reveal white lines across the knuckles of an anxious person talking about what upsets him most and which renders him impotently angry. Empathy allows the observer to employ his own capacity for emotion as a diagnostic and therapeutic tool. Training and experience are essential for knowing in which areas delving will be rewarded with useful information: how to ask questions that are comprehensible to patients of different verbal abilities and cultural background, and which will result in appropriate answers; how to avoid damaging the patient still further with well directed but brutal questions.

There is a great value in the deliberately *vague question*. There are many patients who would be extremely offended to be asked 'Do you hear voices giving a running commentary on your actions?' Those who actually suffered from this symptom might very well not recognize that form of words as representing their experience. It is better to approach the area of enquiry with loose and ambiguous questions: 'Do you sometimes have unusual experiences? What do you feel is the explanation for them?' Such questions are less embarrassing and can be asked of anyone. They are also less directive and allow totally unexpected psychopathological material to be revealed. Vague questions are useful in highlighting the areas for further questioning; more specific questions in these areas then clarify the phenomenological detail.

SYSTEMATIC ENQUIRY

Appearance and *behaviour* are observed for the clinical medical information they carry: does the patient look ill? is he alert, oriented, fully conscious, fluctuating in his mental state? are there any behavioural or neurological abnormalities? Observation is also useful for assessing non-verbal communication (Argyle, 1975). From his posture, gesture, facial expression and so on he betrays his state of emotion, information about his personality and his attitude to the observer and to others, despite his silence or contradictory verbal communication. Obviously, observation of behaviour also indicates psychiatric symptomatology such as tics, catatonic movements, possible hallucinatory perception, feeding and excreting disorders. Posture can be revealing to the acute observer, for instance, the *pharaonic posture*, and the slow deliberate movements of head and neck of the schizophrenic patient. If the patient is mute, observed behaviour is the only source of clinical information, but the importance of observation needs to be stressed also for those patients who do speak. Observation may be valuable to corroborate the patient's complaints, to make clear the degree of emotional involvement he has in his symptoms, or sometimes to contradict his statement; for example, the person who manifests physically extreme anxiety yet denies any worries on enquiry.

Talk reveals *thought*. Listening to and studying the patient's utterances is usually the most important part of assessing his mental state. Thought disorder and the interpretation of abnormalities in use of words, syntax and association of ideas were discussed in more detail in Chapter 8. The flow of talk merits notice. Does he talk volubly and easily or in taciturn monosyllables? Does he just answer questions or speak spontaneously? Is his conversation appropriate to the social metier, and coherent? Is the train of thought readily distracted? Throughout the interview as much as possible of the patient's speech should be recorded verbatim. This provides a clearer flavour of this individual person's inner milieu, and also the data of self-experience will allow another person to evaluate the diagnosis. It is useful, in investigating thought processes, to give the patient proverbs to interpret. Using proverbs that he will not have come across before–'the image maker does not worship the gods'–is preferable as they will prevent an automatic response (Rawnsley, 1985).

As the interviewer enquires about and forms his own assessment of *mood*, he has three areas for exploration: *subjective* and *objective* description of mood, and evaluation of *rapport*. There is much more to mood than just depression or elation; the finer nuances of this person's *subjective* emotional experience must be carefully dug out like truffles, using a sensitive nose and delicate extraction. A person looking forward to an event may be acutely apprehensive, exquisitely excited but rather anxious, hopelessly resigned, and so on; 'afraid of the future' is not an adequate description. Mood can be studied for its direction (depression or elation); its consistency (stable or labile), its appropriateness; its amplitude and the degree of discrepancy between subjective description and objective observation.

Of course there is really no such thing as a wholly objective assessment of mood. The doctor comments on the mood state of his patient from his observation of the patient's demeanour and the general tone of his conversation during the interview. He makes the comment, 'he appears depressed; he is agitated and tense'. In fact, this comment on his patient's emotion abbreviates the empathic process through which he goes to make this judgement. The doctor observes the patient and picks up available cues for mood, relating these to his experience with other patients and other people through his life, and ultimately, to his knowledge of his *own* affective state. His assessment runs–'If I felt how my patient looks, speaks and acts, I would feel profoundly depressed and agitated; he is, on observation, depressed and agitated'.

Rapport is a useful measure of the patient's ability to communicate his feelings to another person. The interviewer needs to make himself into a yardstick, a *constant rapport maker*, against which the patient's ability to make rapport can be measured. To do this, the doctor requires clinical experience and an objectivity in which he knows how he reacts to, and communicates with, many different sorts of people. He knows himself and his own competence well enough to exclude this from the assessment of rapport so that, as far as possible, it is only the patient's capacity for emotional communication that is being tested.

The *ideas* and *beliefs* the patient holds and *abnormalities of perception* he experiences are ascertained and explored during the interview. In ordinary conversation there is a great deal of filling in or editing to eliminate the deficiencies of communication. A person talks and comes to a halt halfway through a sentence for loss of a word. The other person provides the word and thus continues the conversation to both parties' satisfaction. There is a tendency for those coming new to dialogue with the mentally ill to bring into their conversation these social niceties which are used to save embarrassment. The doctor tends to note what he thinks the patient meant to say, as if the latter's thinking processes were similar to his own, rather than concentrating on what he actually said. A lot of significant psychopathology is thus missed. Delusions and hallucinations are not volunteered by the patient as symptoms for the obvious reason that they are not experienced as different from the rest of the person's thinking or perceiving. To the patient, subjectively, a delusion is indistinguishable from any other idea, a hallucination is indistinguishable from any other normal perception. Skill in interviewing therefore comes very much in knowing when to look for a delusion and how to make a clear distinction between what the person experiences and what it reveals phenomenologically.

Passivity or delusions of control, *obsessions*, *compulsions* and *depersonalization* may be easily revealed or made plain with some difficulty. It is important to try and categorize the type of experience as early in the course of treatment as possible, since patients' explanations tend to become contaminated on repeated questioning. When passivity, for example, is suspected, it is generally best to follow up the clues right away and decide once and for all whether the symptom is present.

Assessment of the *cognitive state* includes at least briefly testing for orientation, attention, concentration and memory. Clinical testing is not similar to psychometry in that there is no intention to produce a score at the end of the test. The doctor is concerned with abnormality, and so his assessment depends on the degree of conformity with norms established through his clinical experience and the expectations one might reasonably have for this individual in health. So the expectations for *digit span*, forwards and in reverse, will be different for a 60-year-old office cleaner from a 30-year-old chartered accountant. When a doctor has taken the trouble to learn to standardize his interview technique, cognitive assessment becomes reasonably reliable and is rarely contradicted by formal psychological testing. The examination of the cognitive state overlaps with full neurological assessment and may require much greater neurological detail (Strub & Black, 1977).

The doctor, from specific questions and from the interview in general, needs to form an idea of his patient's attitude to his illness, difficulties and prospects. To what extent does he have *insight* into his condition? Any illness of some severity will alter the patient's world, and view of the world. Insight assesses the awareness of this change by the patient, and his capacity for adapting to this change.

Many textbooks and numerous psychiatric institutions have their own scheme for psychiatric interviewing. This account is a general commentary rather than yet another scheme. Table 22.1 contained a memorandum of key areas to be covered in the history and examination of a psychiatric patient.

Formulation

There is considerable debate as to what comprises the ideal psychiatric formulation. This is probably a chimera, in that a standardized formula for all patients from all psychiatrists is inappropriate. The formulation should be a brief written summary of the case, showing how the interviewer has made sense from his individual clinical picture within his general psychiatric framework.

Usually the formulation starts with a *description* of the patient in his sociocultural context: name; age; sex; occupation; social/cultural/ethnic/ religious group. It then proceeds with the nature of the *presenting complaint* and description of other *prominent symptoms*; the mode of *referral* to the psychiatric service; and *admission status* if appropriate (for example, 'admitted under Section 2 of the Mental Health Act'). There should be a brief account of the *genesis* and *development* of the symptoms. How have they arisen? What explains their development? Why did they occur?

It is important to make a *diagnosis*, that is, to put the illness of the individual into the context of accumulated professional knowledge. Very often a *differential diagnosis* will be given and then it needs to be stated in what order of likelihood the diagnoses are listed and whether the conditions are seen as being mutually exclusive or may be present together. Evidence for and against each diagnosis is enlisted.

Evidence of *aetiological factors* may already have been discussed with the genesis of symptoms. If not, it is summarized with the discussion of diagnosis.

Aetiology implies the use of theoretical models, and usually more than one model–biological, psychodynamic, behavioural, social–should be considered. Any further *tests* and *investigations* required for elucidation should be mentioned.

Prognosis and *management* should be discussed. The former implies the prognosis for this episode and also for life; for morbidity, mortality and for personal relationships. Management should also be reviewed in a comprehensive way that includes physical, pharmacological, psychological, rehabilitative, social and cultural methods, both in the short and long term.

The formulation then is an account based upon understanding and explanation (Chapter 1). It should be flexibly adapted to the individual case and not conform to a rigid structure. Guidelines have been produced for formulating a case (Greenberg *et al.*, 1982).

References

American Psychiatric Association (1980) *Diagnostic and Statistical Manual of Mental Disorders*, 3rd Edn. Washington: American Psychiatric Association.

Argyle M (1975) *Bodily Communication*. London: Methuen.

Greenberg M, Szmuckler G & Tantam D (1982) Guidelines on formulating a case for the MRCPsych examination. *Bulletin of Royal College of Psychiatrists 6*, 160–2.

Leff JP & Isaacs (1978) *Psychiatric Examination in Clinical Practice*. Oxford: Blackwell Scientific.

Rawnsley K (1985) Workshop on the Teaching of Descriptive Psychopathology to Postgraduates in Psychiatry Association of University Teachers of Psychiatry, Leeds.

Rix KJB (1987) *Handbook for Trainee Psychiatrists*. London: Baillière Tindall.

Solzhenitsyn A (1971) *August 1914* (transl. Glenny M, 1972). London: Bodley Head.

Strub RL & Black RW (1977) *The Mental Status Examination in Neurology*. Philadelphia: FA Davis.

Tyrer P & Alexander J (1979) Classification of personality disorder. *British Journal of Psychiatry 135*, 163–7.

World Health Organization (1977) *International Classification of Diseases, Injuries and Causes of Death*, 9th Revision. Geneva: World Health Organization.

-23

Psychopathology and Diagnosis

'There's glory for you!' 'I don't know what you mean by "glory"', Alice said. 'I meant, "there's a nice knock-down argument for you!"' 'But "glory" doesn't mean "a nice knock-down argument"', Alice objected. 'When I use a word,' Humpty Dumpty said in a rather scornful tone, 'it means just what I choose it to mean,–neither more nor less.'

Lewis Carroll *Through the Looking Glass* (1872)

Diagnosis is much more than a word plucked out of the air and pinned onto a hapless 'patient'. It conveys meaning–about the antecedents of the present state, about what other conditions are similar and, most important of all, about what is likely to happen in the future and, therefore, what should be done about it. Diagnosis is a means of communication between doctors; it should encompass a full formulation, rather than just a single word used in an idiosyncratic manner.

The importance of making a diagnosis and the range of diagnoses, is as great in psychiatry as in the rest of medicine; the conceptual differences between different diagnostic categories are actually greater, as *mental disorders* include situational, social, emotional and psychological disturbance, as well as physical illness. Understandably, most of the medical illnesses that have been described were based upon signs or symptoms; this is true also for psychiatry. There is, therefore, a very close association between the observation and classification of 'symptoms in the mind' (Burton, 1621) and psychiatric diagnosis.

In general medicine, diagnosis is based upon the complete clinical process: detailed history-taking; examination of the patient: and carrying out appropriate special investigations. This is true also for psychiatry. However, because of the limitations of its subject, this book does not deal with physical examination, nor with physical (radiological, laboratory) or psychological (psychometric) investigations.

CONCEPTS OF HEALTH AND PSYCHOPATHOLOGY

The late Peter Sedgwick (1981) made the important discovery that 'disease is a human invention... there are no illnesses or diseases in nature': hence the quotation at the beginning of this chapter. He rightly pointed out that humans describe potato blight as a disease solely because they want to grow potatoes: 'if man wished to cultivate parasites (rather than potatoes) there would be no "blight" but simply the necessary foddering of the parasite crop'. Sedgewick claimed that it was the human social meaning attached to the fracture of a septuagenarian femur that constituted illness or disease. 'Out of his anthropocentric self-interest, man has chosen to consider as "illness" or "diseases" those natural circumstances which precipitate the death (or the failure to function according to certain rules) of a limited number of biological species; man himself, his pets and other cherished livestock, and the plant-varieties he cultivates for gain or pleasure'.

Such arguments point us to the fact that medicine is not 'objective, scientific' applied biology but necessarily value-laden. This is true of the disruption of the internal state that 'patients' bring as 'complaints' to the doctor and true also of those complaints which the doctor regards as 'symptoms'. A less extreme view of the effect of social values upon the presentation of illness is the notion of the *sick role* as developed by Talcott Parsons (1951). Whatever the underlying causes of conditions, the role that the subject himself, the patient, chooses to play, and the role that is forced upon him by those around him because of his illness, are highly significant in the way his symptoms manifest.

People differ in the way they perceive, evaluate and act upon, or fail to act upon, the symptoms they experience. This Mechanic (1986) has called *illness behaviour*. Somatic or psychological symptoms do, of course, frequently occur without any evidence of organic disease. When attempting to describe and classify such symptoms, it is helpful to establish a phenomenological basis; conditions are recognized because of the particular characteristics of the patient's complaints, not because of some presumed theoretical notion of cause. The bizarre lengths which result from the application of a preformed theory of disease aetiology to symptoms, rather than developing from *symptoms* to *theory*, is admirably illustrated in Engelhardt's (1981) essay 'The disease of masturbation'. In the nineteenth century masturbation was widely believed to produce many signs and symptoms including dyspepsia, constriction of the urethra, epilepsy, blindness, vertigo, loss of hearing, headache, impotency, loss of memory, insanity, cardiac arrhythmia, rickets, leucorrhoea in women, conjunctivitis and generalized weakness, and it was held to be a dangerous disease entity.

Lewis (1953) pointed out that mental illness could be characterized in terms of psychopathology: 'disturbance of part functions as well as general efficiency'. *Part functions* refer to the different aspects of psychic experience and behaviour described in previous chapters—memory, perception, forming beliefs and so on. Thus Lewis saw a disturbance in perception, for example, hallucination, as a reason for establishing a *case* of mental illness—on psychopathological grounds.

Use of symptoms to form diagnostic categories

The relationship between signs and symptoms in psychiatry was discussed in Chapter 1. Traditionally, symptoms have been divided into those causing suffering and pain (distress) and those causing loss of function (disability). Where the only disharmony is between the individual and his society, the disturbance is not regarded as mental illness. For the great majority of mental disorders diagnostic classification is made according to the profile of symptoms presented. Exceptions to this are: (1) where the aetiology is known, for example, general paralysis of the insane; (2) where the structural pathology is known, for example, Huntington's chorea; and (3) where cause is hypothesized to result from a process without conclusive evidence, for example, *conversion* in hysteria. Descriptive psychopathology is atheoretical in nature and thus allows the development of a purely descriptive diagnostic terminology.

Symptoms are collected into constellations that commonly occur together to form the *syndromes* of mental illness. It is usual to make a distinction between *illness*, with a definite onset after normal health, and the lifelong characteristics of mental handicap or personality disorder.

Another fundamental distinction usually made by psychiatrists and based ultimately upon psychopathology, is that between *psychoses* and *neuroses*. Psychoses 'are major mental illnesses. They are exceedingly hard to define although they are usually said to be characterized by severe symptoms, such as delusions and hallucinations, and by lack of insight' (Gelder *et al.*, 1983); there is loss of contact with reality. Neurosis 'is a psychological reaction to acute or continuous perceived stress, expressed in emotion or behaviour ultimately inappropriate in dealing with that stress'; phenomenological characteristics held in common by neurotic patients include disturbances of self-image, of the experience of relationships and, often, bodily symptoms without organic cause (Sims, 1983).

Psychiatric diagnosis is usually hierarchical; organic syndromes taking precedence over functional psychoses, these over neuroses, and neuroses over situational or adjustment reactions. A patient with schizophrenia and super-added anxiety will usually receive only the diagnosis of schizophrenia. This can be a considerable disadvantage of present practice for planning treatment programmes as, for instance, the prognosis of chronic schizophrenia may be determined more by the presence of neurotic symptoms than by the response of schizophrenic symptoms to treatment (Cheadle *et al.*, 1978). Foulds (1976) used this hierarchical approach to establish a system of classification of *personal illness*, with *delusions of disintegration* at the apex taking priority over intervening levels down to *dysthymic states* as the lowest level.

An example of *categorical* classification is shown in Table 23.1. Various non-categorical methods of classification have also been used. In the *dimensional* approach as advocated by Eysenck (1970), the variations of presentation of mental illness are accounted for on just three dimensions: psychoticism, neuroticism and extraversion/introversion. *Multiaxial* classification codes different sets of information separately (see below, p. 315).

THE PRESENT STATE EXAMINATION

An example of psychiatric phenomenology applied in research is the development of the Present State Examination (Wing *et al.*, 1974): 'The Present State Examination (PSE) schedule is a guide to structuring a clinical interview, with the object of assessing the present mental state of adult patients suffering from one of the neuroses or functional psychoses'. It aims to enquire about the patient's condition and subjective state and record this information in terms of symptoms. When there is conflict between clinical and statistical judgements, clinical judgement is allowed to prevail. Symptoms are aggregated into a list of syndromes. The classification of symptoms is carried out on a computer programme known as 'Catego', which reduces the 500 PSE items to a maximum of six descriptive categories, and thence into one descriptive group for the individual patient.

An aim of the PSE has been to determine whether there are clinically recognizable symptoms upon which all psychiatrists can agree and label in the same way. Wing *et al.* pose two questions: 'First, whether certain psychological

Table 23.1 Classification of Mental Disorders (after Gelder *et al.*, 1983)

Psychoses	Organic disorders
	   Acute organic syndrome
	   Chronic organic syndrome (dementia)
	   Dysamnestic syndrome
	
	Schizophrenia
	Schizoaffective disorders
	Paranoid states
	Affective disorders
	   Mania
	   Depressive disorder	

	Neuroses
	   Depressive neurosis
	   Anxiety neurosis
	   Phobic neurosis
	   Obsessional neurosis
	   Hysteria
	   Depersonalization syndrome
	   Non-specific and mixed
	
	Personality disorders
	Adjustment disorder
	Other disorders
	   Sexual dysfunction and
	     sexual deviations
	   Alcohol and drug dependence
	   Miscellaneous syndromes
	   Psychological factors associated
	     with medical conditions
		Neuroses and related disorders

	Mental retardation Disorders specific to childhood	

and behavioural phenomena which have generally been thought by psychiatrists to be symptoms of mental illnesses can be reliably recognized and described, irrespective of the language and culture of the doctor or patient; secondly, whether rules of classification can be specified with such precision that an individual with a given pattern of symptoms will also be allocated to the same clinical grouping'.

Thus the PSE starts from a psychopathological standpoint. The interviewer is trained to note the presence or absence of listed symptoms in the glossary. Groups of symptoms are collected together into syndromes by use of computerized Catego class. The end-product of the PSE is diagnosis as a research tool based upon phenomenology, and available for study by other workers in other cultures. An example of the relationship between syndromes and symptoms is shown in Figure 23.1.

An example of the use of the PSE involves the terms used for the symptoms of schizophrenia. The *nuclear syndrome* of Wing *et al.* is composed of Schneider's first-rank symptoms. The symptoms they listed as comprising this syndrome in the ninth edition of the PSE are *thought intrusion, thought insertion, thought broadcast, thought commentary, thought withdrawal, voices about the patient, delusions of control, delusions of alien penetration* and *primary delusions*. They make

Syndrome no. (a)	Syndrome name (b)	Symptoms (list II) (c)	
1 (NS)	*Nuclear syndrome*	55 Thought intrusion 56 Thought broadcast 57 Thought commentary 58 Thought withdrawal	62 Voices about patient 71 Delusions of control 81 Delusions of alien penetration 82 Primary delusions

0   No symptoms
1   NS? = Partial delusions only   11
2   NS+ = 1 symptom
3   NS++ = 2+ symptoms

Fig. 23.1 Excerpt from the Present State Examination. From Wing *et al.*, 1974, with permission

the useful point that *thought insertion* is likely to be rated with a false positive if the examiner does not have the symptom in mind but some general approximation to it. *Voices about the patient* implies non-affective verbal hallucinations heard by the subject talking about him in the third person. *Delusions of control* refers, of course, to passivity experiences. *Delusions of alien forces penetrating* or *controlling* the mind or body is a special form of symptom already listed as belonging to the nuclear syndrome. By *primary delusions* Wing *et al.* imply *delusional perception* and give the example of a patient undergoing liver biopsy who felt, as the needle was inserted, that he had been chosen by God.

Table 23.2 First-rank symptoms of schizophrenia (Schneider, 1959) and symptoms from the Present State Examination (Wing *et al.*, 1974)

First-rank symptoms	*Equivalent symptom from Present State Examination*
Delusional	
1 Delusional percept	Primary delusion
Auditory hallucinations	
2 Audible thoughts	Thought echo or commentary
3 Voices arguing or discussing	Voices about the patient
4 Voices commenting on the patient's action	Voices about the patient
Thought disorder: Passivity of thought	
5 Thought withdrawal	Thought block or withdrawal
6 Thought insertion	Thought insertion
7 Thought broadcasting (diffusion of thought)	Thought broadcast or thought sharing
Passivity experiences: Delusion of control	
8 Passivity of affect ('made' feelings)	Delusions of control
9 Passivity of impulse ('made' drives)	Delusions of control
10 Passivity of volition ('made' volitional acts)	Delusions of control
11 Somatic passivity (influence playing on the body)	Delusions of alien penetration

FRENCH CLASSIFICATION

French psychiatric classification in the nineteenth century was firmly based upon the observation and coding of symptoms, according to Pichot (1984). Pinel stated that: 'One must be on one's guard against mixing metaphysical discussions, or certain disquisitions of the ideologists, with a science which consists of carefully observed facts'; while his pupil, Esquirol, produced a nosology 'based predominantly on the symptoms displayed by the patient at one particular time' (Pichot, 1984). However, later in that century a biological basis for illness became accepted, even in those conditions where no organic pathology could be demonstrated. This led to an emphasis on the pattern of development to delineate specific diseases.

The theory of *degeneration*, a process that could be inherited over several generations, was introduced by Morel and hindered the development of French psychiatry. This theory subsequently became the basis for the system of classification devised by Magnan. The subsequent work of Kraepelin, which has so greatly influenced British as well as German psychiatry, and of Bleuler, (which although starting in Switzerland was particularly influential in USA), had different effects in France, especially within the classification of what in Britain would be regarded as schizophrenia. Three terms have been used in France: *schizophrenia*, which incorporated that part of Kraepelin's concept of dementia praecox that excluded the other two, *bouffées délirantes*, more or less equivalent to acute delusional states, and *chronic hallucinatory psychosis*, with chronic systematized delusions.

COMPARISON OF ICD 9 AND DSM III

The *Manual of the International Statistical Classification of Diseases, Injuries, and Causes of Deaths*, 9th Revision (World Health Organization, 1977) is a classificatory system for the whole of medicine. However, for Section V Mental Disorders, 290–319 only, a glossary has been included with the tabulated lists of conditions. Mental disorders are divided in traditional fashion into psychoses (290–299), neurotic disorders, personality disorders and other non-psychotic mental disorders (300–316), and mental retardation (317–319).

Throughout the ICD 9 classification of mental disorders there are categories for 'mixed cases', for 'other' situations, and for 'unspecified' conditions. Although this classification has obvious weaknesses, for example, the term *depression* can be used in any of ten different categories (Figure 23.2; Sims, 1983), it has the great advantage of being readily usable by administrative and other non-medical staff, from the case notes of medically qualified personnel, and also that very few cases coming into psychiatric care will be excluded from all categories. Adequate training in the use of categories and in the meaning of the glossary greatly improves the precision of this classification (Zigmond & Sims, 1983).

The *Diagnostic and Statistical Manual of Mental Disorders*, 3rd Edition (DSM III, American Psychiatric Association, 1980) is specifically designed for mental illnesses. It has developed out of the previous DSM I and II, and has taken into account ICD 9. However, whereas ICD 9 is designed more for administrative and epidemiological work, DSM III is recommended for research as well as clinical use.

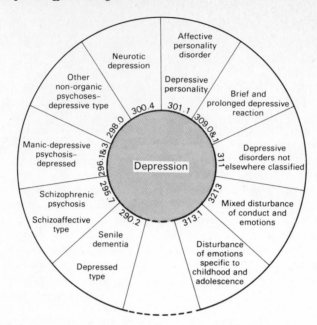

Fig. 23.2 Classification of depression in ICD 9

As far as possible, ICD 9 code numbers are retained in DSM III which enables broad comparability to be maintained, but there are very considerable divergences between the two systems. Like ICD 9, DSM III contains a glossary of the categorical terms, but in DSM III there is a great deal more instruction given on how to use categories. There is for each category a detailed list, entitled 'diagnostic criteria', which normally demands a specific number of characteristics out of the total to be fulfilled for the diagnosis to be given.

Like ICD 9, the DSM III is based upon the description of symptoms as ascertained in clinical interview. It demands clinical skills for adequate use. Although obviously the greatest attention is given to situations where mental disorder is undoubtedly present, it is possible to classify conditions not attributable to mental disorder; for example, where behavioural or psychological problems come to professional attention or treatment although not ascribable to mental disorder.

A disadvantage of DSM III is that it has splintered the generic category of neurotic disorders which is present in ICD 9. Tyrer (1985) has commented: 'in the International Classification of Diseases there are now 9 categories of neurosis and in... DSM III, the number has risen to 21. Does this represent a real advance or is it merely legerdemain?... If these disorders are fundamentally distinct from each other they should show stability over time and have different natural histories. By these criteria the categorisation of neurosis is defective'. What is held in common between different neurotic disorders is more significant than the differences between such disorders, and neuroses have a commonality of possible aetiologies, prognosis, individual methods of treatment and approaches to management services that mark them out from other mental disorders (Sims, 1985). Also, not all the conditions that would generally be thought of as neuroses fit neatly within the diagnostic criteria for particular neurotic syndromes such as anxiety state (Gelder, 1986). There are also problems with DSM III diagnosis of schizophrenia which is over-inclusive when compared with ICD 9 or the Present State Examination. The DSM III designation 'major depressive disorder' is also over-inclusive when compared with other classifications, and for clinical application.

Both ICD 9 and DSM III are in the process of revision. They are therefore not discussed in detail as they are likely to become obsolete. However, they demonstrate some of the principles of attempting to use the symptoms assessed by psychopathology for diagnosis.

Multiaxial classification

DSM III introduces the concept of multiaxial diagnosis, so that different types of clinical information may be evaluated for planning treatment and predicting outcome in each individual: Axis 1 includes mental disorders, excluding Axis 2 which includes personality disorders and specific developmental disorders; Axis 3 is used for physical disorders; Axis 4 for severity of psychosocial stressors, and Axis 5 for the highest level of adaptive functioning in the past year. Axes 1, 2 and 3 are used in normal clinical practice for evaluating treatment and predicting outcome; axes 4 and 5 are for research use.

Child psychiatry now also makes wide use of a five-axis system originally proposed by a World Health Organization Working Party (Rutter *et al.*, 1975). The axes recommended are as follows:
Axis 1. Clinical psychiatric syndrome;
Axis 2. Specific delays in development;
Axis 3. Intellectual level;
Axis 4. Medical conditions;
Axis 5. Abnormal psychosocial situations.

Clinicians have found this system relatively easy to use, and it allows the systematic recording of the broader range of information required for adequate evaluation in child psychiatry. The obvious disadvantage of multiaxial classifications are, of course, their rather complicated nature, resulting in inaccurate usage when applied to general administrative diagnostic recording.

Postscript

Fundamental to psychiatry is the need to understand what the patient is experiencing. Eisenberg (1986) has succinctly summarized the aspirations of the biological school of psychiatry: 'for every twisted thought there is a twisted molecule'. Ironically, if this association were to be achieved it would make the need for expert phenomenological skills more, rather than less, important, as it is likely to remain, from the patient's point of view, more comfortable to have his thoughts than his molecules explored.

USES OF PSYCHOPATHOLOGY

It has been said of William of Ockham, who so courageously navigated the murky and dangerous waters of medieval philosophy and science, that he was 'an empiricist refusing to stretch knowledge beyond the bounds of ascertainable experience' (Leff, 1958). This is the position of descriptive psychopathology: aiming not to draw conclusions beyond the subjective experience of the patient. Every psychiatrist uses phenomenology to some extent but it is a much more valuable tool if used rigorously.

The four practical applications of descriptive psychopathology then are as follows:

1   *Communication*–it enables clinicians to speak and write to each other about the problems of their patients in a mutually comprehensible way. This is clearly of value both in clinical practice and for research.
2   *Diagnosis*–psychiatric diagnosis at the present time is necessarily based upon psychopathology.
3   *Empathy*–the method of empathy, that is using phenomenology to explore the patient's subjective experience, is a rational way of establishing a therapeutic relationship; it enables the therapist to understand the subjective experience of his patient and will give the patient confidence in further entrusting the secrets of his internal environment to the therapist.
4   *The law*–descriptive psychopathology is the only reasonable way of determining what is mental illness, and what are the differences between mental illnesses, from a forensic point of view. Mutual enlightenment in the area between the law and psychiatry, where there is at present so much misunderstanding, will result from a clearer use of psychopathology by both parties.

The patient's symptoms, his sufferings, are a logical starting point for the doctor's sympathy, curiosity, and therapeutic endeavour. To start elsewhere turns medicine on its head and, ultimately, one arrives in a topsy-turvy world like Samual Butler's *Erewhon* (1872) where, 'illness of any sort is considered... to be highly criminal and immoral; and that I was liable, for catching cold, to be had up before the Magistrates and imprisoned for a considerable period...' and, 'if a man forges a cheque, or sets his home on fire or robs with violence from a person, or does any such things that are criminal in our own country, he is either taken to a hospital and is carefully tended at the public expense, or if he was in good circumstances, he lets it be known to all his friends that he is suffering from a severe fit of immorality... and they come and visit him with great solicitude....' You may think this is too far featched; however, it certainly appears to be the situation for some of the dissidents in psychiatric custody (Bloch & Reddaway, 1977).

The ultimate aim of psychiatry is not, of course, knowledge, but to help people to function and feel better; phenomenology is a valuable therapeutic tool. Ideally, it gives the patient, in his doctor, a person who understands what he is feeling but does not try to explain causes in terms of some unconvincing theory. The patient often has a great sense of relief when the doctor, however falteringly, describes back to him the symptoms, or the internal experience which he, the patient, has found so difficult to describe.

NEED FOR RESEARCH

Psychopathology was introduced into psychiatry before there was much emphasis on quantification, population surveys, or experimental method. It is now important for the further development of descriptive psychopathology that more rigorous research methods be applied. Phenomenology has a place in psychiatric research which has not yet been fully exploited.

Investigation of the experience of the individual has to be linked to an understanding of his biology, and it is also important to assess how normal phenomena are distributed within the population. The scientific basis of psychiatry includes, as well as biological and behavioural sciences, epidemiology and phenomenology. Recognition of homogeneity includes both the symptoms within an individual patient and the features of an affected population. The Present State Examination has been discussed earlier as a method of quantifying psychopathological information. In previous chapters mention has been made of Repertory Grids as an experimental method for investigating semantic space.

To introduce experimental methods into research in descriptive psycho-pathology will sometimes involve single case studies in which variables that have been evaluated phenomenologically are altered; for example, Green and Preston (1981) amplified the quiet whispering of a chronic schizophrenic patient during the time he was auditorily hallucinated. He whispered at the same time as he heard voices, and the content of his vocalization corresponded to what the voices were reported to have said, thus demonstrating the disturbance of boundaries of self found in schizophrenia. This type of investigation could be extended further but needs to be coupled with exact enquiry of the phenomena.

It is important for progress, that advances in biological aspects of psychiatry are assisted by high quality psychiatric diagnosis based upon phenomenology that is both reliable (that is, capable of reproduction by the same interviewer at a different time or by different interviewers) and quantifiable. Never were the skills of the clinical phenomenologist more necessary nor more likely to yield beneficial results both in understanding and in therapy. Jaspers (1959) commented: 'phenomenology, though one of the foundation stones of psychopathology, is still very crude'. This is still true, but it is now high time that descriptive psychopathology became more sophisticated.

Phenomenology takes the doctor's art and discipline of observation inside his patient's mind. David Hume (1804) described the lack of examination in medicine in his essay 'Of Polygamy and Divorces'. He tells of the physician brought into the Grand Signior's seraglio in Constantinople:

> he was not a little surprised, in looking along a gallery, to see a great number of naked arms standing out from the sides of the room. He could not imagine what this could mean; till he was told that those arms belonged to bodies, which he must cure, without knowing any more about them than what he could learn from the arms. He was not allowed to ask a question of the patient, or even of her attendants, lest he might find it necessary to enquire concerning circumstances which the delicacy of the seraglio allows not to be revealed. Hence physicians in the east pretend to know all diseases from the pulse, as our quacks in Europe undertake to cure a person merely from seeing his water.

Psychiatry must now come out of the seraglio and use all the available information in the service of its patients, including phenomenology, for diagnosis, for understanding and for treatment.

References

American Psychiatric Association (1980) *Diagnostic and Statistical Manual of Mental Disorders*, 3rd Edn. Washington: American Psychiatric Association.
Bloch S & Reddaway P (1977) *Russia's Political Hospital*. London: Gollancz.

Burton R (1621) *The anatomy of melancholy, what it is. With all the kinds, causes, symptoms, prognostickes, and severall cures of it by Democritus Junior.* Oxford: Cripps.

Butler S (1872) *Erewhon.* London: Cape.

Carroll L (1872) *Through the Looking Glass, and What Alice Found There.* London: Macmillan.

Cheadle AJ, Freeman HL & Korer J (1978) Chronic schizophrenic patients in the community. *British Journal of Psychiatry 132,* 221–7.

Engelhardt HT (1981) The disease of masturbation: Values and the concept of disease. In Caplan AL, Engelhardt DT & McCartney JJ (eds) *Concepts of Health and Disease.* Reading, Massachusetts: Addison-Wesley.

Eisenberg (1986) Mindlessness and brainlessness in psychiatry. *British Journal of Psychiatry 148,* 497–508.

Eysenck HJ (1970) A dimensional system of psychodiagnosis. In Mahrer AR (ed.) *New Approaches to Personality Classification,* pp. 169–207. New York: Columbia University Press.

Foulds GA (1976) *The Hierarchical Nature of Personal Illness.* London: Academic Press.

Gelder MG (1986) Neurosis: another tough old word. *British Medical Journal 292,* 972–3.

Gelder M, Gath D & Mayou R (1983) *Oxford Textbook of Psychiatry.* Oxford: Oxford University Press.

Green P & Preston M (1981) Reinforcement of vocal correlates of auditory hallucinations using auditory feedback: A case study. *British Journal of Psychiatry 139,* 204–8.

Hume D (1804) *Essays and Treaties on Several Subjects,* Volume 1. Edinburgh: Bell & Bradfute.

Jaspers K (1959) *General Psychopathology,* 7th Edn. (transl. Hoenig J & Hamilton MW, 1963). Manchester: Manchester University Press.

Leff G (1958) *Medieval Thoughts.* Harmondsworth: Penguin.

Lewis AJ (1953) Health as a social concept. *British Journal of Sociology 4,* 109–24.

Mechanic D (1986) The concept of illness behaviour: culture, situation and personal predisposition *Psychological Medicine 16,* 1–7.

Parsons T (1951) Illness and the role of the psysician: a socicological perspective. *American Journal of Orthopsychiatry 21,* 452–60.

Pichot PJ (1984) The French approach to psychiatric classification. *British Journal of Psychiatry 144,* 113–18.

Rutter BM, Shaffer D & Shepherd M (1975) *A Multiaxial Classification of Child Psychiatric Disorders.* Geneva: World Health Organization.

Schneider K (1958) *Clinical Psychopathology,* 5th Edn. (transl. Hamilton MW, 1959). New York: Grune & Stratton.

Sedgwick P (1981) Illness–Mental and otherwise. In Caplan AL, Engelhardt HT & McCartney JJ (eds) *Concepts of Health and Disease: Interdisciplinary Perspectives,* pp. 119–130. Reading, Massachusetts: Addison-Wesley.

Sims ACP (1983) *Neurosis in Society.* Basingstoke: Macmillan.

Sims ACP (1985) Neurotic Illness: conserving a threatened concept. *British Journal of Clinical Pharmacology 19,* 95–153.

Tyrer P (1985) Neurosis divisible? *Lancet 1,* 685–8.

Wing JK, Cooper JE & Sartorius N (1974) *The Measurement and Classification of Psychiatric Symptoms: An Instruction Manual for the PSE and Catego Program.* Cambridge: Cambridge University Press.

World Health Organization (1977) *International Statistical Classification of Diseases Injuries and Causes of Death,* 9th Revision. Geneva: World Health Organization.

Zigmond AS & Sims ACP (1983) The effect of the use of the International Classification of Diseases, 9th Revision upon hospital in-patient diagnoses. *British Journal of Psychiatry 142,* 409–13.

Index